# MEN AND MATTERS

# MEN AND MATTERS

BY
WILFRID WARD

*Essay Index Reprint Series*

BOOKS FOR LIBRARIES PRESS
FREEPORT, NEW YORK

First Published 1914
Reprinted 1968

LIBRARY OF CONGRESS CATALOG CARD NUMBER:
68-8503

PRINTED IN THE UNITED STATES OF AMERICA

# PREFACE

WHILE most of the essays in this volume tell their own story, a few words must be said in respect to three of them, entitled: *The Conservative Genius of the Church; St. Thomas Aquinas and Medieval Thought;* and *Cardinal Newman on Constructive Religious Thought.* These three essays deal with different aspects of one subject.

It is becoming more and more generally admitted that Christian belief cannot be adequately justified or preserved for an inquiring generation without taking account of the legacy left us by the special wisdom and insight of the saints and the prophets of old, which reaches its climax in the Revelation of Christ Himself. And it is widely recognized that the corporate society which has ever preserved that legacy in its traditions is the Holy Catholic Church of the Creed. Again, in the difficult task of Apologetic and of interpreting Christianity to successive civilizations, it is now generally recognized that the thought of the expert few is the natural guide to the less gifted many. And here again the theological tradition of a corporate society is invaluable. The claim for Christianity is at its strongest as exhibited, not in the reasoning of a single average mind, but in the life and thought of the Church as a whole and from the beginning. The individual member of the Church participates in thought and life larger and deeper than his own. The crude theory of "private judgment" finds few advocates.

The growing acceptance of the general idea of
Church authority, as opposed to a mere reliance on
private judgment, is witnessed to by the spread of the
Catholic Movement in the Church of England. That
authority has ever been definitely conceived and
jealously guarded by the single polity of the Catholic
and Roman Church, which claims to have represented
continuously the Holy Catholic Church of the Creed.

The element of conservatism in the Catholic
Church which is involved in its very idea is
emphasized in my essay on the Conservative genius
of the Church.

But concurrently with this conservative action of
the Church, Christianity needs for its defence in the
present as in the past active thought, undertaken
with the object of adapting the details of Christian
theology to the exigencies of the times. Without it
conservatism would be fossilism. And this point is
enlarged on in the other two essays to which I have
referred.

It has a very important practical relation to the
situation which has been created—in the Catholic and
Roman Church especially—by the rise of Modernism.
There has actually been, in the course of the past
half century and more, a widespread endeavour to
bring Catholic thought abreast of the times—an
endeavour rendered especially urgent in our own day
by the rapid advance of the sciences. This endeavour
has led some writers into disastrous errors and
excesses. But there are also signs in certain quarters
of reaction to an opposite extreme—to suspicion of
those who have continued to attempt the same difficult
task with greater caution and submission to authority.
It seems to be assumed in some quarters that

submission to ecclesiastical authority must suffice for guidance on the most intricate problems, and that active thought savours of a wanton and dangerous love of innovation. This view I venture strongly to deprecate, on lines laid down in Cardinal Newman's writings, as opposed to the traditions of the Church. For it is the great theological thinkers who have been our intellectual guides in times past—ecclesiastical authority approving. I have in the two essays to which I have just referred endeavoured to point out two things :

(1) The phenomenon before us is no new one. And it behoves us to judge the present in the light of past experience. Again and again the attempt to express Christianity in terms of the thought of the day has led to heresies, and heresies are of course a danger to the Church. But it is the very same attempt made with caution and submission which has gradually formed Catholic theology—and Catholic theology is the great intellectual defence of the Church. It was the active exercise of reason, and not the *fiat* of authority, which wrought out the *Summa Contra Gentiles* and the *Summa Theologiæ* to meet the very special intellectual needs of the thirteenth century.

(2) Alarmists note, in views put forward by those who are endeavouring to make the much needed intellectual adaptations, an apparent resemblance to some Modernist writings, and appeal to this resemblance as justifying their suspicions. Yet, again judging by the past, such an inference is surely unwarrantable. The fact that certain positions are erroneous does not raise even a presumption that others apparently resembling them are not true and even of great importance. The *Augustinus* of Jansenius contained

heresy, yet its author held that he was only repeating in it the substance of what St. Augustine had said. In this contention he was not justified. The differences were of course all-important. But the elements of apparent resemblance between the work of the Saint and that of the founder of Jansenism are undeniable. The Fathers who condemned Nestorius at Ephesus were orthodox ; yet it was only an exaggeration of their teaching which was responsible for the subsequent heresy of the Monophysites which was condemned at Chalcedon. The orthodox position had points of resemblance to each of the opposite heresies. Newman has pointed out that the members of the Church of Neocæsarea suspected St. Basil of a tendency to Arianism, the more so because some of his friends were semi-Arians. But he traces their suspicions to the fact that they themselves, in their zeal against Arianism, had approached the opposite extreme of the Sabellians. That Arianism is false does not make Sabellianism true. That Jansenism is false does not make Pelagianism true. That Gallicanism is false did not prevent the great Bishop Dupanloup from protesting against M. Louis Veuillot's untheological exaggerations of the Papal prerogatives. To make such a protest was not to censure the enthusiastic loyalty which may lead to such exaggerations. It was a zealous but undiscriminating devotion to the doctrine of our Lord's divinity which led some to the extremes of Monophysitism. Thus a writer may be doing a most necessary work in defence of orthodoxy in vindicating a thesis which the alarmists of whom I have spoken will regard as akin to heresy.

Furthermore, even men who have written what is heretical may, like Origen or Tertullian, have done valuable work for Christian thought. We can no more afford now than we could in the fourth century or the thirteenth to lose contributions of value in the difficult enterprise of meeting the anti-Christian thought of the day.

Efforts at a synthesis between the traditionary scholastic teaching and the developments of science and thought are not wanton intellectual indulgences, but attempts to meet an urgent need. Such an endeavour has been made systematically for some years by the Institut de St. Thomas, at Louvain, founded under Leo XIII.'s especial patronage, and the further spread and development of its programme would be welcome to many inquirers.

Some papers read before the Synthetic Society are published in this volume for the first time. Some account of that society is given in the essay on Mr. George Wyndham.

It remains for me to thank the representatives of Mr. George Wyndham for their permission to use extracts from his letters in my essay on him which first appeared in the *Quarterly Review*, and to acknowledge the courtesy of the editors and proprietors of the various reviews in which many of the essays now published originally appeared, in giving leave for their republication.

W. W.

# CONTENTS

# MEN AND MATTERS

## I

## DISRAELI

WHEN the generation to which the present writer belongs was in its youth there was a little book of caricatures of Gladstone and Disraeli which was very popular. One picture depicted the House of Commons. On one side of the table stood Mr. Gladstone, fire flashing from his eyes, as with angry and threatening gesticulation he denounced his chief opponent. The hawk-like face added to the destructive suggestion of his attitude, while the movement of his arm was almost physically menacing. At the other side of the table, impassive, apparently half asleep, with an amused sneer on the face and his hat somewhat drawn over his eyes, sat Mr. Disraeli. Beneath the picture was written an extract from one of his speeches, which ran nearly as follows: "The right honourable gentleman sometimes addresses us in such a tone and with such a manner as to make me sincerely thankful that a very substantial piece of mahogany stands in this House between him and myself."

The contrast between these two men was a never-failing drama before the public eye. The heated

B

earnestness of the one, the cool sarcasm of the other;
the unctuousness of the one, the cynicism of the
other; what critics regarded as an undue parade of
religious principle in Gladstone, and the entirely
secular ideals of his rival—who, nevertheless, liked a
Cardinal, and avowed himself to be "on the side of
the angels,"—this contrast was unfailing and constantly found fresh occasions for its display. Gladstone's attitude towards Disraeli was that of the
righteous man towards one whom he holds to be
without principle and somewhat flippant. Disraeli
treated Gladstone as a solemn person of appalling
energy, with perhaps a suspicion of Pecksniff about
him, who was apt to get very excited; or, as he once
described him, as a "sophistical rhetorician inebriated
by the exuberance of his own verbosity, and gifted
with an egotistical imagination." The two antagonists
used to recall Pickwick and Jingle. The indignant
righteousness of the one provoked the cynical coolness of the other, and *vice versâ*. I am surprised that
this actual comparison never occurred to the clever
cartoonist in *Punch*, who faithfully reflected the
impressions of a large section of the public, and
whose pictures of the two men had much which
suggested it.

The general contrast, when once it had been
outlined, could not fail to remain fixed in the public
mind, and *Punch* returned to it again and again. In
one cartoon of 1873, which appeared just after the
formal announcements and solemn mutual courtesies
between leaders which are customary at the opening
of a session, they figured as "Disralius" and "Gladstonius"—two Roman augurs. Dizzy has his hand
to his mouth in the vain endeavour to conceal his

laughter. " I always wonder, brother," he says, " how we chief augurs can meet on the opening day without laughing." Gladstonius replies with severity, " I have never felt any temptation to the hilarity you suggest, brother, and the remark savours of flippancy." In another cartoon Gladstone is reading Dizzy's *Lothair*, just after its publication. And Dizzy has taken down from his bookshelf a copy of Gladstone's *Juventus Mundi*. Gladstone's frown is severe as he ejaculates · " Hm—flippant! " while Dizzy's " Ha— prosy! " is accompanied by a yawn of extreme bore- dom. After Gladstone's extraordinary display of energy in his Scotch campaign, when he returned to political life in the late 'seventies, *Punch* published a cartoon in which he was represented as a fancy skater performing the most wonderful and exhausting evolu- tions on the ice. Dizzy, looking on from the bank of the pond, has an expression of wonder blended with anxiety, and has just taken down his eye-glass after scrutinizing the performance. " Wonderful! " he exclaims. " Both wind and limb! At our time of life, too, when a fall would be so serious! "

Throughout the cartoons of Disraeli in the late 'sixties and early 'seventies the old tradition was still visible, that he was a clever adventurer—extraordi- narily clever indeed, but not to be regarded as a serious politician. His success in carrying the Reform Bill in 1868 was represented as a wonderful egg dance achieved by an acrobat, and he appeared again and again as a juggler, a harlequin, a tumbler, a conjurer or a rope-walker or an actor, and once as Fagin the Jew coaching his young pickpockets.

In the early 'seventies Disraeli had begun to strike the Imperial note. It took some years before this was generally felt to represent, as it certainly did, a really deep and almost passionate belief. At first it appeared to be a fresh instance of the contrast between his attitude on foreign politics and Gladstone's phase of Little Englandism without at once suggesting a new access in Disraeli of political seriousness and conviction—a quality of which, in his own way, Mr. Gladstone had so large a share. Disraeli's Imperialism was at first believed to be a clever move in the game—a new limelight for the stage effects and dramatic surprises he loved, as when he suddenly bought up the Suez Canal, and thus secured the key to India. And this idea only gradually gave way to a truer one. Even when Disraeli suggested the title " Empress of India " for Queen Victoria, Tenniel's witty pictures in *Punch*—" New crowns for Old," after the " New lamps for Old " of Aladdin's story, and the crowning of Dizzy by Victoria,—represented an impression which had but recently ceased to be widespread. Queen Victoria was to be flattered and kept in a good humour by a new title which cost Disraeli nothing and added nothing whatever to her real power ; and Disraeli was to receive in return the coronet of an Earl to satisfy his ambition.

But in point of fact, in spite of the somewhat theatrical element which, in his Imperialism as in all else, was visible in Disraeli's operations, there is little doubt that he developed in his old age, when the *stimulus* of personal ambition was inevitably less keen —for ambition had been satisfied and his own future was limited by the laws of life to a few years—a really earnest passion for the development of the Imperial idea. The Primrose League, founded in his

honour—with its knights and dames and its coloured
badges—has truly caught this spirit, and is a lasting
monument to it. The machinery is showy and
theatrical. But it represents enthusiasm and hard
practical work in educating the party. The Jingo
songs which accompanied its birth had a touch of the
cheapness and the want of true dignity which were
apt to attend all his own work. But they helped on
the cause and appealed to minds which were worth
winning. Disraeli was thoroughly in earnest in this
last phase of his career, and his imagination was
really fired. It was this development in him which
quite transformed the attitude of the late Lord Salisbury towards his chief, and he did not stand alone.
While some few felt to the end towards Disraeli as
towards a successful adventurer without convictions—
the Acrobat, the Gamester, the Leotard of *Punch's*
pages—they were but a small and negligible minority
in the party. The late Lord Emly, who as Mr.
Monsell had been a devoted Peelite in 1846, and had
followed Disraeli's career with very keen, though
unsympathetic, interest, once said to the present
writer : "People often talk of Disraeli's rise from
nothing to being Prime Minister in 1867 as a marvellous achievement. In my opinion, however, the
change of his position between 1867 and 1878—the
high-water mark of his second innings—was far more
remarkable. In 1867, while there were a few enthusiastic devotees of his genius, the almost universal
feeling, even in his own party, was that he was an
unprincipled adventurer, yet so marvellously clever
that in a difficult time it was best for the party to use
him and to follow him. He was still an outsider ;
and the great aristocracy of England regarded it as

impossible that he should ever be accepted as their
social equal. In 1878 the impossible had happened.
He had won not only power, but general reverence.
Our aristocracy not only accepted him, but treated
him with the utmost respect. I have seen the Duke
of Richmond in his company, and the Duke's attitude
was one of deference, and even of fear."

The publication of Mr. Monypenny's classical
Biography has placed those who in their youth
witnessed with fascination the last two acts of a great
drama in a position to understand nearly the whole.
It was feared by some that when he came to deal with
Disraeli's Parliamentary life his own want of personal
familiarity with the *milieu* in which it was passed
would make Mr. Monypenny fail. No one, I think,
who has read his fascinating volumes can doubt of his
remarkable success. Indeed, much as we may admire
Lord Morley's *Life of Gladstone*, it is more than anything in the vivid dramatic quality that its author fails,
while Mr. Monypenny succeeds. Few things have
ever been written in political biography more dramatic
than Mr. Monypenny's account of the long-standing
duel between Disraeli and Peel, which first made
Disraeli actually "arrive" in political life. It is probable that the very lack of experience which made
some onlookers anxious proved Mr. Monypenny's
best friend; while Lord Morley's political experience
made him somewhat careless in this respect. The
fact that Mr. Monypenny neither remembered those
days nor was familiar with the life of the House
of Commons made him take infinite pains to
collect all the contemporary sources of information
which could make these scenes live for himself, and,
in doing so, he has made them live for others. For

Lord Morley, on the contrary, both the place and, to some extent, the events he describes were matters with which he was personally familiar; and he sometimes seems to assume the same familiarity as already secured on the part of his readers. He has, therefore, not left for posterity anything approaching the vivid picture of the drama of House of Commons debates which Mr. Monypenny has painted. Mr. Monypenny's success makes it all the more tragic that he lived only long enough to hear the first notes of the general acclaim accorded to his work.

Disraeli's success was due before all things to an avowed and unconquerable ambition. He was stimulated rather than cowed by the consciousness that he had to fight against great odds in his own antecedents and in popular prejudice. He openly avowed in a speech of 1844 that personal ambition was his ruling motive. "There is no doubt, gentlemen," he said, "that all men who offer themselves as candidates for public favour have motives of some sort. I candidly acknowledge that I have, and I will tell you what they are. I love fame; I love reputation; I love to live in the eyes of the country, and it is a glorious thing for a man to do who has had my difficulties to contend against." "A member who wants to get on," he was wont to say, "should be constantly in his place in the House. And when he is not there he should be reading Hansard." And he practised what he preached. It was his unflagging pertinacity; his freedom from the drawback of sensitiveness; the determination that he would succeed—the insistence that he had succeeded; the refusal to look in the face the bare possibility of failure, that in the event made his genius triumphant.

Gladstone knew the temper of that fastidious assembly, the House of Commons, well before he entered it, for it was reflected closely enough in the Oxford Union of his time. Disraeli, on the contrary, frequently and seriously misjudged it. The story of his first speech has often been told. The late Sir Rupert Kettle, an eye witness, left in his diary an account of it which Mr. Monypenny never saw, and which helps to complete the picture he gives. Sir Rupert sketched Disraeli as he spoke, and under the sketch is written : " Disraeli, a little dandy Jew, looks about 18." His hair was long ; he was much scented ; he was over-dressed. The imagery congenial to his Oriental mind made his style turgid, a quality most repugnant to the taste of the House. His self-confidence was too transparent to be disguised. He could not, therefore, attain to the touch of diffidence which the House requires in a new aspirant for its favour. And he was a Jew in days when that very fact greatly added to the prejudice against him. The words in Sir Rupert's diary are hasty and inadequate as a description, but they have the touch of life that belongs to contemporary notes.

The next thing was young D'Israeli's maiden speech. He began with all the confidence of a bully to claim indulgence for his first attempt. Then said a few words to O'Connell about his rambling speech. " But I'll spare the honourable and learned gent's feelings." (Laughter.) From this time he tried to do the orator so very much that roars of laughter ended a sentence begun amidst coughs and groans. Even his own Party did not cheer after a sentence or two. [We caught such sentences as] "When the bell of our Cathedral announced the death of a monarch," " See the philosophic prejudice of man," " Nothing is so easy as to laugh," " Oh, give me but five minutes by the clock," " I never attempted anything but I succeeded," and lastly he hooted, to be heard above the noise : " Though you won't hear me now, the time will come when I will make you hear me." So much for him.[1]

In Mr. Monypenny's pages we get one or two further details which show the kind of bombastic imagery which the speech contained. One of the sentences which was laughed down alluded to some one as having "in the one hand the Keys of St. Peter, and in the other the Cap of Liberty." Disraeli complained in conversation that his enemies would not allow him to finish his pictures—and the " cap of liberty" never got into the speech at all, as the speaker's sentence was broken short by the general laughter. However, far from being discouraged, he appears hardly to have been even ruffled. He only awaited another opportunity and took note of rocks ahead which must be avoided. Ten days later he was on his feet again. He was careful this time to indulge in no imagery. The speech was clear and unpretentious and succeeded. He soon won the ear of the House to some extent, but it was long before he was certain of it. His own account of the dogged persistency with which he pursued a speech in March, 1842, on the Consular Service is a good exhibition of his persevering determination.

The affair last night realized all my hopes ; the success was complete and brilliant. I rose at five o'clock to one of the most disagreeable audiences that ever welcomed a speaker. Everybody seemed to affect not to be aware of my existence, and there was a general buzz and chatter. Nevertheless, not losing my head, I proceeded without hesitation for ten minutes, though when I recollected what I

---

[1] This extract was published in *The Times* of Nov. 29, 1912.

had to travel through, and the vast variety of detail which I had perspicuously to place before the House, I more than once despaired of accomplishing my purpose.

In about ten minutes affairs began to mend; when a quarter of an hour had elapsed there was generally an attentive audience; and from that time until near half-past seven, when I sat down, having been up about two hours and twenty minutes, I can say without the slighest exaggeration that not only you might have heard a pin fall in the House, but there was not an individual, without a single exception, who did not listen to every sentence with the most marked interest, and even excitement. The moment I finished, Peel, giving me a cheer, got up and went to dinner.

After the speech Sydney Herbert, as he records, came up to him and asked where he got his mass of extraordinary information. "A most remarkable display," Herbert added, "and it is thought so."

Every move in the game, every sign of success and criticism is recorded in the letters to his sister. In 1842 he realizes that his position is on a new footing. "I already find myself without effort the leader of a party, chiefly youths and new members." The reference is to the Young England party whose most prominent members were the late Duke of Rutland, then Lord John Manners, George Smythe, and Baillie Cochrane. This was a passing phase; but not without its importance. With Disraeli's peculiar temperament, any form of leadership fired his imagination and helped to further success.

I think that Mr. Monypenny makes good his contention that those have wronged the man who ascribed Disraeli's virulent attacks on his old chief three years later simply to the fact of Peel's not giving him office when he came to power in 1841. But they cannot be ascribed primarily to Disraeli's convictions

on the proposed repeal of the Corn Laws. The first
attack had nothing to do with this question. But it
was such a brilliant success in the House that Disraeli
saw his path marked out for him. His primary
motive was neither the indulgence of personal resentment against Peel nor zeal for the retention of the
Corn Laws. It was simply that his own gifts and the
circumstances of the time made his line of action
the best road to the front. The country gentlemen
wanted a man of parts to plead their cause and oppose
Peel. The effectiveness of his first attack on Peel
marked out the method to be chosen—the strong
personal element in the opposition. There was spice
and piquancy in such personal encounters, and they
brought into evidence his most brilliant gifts. They
brought also immediate notoriety : and for a man of
genius notoriety soon comes to mean success, which
was Disraeli's goal.

This most important phase of Disraeli's career is
described at length and with masterly power by Mr.
Monypenny. Its general character has been stereo-
typed in the cartoons in *Punch*, in one of which
Disraeli's incisive criticisms are represented by Dizzy
with his teeth dug into Peel's body hanging on to him
with doglike tenacity. Mr. Monypenny has seen his
opportunity in this historic and prolonged encounter,
and has taken it. The first assault was in 1845, the
occasion being a protest which had been made against
the opening by Government officials of certain letters
addressed to Mazzini, who was living in England.
Peel had defended the Government's action successfully and with great warmth as absolutely necessary
with a view to preventing serious international complications. Disraeli, posing as a friendly critic, ridiculed

nevertheless the meticulous detail in Peel's account of the succession of causes and effects which, had the letters not been opened, must have led inevitably at last to the most disastrous consequences. He compared it to the nursery story of the house that Jack built in which " this is the dog that worried the cat that killed the rat that ate the malt that lay in the house that Jack built." But he ended with some sarcastic banter directed against the note of indignant and even angry righteousness which marked Peel's speech.

The right hon. gentleman will pardon me for observing it, but he displayed an unusual warmth. I am aware that it by no means follows that the right hon. gentleman felt it. The right hon. baronet has too great a mind, and fills too eminent a position, ever to lose his temper ; but in a popular assembly it is sometimes expedient to enact the part of the choleric gentleman. The right hon. gentleman touched the red box with emotion. I know from old experience that when one first enters the House these exhibitions are rather alarming, and I believe that some of the younger members were much frightened ; but I advised them not to be terrified. I told them that the right hon. baronet would not eat them up, would not even resign ; the very worst thing he would do would be to tell them to rescind a vote. (Loud cheering and shouts of laughter.)

There was no mistaking the acerbity that underlay Disraeli's speech, although he professed to speak as a friend of the Government. For the moment Peel's retort was extremely effective, as it was dignified.

It is certainly very possible to manifest great vehemence of action and yet not to be in a great passion. On the other hand, it is possible to be exceedingly cold, indifferent and composed in your manner, and yet to cherish very acrimonious feelings. Notwithstanding the provocations of the hon. gentleman, I will not deal so harshly with him as he has dealt with me. He undertakes to assure the House that my vehemence was all pretended, and warmth all simulated. I, on the contrary, will do him entire justice. I do believe that his bitterness was not simulated, but that it was entirely sincere. The hon. gentleman has a perfect right to support a hostile motion . . . but let him not say that he does it in a friendly spirit.

Had Peel stopped there he would probably have scored decisively against Disraeli. But, led on by his good memory and his habit of quotation, he cited in conclusion Canning's famous denunciation of the candid friend :

> Give me the avowed, the erect, the manly foe :
> Bold I can meet, perhaps may turn, the blow ;
> But of all plagues, good Heaven, Thy wrath can send,
> Save, save, O save me, from the candid friend !

This gave Disraeli a great chance, for Peel's behaviour to Canning in the 'twenties was the passage in his career which his enemies best remembered in his disfavour. Disraeli had to bide his time, for he had already spoken and could not again speak in reply. But he got a friend to bring the subject up again a week later, and began his attack on Peel in good earnest. His speech was a criticism on Peel's whole policy. From beginning to end it was full of brilliant passages. Peel's reference to Canning supplied the poisoned shaft which was discharged at the end.

The right hon. gentleman knows what the introduction of a great name does in debate—how important is its effect, and occasionally how electrical. He never refers to any author who is not great, and sometimes who is not loved—Canning, for example. That is a name never to be mentioned, I am sure, in the House of Commons without emotion. We all admire his genius. We all—at least, most of us—deplore his untimely end ; and we all sympathize with him in his fierce struggle with supreme prejudice and sublime mediocrity— with inveterate foes and with candid friends. (Loud cheering.) The right hon. gentleman may be sure that a quotation from such an authority will always tell. Some lines, for example, upon friendship, written by Mr. Canning and quoted by the right hon. gentleman ! The theme, the poet, the speaker—what a felicitous combination ! (Loud and long-continued cheers.) Its effect in debate must be overwhelming ; and I am sure, if it were addressed to me, all that would remain would be for me thus publicly to congratulate the right hon. gentleman, not only on his ready memory, but on his courageous conscience.

Mr. Monypenny makes the scene more vivid by quoting a description in *Fraser's Magazine* of Disraeli's parliamentary manner.

With his supercilious expression of countenance, slightly dashed with pomposity, and a dilettante affectation, he stands with his hands on his hips, or his thumbs in the armholes of his waistcoat, while there is a slight, very slight, gyratory movement of the upper part of his body, such as you will see ballroom exquisites adopt when they condescend to prattle a flirtation. And then, with voice low-toned and slightly drawling, without emphasis, except when he strings himself up for points, his words are not so much delivered as that they flow from the mouth, as if it were really too much trouble for so clever, so intellectual—in a word, so literary a man to speak at all. . . .

So much for his ordinary level speaking. When he makes his points the case is totally different. Then his manner changes. He becomes more animated, though still less so than any other speaker of equal power over the House. You can then detect the nicest and most delicate inflexions in the tones of his voice ; and they are managed, with exquisite art, to give effect to the irony or sarcasm of the moment. . . . In conveying an innuendo, an ironical sneer, or a suggestion of contempt, which courtesy forbids him to translate into words —in conveying such masked enmities by means of a glance, a shrug, an altered tone of voice, or a transient expression of face, he is unrivalled. Not only is the shaft envenomed, but it is aimed with deadly precision by a cool hand and a keen eye, with a courage fearless of retaliation. He will convulse the House by the action that helps his words, yet leave nothing for his victims to take hold of. He is a most dangerous antagonist in this respect, because so intangible. And all the while you are startled by his extreme coolness and impassibility. . . . You might suppose him wholly unconscious of the effect he is producing ; for he never seems to laugh or to chuckle, however slightly, at his own hits. While all around him are convulsed with merriment or excitement at some of his finely-wrought sarcasms, he holds himself, seemingly, in total suspension, as though he had no existence (*sic*) for the ordinary feelings and passions of humanity ; and the moment the shouts and confusion have subsided, the same calm, low, monotonous, but yet distinct and searching voice is heard still pouring forth his ideas, while he is preparing to launch another sarcasm, hissing hot, into the soul of his victim.

Then comes Mr. Monypenny's own vivid sketch of the scene and its brilliant consequences.

With the aid of this writer we can almost see Disraeli standing with pale face and impassive manner as he delivers his philippic ; hear the tone of every sentence as it falls from his lips ; and follow the emotions of his audience as it listens, now perplexed, now expectant, now hilarious. We have first the low, level speaking in no way remarkable that makes the preparation ; the gradual development of the theme of Peel's disregard of party . . . the feigned humility of his readiness to bow to the rod, and the seeming compliment to Peel's mastery of quotation ; Peel nervous and expectant, the House still puzzled ; the stealthy approach to the position from which the spring is to be made ; the name which is the key-word, dropped as if by accident—" Canning, for example " ; Peel visibly uncomfortable ; the House beginning to be excited ; the drawling allusion to Canning's fierce struggle with " sublime mediocrity "—perhaps aimed at Peel, though all are still doubtful—and " with—candid friends "—when the pause, the inflexion of the speaker's voice, and the direction of his glance convert doubt into certainty ; and then the culminating blow, " Some lines upon friendship written by Mr. Canning, and quoted by the right honourable gentleman " ! and, where a lesser artist would have spoilt all by some crudity of comment, only the restrained but mordant words : " The theme, the poet, the speaker—what a felicitous com-bination ! "

The effect of the speech on the House [Mr. Monypenny continues] was stupendous. " It would have made you cry with delight," wrote George Smythe to Mrs. Disraeli, " to have heard the thunders of cheering " ; and the excitement at the close was so great that it was some time before Graham, who rose to follow, could make himself heard.

Here for a moment I pause. Before taking a further view of Disraeli when he became a real power in the country, as he did in the contest between the Peelites and the old Tories, and continued to be thenceforth, it is necessary to go beneath the surface of events and study the temperament and character revealed in these pages. We must say something of Disraeli's moral character, of the ideals which actuated him over and above the one governing ambition for personal success. We must look at the strong and weak elements of taste and temperament and equip-ment which may be traced to his Oriental blood and the conditions of his early life. In a word, a brief psychological study of the man must precede a further study of his career.

The question has been often asked, Was Disraeli sincere ? and it is not so easy to answer as it might seem to be at first sight. It is like asking if an imaginative child of four believes in fairies. To answer " yes " may be untrue ; to answer " no " equally untrue. In both cases there is a mid-way state of mind. Disraeli had certain most genuine enthusiasms, and up to a certain point sincere beliefs. Yet, his underlying cynicism prevented their being as absolute or sacred for him as political convictions would be for many another. The question, Is any of it more than a game which must be played successfully ? was ever lurking in the depths of his consciousness as he discussed legislative schemes; and this probably helped in concentrating him on his own personal career. Whatever was or was not worth while in relation to the future of the world, to play the game successfully was worth while for himself ; and, moreover, if anything *was* great and worth achieving by him in relation to the good of the country or of the race, it could only be effected by his own success in making his powers appreciated. Only thus could his schemes become operative. Therefore I think that there is a greater unity than Mr. Monypenny sees between the words I have already cited, in which Disraeli avows so frankly his personal ambition in the speech of 1844, and the apparently higher tone taken up in the passage his biographer quotes from *Coningsby*. In *Coningsby*, when alluding to " that noble ambition which will not let a man be content until his intellectual power is recognized by his race," he associates it with the view of life taken by a hero —with " the heroic feeling . . . that in old days

produced demigods; without which no State is safe;
without which political institutions are meat without
salt; the Crown a bauble, the Church an establishment, Parliaments debating clubs, and civilization
itself a fitful and transient dream." It was only by
making himself felt and appreciated that he could
accomplish the hero's aims,—those actions that will live
in history as great and beneficent.

His mixture of sincerity and cynicism is visible, I
think, in a very different field from that of politics—
namely, in his correspondence with the lady who afterwards became his wife, in which he assures her that
while he first thought of marrying her from interested
motives, he has come to love her for herself alone.
The letter is not, I think, substantially insincere; but
the strong expressions calculated to touch a woman's
heart have in them something histrionic, which was
part of his cynicism. Such expressions were hardly
the outpourings of a full heart. He knew them to be
very pleasing to a woman : and his feelings as well as
his interest prompted him to please this particular
woman. "He is to be depended on to a certain
degree," is what his wife writes of him after some
years of experience, and that is probably about the truth.
People have often debated as to whether Disraeli was
sincere or insincere, and have taken sides strongly
for one or the other position. He was not insincere;
he was, to some extent, sincere in most of his enterprises. He was absolutely sincere in his desire for
his own advancement, and other sincere aspirations
became more prominent after he had secured the
satisfaction of this overmastering passion.

Disraeli's sincerity then was real, but with a touch
of underlying cynicism, and this undoubtedly told

against scrupulous conscientiousness. There were
certain great ideals which he meant to realize. If
anything was worth while, they were worth while,
and, to some extent, the end justified the means.
Petty scruples were out of place.

From a very early period his aim was largely the
achievement of a democratic Toryism, the development of Toryism into nationalism. He had not been
in the House of Commons much more than two years
when he wrote to the popular leader, Mr. Charles
Attwood :

I entirely agree with you that a union between the Conservative Party and the Radical masses offers the only means
by which we can preserve the Empire. Their interests are
identical : united they form the nation, and their division has
only prompted a miserable minority under the specious name
of the people to assail all rights of property and person.

He had first to develop popular sympathies in the
Tory party. Later on the Crown and the Empire
occupied a large space in the ideal which he placed
before his followers. He was also actuated in his
method of educating his party by a very permanent
conviction that imagination is the weapon whereby
the greatest things are achieved.

We are not indebted to the Reason of man [we read in
*Coningsby*] for any of the great achievements which are the
landmarks of human action and human progress. It was not
Reason that besieged Troy ; it was not Reason that sent forth
the Saracen from the Desert to conquer the world ; that
inspired the Crusades ; that instituted the Monastic Orders ;
it was not Reason that produced the Jesuits ; above all, it
was not Reason that created the French Revolution. Man
is only truly great when he acts from the passions ; never

irresistible but when he appeals to the imagination.   Even
Mormon counts more votaries than Bentham.

His own temperament was profoundly imaginative, though his was not imagination of the highest
order.   It is true that he kindled at some great
pictures in history, and had brooding dreams, half
true, half purely imaginary, concerning his own Jewish
ancestry.   But his imagination was also most vividly
affected by the passing show of life in its more trivial
and even tawdry aspects.   He loved the stage effects ;
the scene-painting of life.   A fashionable entertainment delighted him ;  the number of servants, the
liveries, the silver or gold plate, the *cuisine* in its
minutest details, the beautiful dresses, the jewels ;
none of it was lost on him.   He loved a gathering of
the English aristocracy, and I have sometimes thought
that the high place which its countenance occupied in
his ideal of his own success, his strong feeling for it,
as ranking high among great things—so far as he
believed anything to be great at all—had something
to do with his eventually gaining its goodwill in spite
of unpromising antecedents.   He wooed our aristocracy
long and persistently ;  he touched its heart.   He won
and even vanquished it at last.   His letters would
seem to show that his own prominent and often distinguished position at gatherings of the great was
among the keen pleasures of his life.   Doubtless it
was to him largely the symbol of the success he had
achieved.   But there was also a strong ingredient of
the Oriental love of magnificence.   He loved the
actual material show.   The almost limitless degree of
this enjoyment, the comparative absence of fastidious
taste in its quality, the love of mere splendour and
rich and lavish display are distinctly un-English.

His imagination, indeed, veritably feasted on scenes of splendour, and he described them in his letters with an unwearied pleasure which strikes one forcibly in reading them. This continues long after the first blush of success. To be the centre of or a prominent figure in a showy fashionable pageant seems to be an almost physical enjoyment to him.

I suppose there were several ingredients in this cup of happiness. It was all a new experience to one of his modest beginnings, and where a more refined taste would shrink from the glare of unwonted splendour, his own theatrical nature basked in limelight as in sunshine. Then there was the peculiar pleasure of what we win by hard work. Again, pleasure is always enhanced by previous abstinence. Tennyson once described in a poem the warm glow of full life which came to him with eating a chop after weeks of vegetable diet. "It felt like strong brandy," he once said in speaking of it. The heavenly peace which sometimes comes in convalescence is another instance of the same law—the strain of illness brings this compensation. Given a vivid, but not a refined imagination, small beginnings, a hard struggle for success, an unappeasable appetite for splendour, and many sources of pleasure are combined. The appetite in question will be both stimulated and satisfied as far as it can be. Satisfied, but hardly sated, for such pleasures seemed, in Disraeli's case, never to pall.

I would add the suggestion that there is something in external grandeur which appeals to a sceptical mind. Whatever is or is not real, the show is there, and it is real for the sceptic himself. So far as it meets his eye, it exists for him. Whatever is or is not truly great, this at least is grand to look at and stimulating to the senses and fancy. I have known several cases in which the taste of the unsophisticated and simple mind in this respect is shared—albeit more moderately —by the sceptic. To the simple mind it is all overwhelmingly real, while to the sceptic it is more certainly real than anything else, for at least it appears and makes a great show, which the unseen does not.

Disraeli's literary gift was remarkable, but, like his imagination, it was not of the first order. It proves of great value to his biographer, for it is the absence of the power of self-expression in many great statesmen that is apt to make political biographies so deficient in the play of human life.

Both *Coningsby* and *Sybil* are invaluable as pictures of Disraeli's mind. His letters also are highly self-revealing, and his early speeches owe much to his literary power. Indeed, Mr. Monypenny tells us that when in later days he had completely caught the House of Commons manner of speaking (not entirely a good manner), his speeches in the House became far less effective as compositions. Those which were made in the days when his literary career was recent, and his sense of literary effect keenest, are far better monuments of his eloquence.

It is hardly an exaggeration to say that the very mediocrity of Disraeli's endowment with the qualities of which I have just spoken contributed immensely to his success in politics. A more sincere man or a less sincere man might have failed. One with a more refined imagination would have failed, and one with less imagination could not have done what he did. Again, the finest literary taste almost invariably means the presence of the artistic temperament—a temperament most fatal to success in action. This weakness never

attacked Disraeli; yet his powers of expression contributed immensely to his success.

To speak first of his sincerity. There is no doubt
that a mere opportunist fails to reach the highest point
in political life. He cannot easily gain followers, or,
if he gains them, he cannot continue to inspire them.
He stands too fatally convicted of egoism. He can
represent no cause. He has no instrument wherewith
to kindle enthusiasm. A mere actor must be found
out in the long run. Thus a less sincere man could
not have "arrived." Yet intense sincerity brings with
it depth of principle and consequent scrupulousness,
which are often a great drawback in difficult enterprises.
And Disraeli's drawbacks were already great enough.
His convictions then were strong enough to fire him
and to enable him to fire others with enthusiasm—not
strong enough to handicap him. His entreaty for office
under Peel in 1841, and his subsequent attacks on Peel,
presented no difficulty as they would have done to one
whose convictions were deeper. Both moves were
largely opportunist. Yet there was enough of conviction in his personal admiration for Peel, and in his
disagreement with Peel's later views on the Corn
Laws; enough of conviction in his criticism of Peel's
triple apostasy on Emancipation, Parliamentary Reform and Free Trade to enable him to make each
move in some sense sincerely, and in the later attack
to take the practical leadership of a party effectively.
The same holds good in other great steps in his
career. When he "dished the Whigs" by his Reform
Bill in '68, though it was a clever move in the game,
it also derived some inspiration from his avowed
devotion to the popular cause. His sincerity reached
its highest point both in itself and in its influence on

others in the Imperialist campaign, which was the last
in his life.

As for his imagination, a highly imaginative man
is apt to outstrip the practical and become a dreamer.
Again, a love of splendour like Disraeli's may become
enervating and lead to complete inaction. With
Disraeli on the contrary, the love of splendour meant
a keen appreciation of the visible symbols of success
and stimulated him to further success. His reception
at the great social functions in which he revelled
witnessed to the position he had won. In firing his
imagination they prompted him to further action.
Moreover his imagination, like Napoleon's, helped
him in larger fields to conceive and to execute great
designs. It was well under the control of his practical
ambition.

But lastly, his considerable literary gift never
meant that high-strung literary temperament which
is so fatal to practical effectiveness. He was never a
morbid or hyper-sensitive man. These are qualities
which prove the deadly foe to persevering and consistent action. The literary temperament often means
that a man is at the mercy of his moods; that he acts
one way one day, another another; that he pursues
one line with intense eagerness for a time and then
tires of it. None of this was true of Disraeli from the
very limitations of his literary genius. It never
carried him away. He kept steadily in view the one
cherished goal. He was not a man who might in one
mood devote himself to Parliamentary work and in
another tire of all hard work. He was not one to
brood over the attacks of his enemies, or to be brought
low by those acute sufferings which attend on thinness
of mental skin. On the contrary, his skin was of the

toughest. He neither had the piercing insight of the artistic temperament nor was the victim of its paralyzing effects on consistent action. His wife said of him that he was very conceited, but not vain; and if the distinction denotes the absence in his self-complacency of undue sensitiveness to the opinion of others, the remark was entirely just. His literary gifts gave him great facility of expression and of mental movement, while they never reached the point which makes the typical literary man ineffective in action. His gift of expression, his imagination and his sincerity were alike helpful and were never obstacles. They were servants and instruments which he had well in hand, and could use with great skill. They were never his masters.

There is a remarkable passage in *Coningsby*, not without its significance in the interpretation of Disraeli's political ideals. Speaking of the two years that followed the Reform Bill of 1832, he writes: "It is hardly possible that a young man could rise from the study of these annals without a confirmed disgust for political intrigue—a dazzling practice apt at first to fascinate youth, for it appeals at once to our invention and our courage; but one which should really only be the resource of the second rate. Great minds must trust to great truths and great talents for their rise, and nothing else."

On the whole, I think that Disraeli was, in his own career, true to this counsel. This does not mean that he was incapable of intrigue or incapable of opportunism; but it does mean that he saw clearly that if he would attain to the great position at which he aimed, such methods must hold a minor place. It

does also mean that he saw in the statesmanlike aims
of which he was conscious, a truer road to success and
one which better satisfied his own ideal than mere
intrigue.   In his own way, he was full of views and
ideas which he desired to realize in the world of
politics, and he believed them to be true enough
and persuasive enough to enable him to gain a
following.

These remarks, while they can only be fully appreciated by the study of Disraeli's career as a whole,
are, in their measure, applicable to the brilliant period
of his career set before us in Mr. Monypenny's second
volume—the account of his rise to the first place in
his party by means of the attack on Peel.   In his
campaign against Peel's proposed repeal of the Corn
Laws, I see the eager and tenacious seizing of an
opportunity.   I do not see either personal resentment or political insincerity, with both of which he
has been credited by Lord Cromer in his well-
known essay on Disraeli.   That he saw a telling
opportunity which made for success he himself
expressly avows.   " The opportune," he writes, in
describing his first speech in the campaign, "has
sometimes more success in a popular assembly than
the weightiest efforts of research and reason."   But,
in using his opportunity, he did not lack conviction.
On the contrary, his action was opportune just because
of the convictions in himself and others which called
at the moment for forcible expression.   The strong
personal element visible in the attacks on Peel was,
I think, carefully designed for effect.   Lord Cromer
ascribes it to resentment against Peel for having
refused him office in 1841.   I take leave to doubt this.
Disraeli was too long-headed to be carried away by

resentment. Two years had passed since the refusal before he attacked Peel at all—a sufficient interval to enable the greatest anger to cool. No; the policy was calculated. It was due to no animosity against Peel. He thought much more about himself than he did about Peel. It was due to a desire to advance himself. The brilliancy of his earliest personal sallies against Peel had already immensely advertised him, and when the Corn Law question came to the front, the very greatness of the opportunity was this, that attacks which had at first brought only immediate notoriety now gave occasion for the assertion of principles which moved men deeply and gained him a following which mere notoriety could never have secured. It was not a mere intrigue. He seized an opportunity for advocating a great policy. Indeed, a merely opportunist course would have greatly weakened his position and laid him open to damaging retort, for his very charge against Peel was one of opportunism. Peel was, he maintained, sacrificing the avowed protectionist principles of the party to a policy dictated by a general panic. He was falling in with the general alarm in order to maintain his place.

This is nowhere expressed by him more clearly than in one of the earliest and most brilliant of these sallies in the House of Commons. "My conception of a great statesman," he said, "is of one who represents a great idea—an idea which may lead him to power, an idea with which he may connect himself . . . an idea which he may and can impress on the mind and consciousness of a nation . . . that is a grand, that is indeed a heroic position. But I care not what may be the position of a man who never originates an idea, a watcher of the atmosphere, a man who, as he says, takes his observations and when he finds the wind in a certain quarter trims to suit it. Such a person may be a powerful Minister, but he is no more a great statesman than the man who gets up behind a carriage is a great whip. Certainly, both are disciples of progress ; perhaps both may get a good place, but how far the original momentum is indebted to their powers, and how far their guiding prudence applies the lash or regulates the reins, it is not necessary for me to notice."

Disraeli, then, was statesmanlike in his maintenance of principle, statesmanlike also in his prescience, while he was bent on success. As to the Corn Laws, he saw then what our generation now realizes, that the true alternative lay, not between the old protective system and out and out Cobdenism, in a Europe which was not prepared to accept the latter alternative, but in relaxing the old protective system as circumstances demanded—gradually and carefully and with a special eye on the interests of agriculture. Common-sense and conviction are alike visible in the following retort to one of Peel's speeches avowedly in favour of complete repeal, but forcible in Disraeli's view only in so far as it proved the desirability of moderating the protective system :

The whole speech only proved the advantage of the principle of a moderate protection. ("Oh!") I am sorry, sir, to have excited that groan from a free trader in distress. (Great laughter.) I want to ask the right hon. gentleman a very important question : Does he believe that he can fight hostile tariffs with free imports ? That is the point. ("Hear, hear!") "Hear, hear!" from the disciples of the school of Manchester! A most consistent cheer! They have always maintained they can ; and if their principles are right, as they

believe they are—as I believe they are not—I can easily
understand that, their premises being assumed, they may
arrive at that conclusion.   They believe they can fight hostile
tariffs with free imports, and they tell us very justly : " Let
us take care of our imports, and everything else will take care
of itself."   But is that the conviction of the right hon. gentleman ?   We want to know that, because if that be his conviction,
why all these elegies over defunct diplomatic negotiations
to preserve commercial treaties ?   If he believes that we can
meet hostile tariffs with free imports, he need not trouble
himself about commercial treaties.   But if the right hon.
gentleman does not believe that, if he has not the conviction
of the school of Manchester, then he is not justified in offering
this measure.

As long as free trade was a sacred dogma among
English economists this position which Disraeli consistently held appeared to them not worth arguing
with.   It was therefore not readily believed in as the
sincere conviction of an acute thinker.   This view of
the case has been taken for the most part by the
historians.   But our own generation is in a position
to do Disraeli more justice.

While, so far as economic principle was concerned,
Disraeli saw more truly than the Cobdenites, we find
incidentally in his speeches at this time a further and
deeper prevision unconnected with the special matter
in hand.   More than once he took occasion to hint at
a future for the Tory party as the champion of democracy—an idea which was anything but congenial to
the country gentlemen whose cause he was pleading ;
and his remarks were the result of a very carefully
thought out view of the signs of the times of which
our own day has witnessed the truth.

Writing in the 'forties of the discussions of 1831
and 1832 on the Reform Bill, he pointed out that the

essence of the English constitution was the balance of the three estates of the realm, the crown, the peers and the "community"—a term which probably described the inferior holders of land whose tenure was not immediate of the Crown.    This last and third estate was so numerous that it appeared only by representation.    But he adds : " In treating the house of the third estate as the house of the *people* and not the house of a privileged class, the ministry and Parliament of 1831 virtually conceded the principle of universal suffrage."

The graphic description in *Coningsby* of the Duke of Wellington's ineffectual attempt to resist this revolution is succeeded by the following account of its sequel :

The Reform Party, who had been rather stupefied than appalled by the accepted mission of the Duke of Wellington, collected their scattered senses, and rallied their forces.    The agitators harangued, the mobs hooted.    The City of London, as if the King had again tried to seize the five members, appointed a permanent committee of the Common Council to watch the fortunes of the "great national measure," and to report daily.    Brooks', which was the only place that at first was really frightened and talked of compromise, grew valiant again ; while young Whig heroes jumped upon club-room tables and delivered fiery invectives.    Emboldened by these demonstrations, the House of Commons met in great force, and passed a vote which struck, without disguise, at all rival powers in the State, virtually announced its supremacy, revealed the forlorn position of the House of Lords under the new arrangement, and seemed to lay for ever the fluttering phantom of regal prerogative.

This view of the significance of the situation, startlingly realized in our own time by the passing of the Parliament Act, determined Disraeli's own political course, and it appealed, in many respects, to his sympathies. The future, he saw, was with the democracy. The hope for the Tory party lay not in an unintelligent refusal to recognize the inevitable, but in forming an alliance between the aristocracy and democracy which might make the party once more a real power in the altered conditions of the constitution.

Speaking in 1846, he said : " If we must find new forces to maintain the ancient throne and immemorial monarchy of England, I, for one, hope we may find that universal power in the invigorating energies of an educated and enfranchised people." And later on, in a telling retort to Roebuck, the member for Bath, he hints that his sympathies as well as his reason are in the same direction. This passage is worth quoting as a sample of Disraeli's speaking. Roebuck had recalled the old charge that Disraeli first aspired to Parliament with the assistance of two Radicals— Hume and O'Connell—and suggested that he might come back into his (Roebuck's) camp. Disraeli retorted as follows :

I am not in a condition to have had hereditary opinions carved out for me, and all my opinions, therefore, have been the result of reading and thought. I never was a follower of either of the two great aristocratic parties in this country. My sympathies and feelings have always been with the people from whom I spring ; and when obliged as a member of this House to join a party, I joined that party with which I believe the people sympathize. I continue to hold substantially the same opinions as I have always professed ; and when the hon. member talks of my going "into his camp," I never heard that he had a camp. How the solitary sentry talks of his garrison ! He a leader of the people ! In my opinion, there is no greater opponent of real democracy than a modern Liberal.

I emphasize these two declarations as indicating the point for which I am contending : that Disraeli's programme all along was determined by larger views than those whereby the mere opportunist seeks for immediate success. Such declarations of democratic sympathy could not have been especially welcome to the aristocratic section of the Tory party, with which Disraeli was at the moment identifying himself. Had he looked only to immediate influence, had his method been confined simply and solely to strengthening his position with the party, he would not have gone out of his way to proclaim views so widely unwelcome to them.

Taking, then, the two instruments which Disraeli advocated for the attainment of success—great talents and great truths—it is clear enough that there was no lack of what he himself regarded as great truths in his first important Parliamentary campaign—his attack on the proposed repeal of the Corn Laws. When we come to the exercise of his great talents on the occasion, the record is not so entirely satisfactory. Disraeli's talents included prominently an extraordinary gift for personal attack which was apt to degenerate into invective. In the acute tension of this memorable struggle, it was natural enough that he should use to its utmost extent this his special gift. Moreover, he had tested its effect on the House of Commons in attacking Peel before the Corn Law struggle began, and with brilliant results.

Up to a certain point his attacks on Peel in 1846 were justifiable. They belonged to that opportunism

which may be regarded as legitimate. Peel's action
offered an extraordinarily good target. Although the
absolute sincerity of his conversion to Cobdenism is
undeniable, his party had been elected as staunch
protectionists. The mandate of the people was not,
indeed, in those days as imperative or as exacting as
it is now. Still, it had to be reckoned with, and the
mandate to the Tories was based on a protectionist
programme. The potato famine in Ireland had
thoroughly alarmed Peel, and he had come to think
that the repeal of the Corn Laws was the only wise
course under the circumstances. He recognized in
the first instance the almost impossibility of the Tory
protectionist party undertaking this measure. He
resigned, and Lord John Russell was sent for by the
Queen. Repeal was obviously a measure naturally
falling to a Liberal administration. When, however,
Lord John had failed to form his ministry, Peel took
office again with the avowed object of reversing the
policy which was an essential part of the original Tory
programme. So far as Disraeli confined himself to
scathing attacks on this course of action, he was
playing the game fairly enough. In one of his wittiest
and most effective speeches he pilloried Peel by the
following ludicrous comparison :

Sir, there is a difficulty in finding a parallel to the position
of the right hon. gentleman in any part of history. The
only parallel which I can find is an incident in the late war in
the Levant, which was terminated by the policy of the noble
lord opposite. I remember when that great struggle was
taking place, when the existence of the Turkish Empire was
at stake, the late Sultan, a man of great energy and fertile in
resources, was determined to fit out an immense fleet to
maintain his empire. Accordingly a vast armament was

collected. The crews were picked men, the officers were the ablest that could be found, and both officers and men were rewarded before they fought. (Much laughter.) There never was an armament which left the Dardanelles similarly appointed since the days of Solyman the Great. The Sultan personally witnessed the departure of the fleet ; all the muftis prayed for the expedition, as all the muftis here prayed for the success of the last general election. Away went the fleet, but what was the Sultan's consternation when the Lord High Admiral steered at once into the enemy's port. (Loud laughter and cheers.) Now, sir, the Lord High Admiral on that occasion was very much misrepresented. He, too, was called a traitor, and he, too, vindicated himself. " True it is," said he, " I did place myself at the head of this valiant armada ; true it is that my Sovereign embraced me ; true it is that all the muftis in the empire offered up prayers for the expedition ; but I have no affection for war, I see no use in prolonging the struggle, and the only reason I had for accepting the command was that I might terminate the contest by betraying my master." (Tremendous Tory cheering.)

This speech and its fellows were immensely effective, and in delivering them Disraeli was above serious criticism on the score of excessive personalities. But in the exuberance of success he went much further. He attacked Peel's whole political character. He denounced him as an out-and-out opportunist, a mere trimmer. " Nursed in the House of Commons," he said in one speech, " entertaining no idea but that of Parliamentary success, if you wish to touch him to the quick you must touch him on the state of the poll."

When Peel impressively spoke of looking in his policy to the verdict of posterity, Disraeli contemptuously retorted that the only future to which such statesmen as he were sensitive was " the coming quarter-day." He taunted Peel with his whole past

career,—his political apostasy on emancipation, on
Parliamentary reform, as well as on the fiscal question. Peel's present, he argued, was but in keeping
with his past. Here Disraeli laid himself open to a
most damaging retort. He had in 1841 besought
Peel to give him office. There is nothing unjust or
unreasonable in condemning utterly on a specific point
the policy of a Minister whom nevertheless one may
have respected and trusted sufficiently to join his
administration. But if Peel were the utterly untrust-
worthy opportunist whom Disraeli was now describing,
how came it that Disraeli himself had only five years
earlier desired to join his ministry ? Peel drove home
this argument with great dignity and effect. " If," he
said, "after reviewing my whole public life—a life
extending from thirty years previously to my accession
to office in 1841—he then entertained the opinion of
me which he now professes, . . . it is a little surprising
that in the spring of 1841, after his long experience of
my public career he should have been prepared to
give me his confidence. It is still more surprising
that he should have been ready, as I think he was, to
unite his fortunes with mine in office, thus implying
the strongest proof which any public man can give of
confidence in the honour and integrity of a Minister
of the Crown."

This speech was followed by the famous reply of
Disraeli which is quoted as the classical instance of
his mendacity. Disraeli admitted that there had been
some communication between him and the Government, originating in a confidential friend of Sir Robert
Peel. But he denied having asked for office. He
added, however : " It is very possible if in 1841 I had
been offered office—I dare say it would have been a

very slight office—but I dare say I should have accepted it."

A year earlier he had already denied in a speech to his constituents that he had ever asked for office. And even Mr. Monypenny does not venture to acquit Disraeli of sheer untruthfulness in these denials. Yet one may venture to take a more favourable view and to believe that these denials may well have been simply due to a lapse of memory. The present writer came across a curiously parallel case in dealing with the letters of Cardinal Newman, a case in which this explanation was undoubtedly the true one. Newman was charged in the *Standard* newspaper in 1869 with having in a letter to a friend designated the advanced champions of Papal Infallibility as "an insolent and aggressive faction." Newman publicly denied that he had ever used such words, but admitted that they were not alien to his sentiments. In the end it was proved that he had used them. He remembered accurately, that is, his state of mind, but he had a strong impression that he had not expressed it. So, too, Disraeli did not deny that he had been ready to accept office, but only that he had actually asked for it. No one who knows anything of Newman's character would doubt for a moment that his was simply a case of a keen and over-confident memory going wrong.

In Disraeli's instance the letter in which he asked for office was such that it might easily have remained in his mind as having been rather a remonstrance at getting nothing than a direct request for office. It was written not before Peel formed his ministry, but when he had nearly completed it. The burden of the letter *was* a remonstrance and a reminder

of his services to the party and of the intimation he
professed to have received from a member of Peel's
Cabinet that those services would be rewarded. Peel,
in his reply, dwelt entirely upon this charge of break-
ing a promise, and Disraeli's further rejoinder dealt
exclusively with this point, and did not renew the
request for office. It is surely by no means improbable
that the correspondence may have dwelt in his mind
as only a remonstrance—which carried, no doubt, the
implication that if at the eleventh hour he was offered
some post he would accept it, but did not include a
positive request for office. Mr. Monypenny tells us
that Disraeli kept no copy of his letter ; and it was
obviously written in a hurry. This view of the case
is at least quite a conceivable one, sufficiently within
the realms of possibility to call, in any case, for a
suspension of judgment. And when we consider the
overwhelming damage which would have been inflicted
on Disraeli if the letter had been found and published
by Peel, we may feel that, whatever view we hold of
his morality, his sagacity would have prevented his
taking the risk involved in his two denials had he
accurately remembered the letter.

This phase, then, in Disraeli's attack on Peel,
while it is fairly open to the charge that he was
carried away in the heat of the struggle into giving
a more damaging estimate of Peel's political character than he really entertained, does not, in my
judgment, at all certainly include the serious blot
on his veracity of which his enemies have made
so much. Let us recall his own words in reference
to Peel himself as to the duty of generous judgment in the case of a great statesman. "In passing
judgment on public men, it behoves us ever to take

large and extended views of their conduct, and previous incidents will often satisfactorily explain subsequent events which, without their illustrating aid, are involved in misapprehension or mystery."

The account of these years would be far from complete if it did not give us (as Mr. Monypenny does) a picture of Disraeli's social triumphs. His own description of these to his beloved and sympathetic sister Sarah illustrate the excessive imaginative pleasure he took in this aspect of his life—a characteristic of which I have already spoken,—and his transparent satisfaction at all the attentions that were paid to him.

Here is an account written to his sister of an entertainment by the Londonderrys (after a review in Hyde Park), which "was so magnificent," as he declares in the course of his description, "that everybody lost their presence of mind."

July 11, 1838.

Yesterday, the day being perfect, there was a splendid review in Hyde Park. I saw it admirably from Mrs. Wyndham's. The De La Warrs, Rolles, Lawrence Peels and Dawsons were there, but no one was allowed to be on the drawing-room floor, lest there should be an appearance of a party, except old Lord Rolle and myself to be his companion. Lord R. sat in the balcony, with a footman each side of him, as is his custom. The Londonderrys, after the review, gave the most magnificent banquet at Holdernesse House conceivable. Nothing could be more *recherché.* There were only 150 asked, and all sat down. Fanny was faithful and asked me, and I figure in the *Morning Post* accordingly. It was the finest thing of the season. Londonderry's regiment being reviewed, we had the band of the 10th playing on the staircase, the whole of the said staircase (a double one) being crowded with the most splendid orange trees and Cape jessamines ; the Duke of Nemours, Soult, all the "illustrious strangers," the Duke and the very flower of fashion being assembled.   The banquet was in the gallery of sculpture ; it was so magnificent that everybody lost their presence of mind.   Sir James Graham said to me that he had never in his life seen anything so gorgeous.   "This is the *grand seigneur* indeed," he added.   I think it was the kindest thing possible of Fanny asking me, as it was not to be expected in any way.   The splendour of the uniforms was remarkable.

The Disraeli atmosphere is equally visible in the following account by Mrs. Disraeli of a function at the Duke of Buckingham's at Stow in 1845, at which the Queen was present :

We were for the first hour in the vestibule, like a flock of sheep, half lit up, and no seats or fire, only a little hot air and a great deal of cold wind ; a marble floor.   Fancy, dear, shivering Dizzy, and cross-looking Mary Anne, in black velvet, hanging sleeves looped up with knots of blue, and diamond buttons.   Head-dress, blue velvet bows and diamonds. After a time we passed Her Majesty and the Prince, the Duke and Duchess and the rest standing behind, the Duke giving our names exactly the same as an ordinary groom, and we making our curtseys and bows.   About eleven, or soon after, Her Majesty retired, and then all became joy and triumph to us.   First, Sir Robert Peel came to us, shaking hands most cordially, and remained talking for some time ; then Lord Nugent, introducing his lady, Colonel Anson, Sir James Graham, Lord and Lady de La Warr, Lord Aberdeen. The Duke almost embraced Dizzy, saying he was one of his oldest friends ; and then he offered me his arm, taking me all through the gorgeous splendid scene, through the supper room and back again, down the middle and up again—all making way for us, the Queen and your delighted Mary Anne being the only ladies so distinguished.   After this I retired to a sofa, with the Duchess, who told me that Her Majesty

had pointed Dizzy out, saying : " There's Mr. Disraeli." Do
you call all this nothing ? The kind Duchess asked me to
luncheon the next day and to see the Queen's private
apartments.

A hasty reader of these triumphant records of
Disraeli's own social successes, written by himself and
his wife, might be inclined to class him among the
snobs. But this would be a mistake. His underlying
cynicism, his belief in his own genius and in the greatness of the Jewish race largely qualified his feelings
towards that great world which he recognized nevertheless as so important in the visible drama of public
life. He had not the soul of a snob.

Disraeli's interviews with Louis Phillippe while in
Paris in 1842, probably kindled his imagination yet
more than the scenes of the great world in his own
country. He was received with great distinction.
He discussed international politics with the French
King. The visit was repeated in 1845, and led to
interviews with Guizot and a correspondence with
Lord Palmerston on the relations between the two
countries.

Here is Disraeli's account of his first dinner at the
Tuileries :

On Saturday last I received a command to dine at the
Tuileries on the following Monday at 6 o'clock. I was
ushered, through a suite of about twenty illuminated rooms,
to the chamber of reception, where I formed one of the circle,
and where I found seated the Queen of Sardinia, at present
a guest, and her ladies. Soon after the Court entered and
went round the grand circle. I was the only stranger, though
there were sixty guests. Dinner was immediately announced,
the King leading out the Queen of Sardinia, and there were
so many ladies that an Italian princess, duchess or countess

fell to my share. We dined in the gallery of Diana, one of the *chefs-d'œuvre* of Louis XVI. and one of the most splendid apartments perhaps in the world. . . . In the evening the King personally showed the Tuileries to the Queen of Sardinia, and the first lady in waiting, the Marquise de Dolomieu, invited me, and so did the King, to join the party, *only eight*. It is rare to make the tour of a palace with a King for the cicerone. In the evening there was a reception of a few individuals, but I should have withdrawn had not the King addressed me and maintained a conversation with me of great length. He walked into an adjoining room, and motioned me to seat myself on the same sofa. While we conversed the chamberlain occasionally entered and announced guests. " S. A. le Prince de Ligne," the new Ambassador of Belgium. " J'arrive," responded His Majesty very impatiently, but he never moved. At last even majesty was obliged to move, but he signified his wish that I should attend the palace in the evenings. . . .

You must understand that I am the *only* stranger who has been received at Court. It causes a great sensation here. There is no Court at present, on account of the death of the Duke of Orleans ; and the Ailesburys, Stanhopes and Russian princes cannot obtain a reception. The King speaks of me to many with great *kudos*.

In a later reminiscence of Louis Phillippe we have a very curious account of one personal peculiarity of that King which recalled his earlier life of vicissitude and adventure :

In the King's time there never was a dinner given at the Tuileries, no matter how stately, without a huge smoking ham being placed, at a certain time, before the King. Upon this he operated like a conjurer. The rapidity and precision with which he carved it was a marvellous feat ; the slices were vast, but wafer-thin. It was his great delight to carve this ham, and indeed it was a wonderful performance. He told me one day that he had learnt the trick from a waiter at

Bucklersbury, where he used to dine once at an eating-house
for ninepence per head.

One day he called out to an honest Englishman that he
was going to send him a slice of ham, and the honest Englishman—some consul, if I recollect right, who had been kind to
the King in America in the days of his adversity—not used
to Courts, replied that he would rather not take any. The
King drew up and said : "I did not ask whether you would
take any ; I said I would send you some." A little trait, but
characteristic of the dash of the *grand seigneur*, which I often
observed latent in L. Phillippe, though from his peculiar
temperament and his adventurous life of strange vicissitude
he was peculiarly deficient in dignity. . . .

There can be little doubt that this period of rapid
rise to fame was a very happy one in Disraeli's life—
perhaps the happiest. The opportunity had been
quite unlooked for, and the change in his position
from a merely clever and somewhat erratic member
of Parliament to one of the most prominent men in
England, was extraordinarily rapid. There were the
special sweets of confident anticipation. He was also
comparatively young and capable of keen feeling.
There were still living and in constant intercourse
with him his devoted wife and his sister, Sarah. The
full sympa ,, of both of them in the drama of his
career was an important ingredient in his cup of
happiness. His greatest acts of constructive statesmanship no doubt belong to a later period. He was
twice Prime Minister, and in his first tenure of that
office he realized by the Reform Bill of 1867 one of
his ideals, namel; the attempt to enlist on the side
of the Tory cause "the invigorating energies of an
educated and enfranchised people." During his second
reign he devoted himself, as has already been said, to

the development of the Imperial idea in his party. He brought into prominence the position of England as an Imperial Power, and substantially increased her influence on Continental politics. But before his first innings his sister Sarah was dead; and before his second his wife had been taken from him. He was elderly in 1867, old in 1873. "It has all come too late," he said.

Of these later days I shall not now speak in detail, as Mr. Monypenny's volumes have not told us their inner history.

## II

## LORD CROMER ON DISRAELI

I REFERRED in my last essay to Lord Cromer's remarkable study of Disraeli, written originally in the *Spectator* and afterwards published as a volume. It contains passages that are full of insight. But it includes a severe indictment. "Disraeli," Lord Cromer writes, was a "political adventurer" who "used his genius to found a political school based on extreme self-seeking opportunism. In this respect he cannot be acquitted of the charge of having contributed towards the degradation of English political life." This charge, which I cannot accept as just, supplies a suitable theme for some further observations on a singularly intricate character.

It has called forth indignant protests from Disraeli's admirers. Indeed, it is not to be wondered at that the generation which knew the Disraeli of the 'seventies should resent an account which ranked the great Tory statesman of their youth as nothing better than an unprincipled and self-seeking adventurer. I venture to think that all the most interesting passages in Lord Cromer's analysis of Disraeli's character may stand, while yet one may strongly join issue with him on his disparaging conclusion. A self-seeking adventurer and opportunist is one who lacks, or at least does not act upon, political convictions, and has no other aims besides his own personal advancement. I do not think this can possibly be said of Disraeli in the face of obvious facts. His active mind was full of views and aims quite unconnected with his personal advancement. No doubt there was an element of opportunism in his early career, and he had a passion for success. He conceived a determination which hardly any one in his position would have ventured to conceive, that he would rise to the very top of the political ladder ; and only an indomitable pluck which was not over sensitive to petty scruples could have enabled him to realize that ambition. For him to get into Parliament at all was difficult. He had to look for help where he could get it. And, agreeing with neither party, he did avail himself of assistance from members of both. Had Disraeli at the outset relied for success on nothing but the scrupulous advocacy of political ideals, he could never have become a great statesman at all. He would not have had the chance, for he would never have got to the front.[1] Lord Cromer seems to me to ignore this. He deals with Disraeli's earlier career as though it were exclusively an index, and a complete index, to his inspiring motives and ideals, quite apart from his sheer necessities. It might be so in the case of one who began political life

---

[1] That Disraeli's cleverness helped him to the front is not inconsistent with the fact that it created a certain mistrust of him in his party later on, and was so far detrimental rather than helpful to his influence when he became leader. Simple and straightforward minds could not quite understand him. I say this in reply to a critic who lays stress on this latter fact as inconsistent with what I say in the text. I do not see the inconsistency. The qualities which bring an obscure man to the front— the clever use of opportunity and insistent pushing—are not necessarily those which inspire complete confidence when he has arrived.

with such advantages as William Pitt, for whom an independent position was secure from the first. Pitt was free to concentrate his energies on public objects with little or no *arrière pensée* to personal advancement. With Disraeli it was otherwise. He had to push to the front rank. It was only after he had got there that he could adequately display his larger aims as a statesman.

But even in his early career Disraeli was not opportunist at the cost of being false to his convictions. He never for a moment pretended to endorse the views of the leaders of the Whig party, though he had friends in the rank and file. On the contrary, he consistently denounced them. His vehement personal attacks on Peel may have been largely prompted by opportunist motives. Grant Duff relates in his Diary that Disraeli excused his action to Peel's daughter on that very ground. "It was a splendid opportunity for a young man," he said. And he added: "Did you ever see a little dog bark at a big dog? I was that little dog." But while these personal assaults on Peel brought him to the front, they involved no unfaithfulness to conviction. Disraeli adhered consistently to Peel's earlier policy (in which he had concurred) of moderate Protection, of a modification of the Corn Laws as opposed to their repeal. It was Peel who changed, and not Disraeli. Thus Disraeli cannot be justly accused of any desertion of political principles. It can only be said that he advocated what were his genuine views in such a manner as to tell for his own advancement. To depict him as merely an opportunist is, indeed, to miss the very essence of his genius. The thorough-going opportunist is a trimmer. He is the antithesis to the man of ideas. And the author of *Coningsby* and *Sibyl* was pre-eminently a man of ideas. This, indeed, Lord Cromer elsewhere in his essay to some extent recognizes. But he nowhere recognizes that it was to the ideas and not to opportunist methods that Disraeli mainly looked for achieving success. I cited in my first essay his remark in *Coningsby* that the second-rate man succeeds by intrigue, the first-rate man by great talents and great truths. Disraeli regarded himself as a first-rate man, and he meant to tread the first-rate man's path to success.

Lord Cromer makes the same mistake as do those who accuse indiscriminately of selfishness all who seek after their own happiness. Ambition, like the desire for happiness, is natural to man. It is hard to get away from either : but we may seek happiness either by satisfying our higher nature which prompts us to beneficence, or by purely selfish pleasure. And a statesman may gratify ambition for success by striving merely to be prominent, or to be really great. Disraeli certainly aimed at the latter. And no mere opportunist can become a great leader of men. Lord Cromer does not exaggerate the degree of Disraeli's ambition, but he mistakes its quality.

An element of opportunism is found in every practical statesman. But it was not more conspicuous in Disraeli,—in his later life at all events—than it was, for example, in Palmerston. In the great measures of his first premiership—the extension of the franchise and the removal of Jewish disabilities—his action was the reverse of opportunist in the ordinary sense. He opposed rather than fell in with the current of traditional opinion in the Tory party, and was actuated by his own long-standing ideals.

Then, again, his foreign policy, during his second tenure of highest office, lifted English statesmanship once again, as Palmerston had lifted it, above the somewhat parochial standpoint of Mr. Gladstone and of the Manchester school. Doubtless there were startling actions which were denounced by critics as theatrical. But they were often justified by the event. One of his severest critics—Grant Duff—who had laughed at Disraeli's rather sensational purchase of the Suez Canal shares, which secured for England the key to India, had the candour to admit in later years that it had proved an immense financial success.[1] When our ships appeared suddenly at the Dardanelles in 1877, and when the Indian troops were sent to Malta, people talked of a *coup de théâtre*, but the demonstration had its effect on the Russians.[2] The treaty of St. Stefano and the Berlin Congress were largely due to what Russia took to be signs that England was in earnest and prepared to act.

Lord Cromer's criticism on Disraeli's policy of democratic Toryism, while undoubtedly it has some force, nevertheless fails to face the crux of the question as a practical one, namely, that the alternative policy of making the Tory party dependent on the middle classes was, in the 'fifties and 'sixties, impossible. The alliance between the bulk of the middle classes and the Liberals was very closely cemented. The wage-earning class was, so to say, much more open to an offer from the Tories. This was decisive for a practical statesman, though I admit that a special

[1] *Out of the Past*, by Sir M. E. Grant Duff (Murray), vol. ii. p. 207.

[2] The general impression on the Continent had been that India would be a source of embarrassment in case of war. But the arrival of Indian troops in Malta set free our own troops for active service elsewhere.

alliance with the shopkeeping classes would in any case have been very repugnant to Disraeli's prejudices. There is, no doubt, some truth in Lord Cromer's contention that the middle class, which has a certain stake in the country, would form a more reliable support for Conservatism than the wage-earning class. That class is the demagogue's natural prey. It has less to lose by revolution, and has less knowledge and critical power wherewith to appraise the real value of a specious promise. Radicals can always go " one better " than Conservatives in the demagogue's bids for support. But in the 'fifties and 'sixties the alliance between the middle class and the Whigs was too firm to be broken.

Mr. Monypenny's remarks on Disraeli's consistency (in the first volume of his biography) are, I think, very just. So far as ideas go, Disraeli was from first to last consistent. His faith in democracy, his reverence for traditional institutions, his dislike of the Whig oligarchy, his desire to secure a modification of the Corn Laws, but without the sacrifice of agricultural interests, his sympathy with the people before such sympathies had become fashionable—all these are visible in Disraeli's public utterances from first to last. He had not, as Mr. Monypenny happily expresses it, "the self-conscious consistency of the moral precisian "; but certain cardinal ideas possessed him, and possessed him consistently. Why then was he accused of inconsistency ? Because the world is apt to measure consistency in a statesman rather by the etiquette of party allegiance which it understands than by ideas which it does not understand. Yet, as Mr. Monypenny says, " A man with a perfectly consistent party record will be more likely to win

E

distinction as a good partisan than as a great statesman. If we are to measure consistency by ideas,"
Mr. Monypenny continues, "Disraeli is the most consistent [among his contemporaries], and yet more than
any of the others he was to suffer throughout his
career from the reputation of political time-server and
adventurer acquired in these early and errant years.
In one sense this reputation was wholly unjust; in
another it had not been unprovoked, nor, indeed,
wholly undeserved. In his guiding principles and
ideas he had changed far less than most of his judges
and critics, but the world, which looks only to exter-
nals, saw that he had been in communication, if not
in co-operation, with men at the opposite poles of
politics, and drew its conclusions accordingly. He
had been too eager in his desire for 'tangible and
immediate success, too reckless in his disregard for
the conventions of political life; and he had thus
aroused in many a distrust which he was never wholly
to allay." [1]

At the same time, while I admit Mr. Monypenny's
plea that Disraeli was essentially consistent, it cannot
be denied that his irrepressible habit of banter sometimes suggested a lower standard of political consistency than he really acted on. For example, the
racy passage on party allegiance in his now forgotten
novel, *The Young Duke*, which was avowedly autobiographical, must have confirmed the solemn critics
in their estimate of him as a political *farçeur*.

Am I a Whig or a Tory? I forget. As for the Tories,
I admire antiquity, particularly a ruin; even the relics of the
Temple of Intolerance have a charm. I think I am a Tory.

[1] *Life of Disraeli*, I. p. 277.

But then the Whigs give such good dinners, and are the most amusing. I think I am a Whig. But then the Tories are so moral, and morality is my forte ; I must be a Tory. But the Whigs dress so much better ; and an ill-dressed party, like an ill-dressed man, must be wrong. Yes ! I am a decided Whig.

And yet—I feel like Garrick between Tragedy and Comedy.

I think I will be a Whig and Tory alternate nights, and then both will be pleased ; or I have no objection, according to the fashion of the day, to take place under a Tory ministry, provided I may vote against them.

Disraeli's political seriousness and earnestness is, I think, the true problem, not his sincerity. Sincerity is sometimes understood to mean frankness. If so, he was the most sincere of politicians. It is his own naked avowals that fame was his chief object that have put weapons into Lord Cromer's hands. Political sincerity may again mean consistency. If so, Disraeli has a strong case—stronger than that of his two chief opponents—Peel and Gladstone—each of whom can be charged with at least two famous reversals of their own policy. But sincerity may also mean depth and seriousness. How deeply and how seriously do public objects, which we genuinely desire, move us ? How deep is their force as motives ? Johnson denied depth of sincerity to the butcher who descanted on patriotism. "When," he remarked, "a butcher says his heart bleeds for his country, he has, in fact, no uneasy feeling." How far were Disraeli's real convictions deeply serious ? How far did a certain underlying cynicism accompany all his aspirations ? Here we have an interesting question which cannot be answered without a study of Disraeli's very peculiar

mental temperament. This has been a puzzle to the
ordinary Englishman—largely, no doubt, because of
the Oriental element in it on which Lord Cromer
dwells. The aims and motives of the Oriental puzzle
us much as a cat puzzles us. We know when a dog
is pleased and what he wants; but the emotions of a
cat are often shrouded in mystery for us. Indeed,
one of our poets once compared a cat to the
mysterious Oriental, a bustling collie dog to the
straightforward Western. But we have, moreover,
to consider in Disraeli not a type—for he had many
qualities distinctly English (his courage and pertinacity
for example)—but a very unique individual.

The twelfth Duke of Somerset—Disraeli's old
friend long before he entered the House of Commons
—has left it on record that he once asked Disraeli in
early years what he considered the most desirable life.
Disraeli replied: " A continued grand procession from
manhood to the tomb." [1]  Grant Duff records in his
Diaries how, at the great party given to open the
Foreign Office when Disraeli was Prime Minister in
the 'seventies, after handing the Princess of Wales
to her carriage, he came back and saw, waiting in
the hall, the Duchess of Somerset, who had been
so kind to him in the days of his struggling
youth. The whole drama of life seemed to flash
upon him suddenly. He turned to her and said:
"Isn't it all a play?" Life was to Disroeli always
something of a drama in which he meant to play a
prominent part—a pictorial procession of great men,
among whom he meant to be conspicuous. He
had a touch of megalomania, and a touch of the
theatrical. Without for a moment saying that his

[1] *Disraeli*, by W. Meynell (Hutchinson), p. 185.

conception of life was immoral, I think it is true
to say that it was somewhat non-moral. His
immediate aims grew far larger and less personal
after he had attained success ; he concentrated on
important public objects and conceived a great policy
of Imperialism ; but his dramatic way of viewing life
never left him. It was an unalterable trait in his
mental character.

We see it plainly in the graphic accounts of his
doings and triumphs contained in his early letters to
his friends. As quite a lad he was sent to Abbotsford
to negotiate on Murray's behalf with Lockhart and
Sir Walter Scott concerning the founding of a newspaper—the *Representative.* He writes from thence
with all the airs of an ambassador. The proposed
journal is to be a great international power, a " mighty
engine." Its writers are to include the greatest men
of the day, foreigners as well as Englishmen. The
delicate negotiations with Abbotsford are shrouded in
mystery. The eminent personages concerned are
alluded to, not by their names, but by a prearranged
code. Murray is warned to stay in London, as the
chief actors may find it the best diplomacy to come
up quite suddenly. His friends, amused at his pose,
dubbed him "the young plenipotentiary."

The letters to his sister Sarah, during his foreign
tour of 1830, are, again, intensely dramatic. They
evince the fascination which the mere drama of life,
with its startling and picturesque incidents, had for
him. To play a conspicuous part in this drama was a
passion so overwhelming that at first he thirsted even
for notoriety in default of fame of higher quality.
We have often heard of Disraeli's extravagant dress
in his early years. Perhaps few people before Mr.

Monypenny's volumes appeared had realized quite how far it went, or appreciated his love of making even a momentary sensation by it and being stared at. I dwell on this fact, as I think it is really indicative of a marked and permanent feature in his character which had serious consequences. When he went for a foreign tour with his friend Meredith in 1830, the account of his performances in this line would be almost incredible, but for unquestionably authentic records. He appeared to change one fantastic dress for another almost every day. Meredith thus describes his appearance when Disraeli came to see him some time before they started on their travels : " He came up Regent Street when it was crowded, in his blue surtout, a pair of military light blue trousers, black stockings with red stripes, and shoes ! 'The people,' he said, 'quite made way for me as I passed. It was like the opening of the Red Sea, which I now perfectly believe from experience. Even well-dressed people stopped to look at me.' I should think so ! " adds Meredith.

On his first meeting a few days later with Lytton Bulwer at dinner in Hertford Street, his appearance was thus described by his host : " He wore green velvet trousers, a canary-coloured waistcoat, low shoes, silver buckles, lace at his wrists, and his hair in ringlets."

In the course of his wanderings he broke out into fresh extravagances. He spent part of his time at Malta in company with Mr. James Clay—afterwards a well-known member of Parliament. One week they went yachting, and Disraeli donned a fresh costume to suit the occasion, which he thus describes to his brother :

' I have spent very agreeable hours in a yacht which Clay has hired, and in which he intends to turn pirate. The original plan was to have taken it together, but Meredith was averse to this, and we have become his passengers at a fair rate, and he drops us whenever and wherever we like. You should see me in the costume of a Greek pirate. A blood-red shirt, with silver studs as big as shillings, an immense scarf for girdle, full of pistols and daggers, red cap, red slippers, broad blue-striped jacket and trousers.

His overweening self-confidence made him think his extravagance impressive and thoroughly welcome. He assumed the languor of an *exquisite*, and gave himself the superior airs of an intellectualist who looked down on the ordinary sports of youth. He writes as follows from Malta :

Here the younkers do nothing but play rackets, billiards and cards, race and smoke. To govern men you must either excel them in their accomplishments or despise them. Clay does the one ; I do the other ; and we are both equally popular. Affectation tells here even better than wit. Yesterday at the racket court, the ball entered and lightly struck me. I took it up, and, observing a young rifleman, I humbly requested him to forward its passage into the court, as I really had never thrown a ball in my life. This incident has been the general subject of conversation at all the messes to-day.

Unfortunately, Sir William Gregory has left an account derived from Clay himself of the impression Disraeli made on his company, which tells a very different story :

"When the two got into society," Sir William writes, " Disraeli made himself so hateful to the officers' mess that, while they welcomed Clay, they ceased to invite ' that damned bumptious Jew boy.' "

It seems that when he did dine with the officers he appeared in Andalusian dress, "in his majo jacket," writes Meredith, "white trousers, and a sash of all the colours in the rainbow. In this wonderful costume he [also] paraded all round Valetta, followed by one half of the population of the place, and, as he said, putting a complete stop to all business."

When he gets to Yanina he is intoxicated with the general splendour and colour of the costumes and the Oriental air of the place, and is prompted to don an entirely fresh costume *à la Turque.* It is all described by him in a letter to Benjamin Austen:

I can give you no idea in a letter of all the Pashas, and all the Silictars, and all the Agas that I have visited and that have visited me ; all the pipes I smoked, all the coffee I sipped, all the sweetmeats I devoured. . . . For a week I was in a scene equal to anything in the *Arabian Nights*—such processions, such dresses, such *cortèges* of horsemen, such caravans of camels. Then the delight of being made much of by a man who was daily decapitating half the Province. Every morning we paid visits, attended reviews, and crammed ourselves with sweetmeats; every evening dancers and singers were sent to our quarters by the Vizier or some Pasha. . . .

I am quite a Turk, wear a turban, smoke a pipe six feet long, and squat on a divan. Mehemet Pasha told me that he did not think I was an Englishman because I walked so slow : in fact, I find the habits of this calm and luxurious people entirely agree with my own preconceived opinions of propriety and enjoyment, and I detest the Greeks more than ever. You have no idea of the rich and various costume of the Levant. When I was presented to the Grand Vizier I made up such a costume from my heterogeneous wardrobe that the Turks, who are mad on the subject of dress, were utterly astounded. . . .

Further details of the costume are given by

Meredith : "Figure to yourself," he writes to a friend,
" a shirt entirely red, with silver studs as large as
sixpences, green pantaloons with a velvet stripe down
the sides, and a silk Albanian shawl with a long fringe
of divers colours round his waist, red Turkish slippers,
and, to complete all, his Spanish majo jacket covered
with embroidery and ribbons." " Questo vestito
Inglese o di fantasia ? " asked a little Greek physician
who had passed a year at Pisa in his youth. " Inglese
e fantastico," was Disraeli's oracular reply.

Throughout his travels we see both his keen sense
of the dramatic and his love of splendour. This could
easily be illustrated at great length.

When he is in Spain he writes from Cadiz : " The
white houses and the green jalousies sparkle in the
sun. Figaro is in every street, Rosina in every
balcony." From a score of letters in the same strain
I select a quotation from one to his mother, written
from Granada :

A Spanish lady with her fan might shame the tactics of
a troop of horse. Now she unfurls it with the slow pomp
and conscious elegance of a peacock. Now she flutters it
with all the languor of a listless beauty, now with all the live-
liness of a vivacious one. Now, in the midst of a very tor-
nado, she closes it with a whir which makes you start, pop !
In the midst of your confusion Dolores taps you on the elbow;
you turn round to listen, and Florentina pokes you in your
side. Magical instrument ! You know that it speaks a particular language, and gallantry requires no other mode to
express its most subtle conceits or its most unreasonable
demands than this slight, delicate organ. But remember,
while you read, that it is not here, as in England, confined
alone to your delightful sex. I also have my fan, which
makes my cane extremely jealous. If you think I have
grown extraordinarily effeminate, learn that in this scorching

clime the soldier will not mount guard without one. Night wears on, we sit, we take a *panal*, which is as quick work as snapdragon, and far more elegant; again we stroll. Midnight clears the public walks, but few Spanish families retire till two. A solitary bachelor like myself still wanders, or still lounges on a bench in the *warm* moonlight. The last guitar dies away, the cathedral clock wakes up your reverie, you, too, seek your couch, and, amid a gentle, sweet flow of loveliness, and light, and music, and fresh air, thus dies a day in Spain.

When he gets to the East the drama heightens. A touch of the theatrical comes out in a phrase he uses in a letter to Mrs. Austen: "All was like life in a *pantomime* or an Eastern tale of enchantment."

Of course, he imagined himself as playing a central *rôle* in this fascinating drama of life, and his methods were marked by dramatic effects. This was apparent in his later career, as well as in his earlier struggle for place. But these effects did not ever consist in a mere skilful playing to the gallery with a view to winning applause—the course of a systematic opportunist. On the contrary, just as he irritated the officers at mess, so he later on irritated many of his constituents by his affectations and showy dress, and eventually irritated the House of Commons in his first speech by his turgid and bombastic eloquence. No doubt the resolute determination to get on made him gradually correct faults which offended those on whom his success depended. But in the first instance he was acting in the drama of life a part suited to his own sense of what that drama should be. And thus he was dramatic in pursuing even his highest political ideals. He was making history. History was for him a scenic drama, and he cared only for its stirring pages.

His Oriental love of magnificence never woke a
response in his English followers. It did not in early
years contribute to his personal popularity—rather
the reverse. But it had a large part in the picture of
his own life which satisfied his ideal. Probably he
needed appreciative sympathy from some—and he
got it from Bulwer, from his wife, and, more than
all, from his sister Sarah, to whom he was so
devoted and who so entirely shared his own likes and
dislikes. Sarah Disraeli died before her brother
became Prime Minister in 1867, and pathetic is the
record by Sir Philip Rose of Disraeli's reply to a
word said to him on this subject. Rose lamented that
Sarah had not lived to see the great day, and Disraeli,
deeply affected, could only reply in a few broken
words: "Ah! poor Sa, poor Sa; we've lost our
audience, we've lost our audience!"

Grant Duff—not perhaps a wholly sympathetic
critic, but a faithful raconteur—used to declare that
Disraeli involuntarily let out the feeling he had that
he was taking part in a dramatic representation by
referring to Her Majesty's Government in a speech
as "Her Majesty's Company."

Dramatic surprises were, of course, to the end a
characteristic feature in Disraeli's policy. During the
few years of his glory in the 'seventies, a stern Whig
critic remarked, "Lord Beaconsfield has taken John
Bull to Cremorne. The old fellow rather likes it, but
there will be a morrow to the debauch." His sense
of the dramatic did not desert him as the drama drew
to a close. Some one asked him when he got to the
House of Lords how he liked it. He replied: "I
feel that I am dead, but in the Elysian fields." Lord
Ronald Gower has given an account of him sitting

looking into the fire in his last years, conjuring up the picture of old friends who were dead, and murmuring : " Dreams, dreams, dreams ! "

With the frankness that characterized him throughout, he faced the inevitable end.  As he drove with Lord Salisbury from one polling booth to another during the election of 1880, and saw that a Liberal victory was inevitable, he remarked, " What a difference age makes: to you, I suppose, all this is agreeable excitement, to me it is the end of all things."

One more word as to Disraeli's determination to succeed.  Most people have heard of his shouting out to a hostile House of Commons after his first speech, " The time will come when you will hear me."  Ten years earlier he had advised a friend to keep his letters, as they would some day be worth ten guineas apiece.  Most people have heard of his telling Lord Melbourne, after he had been in the House two years, that he meant to be Prime Minister.  Not so many, perhaps, have heard that Lord Melbourne, who had treated the remark at the time as the vagary of an eccentric, lived to see him, in 1848, chosen leader of the party in the Commons, and, on hearing the news, exclaimed : " By God ! the fellow will do it yet."  I desire, however, here to emphasize a further point.  He wanted not only fame, but the sweets of fame.  And he wanted them while he could enjoy them.  He was an epicure in his ambition, though he would toil for his pleasures.  He once said that he must get fame as a young man, and could not be satisfied with waiting for it until old age.  Anyhow, he pooh-poohed the idea of posthumous fame being worth anything.  When he published the first part of his only epic poem, he introduced it to the public with these words : " I am not one who finds consolation for the neglect of my contemporaries in the imaginary plaudits of a more sympathetic posterity. The public will decide whether this work is to be continued and completed. If it passes its vote in the negative, I shall, without a pang, hurl my lyre to limbo."

One of his characters in *Contarini Fleming* gives utterance to the same sentiment in the following words : " A man of great energies aspires that they shall be felt in his lifetime ; that his existence should be rendered more intensely vital by the constant consciousness of his multiplied and multiplying power. Is posthumous fame a substitute for all this ? "

The passion for fame seems to have cost him at moments when he doubted of success all the pain that a hopeless love passion sometimes costs—if we are to take as autobiographical another passage in the same novel : " To feel the strong necessity of fame . . . with no simultaneous faith in your own power " causes " despondency for which no immortality can compensate."

This thirst for immediate results, this determination that the excitement of political fame should come at once, was, I think, illustrative of his view of life as a drama and no more. It meant a certain want of deep faith, and consequently of the deepest seriousness. There was a touch of scepticism and irony underlying his fascination in the drama. Yet his fascinated interest in it all contributed to the picturesqueness and the attractiveness of his own life. Of this I shall say more directly.

One quality he possessed which is often lacking in

Englishmen—extreme frankness. Personal ambition
was openly proclaimed by him—in words quoted
in my last essay—as the ruling motive of his life.
This out-spokenness was opposed to English virtues
and to English vices alike. Most Englishmen,
while they are prepared to respect avowed ambition, if it is an ambition to do great things for one's
country or for the world, are not prepared to respect
what seems to be mere self-seeking, still less its
open avowal. But again, to this high standard
among Englishmen, often corresponds what may fairly
be called a vice—a touch, at all events, of hypocrisy.
A Frenchman once defended it by saying, " L'hypo-
crisie est l'hommage que la vice rend à la vertu."
Many Englishmen, whose ruling passion is personal
ambition in the same sense as it was with Disraeli,
profess to be actuated rather by public-spirited motives
which in reality have no effect on them at all. Even
to themselves they will not own the truth of which
they are ashamed as Disraeli did without shame. Mr.
Snodgrass protested : " It was not the wine, it was the
salmon." Disraeli was destitute both of the English
scruple, and of its corresponding vice.

In all this the fates provided him with a most
effective foil in the person of his famous antagonist
—Mr. Gladstone. A great friend of Gladstone's
once said to me when I had been deprecating in conversation with the great man a certain want of ambition in a character under discussion : " You must not
say that to *him ;* he thinks all ambition wrong." This
was certainly the antithesis to Disraeli's frank avowals.
If Disraeli often had the mannerism of his cynical
indifference, Gladstone had to an intense degree the
mannerism of his earnestness. And it led hostile

critics to charge him with a lack of the deepest sincerity
on precisely the opposite grounds from those on which
Disraeli's sincerity was impugned. Mr. Monypenny
has, as I have said, shown conclusively that Disraeli,
in spite of untoward appearances was, nevertheless,
from first to last consistent in his political views. It
is difficult to maintain the same in respect of the man
who began life, in Macaulay's phrase, as the "rising
hope of the stern, unbending Tories," and ended it
an extreme Radical, as Radicalism was conceived
in the 'eighties. Consistency is again not the obvious
characteristic of the man who in 1882 was zealous
for coercion in Ireland, and in 1885 an enthusiastic
advocate of Home Rule. One who greatly admired
Gladstone—the late Mr. Aubrey de Vere—was so impressed by the unexpected changes in his policy that
he compared his proceedings to the knight's moves at
chess.

It is not to my purpose to go further into the
causes of Mr. Gladstone's political variations. Bismarck, I believe, held that his extraordinary fertility
of speech was responsible for them, as it enabled him
to find the best reasons for doing what party motives
really prompted. "His eloquence is his bane,"
Bismarck is said to have remarked, "not so much
because he can persuade others of a bad case, but
because he persuades himself." Be this as it may,
Gladstone's intense mannerism of conscientiousness
was in marked contrast to Disraeli's mannerism of
cynical indifference. And his critics taxed him with
talking too much of an inflexible conscience which
proved so plastic, while Disraeli's critics accused
him of an unscrupulousness which was naked and
unashamed.

A friend of mine once told me that he had heard Gladstone's character discussed in Carlyle's presence, and some one asked Carlyle : " Do you think he really has a conscience ? " Carlyle reflected, and then replied : " I think he has a conscience, but it is a very peculiar conscience. It is a conscience which moves in turn to every point of the compass. It is what I call a rotatory conscience." Labouchere, who regarded Gladstone as an out-and-out opportunist, in spite of his protestations of profound conscientiousness, is reported to have said : " I don't mind Mr. Gladstone playing with three aces up his sleeve ; but I do object to his trying to persuade us that Almighty God put them there." That sayer of good things—Dr. Magee, Archbishop of York—was once listening to a conversation on Gladstone's sudden change in respect of Home Rule which some one described as Gladstone's "method of dealing with the Irish question." " No, no," interpolated Magee, " not dealing—shuffling ! "

Mr. Gladstone's earnestness in conversation, his thirst for information, his absence of pretension, had their own attractiveness, for all that might be said of his instability. And I think, too, that both Disraeli's rather cynical frankness and his love of the pictorial and dramatic had a very attractive side. Determined though he was to make his mark, he had little or no egotism. " He seldom talked of himself," is the testimony of one who saw him often in later years. His mind was objective, and not at all introspective. He looked at himself with profound interest, but from outside. There was a certain simplicity in him, and some strong and lovable feelings shine forth in him clear as crystal, as, for example, his home affections. These are conspicuous in his love for his wife, and for his sister Sarah, notwithstanding occasional histrionic expressions in his correspondence with the former. Queen Victoria, an excellent judge of men, was fascinated by him, and the following graphic word-picture of their relations, published in the *Quarterly Review* after her death, is worth citing :

He was never in the least shy ; he did not trouble to insinuate ; he said what he meant in terms the most surprising, the most unconventional ; and the Queen thought that she had never in her life seen so amusing a person. He gratified her by his bold assumptions of her knowledge, she excused his florid adulation on the ground that it was " Oriental," and she was pleased with the audacious way in which he broke through the ice that surrounded her. He would ask across the dinner-table, " Madam, did Lord Melbourne ever tell your Majesty that you were not to do this or that ? " and the Queen would take it as the best of jokes. Those who were present at dinner when Disraeli suddenly proposed the Queen's health as Empress of India, with a little speech as flowery as the oration of a maharajah, used to describe the pretty smiling bow, half a curtsey, which the Queen made him as he sat down. She loved the East, with all its pageantry, and all its trappings, and she accepted Disraeli as a picturesque image of it. It is still remembered how much more she used to smile in conversation with him than she did with any other of her Ministers.

Truly dramatic is the story of Disraeli's friendship with Mrs. Brydges Willyams, a Spanish Jewess of the da Costa family, which belongs to a period subsequent to that dealt with by Mr. Monypenny. Mrs. Willyams conceived an enthusiastic admiration for him and entreated him to meet her. Her pertinacity eventually won the day, and he kept tryst with her as she asked at the fountain in the Crystal Palace. The meeting ended in a friendship. She was rich. She

F

was determined to help his career substantially. She left him all her fortune when she died. She devoted herself to him as long as she lived. I will quote two letters to Mrs. Willyams of the year 1862, each of which is in Disraeli's flowery and imaginative manner :

I am quite myself again ; and as I have been drinking your magic beverage for a week, and intend to pursue it, you may fairly claim all the glory of my recovery, as a fairy cures a knight after a tournament or a battle. I have a great weakness for mutton broth, especially with that magical sprinkle which you did not forget. I shall call you in future after an old legend and a modern poem, " The Lady of Shalott."

\*        \*        \*        \*        \*        \*

December 8, 1862.

They say the Greeks, resolved to have an English king, in consequence of the refusal of Prince Alfred to be their monarch, intend to elect Lord Stanley. If he accepts the charge, I shall lose a powerful friend and colleague. It is a dazzling adventure for the house of Stanley, but they are not an imaginative race, and I fancy they will prefer Knowsley to the Parthenon and Lancashire to the Attic plains. It is a privilege to live in this age of rapid and brilliant events. What an error to consider it a utilitarian age ! It is one of infinite romance. Thrones tumble down, and crowns are offered like a fairy tale ; and the most powerful people in the world, male and female, a few years back were adventurers, exiles, and demireps. *Vive la bagatelle !* Adieu. D.

The drama of a religious service interested Disraeli more than a sermon. Dean Stanley used to tell how he met him one day when he (the Dean) was going *incognito* to hear the service at Westminster Abbey. Disraeli remarking, " I like these Haroun al Raschid performances," went with him. Every one made way for them, and for a short time Disraeli listened to the sermon, but soon began to fidget, being obviously bored. " A very remarkable discourse," he said, "but an engagement summons me. I have been deeply interested—the multitude, the lights, the surrounding darkness, the courtesy—all most remarkable. Good-bye, my dear Dean."

The contrast to Gladstone was completed by Disraeli's unfailing sense of humour. Disraeli's own consciousness of this contrast is illustrated in the following anecdote related by Lord George Hamilton in a letter to myself, from which the writer allows me to quote :

In the Parliament of 1868 (writes Lord George) there were a number of young members on the Conservative side like myself who had been in the habit of taking a good deal of exercise. As members of Parliament we used once a week to row in an eight on the river at Maidenhead, and it was suggested that as a joke we should ask Dizzy to steer us. I went up to him and made the suggestion that if he would undertake that duty we would challenge an eight on the other side with the Prime Minister (Mr. Gladstone) as coxswain. He replied : "All right, my dear boy, but the other damned fellow won't do it, you know."

I submit that so far as there is an element of truth in Lord Cromer's contention that Disraeli was not a wholly trustworthy guide in politics, the fact is due not to his being a self-seeking adventurer without principle—an unjust charge suggested in part by his own cynical avowals of his thirst for fame—but to that imaginative temperament which was in many ways so attractive. Self-seeking was not more marked in him than in many another. It did not involve a sacrifice of conviction to self-advancement. He had at the outset to choose between two parties with neither of which he agreed. A very moderate Tariff Reformer in our own day may pursue his honest aims by allying himself either with Unionist Free Traders or with Tariff Reformers. He agrees with neither. By either alliance he works against the fanatical Tariff Reformers, either as a foe from without, or as a drag on the wheel from within. He is free to be opportunist in his choice because neither alliance means sacrifice of conviction. It was not Disraeli's self-seeking opportunism which prevented his being a wholly safe guide ; it was rather his imaginative and dramatic way of looking at life and his love for startling effects—for green trousers in Regent Street. While imaginative genius may display itself in very remarkable intuitive insight in particular fields, its action is uncertain. It often fails in that careful attention to facts and consequences lying outside the particular field which more systematic and prosaic methods ensure. It is too personal, and apt to be wilful. Mrs. Jellyby may have worked with great insight for the natives of Borrioboola Gha, but she was not a successful mother to Caddy. Where Disraeli saw truly, indeed, he might be dramatic in his methods without doing any one much harm. But one who is bent on being sensational may indulge his passion in other fields in which his touch is less sure, and with serious consequences. And he may neglect very necessary work which does not offer scope for his peculiar genius or interest his moody temper. Duty is often dull, and dulness was Disraeli's pet aversion. Hence a certain mistrust of Disraeli is compatible with recognition of his great qualities as a statesman in some departments. At the same time, more tangible instances of evil consequences from his peculiar temperament must be adduced than have yet been formulated, before the indictment against him becomes very damaging.

It is notorious that moral standards in public life were exceptionally high in the years that followed the European convulsions of the later years of the eighteenth century and the earlier of the nineteenth, and I do not deny that there is at present apparently an increase of adventurous and opportunist statesmanship which plays for its own hand. But the cause I would suggest is to be sought rather in the peculiar political conditions of our time than in the example of Disraeli. It is to the excesses of the present party system, and, I may add, to the excesses of modern democracy, that I venture to ascribe the undeniable fact that principle is less uncompromising and opportunism more marked in the political personages of to-day than it was with those belonging to the age of our fathers.

When party allegiance is carried to an extreme, individuality is crushed, and inflexible assertion of principle becomes far harder in practice. The call to subordinate personal convictions to party decrees is so constant that political independence becomes an impracticable attitude. It may banish a man from public life altogether. Again, when we have to gain the approval of the least educated classes before a policy can become practical politics, statesmen are almost driven to the arts of the demagogue. And this lowers the standard of political honesty. So far as the excesses of the present party system are responsible for the diminution of political principle, the remedy is to be sought, not in revolting from Disraeli's example as immoral, but in attempting to realize one of his own early dreams—the formation of a National party, the aims of which should be higher and more public-spirited than those of either of the existing political divisions.

# III

# GEORGE WYNDHAM

MUCH was written of Mr. George Wyndham in a generous and ungrudging spirit at the time of his death. His charm, his grace, both physical and mental, his versatility as soldier, man of letters and statesman were all commemorated; his great Land Act in Ireland received the fullest acknowledgment. People were really moved at his death, and with a few exceptions the chief organs of public opinion for a brief space gave whole-hearted acknowledgment to what public opinion held that he had done well. Then the world went on its way and resumed the absorbing interests from which it had turned aside for a moment to bestow attention on the sudden extinction of a brilliant light.

Yet most of the kind things that were said might have been true of one whose gifts were immeasurably inferior to George Wyndham's. Many of us feel, as Mr. Balfour said in the House of Commons at the time, that Mr. Wyndham's gifts have not received their full meed of praise, partly because they never found the theatre whence they could be so exhibited as to be unmistakable to the world at large.

" What is truth ? " asked Pilate. " What is fame ? " is a question similar in its apparent simplicity and in its real difficulty. A man's greatness is apt to be

measured by the test which is most of all affected by
the chapter of accidents, namely, visible success.
That is the most obvious test, but it is superficial and
often wholly inadequate. William Watson has told
us in memorable lines that " the facile conqueror " may
be less great than " he, who, wounded sore, . . . sinks
foiled, but fighting evermore." Failure may be more
splendid than success. But in the case before us the
large measure of success actually achieved may be a
serious obstacle to the general recognition of the
splendour of the man's failures. Those who wish to
discourse on this latter aspect of his career have not
before them the inspiring task of rescuing from
obscurity an unknown genius who was crushed and
crowded out in the struggle of life by adverse circumstances. We are dealing on the contrary with one
who for years seemed to be fortune's spoilt child ;
whose circumstances and position were, by comparison with many men of genius, splendid ; who was
a member of the Government at an age when most
men have not yet got into Parliament; who was a
Cabinet Minister in the front rank in his thirties.
Yet it remains true that George Wyndham's true title
to greatness can only be measured by taking into
account powers and actual work that gave sure
promise of greater public successes than he ever
attained, and even by computing the elements of
tragedy in his life. The test supplied by tangible
success is in his case an eminently inadequate test. If
it remains unchallenged he will not be to posterity
what he really was in life.

Mr. Wyndham went to the War Office as Under-
Secretary in 1899. And his work there stood out at
once, in the eyes of those who came across it, as

something on quite a different plane from that of the
ordinary official, even of first-class ability. Helped
no doubt by his early soldier life, he studied the
requirements of our army with the large outlook of a
true statesman. To the end of his life his speeches
on this subject were most memorable. The impression he made on Lord Lansdowne, his chief at
the War Office, is thus recorded by him in a letter
to the present writer :

> You ask me to give you in a few sentences my impression
> of George Wyndham's work at the War Office. It was my
> good fortune to have him for my colleague during the last two
> years of my service as Secretary of State. The War Office
> was not then, and I suppose never has been, exactly a bed of
> roses. Old problems of army organization were still unsolved,
> new problems concerning the arms, ammunition and equip-
> ment of the forces were constantly arising, and the machinery
> of the Office itself, recently reconstructed, was not yet
> working smoothly. On the top of all this came the South
> African War, with its new responsibilities, its revelations and
> its disappointments. The stress was severe, and the repre-
> sentative of the Department in the House of Commons had,
> so far as the Parliamentary burden was concerned, to bear by
> far the heaviest share of the load. George Wyndham bore it
> with infinite patience and good temper, and with untiring
> resourcefulness. Inside the Office he was a tower of strength,
> a keen and thorough worker, always intent upon getting at
> the root of things. He had a rare power of handling difficult
> and complicated questions, and although he could grasp
> details and expound them with unrivalled lucidity, he never
> lost himself in them. I cannot conceive an abler or a more
> delightful colleague.

It was while he was at the War Office that
Wyndham made perhaps his greatest speech in the
House of Commons, in which to a knowledge of his

own subject he added a keen realization of the situation
created by the South African War, which was putting
so many English homes in mourning. This combination called out the greatest gifts of an orator. After
that speech he was freely spoken of as a future Prime
Minister. It was thus at the War Office that he won
his spurs. Yet, when, nearly four years later, he was
offered the post of Secretary for War, his loyalty to
the cause of Ireland, to which he had by then devoted
his whole heart, made him decline it. Here, then,
was one sphere in which he showed his splendid
powers and equipped himself for a great work for
which he all but found his opportunity. That he just
missed that opportunity was in its circumstances
almost tragic. For had he then gone to the War
Office, he would have escaped the check in Ireland
that threw back his political career, and he would have
been supreme in a sphere which he had almost
completely mastered.

But the tragedy of adverse circumstance was far
greater in Ireland itself. Here he had actually found
both his field and the position in which he could
control it. After a brief space he had the most
influential position which exists in that country—he
was Chief Secretary and in the Cabinet. He realized
one great scheme in the Land Purchase Act. Those
who watched things closely saw the extraordinary
gifts which this measure displayed. " I doubt,"
writes Lord Lansdowne, " whether any one else
could have carried the great Land Act which will
always be associated with his name, and which will be
a monument to him *ære perennius.*" The rest of his
programme remained unfulfilled, and its details were
never disclosed to the public. A large section of his

party spoke of his "Irish failure." Yet those who worked with him held that what was great in his plans as an Irish statesman was as visible in schemes that were never realized as in the initial success. The world in summing up a man's fame deducts failure from success, but sometimes a truer estimate is gained not by subtraction but by an addition sum in which much that fails is added to what succeeds. Had George Wyndham come to Ireland merely as an able Chief Secretary with a safe programme, as a party politician who meant to climb the ladder, we should, it is true, have never heard of the Devolution Scheme—as it was called, though Wyndham never used the phrase or accepted this scheme of Lord Dunraven. But we should never have had the Land Act. Both the measure which succeeded and the policy of conciliation which failed told of qualities in themselves great. It needed his immense energy, his enthusiasm, his grasp of detail, his idealism, his concentration on one object, to gain in a brief space such knowledge and insight into the conditions of the country as were necessary to formulate that far-reaching land legislation. But these very qualities led him to study the Irish question all round, not as a party man with the predetermined limitations of a party programme, but as an honest student of Irish history and Irish social conditions, and to conceive an ample programme of which the Land Act was but a part.

He bound himself heart and soul to Ireland. "Ireland," he wrote to a friend in March, 1902, "is in a more plastic state than at any period in my recollection since 1887. Now is the time for moulding her. But this absorbs me mind, body and soul." There are many who remember the joyous enthusiasm

with which he began his work. The dramatic side of
his position in Ireland appealed to him. " I feel like
a Ghibelline Duke in the land of the Guelphs," he
said. When the Land Act was on the eve of passing,
he felt the peculiar joy that comes when concentrated
labour and inspiring dreams are about to be realized
in action. " I 'do' believe that a benignant spirit is
abroad," were the words he chose at this time for an
autograph album. The picture of him, radiant and
even triumphant, turning from one group to another
with a special word for each, as he addressed the
House in the debate on the second reading of his Bill,
must still dwell in the memory of many.

The Bill became law. Troubles were not at once
over. But it was recognized as a great, a very great,
and beneficent measure, the greatest contribution
towards the settling of the Irish question which that
generation had seen. In its author's eyes, however,
it was but the beginning of his work. In the months
that followed he continued to elaborate his schemes
for the country. He refused promotion to other offices,
which the ordinary Chief Secretary would have grasped
at, as an escape from difficulties which soon became
visible on the horizon. He continued to reduce his
plans to practical detail. Such concentration is the way
of the greatest rulers, but one must be an autocrat
like Napoleon to realize all the designs so conceived.
They may be impossible to the party statesman in a
democracy. The policy of conciliation was wrecked
on the rocks of party politics. Its bare discussion
(Wyndham never committed himself finally to any
detailed scheme) was viewed almost as treachery by
the Ulster extremists.

But the tragedy lay in something deeper than

the defeat of any single item of his programme.
Few men are capable of thinking out a programme
which needed so profound a study of the country,
and making it practical. Wyndham believed himself to be capable of this. Many of his friends
thought the same. The tragedy lay in the hard
work and the keen vision of what was possible and
of his own capacity to do it, while the inexorable
conditions of our democracy defeated his plans, not as
it seemed to him by a reasoned opposition, but by
that blind and all-powerful party prejudice, which
makes democracy so often fatal to the schemes of
genius. Wyndham's outlook at starting was simply
that of a Unionist by tradition. And to the end
he was no advocate of Home Rule. But, by force of
study and experience of the country, he came to hold
that, if men strove to emancipate themselves from
party prejudice, Ireland might be developed on
genuinely Irish lines. And this would in all probability have included in course of time a certain limited
concession to the Irish desire for self-government.
"What I preached, in season and out of season," he
wrote two years later, "was that all, no matter to what
party they belonged, and what extreme views they
might hold, should endeavour to agree on practical
proposals of a moderate character." It was the clear
vision of what he could do as he stood but one foot
below the commanding summit whence he might have
actually achieved it that made his enforced descent a
veritable tragedy. According to the world's verdict
this episode brings a heavy deduction from the figures
which stand to the account of his fame. If statesmanship means solely the careful calculation of what party
conditions will admit of, such a verdict may pass. If,

however, the highest statesmanship means the accurate
perception of the needs of a country and insight as to
how they are best met, there are those who hold that
such a verdict must not only be discounted but
reversed.    The ideals which caused his overthrow
bring, according to this view of the case, an immense
accession to the figures which stand to the account of
his genius.    The failure was in party diplomacy; the
success was in formulating those measures which
mark a great ruler.    So at least many of us think;
and the only real test whether or no we are right
in so thinking was denied to him—namely, a fair
trial.

This was the great tragedy of his public life.    The
case of a man of great imagination, who is unpractical,
is not an uncommon one.    But it has not the peculiar
element that made Wyndham's failure so tragic.    On
the contrary, where the dreamer is impotent, Wyndham
was powerful.    He had the rare combination of power
of imaginative conception with grasp of detail and
the ability to reduce his plans to practice.    Vivid as
was the life of imagination which he lived, it never
made him a dreamer.    When the whole instrument
was under his own control, he could reduce to practice
his own complicated schemes.    The programme for
his Irish campaign was the result of brooding
imagination, of laborious study and penetrating
observation, with the one object of discovering what
was best for the country.    But it is the condition
of democratic government that one must often be
satisfied with the second best.    A man whose insight
is ahead of public opinion, and who concentrates his
whole attention on discovering the best, therefore
fails by his very success.    The intense hopefulness of

Wyndham's nature prevented his learning effectively this painful fact until it was too late as far as Ireland was concerned. His very consciousness that he had faced the intrinsic difficulties of his schemes made him forget the extrinsic. The semblance of supreme power in a Chief Secretary who was in the Cabinet made him misjudge—not what was practicable in the country for an autocratic ruler—but the forces which, in fact, limited his own power. The tragedy was that of one who believes himself to see clearly what is needed and how he himself can do it, and is on the point of doing it when he finds himself bound hand and foot and unable to move.

He was never again so near to realizing in action his great powers in the field of practical politics. He never held office again. He made memorable contributions to debates—notably on the education question and on army matters. But he had had a rebuff and had to bide his time. His friends were confident that that time would come. But it did not. Death put an end to such hopes.

And in literature as in politics he showed powers which never had a quite adequate field for their exercise, great literary gifts were visible in a few memorable works—the Introduction to *Shakespeare's Sonnets*, the Preface to North's translation of *Plutarch's Lives*, the Essay on the Poetry of Ronsard, the Addresses on the Springs of Romance in the Literature of Europe and on Sir Walter Scott, and some very perfect translations. But his gifts never found expression in the *magnum opus* that so great a master of thought and style alike could and would some day have given us. What he accomplished was of the first order in quality, and won high appreciation from

the experts, but the full reach of his mind and knowledge was never represented in his published works.
The very richness of his mind made him need time
to make his thoughts "marketable," to reduce them
to the form which the practical requirements of
literature and life demand. Thoughts which crowded
his own exceptional intellect and imagination as one
whole needed to be broken up and subdivided for
others.

I remember one address of his as Lord Rector of
Glasgow University which was so packed with thought
that it would have formed the subject of a great work.
As it stood, while careful readers and thinkers saw
how pregnant were its suggestions, it inevitably
passed over the heads of an audience which needed
for its comprehension subdivision, explication, and
illustration for which the opportunity gave him no
time or scope. And this instance is typical of many
another. Those who had the best opportunity of
knowing his mind felt that his work hitherto had been
an elaborate preparation for the day when complete
and unmistakable public achievement should bring
home to the world at large the full extent of gifts
which were known to many friends. That day never
came. He was cut off at the very season at which
his powers were attaining their full ripeness for
practical use, and when experience was making him
more fully alive to the necessary conditions for
effectively conveying to others the stores of his own
mind.

In estimating George Wyndham, then, one must
speak primarily of what he was, and of what he
thought and planned. He and his work can no more
be gauged by his visible successes than Burke's

speeches can be estimated by their effect on the
House of Commons. When Burke rose, the House
soon emptied. Yet to us, who now read the speeches
at leisure, their greatness is unmistakable. Similarly
the interest of Wyndham's mind and his potential
statesmanship are something far greater than what the
chapter of accidents allowed him to impress unmistakably on the world at large. This was due partly, as
in Burke's case, to certain defects in the man's power
of making himself felt at once by the many; but in
the field of practical statesmanship which Burke never
occupied it was due far more to accidental conditions specially hampering to his peculiar genius.

What Wyndham thought and planned will not be
known fully until a selection from his correspondence
and private memoranda is published. But an idea
of his methods and personality may be gained by the
study of his speeches and writings, and to these may
here be added some account of the man as he was
known to his many friends.

The two salient gifts that ran through all his work,
in literature as well as in politics, were just those
which were noted by Lord Lansdowne at the War
Office, and by his colleagues in Ireland—the imaginative and intellectual perception which went to the
core of things, and his grasp of detail. These gifts
are generally the possession of different persons.
The genius who makes an outline sketch of a scheme
is not generally the man who fills in the details
and makes it practicable. The man who writes the
most brilliant essay is not, as a rule, the man who
undertakes research that is thorough and exhaustive.
Wyndham could do both. This is a combination
people are slow to believe in. Wyndham's "viewiness"

in politics was to many a proof that he was not
practical. So, too, in literature. His delicate style
and poet's sense of form in his writing made people
slow to believe in the extent of his research and
even in the depth of his thought. Yet in both fields
he was untiring and thorough. Those who were with
him in the War Office and in the Irish Office know
the infinitude of labour he spent in accumulating
detail. I often saw him after a full eight hours spent
in the British Museum, while he was writing his
short introduction to *Shakespeare's Sonnets*. Like
all real workers, he did not spare himself. Half a
page of published work might represent what it had
taken days, perhaps weeks, of reading to discover.
The extent of his reading in a man who led a busy
life of action surprised many who talked much with
him on literature or on history. I once asked him
when he had found time for it. He told me that
the bulk of it was done in his soldier days. He was
quartered, I think, in Cyprus, for many months, and
used to parade his men at six or seven in the morning and read from breakfast to an eight o'clock
dinner. This intellectual orgy was most characteristic, and that he remembered what he read after a
spell of uninterrupted work which would reduce most
brains to stupidity was a testimony to his splendid
powers. The extent of his reading and the extent of
his study of detail in politics were as remarkable as
the gifts of thought and imagination displayed in the
use of his knowledge.

But besides that imaginative insight which
belongs to the speculative intellect he had also the
imagination of the poet which threw a halo round his
everyday tasks. The poetry of life's drama is often

G

visible in historical retrospect. But the actors are seldom fully alive to it at the time. Wyndham, however, was alive to the drama while he was working hardest. Thus he drank deeper than most men of the cup of life.

All this was apparent in his conversation. At its best it was wonderful. There was an animation which infected the company in which he talked. It had humour and humanity. He made everything he dealt with seem intensely worth while ; and the width of his information on his favourite topics never made him prosy. At times, at the small dinners of The Club—which still endeavours to preserve the traditions of Johnson and Burke and Gibbon—he would take his part in talk on poetry, and he and Edward Pember would discourse with ample quotation on Byron or on Browning. But his talk on wider and more theoretic subjects was even better. Perhaps it seemed at times to unsympathetic listeners a little overpowering, and he would be impatient of interruption. But if a listener was prepared to make the self-sacrifice involved in playing avowedly only a secondary part, he would be amply rewarded.

Yet his way of talking had in it certain qualities which might prevent its conveying at once and to all some of his most remarkable endowments. Most of these qualities were veritably " qualities " as opposed to "defects." For one thing, his imaginative thought was so crowded and it took in at a glance so wide a field, that his first utterance might be in the highest degree cryptic. It might appear, especially to prosaic or legal minds, almost nonsense. Analogies were thrown together, drawn from regions the most distant from each other. Extreme paradox might be apparent in the first sketch he threw out of a really pregnant view. Yet if one cross-examined him patiently, and at length, the utterance in question would stand it. The chaos was gradually reduced to order. Strong underlying common-sense was often revealed, after some incidental paradox and exaggeration had been reluctantly discarded. Exact and orderly thought was found to lie at the root of the most startling and vague sentences. Again and again the present writer has in the course of an hour or two (for it might take that time) drawn from Wyndham a most able and explicit development of what had scared and even driven away from the group of talkers some who took half a dozen obscure sentences to be merely the characteristic flights of a strange and active fancy, not to be regarded seriously.

Another peculiarity which sometimes detracted from his persuasiveness in writing as well as in speaking, was his fine sense of words. In this he was both an artist and, to some slight extent, a pedant. The words were usually chosen with a very delicate sense of their fitness. But he once owned that he liked to create surprise by them—to put forward the word his hearer did not expect. This was apt to concentrate attention too much on the form of his speech. Hence at moments there was a touch of preciousness almost a semblance of affectation in the phrases of one who was essentially the reverse of an affected man; who was really intent on thought and the reality of things, though he loved beauty as well. I think this quality somewhat damaged his effectiveness in the House of Commons. And an over-great sensitiveness to hostile opinion in the House had at times a similar effect in lessening the persuasive power of one who was a real orator. A hostile or unsympathetic atmosphere seemed to put something out of tune in the delicate mechanism of his mind. It brought a note of anxiety, unnatural to one who was most at home when he was sanguine or even triumphant.

But the form of his diction was a more frequent if a less serious obstacle to complete success than the nature of his audience. On one occasion he said to a friend before rising in the House: "I mean to speak in chiselled sentences." The "chiselled sentences" were very beautiful, perhaps too beautiful. Their carefully elaborated symmetry told of a mind divided between the form and the matter. The peculiar force of utter concentration on the argument was, at such times, wanting. He lacked the complete persuasiveness attaching to a speaker who is so full of his subject as to be wholly careless of form. Carlyle found a stumbling and halting speech of the Duke of Wellington the most persuasive of all that he heard in the House of Lords, because it carried with it the sense of concentrated conviction. Wyndham in reality spoke with deep conviction, but his attention to form, and the nature of the form actually chosen, were apt sometimes to diminish the sense of conviction he conveyed to others. When this impediment was absent, when over-great subtlety too was absent, when he almost forgot niceties of form, and the human touch prevailed over all else, then the great powers of imagination and reasoning apparent in his speeches were realized to the full by his hearers. On such comparatively rare occasions he could hold the House as only the greatest orators hold it.

Experienced members have assured the present writer that they have never seen that fastidious

assembly so profoundly moved as it was by his speech
on the war on February 1, 1900. That speech even
now appeals to those who read it as a great one. A
little exercise of historical imagination will make its
reader realize why it moved the House of Commons
and the country so profoundly. His words had that
note of concentration on the realities of a great crisis,
of rising above the petty conventions of party politics,
which marked Wyndham's work in Ireland later on.
It was a moment when Englishmen had just become
alive to the fact that the South African War was an
enterprise which called for the whole-hearted devotion
of a nation; when many families had that deep and
tragic realization of the situation which is brought
about by the death of kinsmen on the battlefield;
when the nation was, in fact, rising splendidly to the
demand on it; when the army had to recover from
grave reverses. The Government was asking for the
money that was needed to strengthen our armaments.
The nation was preparing for a generous response,
and this moment was chosen, in accordance with the
most futile traditions of party politics, to move an
amendment to the Address which included a vote of
censure on the Government for its "want of knowledge, judgment, and foresight in their preparations
for the war." Wyndham stripped the proposal of its
conventional character, and insisted that it should be
translated into terms of reality. If the vote were
carried, it would mean that to the strain of the war
was to be added the distracting turmoil of a general
election, and all the confusion attending on a change
of Government. And this on the strength of criticism
which was obviously nothing better or more sincere
than that party fault-finding which was just the rule

of the parliamentary game. Wyndham fairly amazed the House by the thoroughness of his detailed justification of the Government. But, even apart from the weakness of the attack, it was a moment at which such party manœuvring was unworthy and most inopportune. Let us have, Wyndham pleaded, all such criticism from Liberal members as may help the Government to carry out the great national task successfully. But a vote of censure at such a moment was the negation of patriotism and the *reductio ad absurdum* of party manœuvring.

His peroration was long remembered. He appealed to a wider public opinion, which took account of facts, against this petty move which took account only of the chessboard of the party game.

We who are initiated in these manœuvres, which though, perhaps, in ordinary times pardonable, are at this moment inopportune, may understand them ; but no one else will. The taxpayer who is prepared to foot this Bill, whatever it may be, and who is perhaps even now thinking of taking his children back from school and of foregoing his autumn holiday, he will not understand it. Our critics abroad, who are not too indulgent, they will not understand it. Our fellow-subjects in Natal, who have perhaps seen their sons die on the battlefield, and their homesteads destroyed, they will not understand this amendment and this debate. Our kinsmen in America, who are watching the vicissitudes of this war, they will not understand it. The legislatures of every single colony in our Empire, which have shown such a whole-hearted and single-minded concentration upon the Imperial aspects, and upon none other, of our present difficulties, will not understand it. Let us, let this honoured and ancient assembly, of which they are all offshoots and children, bear that in mind. It is usual, Sir, to conclude such a speech in defence, or, as I would prefer to say, in explanation of the conduct of the Government with an appeal to the House to reject the vote of censure which is proposed ; but I am sure that in this case such an appeal is unnecessary. I shall have to make an appeal upon questions of practical importance and living moment. I shall have to ask this House for large financial facilities in order that this war may be prosecuted to the only conclusion which the country would tolerate. I shall have to ask the House for still further financial facilities in order that our system of military defence may be placed upon a sound and lasting basis. I do not ask the House to reject this vote of censure. No, Sir ; this House, which is the fountain of our Imperial resources, and which is the ultimate guardian of the nation's honour, will not commit itself to an action which, if perpetrated, would make the mother of parliaments a laughing-stock to the world.

Here we have all the simplicity of great oratory ; but, as I have said, it was not always so in Wyndham's speeches, or in the discourses to his friends which formed part of his table talk.

There was at times something of the moodiness of the poet in Wyndham's talk, something also in extravagant phrases chosen which might suggest a very different man from what he was. The real man was seen in the hunting-field, as he was seen by his secretaries working with immense industry and splendid intelligence at the most complicated details of the regular business of Ireland, or at schemes for the improvement of the country. In both cases there were courage, practical capacity and thoroughness. His facility in doing what was difficult to other men never made him slipshod. But just as the fop in Nelson hardly prepared men for the great sailor and commander, so some of Wyndham's conversation in which the sensitive poet and the fastidious scholar stood revealed did not prepare men for his thoroughness, and made those who were not actually in contact

with it even sceptical as to its existence. In the
House of Commons, too, the graceful figure and the
graceful action and the graceful phrases would often
suggest something in which ornament was so predominant that many refused to look further. The present
writer has had hot arguments with members of the
House who could not be brought to regard Wyndham
as much more than a brilliant ornament with neither
taste nor talent for real business or hard work. It
is true that mere plodding was not to his taste
—and this gave a superficial plausibility to such an
estimate. But, given a crisis or a cause which roused
him, he displayed unmistakably the combination of
imaginative glow with hard work which is the true
realization of the saying that genius involves an infinite
capacity for taking pains.

Perhaps I only complete the statement of what has
already been implied if I add that he led constantly
and intensely two lives, one of the imagination and
affections, and the other of laborious action. I do not
deny that the poet in him weakened in some degree
the man of action. The life of imagination brought,
as I have said, a certain moodiness. It brought undue
sensitiveness. Here he differed from Disraeli, whose
skin remained tough in spite of his literary and imaginative gifts. But it was surprising how vigorous both
lives were in Wyndham. The public is very slow
indeed to believe in such a combination. Men are
apt to judge by general rules, and exceptions must be
proved to the hilt that they may be acknowledged.
More than ever in our own day people are supposed
to have one line, and one only, in which they really
excel. Members of the House of Commons and
many who only casually conversed with him were

therefore apt to take him as a brilliant amateur in
fields where he really was the equal, nay the superior,
of many professionals. True—be it said again—it
needed a crisis, or a stimulating cause, to bring out all
his powers. But those who from experience had
been gradually convinced of their great reach felt
confident that such a crisis must arise and again give
him his opportunity and his stimulus, as the land
question in Ireland had given them, and that he
would some day suddenly stand before all the world
as the man of the hour. Hence the close of a career
admittedly brilliant comes before many, as it does
before Mr. Balfour, as a tragedy; for the "what might
have beens" stand before them in Wyndham's case
as possibilities so vivid as to be little removed from
certainties.

The man has gone. We have his speeches. We
have his written works. Neither reveal him fully.
The written works are highly specialized, and do not
give the reach of his mind, or give it only in occasional
glimpses. We shall see the man better whenever a
selection is published from his poems and his letters.
These will indicate his touch on life as a whole. His
letters have very much of the quality of his talk.
They are intensely alive. They have occasionally
the touch of preciousness in the use of words, the
vivid and at moments fantastic imagination, the exaggerated phrases, as well as the underlying core of
profound thought which were observable in his conversation. I am allowed, in order to give actuality
to my words in a day when we often get fancy
pictures not at all resembling the originals, to quote a
few specimens of his letters to myself, often thrown off
at white heat.

Wyndham would at times in his letters philosophize subtly on political life, or on the art of oratory; or he would analyze his own sensations in enacting the drama before him. This shows a habit of mind which is very rare indeed in a man of action. Here is a study of the conditions of mob oratory, written on the occasion of his speech at the Congress of April, 1906, on the proposed Education Bill:

It is a great tax to speak in that Hall. Two ladies who were there to-day told me that the echo made Balfour hard to follow and that it was a strain to hear me. One has to discard most of a speaker's devices. No one can see the speaker's expression and—if they have to listen intently—no one can be affected by inflections of the voice.

So the speaker has to aim at broad, simple effects. But that entails severe mental concentration and, all the time, there is a dead weight to be lifted without much help from the audience. *Nobody* could speak to a *hostile* audience in that arena. To say that, is to say that a speaker has to discard his principal function, *i.e. pleading.* He must Declaim and Declare, *i.e.* physically make striking, and mentally make simple, what everybody is prepared to admit.

And yet, I agree with you about the concourse. The facts that so many people have come from so many places to be in one place for one purpose, make one great fact—of sense, and thought, and feeling. The *ingredients* make the magic broth. The speaker has but to stir it with a *big wooden* spoon.

More entirely a record of his own sensations is the following, written amid his own election campaign of the same year:

I have been speaking all over the country to good audiences. It is a strange experience and, I imagine, a bad one on the whole. To be the centre of cheering and yelling for nearly five weeks cannot be good for the soul, the mind or the body. The general impression to me is always barbaric and sometimes savage.

But it has a good side. All barriers of birth, and wealth, and education are cast down. You make real intimate friends of men whom otherwise you would never have known. The intimacy of naked contention is bracing, though primitive. And there are pretty touches. . . . But, in the main, the whole business is blatant and barbaric.

He would dream of the past at the end of the year, and his memories would bring the veritable poet's touch on the beauty and interest of life. In thanking for a Christmas present on the last day of 1899, he writes :

I am alone here with memories and work. But I am not at all unhappy. I begin to see that it will not be so very terrible to be old and alone. We are led on to understand the eternity of all fair things by intimate experience, and apart from metaphysical speculation.

Now that Westminster, that kind heart and chivalrous gentleman, is dead ; that A. is away ; B. married ; my little Percy going to Eton in less than a year ; myself without a prospect beyond labour at the demands of the moment ; the whole past twelve years rise up and sing together of the loving-kindness and beauty which has been round me. No gentle act or graceful movement of those who have adorned my life can ever die.

So I sit alone at the end of this year of travail and anxiety, rejoicing. And I thank you from a full heart for your gift and friendship.

Again, at the end of 1906 :

At last, to-night, I finish this working year.

We buried the Education Bill this afternoon. I have won my election, made speeches, published my little book, made new friends, fought old enemies. I have lived, and life is wonderful.

His letters show a vividness and a theoretic quality in his views on politics which are very rare in an Englishman. At times this meant, as it did with Disraeli, a very sure prescience as to the necessary consequences of events whose causes he recognized so clearly; but even when it led only to *impromptu* and irresponsible suggestions it made his writing intensely stimulating. The following comment by him on the prospects of English Democracy will bring this quality of his mind before the reader, and his concluding sentence suggests the wealth of thought and labour he expended on this and kindred topics.

My knowledge—such as it is—informs me that "Democracy" has never lasted a whole generation. Ferrero's new history of Rome demonstrates this. When an oligarchy, based on war and farming, perishes, you get a good two generations, or three generations of "Roman Equites." The prudent and thoughtful oust the political militia. But they always invoke Democracy after thirty or sixty years. Then Democracy develops the "cry" and the "caucus," and so dies, giving place to Bureaucracy, or Cæsarism, or a combination of the two. My "little knowledge" tells me that this is our disease. But my astonishing—at forty-seven years of age—credulity and buoyant animal spirits say to me, "Tush! The English will do something that no one else has done."

If it were possible to tell one's friends all that one thinks and writes and does, I should like to show you all the memoranda I have written during the last year. But that would take as long as it has taken to play my part in this obscure drama.

In his writing, as in his conversation, the kaleidoscope of his mind produced such surprising pictures abruptly succeeding one another, that I hesitate to

give the most characteristic instances, for the reader
has not the opportunity which conversation affords of
learning by cross-examination how fully thought-out
were trains of reasoning, which he suggested without
developing them, or how real was the connexion in his
mind between things objectively poles apart. I will
content myself with one—by no means among the
strongest—which shows the official at the War Office
indulging in feelings and conceits suggested by his
surroundings. That office has had in the last twenty
years many distinguished occupants—Sir Henry
Campbell-Bannerman, Mr. Arnold-Forster, Lord Haldane, Lord Midleton, Colonel Seely, and others.
But it is safe to say that neither the old premises
in Pall Mall nor the buildings in Whitehall ever
inspired any of these men with the combination of
theories and emotions to which the following letter
gives expression.

After a day spent in grappling with complicated detail, I
find that nothing short of philosophy or poetry is of the least
use to me. I tried a novel the other day, *The Open
Question*, and it aggravated me beyond belief. I want the
very best and prefer it in a different form and remotely aloof
from everyday life. I have bought a Latin Prayer Book—
our Prayer Book, 2nd ed., 1574—and find the Psalms very
stately and soothing. A little Latin goes a long way. But
when your business consists in ploughing like a liner through
seas of slipshod English, you need the very opposite: a
dead language, clean-cut and frigid poetry, or abstract
thought. . . .

I have been inside a good many machines; the Army,
Irish Office, Colonial Expansion; Fleet Street; literary
coteries, and now inside, and of, another office; and no doubt
such experience affects me. The multiplicity of the parts
defying philosophic comprehension and the dead weight of

each dragging down individual energy, drive home the lesson that no individual, or race, or age, or movement embracing many nations and some centuries, is likely to give a decisive cast to the direction of development or even to reconcile any considerable number of divergent forces. But this does not daunt me. I see the universal Flux : but I believe in the choric Dance. In some ways business is a capital exercise or drill. It gives you a number of occasions every day for doing the right thing in the right way. This is capital practice. But far from thinking that mere honest effort at complicated jobs would serve mankind as a substitute for philosophy, religion and art, I do not believe that the second-class clerks could work as they do if we had not all the abstract speculations of 3000 years behind us. We either draw inspiration ourselves, or else we imitate others who drew it, from the half-truths arrived at by lonely thinkers.

But, my goodness ! how much more of courage and com-passion and patience and sincerity is needed if the world is to go any better than it has done ! And what is to be done for the people who are outside the worlds of thought and of action ? For the young lady who lost her temper last week because she was not invited [to a party], or for the officer who resigns his commission when his profession interferes with his shooting ?

All these extracts tell of the active, seething imagination of the man. But he could write of politics in a very concrete and practical vein. I must not, however, cite letters dealing with topics of acute political controversy which might provoke discussions that would distract attention from the real matter in hand. I will confine myself to quoting a long and closely reasoned letter on the attempts of 1906 at a compromise on the education question—attempts which he regarded as profoundly illogical.

I am deeply concerned over the so-called Education Com-promise. It makes me sad to feel how remote I am from

my countrymen, and how remote they are—with all their
excellent qualities—from the rudiments of philosophic thought.
It is dear of them to jump at a compromise, but silly to jump
before looking. They will look afterwards. They will look
back and say, " If we had only known." Yet they do not
realize that they preclude themselves from knowing now—or
ever—owing to their inveterate distrust of thinking. Any
man who thinks on these occasions, and shows that he is
thinking, is suspect. I am suspect. But I *must* think ; and
I *will* believe that it is wise to do so. Yet I am nearly
powerless. I thought and spoke on Wednesday. *The Times*
suppressed my speech. *The Morning Post* published a sketch
of the rest, and suppressed all that I said on education.

. . . Will you help me to make them see before the
smash that there are only two ways of approaching the problem ? (1) To start from uniformity of religious instruction ;
and (2) to start from unity of the national system of education. Or, putting it another way, (1) To start from a neutral
religion ; and (2) to start from the neutrality of the State to
all religions.

From whichever point you make your departure, you
must—I admit and assert—make illogical exceptions to fit in
with present practical needs.

But—and here is the whole matter—if you start from a
fair theory, *cela ne pêche pas par la base.* No wrecker can find a
cranny in your foundation, insert his crow-bar, and overthrow
the whole edifice.

If, on the other hand, you start from an unfair theory—as
this bill does—no amount of charity and ingenuity is of any
avail.

Here it is, in the black and white of Clause I., that the
State's *imprimatur* is to be affixed only on undenominational
teaching. If once you say that, " contracting out " is a necessary consequence. You may mitigate its secular evils by
lavish grants ; but you cannot eradicate the stigma. It
makes me sad and sick. Think of the irony of the situation.
On Tuesday the House of Commons, by 5 to 1, supported a
motion in favour of relieving Roman Catholics from important,
but largely sentimental, grievances. The accession oath, the

prohibition on the appointment of a Roman Catholic Lord-Lieutenant of Ireland or Lord Chancellor are grievances. They are antiquated insults and irrational disabilities. We said so on Tuesday by 5 votes to 1. Yet, because Englishmen will not, or cannot, think, on Thursday, in the same week, within forty-eight hours, we say by nearly 2½ votes to 1, that new disabilities—not sentimental and antiquated, but modern and practical—are to be imposed in respect of education for all the Catholic youth in the country.

Nothing can wholly amend that original defect.

But the Bill has been "guillotined." Clause I. goes through automatically on Monday.

I deplore, but accept perforce, that situation.

What really kills me is that your people and our people, who want to be kind, can't think enough to gauge the consequences of that initial mistake.

They say, "If the Government makes the grant big enough, what does it matter?" They say *that* because they will not, or cannot, *think*. Help me to make them think.

On their own absurd basis, this Bill is valueless unless it is a settlement. Very well.

(1) The cost of education has increased, is increasing, and will increase.

Consequently, any *fixed* grant which is fair to-day will be unfair next year, grossly unfair in five years, and utterly useless in ten years. Therefore, instead of haggling for sixpences, they must insist on paying only a quota for the rights of citizenship. They must say, "We think it unfair to pay rates for your religion. We think it sad to be excluded from your national system of education, and bad for that system. But you will have it so. How much are we to pay? Isn't a shilling in the pound enough? We have 300,000 Catholic children. A child's education costs about £3 a head. Is not 900,000 shillings—£45,000 a year—a sufficient tax on our religious convictions?"

Supposing that the House sees the force of that—*i.e.* that for a *permanent* settlement the private contribution must be a *quota*, and not a fixed grant—then point out: II. Population increases. When new schools are wanted, you must give us building grants for the same proportion of 19 : 1. If we need £20,000 for new schools, you must pay £19,000, and we will find £1000.

I don't know why I trouble you with all this.

At this moment I feel as if I lived in a community of deaf men. The more I talk the more worried they look . . . and nothing happens.

The letter is a long one, but I must allow myself to quote its extremely characteristic conclusion :—

Let us quit all this hopeless, helpless dumb show of hypnotized Democracy going to its appointed doom of Bureaucracy and Cæsarism, now as ever, and everywhere — *quod semper et ubique.*

Let us laugh ! We ought to laugh. Surprise is the basis of laughter. And what can be more surprising than to see the leaders of Nonconformity in the House of Commons, bribed by Baronetcies, abrogating the Constitution, and laughing—as well they may—at the spectacle of the Anglican Archbishop ramming Nonconformity down my throat with the butt end of his crozier ? They laugh. Had I not better laugh, too ? " Taking it in good part " is, I believe, the classic phrase for acquiescing in comic turpitude.

But I have not quitted this grim subject. I must, or I shall forget to laugh, and increase the merriment of others by getting angry. That would be absurd, when neither Anglican, nor Catholic, nor Educationalist, nor Unionist, are willing to think of anything but their Christmas holidays.

A word must be said of Wyndham's interest in religious subjects which, in later years, was marked. His interest in the education question was indeed but one instance of this. The early cult of beauty which was natural to his artist's nature had in it, perhaps, a touch of paganism. Later on, the beauty of Catholic ideals drew him. He wrote well and even

H

profoundly on the practical necessity of dogma in order to safeguard religion.

He was one of a group of persons interested in the philosophy of religion, who in 1896 founded the Synthetic Society. Wyndham and the present writer were for a time its honorary secretaries, and among our colleagues were Mr. Arthur Balfour, the present Lord Haldane, Mr. Henry Sidgwick, Dr. Talbot, now Bishop of Winchester, Father Tyrrell, Baron von Hügel, Sir Alfred Lyall, and Sir Oliver Lodge, as well as two veterans who had helped to found the old Metaphysical Society in 1869, namely R. H. Hutton and Dr. Martineau. I name those who most regularly attended our early meetings.

Wyndham took but little part in the formal debates, but in conversation at the small dinners which preceded them he was often very brilliant, and the topics discussed by the Society set him thinking. The following defence of dogma, called forth by an Essay written by one of our members, is surely a remarkable piece of tersely expressed reasoning.

I have read X. and should like to discuss him with you. He writes with lucidity and persuasion. But there is a third position between his and Sabatier's. A man may accept Sabatier's view that the relation of dogma to religion is best illustrated by the relation of language to thought, and may, yet, attach an importance to dogma so great as to justify him in accepting a convinced believer's attitude towards dogma as the only adequate recognition of the magnitude of that importance. Even in literature we decline to bring Shakespeare or Chaucer "up to date ": we prefer, if we can, to read Dante or Homer, however haltingly, in their own Tuscan and Greek. I heard an interesting sermon by Adderley to-day, in which he justified the acceptance of the "Real Presence" and the rejection of "transubstantiation." It would have made a good point of departure for a symposium. His point was that the doctrine of Transubstantiation was only an explanation of the dogma of the Real Presence given, necessarily, in the terms of philosophy then current but now obsolete. Adderley would no doubt argue that, in such a case, the relation of dogma to religion may not only be illustrated by the relation of language to thought, but that it actually is more a question of language than of belief. Carrying that backwards to Sabatier's extreme position, my supporter of a *tertium quid* would handle the Incarnation on similar lines. He would say that in the birth of our Lord there was a manifestation of Divinity on Earth so momentous and so singular as to find an *adequate*, though no doubt *inaccurate* expression, only in the doctrine of the Incarnation. No other form of thought would give him a sufficiently splendid symbol, he would therefore accept that form of thought whilst admitting that in thought and still more, of course, in language it partook of human thought and human language belonging to the age in which it was conceived and to the ages during which it was crystallized. But, just because he makes that philosophic concession, he could and would see much gain in keeping to the form both of thought and language and much risk in any ephemeral attempt to re-think and re-write the symbol.

Some of the opponents of dogma amused him, as he shows in the following note of 1906 :

I have a letter before me from a man who holds that dogmatic teaching of the Christian or any other religion is immaterial. He would teach the religion of citizenship. This turns out to be the teaching of boys not to spit in public places.

There were seasons when Catholic ideals strongly affected his life, and he welcomed the Catholic revival in the Church of England ; but perhaps his sympathies in this matter somewhat outstripped his convictions.

There were very noble and winning traits in a

character not wholly consistent. Though intensely ambitious, he had that devotion to great aims for their own sake which deliberately sacrifices ambition. If going to Ireland satisfied his ambition, his line of action after he was installed went at times in the teeth of his own interests. He studied before all things what was best, not for himself, but for the country. He refused to adopt opportunist courses which would have benefited him personally and averted disaster. He declined, as has been said, offers of official promotion, preferring what only his sanguine and absorbing devotion to the task he had set himself prevented his seeing to be a forlorn hope.

And when resignation of his office was inevitable, and he felt himself to be left almost alone, no word of reproach was ever heard from him. He sadly quoted to one, near to him by friendship and relationship, Chaucer's lines :

> Let not this wretched woe your herté grieve
> But manly set the world in six and seven,
> And if thou die a martyr, go to Heaven.

He was indeed loyal in his friendships, and would do impulsive things for his friends such as are done by the Don Quixotes of the world, but very seldom by those whose lot is cast in the cold calculating atmosphere of public life. Life in the great world is apt to wear off such finer promptings. They are keen in many a boy. Wyndham was something of a boy to the end. His boyish love of the glittering toys of life made him enjoy the glamour of the great world ; but the same youthfulness kept untarnished much of the generous and uncalculating spirit which that world is apt to kill.

This generosity, while it was graceful in his friendships, might even verge on the heroic in its other aspect of which I have just spoken—his devotion to public causes. He could lose himself in his cause. And his heart would be so much set on its success that defeat became tragic. Here I return to the note I touched at starting—the element of real greatness revealed mainly in his failures. The average man of the world held it to show a want of the tough fibre of a work-a-day statesman that he nearly broke his heart when he had finally to give up his Irish schemes. Many of his critics saw no more than this, and were incapable of understanding that Wyndham's unhappiness was largely the result of a depth of conviction and a concentrated devotion by which alone the very greatest things are done. In a lesser degree his keen sense of inevitable consequences and his genuine patriotism made him suffer acutely in other public defeats—notably in August, 1911, when the Parliament Bill was passed. Weeks of ungrudging labour with results that made him intensely sanguine were succeeded by the rebuff of August 10th. To a mechanical mind the depth of his disappointment at that time might seem extravagant. But it stood for a fine quality of insight and a public spirit which is especially rare in our own day. And these allied him on one side with the confessors and with the men of genius.

All this must be remembered in trying to think of him as he really was. The estimate of kindly but undiscerning public opinion will not suffice. We must add to it

> . . . all the world's coarse thumb
> And finger failed to plumb.

And these lines of Browning are followed by others which give truly the same aspect of Wyndham's nature—the aspect that told of genius and made for tragedy. Of Wyndham, if of any one, it is true that he was haunted by a crowd of thoughts and hopes which in the nature of the case could never have been realized, and which yet stamped him as something apart from the many :

> Thoughts hardly to be packed
> Into a narrow act,
> Fancies that broke through language and escaped ;
> All I could never be,
> All, men ignored in me ;
> This, was I worth to God, whose wheel the pitcher shaped.

While then the obituary writers pictured him as the gallant knight, graceful, brilliant, accomplished, I prefer to think of that side of him—a very real side— which allies him with those who have worked and suffered for great causes, the extent and quality of whose labour has been only half recognized, who have seen enough to know sadly how little actual life fulfils the highest dreams which come to men in moments of illumination. Let this thought be set down in his own words which stand before me in his own hand- writing. They are headed " Illumination," and they run thus :

> To have known this once : and so to take our part
> With the great masters who have left behind
> No miniature perfections of their art ;
> But one vast work, unfinished and unsigned,
> That should have told the secret of their heart,
> And tells of hands grown old, and eyes worn blind.

But a record of one who loved Browning's brave boast that he would " greet the Unseen with a cheer," must not conclude on such a note as this, though it is the deepest and truest. To the end Wyndham was full of hope, full of purpose. If he stumbled it was to rise again and work in new fields. And I will conclude by quoting words of keenness as to the future, written only a month before he was taken away. His newly inherited property gave him a congenial field of work. And here the whole instrument was under his own control, as it could never be in the political field of a democracy. For the moment he dreamed of it as giving him full scope for the future, while the possibilities of his beautiful library fed his literary imagination. It is not at all likely that he would have given up politics as his letter hints. But his habit of absorbing himself in what he worked at probably made it a necessity to think of the task directly before him as the one thing that was worth while and was to occupy his future time.

For myself—apart from politics, finance, and the round of duty—I am absorbed in two subjects : Rural England and my library. "We know what we are, but we know not what we may be." I may, perhaps, take office again. But I doubt it. *Inveni portum.* My work, I am almost persuaded, must be to tackle the problem of Rural England ; and my play, I am convinced, to finish my library. The two together would give me happy and useful employment for twenty years.

I am attacking "Rural England" (1) by action, based on study of the past—from Domesday Book onwards—and on modern science—"so called." I think best in action and experiment. So I have given the go-by to theory and have already pumped water several miles over considerable hills ; built cow-sheds ; bought a motor-trolley to supersede four cart-horses, and done much else which will, I believe, put back this bit of England to where it stood in the seventeenth century and afford working models to [those] who lack my capital and imagination. It is jolly work.

(2) But I attack "Rural England" also with my pen and have written a "private" essay that has been "highly commended" by Lansdowne and Milner.

As for my play . . . I have finished the structure of the library and nearly filled it with books. There are six desks for people who mean business. It is inspired by Wells, Merton, San Marco at Florence, etc. But [it] will be a place at the top of the house in which you and X. and I and others can read and write. Party Politics leave me cold. But the countryside of England and the literature of Europe make me glow. . . .

Incidentally to the two main purposes of my life, I am finishing a chapel in the basement.

It is exhilarating to make things yourself. The carpenter and I, without architect or contract, have made the library, the chapel, the new cow-farm and much else. When I told X. a few weeks ago that this would be my work and *not* party politics, he was shocked. But after seeing what I was at he came round to my view. Some people inherit an estate and go on as if nothing had happened. I can't do that. My father never told me anything about this place. I lived and worked in Cheshire and Ireland ; suddenly I find myself responsible for farming myself 2400 acres, and for paying sums that stagger me by way of weekly wages and repairs. So I ask myself, " What are you going to do ? " I mean to use all my imagination and energy to get something done that shall last and remind.

# IV

# MR. CHESTERTON AMONG THE PROPHETS

EVER since Mr. Chesterton began to be prominent the present writer has had frequent discussions with his friends on the nature and extent of his gifts. And it is curious that the books of one man should provoke such opposite judgments in his readers. Setting aside the epithet "brilliant," which seems allowed on all hands, the difference is very complete. The critics from whom I dissent speak of his thought as "superficial"; I find it penetrating. They talk of him as asking us to believe impossible paradoxes. I find him pre-eminently the propounder of the maxims of common-sense—of maxims and principles so clearly true when they are stated that they might be called truisms. They regard him as primarily a purveyor of acrobatic feats of the intellect—exciting and enjoyable, as any amusing "show" is enjoyable, but not to be taken seriously. I have found him, before all things, quick to defend truths of great practical moment, and the effective opponent of plausible and misleading theories—a very serious and important *rôle*. They class him with brilliant writers of the hour, who have no claim to teach the age a serious lesson or to doing more than interest us in their own whims and prejudices by stating them with lucidity and enforcing them with telling epigrams. I associate him with those writers of the past who have decried mere ingenuity in theorizing, and striven to find the path of philosophy traced by Nature herself. I class his thought— though not his manner—with that of such men as Burke, Butler, and Coleridge. When his work on *Orthodoxy* appeared, it seemed to me a triumphant and irrefragable confutation of their view ; I found it regarded by them as a confutation of mine.

The proverb which begins with the words *de gustibus* is an old one. I should not discuss further a view I do not share, but that it appears to me (who am not, of course, an impartial judge) that I do see the qualities in Mr. Chesterton's work which have made such critics take their view, but that they do not see—hardly even look for—those which have made me take mine. And while the former qualities are at all events reconcilable with my view, the latter are not so with theirs. If this is so, I may claim a victory on the ground of De Maistre's aphorism : " Truth can understand error, but error cannot understand truth."

Let me take *Orthodoxy* as a basis for illustrating the above statement. If any one opens it with a predisposition to take what I may call the frivolous view of Mr. Chesterton, he will find in skimming its pages plenty to confirm such a view. " How can I take a man seriously," he will say, " who gives as the primary fact in all his philosophy the belief he has ever had in fairies[1] ; who laughs at conscience and the ' inner voice,' and tells you that ' the most

[1] Page 85.

horrible of all horrible religions is the worship of
the God within '[1]; who is so little alive to the
history of all civilizations, except the Chinese, as to
say that there is in the world 'no tradition of
progress'[2]; who tells us that if we credit any deviation from fixed law (and, of course, even free will
is a deviation from fixed law), the most stupendous
miracle is as easy of belief as the smallest; who
takes his metaphors from taxicabs and tramcars in
Battersea; from the Inner Circle trains and Gower
Street Station and the like—nay, who devotes half a
page to explaining that seriousness is not a virtue,
and that one should not take oneself seriously at all;
that seriousness, moreover, is easy but undesirable?
If such a man sums up on the side of obscurantism
and against modern thought, it is just what was to be
expected—it is all one huge paradox. He does not
at bottom really believe what he says, or expect
others to believe him. To unravel and refute his
arguments is not worth while. It is as little worth
while as to analyze the fallacies in Whately's proof
that Napoleon I. never existed."

This way of looking at the book might be
elaborated and illustrated much more fully. In maintaining that it is a false way I must begin by admitting
that one statement of Mr. Chesterton's is not serious,
namely, that in which he seems to say that he is not
to be taken seriously. This starting-point, which is
mine, is at all events as fair as that of his critics. It
is a case of assumption for assumption. They assume
that he is mainly frivolous; I that he is intensely in
earnest. To them—starting with their assumption—
all the brilliant epigrams with which *Orthodoxy* is

[1] Page 136.  [2] Page 266.

packed from start to finish, seem to be extraordinary
feats of intellectual agility—the renewal, under nineteenth-century conditions, of the dialectical tournaments of the thirteenth : and in those tournaments
it rejoiced a skilled disputant to have to defend what
was neither probable nor true, as it gave all the more
scope for his ingenuity. To me—starting with mine
—this aspect of ingenious paradox appears simply
accessory. I regard it partly as a concession, which
has become habitual on the part of the writer, to the
taste of an age which loves to be amused and hates
being bored. It is the administration of intellectual
stimulants, or the application to a lethargic and tired
and rather morbid world of a tremendous shower
bath, in order to brace it and renew its normal
activities. The net result, however, of Mr. Chesterton's
awakening treatment is not mere stimulating paradox,
but, rather, a douche of startling common-sense.

I shall attempt in the following observations, first,
to justify the claim I make for Mr. Chesterton's book
that it is a contribution of very high utility to religious
thought, and then to examine his mannerisms—which
on the one hand may be said to impair the dignity
of his writing, and sometimes discredit as mere paradoxes the truths he has at heart, but on the other
hand certainly make the book racy and stimulating.

Mr. Chesterton disclaims novelty for his views.
His disclaimer is just, in the sense that in religious
thought, as Macaulay said sixty years ago, the fundamental arguments on either side are unchangeable.
For the most part, " What is new is not true, and
what is true is not new." But that kind of novelty
which is afforded by fresh vividness and reality given
to old truths we find most signally in Mr. Chesterton's

pages. Novel, it may be, his views are not. Original
in him they most certainly are. He tells us, indeed,
that he has never read the chief Christian apologetic
writings at all. He has discovered his arguments for
himself, and herein lies half the interest and value of
his book. It is the record of the past experience of
one who was brought up amid influences which made
him an Agnostic, and was converted to Christianity.
The depth of the Christian philosophy met the
difficulties of an active and penetrating mind that had
again and again found the shibboleths of typical
modern speculative thinkers incoherent, mutually
destructive, or even self-destructive.

Again, his views are original in their mode of
presentment. "It is the very triumph of originality,"
writes a great religious thinker, "not to invent or
discover what is perhaps already known, but to make
old things read as if they were new, from the novelty
of aspect in which they are placed. This faculty of
investing with associations, of applying to particular
purposes, of deducing consequences, of impressing on
the imagination is creative." Some of Mr. Chesterton's most striking pages are an exposition of arguments already used by well-known writers. We find,
for instance, Butler's argument—urged in his sermons
—on the adaptation of human nature to the Christian
virtues. We find illustrations of Tertullian's *testimonium animæ naturaliter christianæ.* I do not say
that Mr. Chesterton gives us again all that Tertullian
and Butler have given us. But in his record of the
way in which these arguments presented themselves
to him, and of the way they drove out modern theories
too shallow to stand against them, we have most
timely evidence of the ever-living power of thoughts

not themselves new.    And we often get a sight of
aspects hitherto overlooked, and yet most wholesome
for the times.    Again, when he mercilessly demolishes
the confused thought which treats mathematical
necessity and scientific uniformity as equally unalterable in the nature of things, he is saying over again
what W. G. Ward and Dr. McCosh said fifty years
ago in answer to John Stuart Mill; yet, in Mr.
Chesterton's context and in the record of the place
which these arguments held in his own mental history,
there is an actuality and point which was necessarily
absent from more formal disquisitions.    So, too, with
Mr. Chesterton's most important contention against
naturalism, that reason cannot be the highest product
of the evolution of merely non-rational forces—that
there must be reason behind the process—we have
an argument made familiar to our own generation by
Mr. Arthur Balfour's books and Archbishop Temple's
Bampton Lectures; yet in Mr. Chesterton it is
original.    So, too, is the view of scepticism as the
suicide of thought—though its main argument, including the metaphor of the sceptical thinker sawing
off the branch on which he sits, is, of course, familiar.
In each case we have all the drama of personal conviction and history—and, in addition, the extraordinary
richness and copiousness of illustration in which Mr.
Chesterton is unrivalled.

Of the occasional grotesqueness of his illustrations
I will speak later on.    But, whatever may be said in
criticism of this attribute, their cogency is unimpaired
or even enhanced by it.    And, after all, in a civilization in which, among the most highly educated,
religious scepticism is nearly as common as it was in
the Roman Empire of the first century of our era,

this is what matters most. In some instances old arguments come upon us in these pages with a new force which is almost startling.

The net result of the book and its *rationale* appear to me—to put it briefly—to be the help it gives us in substantiating the following position, which it is not to Mr. Chesterton's purpose to draw out. Cardinal Newman has written with keen perception in the *Apologia*, on the confusion which modern investigations have introduced into the religious views of many thoughtful persons. This was a subject on which the Cardinal felt strongly long before the danger was generally recognized as imminent. He referred to it as early as 1827, in the first of his University Sermons —which Mr. Chesterton has probably never read, though some of its thoughts appear in his pages. This confusion has led many to abandon Christianity and to return to the old work of formulating original philosophies of life. The effect Mr. Chesterton's work had on the present writer was not to diminish his sense of the difficulties of which, perhaps, Mr. Chesterton, in his sense of victory, makes too light; but to bring into relief the shallowness of thinkers who have allowed new difficulties in detail to lead to doubts of Christianity itself.

Mr. Chesterton brings out forcibly the depth of those elements in the Christian view of life which modern difficulties leave untouched, and, consequently, the weakness of those who have so lightly set it aside. He brings home to us also the impotence of individualism to find any substitute comparable to the corporate faith it is destroying. We, who are brought up Christians, may reflect on some of the primary sources of the life-giving power of our religion as little

as we reflect on the air we breathe. They are too
much a matter of course to be noticed. But the story
of one who was brought up without Christian faith,
felt profoundly the want of it and the incoherence of
its substitutes, and had the earnestness and activity of
mind to formulate for himself many of its underlying
principles,—which by ourselves are merely practically
taken for granted and partly acted on without being
explicitly recognized,—makes us recognize these
principles explicitly. It brings into relief, most valuable
for our own times, the profound answers Christianity
has already given to profound difficulties. Men like
Tatian and St. Justin gave the same personal testimony to the full depth of the Christian message in
the early days of our era. But their task was far
more obvious, for the Empire was pagan. It is just
because we feel we know Christianity so well that we
risk, in some sort, ceasing to know it. Great thoughts,
through becoming stale and mechanical, may be as
little helpful to our own civilization as to a civilization
to which they were unfamiliar. Their being too old
may be as much against their general influence as
their being too young. To see them strike with all
the force of youth on a gifted mind makes them young
again to us. Thus the spectacle of this intensely
active and earnest modern intellect, with all its array
of paradox and quaint conceit, with its disdain of
conventionality, its wilful indulgence in exaggeration,
its streaks of irreverent imagination thrown across
deeply reverent thoughts, its occasional exhibition of
honest Philistine human nature unrestrained by
fastidious taste—the spectacle, in short, of Mr.
Chesterton's whole, forcible, energizing self, with its
strength and its defects, fired by the Christian dogma

and ethics, as though he had lived in the days of Nero or Marcus Aurelius, is just the tonic which a jaded generation needs. And it reminds us how much that is indispensable in the inheritance of Christendom our own age has ceased adequately to realize and is in danger of lightly abandoning.

Mr. Chesterton is impatient with modern thought —sometimes even unfair to it—but often exhibits its weaknesses with the skill of a logical detective. One point on which he insists is the profound answer already given by Christianity to a profound difficulty which has baffled so many typical modern thinkers— optimists and pessimists alike. Christianity recognizes existence as supremely momentous, and the human soul as of supreme value. The world and the soul are, for the Christian, intensely worth working for and worth improving. Yet Christianity recognizes to the full how profound is the *need* of improvement. Thus we have the two great motives for work : that it is sorely needed and that it is intensely worth while.

The modern thinkers who set aside the Christian view lose one or other of these essential motives. The believers in a mechanical law of progress are at one with optimists in denying the former ; the pessimists deny the latter—not to speak of the necessarians who deny the possibility of all effort except what is inevitable, and leave us, therefore, no stimulus at all. In this thought alone—and it recalls the old *Agnosce Christiane dignitatem tuam—* we have a contrast between Christianity and its modern proposed substitutes, which evidently made the acceptance of "orthodoxy" to Mr. Chesterton a veritable emancipation. It is but one of the many

I

sides of Christianity in which he found wisdom and
help towards accepting things as they are, and seeing
their meaning and place in life ; a wisdom tested by
the ages during which the Christian religion has been
acted on by the whole Church. The ingenious con-
jectures of private judgment, on the other hand, are
merely personal, untested and *à priori*, and are likely
enough to change with each clever philosophy which
comes before the mind.

Mr. Chesterton's work is, as I have said, autobiographical ; and while I must leave those who
would master the whole process of his conversion
to what he terms "orthodoxy"—that is to Christianity with a strong Catholic bias—to read what it
would take too long to summarize here, I will now
proceed to give and to illustrate in his own words
some main steps in the process.

In a powerful chapter he brings before us the
sense which early possessed him of the utter confusion
introduced by "private judgment," after the sixteenth-
century Reformation, into a scheme which had been
profoundly coherent. This confusion resulted not
merely from the collapse of many Christian beliefs,
but from the disintegration and loss of proportion
consequent on the rejection of Catholic tradition.
The Christian virtues were distorted by those who
did not deny them. And this process, first rendered
possible by the principles of the Reformation, has
continued to our own time.

Each virtue was taken up by some individual as a
hobby and exaggerated, and stripped of the correctives
which Christian tradition, with its profound sense and
experience of the nature of the whole man, had
supplied to such exaggeration. The chapter is rightly

called the "Suicide of Thought," although, at first sight, this title applies only to the portion which deals with the accompanying sceptical excesses of the intellect. But it really applies equally to the tendency of virtues to run to absurd excesses, if they are not checked by the authority of the Christian Church—for such excesses are due to the one-sidedness of the individual thinker. Charity is allowed to run riot until it becomes so fond of all men and so indulgent to them that it denies the reality of sin. Modesty and humility are Christian virtues. But they take a wrong turn in the modern sceptic, and make him so modest as to doubt of his own power to be sure of the validity of the Divine reason, and of the value of those aims and standards which are the very condition of an action being worth while. Oppression and tyranny among those in authority have ever been among the evils against which great Christian saints have protested, but the modern critic of authority here again runs wild and attacks indiscriminately the uses as well as the abuses of authority. In point of fact, there is a profound principle involved in the action of authority, even in checking the human reason. It checks the suicidal excesses to which, in fallen man, the reasoning faculty tends. For reason, if allowed to run riot, will, as history shows, question even the initial faith which makes us trust its own validity. Against such sceptical excesses of rationalism authority rightly protests, and in doing so is the guardian and friend of reason and not its opponent.

Take another aspect of modern excess—pragmatism. Here again the claim to believe what works well and fits in with the necessities of the human mind is valid. But when this is pressed to a denial of objective truth, we have another instance of the insistence on one aspect to the exclusion of another equally necessary—for the sane and healthy human reason absolutely demands some knowledge of objective truth.

These are some specimens of Mr. Chesterton's illustrations of his thesis—but his own words are so forcible that I proceed to give them :

The modern world is not evil ; in some ways the modern world is far too good. It is full of wild and wasted virtues. When a religious scheme is shattered (as Christianity was shattered at the Reformation), it is not merely the vices that are let loose. The vices are, indeed, let loose, and they wander and do damage. But the virtues are let loose also ; and the virtues wander more wildly, and the virtues do more terrible damage. The modern world is full of the old Christian virtues gone mad. The virtues have gone mad because they have been isolated from each other and are wandering alone. Thus some scientists care for truth ; and their truth is pitiless. Thus some humanitarians only care for pity ; and their pity (I am sorry to say) is often untruthful. For example, Mr. Blatchford attacks Christianity because he is mad on one Christian virtue : the merely mystical and almost irrational virtue of charity. He has a strange idea that he will make it easier to forgive sins by saying that there are no sins to forgive. Mr. Blatchford is not only an early Christian, he is the only early Christian who ought really to have been eaten by lions. For in his case the pagan accusation is really true : his mercy would mean mere anarchy. He really is the enemy of the human race—because he is so human. . . .

. . . Humility was largely meant as a restraint upon the arrogance and infinity of the appetite of man. He was always outstripping his mercies with his own newly-invented needs. . . .

But what we suffer from to-day is humility in the wrong place. Modesty has moved from the organ of ambition.

Modesty has settled upon the organ of conviction ; where it was never meant to be. A man was meant to be doubtful about himself, but undoubting about the truth ; this has been exactly reversed. Nowadays the part of a man that a man does assert is exactly the part he ought not to assert—himself. The part he doubts is exactly the part he ought not to doubt—the Divine Reason. Huxley preached a humility content to learn from Nature. But the new sceptic is so humble that he doubts if he can even learn. Thus we should be wrong if we had said hastily that there is no humility typical of our time. The truth is that there is a real humility typical of our time ; but it so happens that it is practically a more poisonous humility than the wildest prostrations of the ascetic. The old humility was a spur that prevented a man from stopping ; not a nail in his boot that prevented him from going on. For the old humility made a man doubtful about his efforts, which might make him work harder. But the new humility makes a man doubtful about his aims, which will stop him working altogether. . . .

The sages, it is often said, can see no answer to the riddle of religion. But the trouble with our sages is not that they cannot see the answer ; it is that they cannot even see the riddle. They are like children, so stupid as to notice nothing paradoxical in the playful assertion that a door is not a door. The modern latitudinarians speak, for instance, about authority in religion not only as if there were no reason for it, but as if there had never been any reason for it. Apart from seeing its philosophical basis, they cannot even see its historical cause. Religious authority has often, doubtless, been oppressive or unreasonable ; just as every legal system (and especially our present one) has been callous and full of cruel apathy. It is rational to attack the police ; nay, it is glorious. But the modern critics of religious authority are like men who should attack the police without ever having heard of burglars. For there is a great and possible peril to the human mind : a peril as practical as burglary. Against it religious authority was reared, rightly or wrongly, as a barrier. And against it something certainly must be reared as a barrier, if our race is to avoid ruin.

The peril is that the human intellect is free to destroy itself. Just as one generation could prevent the very existence of the next generation, by all entering a monastery or jumping into the sea, so one set of thinkers can to some degree prevent further thinking by teaching the next generation that there is no validity in human thought. It is idle to talk always of the alternative of reason and faith. Reason is itself a matter of faith. It is an act of faith to assert that our thoughts have any relation to reality at all. If you are merely a sceptic, you must, sooner or later, ask yourself the question, "Why should anything go right; even observation and deduction? Why should not good logic be as misleading as bad logic? They are both movements in the brain of a bewildered ape?" The young sceptic says, "I have a right to think for myself." But the old sceptic, the complete sceptic, says, "I have no right to think for myself. I have no right to think at all."

There is a thought that stops thought. That is the only thought that ought to be stopped. That is the ultimate evil against which all religious authority was aimed. It only appears at the end of decadent ages like our own; and already Mr. H. G. Wells has raised its ruinous banner; he has written a delicate piece of scepticism called *Doubts of the Instrument*. In this he questions the brain itself, and endeavours to remove all reality from all his own assertions, past, present and to come. But it was against this remote ruin that all the military systems in religion were originally ranked and ruled. The creeds and the crusades, the hierarchies and the horrible persecutions, were not organized, as is ignorantly said, for the suppression of reason. They were organized for the difficult defence of reason. Man, by a blind instinct, knew that if once things were wildly questioned, reason could be questioned first. The authority of priests to absolve, the authority of popes to define, the authority even of inquisitors to terrify: these were all only dark defences erected round one central authority, more undemonstrable, more supernatural than all—the authority of a man to think. We know now that this is so; we have no excuse for not knowing it. For we can hear scepticism crashing

through the old ring of authorities, and at the same moment
we can see reason swaying upon her throne. In so far as
religion has gone, reason is going. For they are both of the
same primary and authoritative kind. They are both
methods of proof which cannot themselves be proved. And
in the act of destroying the idea of divine authority we have
largely destroyed the idea of that human authority by which
we do a long division sum. With a long and sustained tug
we have attempted to pull the mitre off pontifical man ; and
his head has come off with it. . . .

This bald summary of the thought-destroying forces of
our time would not be complete without some reference to
pragmatism ; for though I have here used and should everywhere defend the pragmatist method as a preliminary guide
to truth, there is an extreme application of it which involves
the absence of all truth whatever. My meaning can be put
shortly thus. I agree with the pragmatists that apparent
objective truth is not the whole matter ; that there is an
authoritative need to believe the things that are necessary to
the human mind. But I say that one of those necessities
precisely is a belief in objective truth. The pragmatist tells
a man to think what he must think and never mind the
Absolute. But precisely one of the things he must think is
the Absolute. This philosophy, indeed, is a kind of verbal
paradox. Pragmatism is a matter of human needs ; and one
of the first of human needs is to be something more than a
pragmatist. Extreme pragmatism is just as inhuman as the
determinism it so powerfully attacks. The determinist (who,
to do him justice, does not pretend to be a human being)
makes nonsense of the human sense of actual choice. The
pragmatist, who professes to be specially human, makes nonsense of the human sense of fact.

I regret that space will not allow me to quote the
fine criticism in this connexion passed by Mr.
Chesterton on Renan and Anatole France ; some
of Mr. Chesterton's words on the former recalled to
the present writer Archbishop Alexander's admirable

lines of forty years ago on the joint efforts of Strauss and Renan to construct a Christ whose reality would respond to all the tests of naturalism, and be simply human as humanity is known to the German *savant* and the French *littérateur*, and their utter failure to produce a consistent whole.

> Divinely gentle, yet a sombre giant,
> Divinely perfect, yet imperfect man ;
> Divinely calm, yet recklessly defiant,
> Divinely true, yet half a charlatan.
> They torture all the record of the Life,
> Give what from France and Germany they get ;
> To Calvary carry the dissecting knife,
> Parisian patchouli to Olivet.

Mr. Chesterton's own summary, given at the end of this remarkable chapter, is at once brief and forcible. As with Christianity, so with Christ, even apart from actual falsehood, the moderns lose all sense of proportion and of the greatness of the whole. The large supernatural sanity of the Divine figure is not seen, for it is broken up in their human categories. Each piece, separate from the whole which explains it, becomes not sane but insane—and therefore unintelligible as a guide in life :

> . . . There is a huge and heroic sanctity of which we moderns can only collect the fragments. There is a giant of whom we see only the lopped arms and legs walking about. They have torn the soul of Christ into silly strips, labelled egoism and altruism, and they are equally puzzled by His insane magnificence and His insane meekness. They have parted His garments among them, and for His vesture they have cast lots ; though the coat was without seam, woven from the top throughout.

I have referred above to Mr. Chesterton's criticism of modern pessimism. I think that it formed the turning-point in his adoption of Christianity. He rejected pessimism, but he was no optimist. His acceptance of the universe, he tells us, was not optimism, but something akin to the loyalty shown in patriotism. The optimist will "defend the indefensible," he will be "the jingo of the universe," he will be "less inclined to the reform of things, more inclined to a sort of front bench official answer to all attacks, soothing every one with assurances. He will not wash the world, but whitewash the world." This is not in accordance with the nature of things. Devotion to the world, as to one's country, should not mean a false contentment which denies its imperfections. Patriotism should first show itself in the effort to make our country great, not in a passive, uncritical assurance that she is already perfect. Rome became great, Mr. Chesterton reminds us, just because men loved her and worked for her. They did not, in the first instance, love her because she was great. Here again, and decisively, Mr. Chesterton finds the truth in regard of our attitude towards the universe in the Christian ideal. He requires a love of the universe as passionate as that of the optimist, a dissatisfaction with it as profound as that of the pessimist. At first sight this appears to be a desire for incompatible objects. How can you intensely love an evil world? Yet if the world be good enough to prompt intense love, how can it inspire the passionate zeal of the reformer? Mr. Chesterton found the desired combination in Christianity. It was God's world of men, yet man had fallen. To help to recover the lost ideal, and to work for this with devotion, similar to

that which makes us long that our Fatherland should
fulfil her highest possibilities—here was passionate
love without optimism; intense zeal for reform and
recognition of evil without pessimism.

A crucial illustration of the difference between
Christianity and pessimism is to be found in the
Christian attitude towards the suicide and the martyr
respectively.  At first sight the two would seem to be
similar.  Each of his own accord gives up his life.
Modern thinkers have tried to identify them.  Such
an attempt is a fresh instance of their carelessness to
probe the true depths of Christian sentiment.  For
the Christian, the two men are not only not the same,
but they are poles apart.  They are the ideal coward
and the ideal hero respectively.  The suicide is the
exponent in action of sheer pessimism—the traditional
stake at the cross roads marking his grave reminds us
that he has committed the one sin unpardonable by
Christianity.  The martyr, on the other hand, is the
very type of the Christian hero; he sacrifices himself,
even his life, to the cause of the Church—his blood is
the seed of Christianity.  This thought and contrast
I have never seen analyzed so subtly as it is in Mr.
Chesterton's pages.

Martyr and suicide alike care little for life.  Yet
in the carelessness of life which they show there is a
difference of temper and motive which makes one the
very antithesis of the other.  " A martyr is a man
who cares so much for something outside him that he
forgets his own personal life.  A suicide is a man who
cares so little for anything outside him that he wants
to see the last of everything.  One wants something
to begin, the other wants everything to end."  This
analysis is carried further and deeper elsewhere in the

book.   Here it comes as the culmination of the philosophy which calls for the combination which makes life and effort worth while—the recognition that there are great causes, great reforms worth striving for in the world ; great evils, and some great goal to be attained which make the effort to reform them intensely worth while.

The chapter entitled the " Paradoxes of Christianity " contains, perhaps, the most valuable writing of the whole book, and indicates the general line of argument on which Mr. Chesterton arrived at his convictions.   He starts with the expression, after his own unconventional and forcible manner, of the practical way in which conviction is reached ; and here again he has rediscovered the path already travelled by a great thinker.   For he gives us a rough and unphilosophical expression of the line of reasoning in a book which he has, perhaps never read —Cardinal Newman's *Essay in Aid of a Grammar of Assent.*   He tells us, in popular language, that it is by the cumulative argument, by the " illative sense," which cannot express all the latent reasons which influence its decision, that he, like others, really reached his conclusions :

. . . A man is not really convinced of a philosophic theory when he finds that something proves it.   He is only really convinced when he finds that everything proves it. And the more converging reasons he finds pointing to this conviction, the more bewildered he is if asked suddenly to sum them up.   Thus, if one asked an ordinary intelligent man, on the spur of the moment, " Why do you prefer civilization to savagery ? " he would look wildly round at object after object, and would only be able to answer vaguely : " Why, there is that bookcase . . . and the coals in the coal-scuttle . . . and pianos . . . and policemen."   The whole case

for civilization is that the case for it is complex.  It has done
so many things.  But that very multiplicity of proof which
ought to make reply overwhelming makes reply impossible.

And then we come to direct autobiography—so
interesting and pertinent that it must be quoted; yet
it is far too long to be quoted in full :

All I had hitherto heard of Christian theology had
alienated me from it.  I was a pagan at the age of twelve,
and a complete agnostic by the age of sixteen ; and I cannot
understand any one passing the age of seventeen without
having asked himself so simple a question.  I did, indeed,
retain a cloudy reverence for a cosmic deity and a great
historical interest in the founder of Christianity.  But I certainly regarded Him as a man. . . . I never read a line of
Christian apologetics.  I read as little as I can of them now.
It was Huxley and Herbert Spencer and Bradlaugh who
brought me back to orthodox theology.  They sowed in my
mind my first wild doubts of doubt.  Our grandmothers were
quite right when they said that Tom Paine and the free-
thinkers unsettled the mind.  They do.  They unsettled
mine horribly.  The rationalists made me question whether
reason was of any use whatever ; and when I had finished
Herbert Spencer I got as far as doubting (for the first time)
whether evolution had occurred at all.  As I laid down the
last of Colonel Ingersoll's atheistic lectures, the dreadful
thought broke across my mind: "Almost thou persuadest
me to be a Christian."  I was in a desperate way.

Mr. Chesterton proceeds to summarize first the
contradictory charges made against Christianity :

Thus certain sceptics wrote that the great crime of Christianity had been its attack on the family ; it had dragged
women to the loneliness and contemplation of the cloister,
away from their homes and their children.  But, then, other
sceptics (slightly more advanced) said that the great crime of
Christianity was forcing the family and marriage upon us ;

that it doomed women to the drudgery of their homes and
children, and forbade them loneliness and contemplation.
The charge was actually reversed. Or, again, certain phrases
in the Epistles or the Marriage Service were said by the anti-
Christians to show contempt for woman's intellect. But I
found that the anti-Christians themselves had a contempt for
woman's intellect; for it was their great sneer at the Church
on the Continent that "only women" went to it. Or, again,
Christianity was reproached with its naked and hungry
habits; with its sackcloth and dried peas. But the next
minute Christianity was being reproached with its pomp and
its ritualism; its shrines of porphyry and its robes of gold.
It was abused for being too plain and for being too coloured.

But then, too, the men of science accused Christianity of being a "light," confined at first to one
people, and not common to all. This was immoral
favouritism. Yet science itself, like Christianity, has
originated in a few, and was never extended to all.
Such is the necessary history of all higher knowledge,
of which the chosen and gifted few are the pioneers.
In view of such careless and flimsy attacks, Mr.
Chesterton began to think that, in the opinion of its
critics, "any stick was good enough to beat Christianity with." There was something in the temper of
the attacks on Christianity which looked suspicious,
over and above their inconclusiveness. Perhaps, after
all, the unreason and eccentricity were on the side of
its assailants, the sanity and common-sense on the
side of Christianity itself.

. . . Perhaps, after all, it is Christianity that is sane and
all its critics that are mad—in various ways. . . . The modern
man thought Becket's robes too rich and his meals too poor.
But then the modern man was really exceptional in history;
no man before ever ate such elaborate dinners in such ugly
clothes. . . . The fact that Swinburne was irritated at the

unhappiness of Christians, and yet more irritated at their happiness, was easily explained. It was no longer a complication
of diseases in Christianity, but a complication of diseases in
Swinburne. The restraints of Christians saddened him
simply because he was more hedonist than a healthy man
should be. The faith of Christians angered him because he
was more pessimist than a healthy man should be.

Yet in this suggestion, Mr. Chesterton is conscious
of something wanting. The moderation of sanity,
the common-sense of mere humdrum human nature,
was not characteristic of Christianity. And here, by
a gradual process, we see Mr. Chesterton rising to the
conception of its supernatural character—to something
answering to intense feeling in man, something not
fathomable or reducible to complete logical consistency
by our finite intellects, but on the contrary presenting
mysteries and paradoxes to us, who see through a
glass darkly. This view we see gradually unfolding
itself in these pages—never, perhaps, adequately
analyzed, yet throughout implied. Only our relations
to another world can remove the constant check
imposed by reason on man's deepest feelings and
aspirations, when he follows exclusively the common-
sense maxims of this world. This world is not
adequate to our self-realization. Man cannot be
explained apart from his relations to God and the
truths of faith. Logic stands aside where mystery
begins; and adoration and self-abasement take its
place. Intense feeling is justified in a sphere in
which logic cannot without a divine revelation reach
the facts. We have the Man-God as the culminating
dogma; the "frenzy" of the crusader is the type of
the feeling which becomes reasonable in view of truths
so far above reason. The sanity of Christianity had

in it as much "frenzy" as belongs to insanity, but it responded to supernatural facts and not to illusions.

Nevertheless it could not, I felt, be quite true that Christianity was merely sensible and stood in the middle. There was really an element in it of emphasis and even frenzy which had justified the secularists in their superficial criticism. It might be wise, I began more and more to think that it was wise, but it was not merely worldly wise; it was not merely temperate and respectable. Its fierce crusaders and meek saints might balance each other; still the crusaders were very fierce and the saints were very meek, meek beyond all decency. Now it was just at this point of the speculation that I remembered my thoughts about the martyr and the suicide. In that matter there has been this combination between two almost insane positions which yet somehow amounted to sanity. This was just such another contradiction; and this I had already found to be true. This was exactly one of the paradoxes in which sceptics found the creed wrong; and in this I had found it right. Madly as Christians might love the martyr or hate the suicide, they never felt these passions more madly than I had felt them long before I dreamed of Christianity. Then the most difficult and interesting part of the mental process opened, and I began to trace this idea darkly through all the enormous thoughts of our theology. The idea was that which I had outlined touching the optimist and the pessimist; that we wanted not an amalgam or compromise, but both things at the top of their energy; love and wrath both burning. Here I shall only trace it in relation to ethics. But I need not remind the reader that the idea of this combination is indeed central in orthodox theology. For orthodox theology has specially insisted that Christ was not a being apart from God and man, like an elf, nor yet a being half human and half not, like a centaur, but both things at once and both things thoroughly, very man and very God.

This character of great opposites in Christian belief is further brought out in the following passage on the greatness and littleness of man according to the Christian view of life:

The average pagan, like the average agnostic, would merely say that he was content with himself, but not insolently self-satisfied, that there were many better and many worse, that his deserts were limited, but he would see that he got them. In short, he would walk with his head in the air, but not necessarily with his nose in the air. This is the manly and rational position, but it is open to the objection we noted against the compromise between optimism and pessimism—the "resignation" of Matthew Arnold. Being a mixture of two things, it is a dilution of two things; neither is present in its full strength or contributes its full colour. This proper pride does not lift the heart like the tongue of trumpets; you cannot go clad in crimson and gold for this. On the other hand, this mild rationalist modesty does not cleanse the soul like fire and make it clear like crystal; it does not (like a strict and searching humility) make a man as a little child, who can sit at the feet of the grass. It does not make him look up and see marvels; for Alice must grow small if she is to be Alice in Wonderland. Thus it loses both the poetry of being proud, and the poetry of being humble. Christianity sought by this same strange expedient to save both of them.

It separated the two ideas and then exaggerated them both. In one way Man was to be haughtier than he had ever been before; in another way he was to be humbler than he had ever been before. In so far as I am Man I am the chief of creatures. In so far as I am *a* man I am the chief of sinners. All humility that had meant pessimism, that had meant man taking a vague or mean view of his whole destiny —all that was to go. We were to hear no more the wail of Ecclesiastes that humanity had no pre-eminence over the brute, or the awful cry of Homer that man was only the saddest of all the beasts of the field. Man was a statue of God walking about the garden. Man had pre-eminence over all the brutes; man was only sad because he was not a beast, but a broken god. The Greek had spoken of men creeping on the earth, as if clinging to it. Now Man was to tread on the earth as if to subdue it. Christianity thus held a thought of the dignity of man that could only be expressed in crowns rayed like the sun and fans of peacock plumage. Yet at the same time it could hold a thought about the abject smallness of man that could only be expressed in fasting and fantastic submission in the grey ashes of St. Dominic and the white snows of St. Bernard. When one came to think of *one's self*, there was vista and void enough for any amount of bleak abnegation and bitter truth. There the realistic gentleman could let himself go, as long as he let himself go at himself. There was an open play-ground for the happy pessimist. Let him say anything against himself short of blaspheming the original aim of his being ; let him call himself a fool, and even a damned fool (though that is Calvinistic) ; but he must not say that fools are not worth saving. He must not say that a man, *quâ* man, can be valueless. Here again, in short, Christianity got over the difficulty of combining furious opposites, by keeping them both, and keeping them both furious. The Church was positive on both points. One can hardly think too little of one's self. One can hardly think too much of one's soul !

The greatness of the soul and the great scale on which Christianity exercised our feelings of wrath and of pity were out of keeping with a view of life which contemplated no more than what this world alone shows to us :

. . . The spirits of indignation and of charity took terrible and attractive forms, ranging from that monkish fierceness that scourged like a dog the first and the greatest of the Plantagenets, to the sublime pity of St. Catherine, who, in the official shambles, kissed the bloody head of the criminal. Poetry could be acted as well as composed. The heroic and monumental manner in ethics has entirely vanished with supernatural religion. They, being humble, could parade themselves ; but we are too proud to be prominent. Our

K

ethical teachers write reasonably for prison reform ; but we
are not likely to see Mr. Cadbury, or any eminent philan-
thropist, go into Reading Gaol, and embrace the strangled
corpse before it is cast into the quicklime. Our ethical
teachers write mildly against the power of millionaires ; but
we are not likely to see Mr. Rockefeller, or any modern
tyrant, publicly whipped in Westminster Abbey.

In truth, this combination of love and wrath,
gentleness and fierceness, was a characteristic note of
Christianity. Each aspect represented something great
in our nature. And Christianity alone showed how
the two could be combined in their fullest intensity :

> . . . The real problem is—Can the lion lie down with the
> lamb and still retain his royal ferocity ? That is the problem
> the Church attempted ; that is the miracle she achieved. . . .
> Those underrate Christianity who say it discovered mercy ;
> any one might discover mercy. In fact, every one did. But
> to discover a plan for being merciful and also severe—that
> was to anticipate a strange need of human nature. . . .
> . . . Any one might say, " Neither swagger nor grovel " ;
> and it would have been a limit. But to say, " Here you
> can swagger, and there you can grovel "—that was an
> emancipation.
> This was the big fact about Christian ethics ; the dis-
> covery of the new balance. Paganism had been like a pillar
> of marble, upright because proportioned with symmetry.
> Christianity was like a huge and ragged and romantic rock,
> which, though it sways on its pedestal at a touch, yet, because
> its exaggerated excrescences balance each other, is enthroned
> there for a thousand years. In a Gothic cathedral the
> columns were all different, but they were all necessary.
> Every support seemed an accidental and fantastic support ;
> every buttress was a flying buttress. So in Christendom
> apparent accidents balanced. Becket wore a hair shirt under
> his gold and crimson, and there is much to be said for the
> combination ; for Becket got the benefit of the hair shirt,

while the people in the street got the benefit of the crimson and gold. It is, at least, better than the manner of the modern millionaire, who has the black and drab outwardly for others, and the gold next his heart. But the balance was not always in one man's body as in Becket's; the balance was often distributed over the whole body of Christendom.

One more extract shall be given, in which we see Mr. Chesterton casting his eye along the story of the early centuries of our era, and noting with the eyes of a Christian poet what he calls the Romance of Orthodoxy. He notes the spectacle of the Church, the great war-chariot of Christ or His war horses, driven with infinite skill and avoiding the excesses of heresy on either side. The passage is as characteristic as anything in the volume, marked by real inspiration and imagination, yet touched—in this case only slightly —by the unconventional colloquialism which we must put up with, for it is part of the Chestertonian style which *is* the man :

. . . People have fallen into a foolish habit of speaking of orthodoxy as something heavy, humdrum and safe. There never was anything so perilous or so exciting as orthodoxy. It was sanity : and to be sane is more dramatic than to be mad. It was the equilibrium of a man behind madly-rushing horses, seeming to stoop this way and to sway that, yet in every attitude having the grace of statuary and the accuracy of arithmetic. The Church in its early days went fierce and fast with any war horse ; yet it is utterly unhistoric to say that she merely went mad along one idea, like a vulgar fanaticism. She swerved to right and left, so as exactly to avoid enormous obstacles. She left on one hand the huge bulk of Arianism, buttressed by all the worldly powers to make Christianity too worldly. The next instant she was swerving to avoid an orientalism, which would have made it too unworldly. The orthodox Church never took the tame

course or accepted the conventions ; the orthodox Church was
never respectable.   It would have been easier to have accepted the earthly power of the Arians.   It would have been
easy, in the Calvinistic seventeenth century, to fall into the
bottomless pit of predestination.   It is easy to be a madman :
it is easy to be a heretic.   It is always easy to let the age
have its head ; the difficult thing is to keep one's own. . . .
It is always simple to fall ; there are an infinity of angles at
which one falls, only one at which one stands.   To have fallen
into any one of the fads, from Gnosticism to Christian
Science, would, indeed, have been obvious and tame.   But to
have avoided them all is one whirling adventure ; and in my
vision the heavenly chariot flies thundering through the ages,
the dull heresies sprawling and prostrate, the wild truth
reeling but erect.

I have quoted enough, I think, to justify me in
my emphatic assertion that Mr. Chesterton is to be
taken seriously.   Yet he may be taken too seriously.
And then there will come a reaction.   He is very serious
in his main purpose ; and his very seriousness has its
share in making him unconventional and startling.
In the fullness of his heart he becomes colloquial.
And in conversation we can say strong things—
violent and exaggerated things—without detriment to
seriousness of purpose.   Moreover, we can be provoked into saying false and indefensible things, which
do not much matter, for spoken words can be corrected,
or afterwards laid aside with a laugh if challenged.
It is by this standard that Mr. Chesterton must be
judged ; and I think that to many who forget the
above considerations his written words are unpersuasive.

At times he does not answer an enemy at all, but
spends a page in refuting a travesty of his position
which no one worth convincing holds.   He tells us,

for example, that "an imbecile habit has arisen in
modern controversy of saying that such and such a
creed can be held in one age, but cannot in another."
His criticism is that "you might as well say that a
certain philosophy can be believed on Mondays, but
cannot be believed on Tuesdays." As a protest
against fanatical worshippers of the Zeitgeist this
may have some meaning ; although in cases where
Mr. Chesterton's parallel is accurate it is too obvious.
But as a serious reply to persons really worth arguing
with, it is little less than absurd. What is generally
meant by the statement Mr. Chesterton attacks is that
some beliefs connected with religion are possible in
one stage of civilization and education, impossible in
another. The popular setting and explication of a
creed changes. Creeds are arrayed, I need hardly say,
in popular legend and illustrated in terms of contemporary science, and these do unquestionably yield to
the pressure of advancing knowledge. It is not (as
Mr. Chesterton assumes) a fundamental philosophy that
changes, but that concrete embodiment of it which
includes popular superstitions. The educated Indian
will not now believe with his ancestors that the world
rests on the back of a tortoise. Among Christians
themselves—to avoid ground even conceivably dis-
putable—many beliefs were possible before Coper-
nicanism prevailed which are now impossible.
Christians could once believe literally the saying of
the Psalmist, *terra in æternum stat.* They could
regard the Ascension as the rising of Our Lord from
a stationary earth to a local heaven above the blue
sky. They could regard such pictures as the frescoes
of Orcagna in the Campo Santo at Pisa as representing a literal fact as to the prospect for our souls after

death.   Mr. Chesterton is, of course, justified in protesting against the idea that an entire religious creed
belongs only to an epoch, and not to mankind as such.
He may rightly protest, moreover, against changes in
detailed popular beliefs, really made to suit the whim
of one generation, and advocated under cover of a
peremptory law of progress.   But the value of such
writing as his is that it often gives a truth with startling distinctness.   In this instance it does nothing of
the kind, but appears to state a falsehood and to miss
the force of the position it criticizes.   The stage of
Silas Marner's life, in which he believed that the lots
revealed the decision of God, was succeeded by the
disproof of this belief.   Superstition was driven out
by experience.   Henceforth his belief of God's action
in the world had either to be held differently or
entirely abandoned.   And there is, of course, a similar
advance in experience and education in the history of
any civilization.

   Again, Mr. Chesterton's tirade against liberal
theology seems to me to miss the mark.   I differ from
such extreme liberalism, of course, as much as Mr.
Chesterton does, but I quite differ from him as to
why it claims to be liberal.   Its devotees claim for
it that it is liberal because it leaves you free to reject
much on which orthodoxy insists.   They hold no
doubt (among other unorthodox tenets) that miracles
are impossible.   I agree with Mr. Chesterton that
this belief is often in individuals based on an irrational
*à priori* assumption.   But Mr. Chesterton speaks of
liberal theology as though it claimed to be liberal
on the ground of its enforcing this belief.[1]   He
treats it to much epigrammatic and scornful invective

----

[1] Page 254.

on the basis of its intolerance. Some liberals are, no doubt, intolerant : but the liberal school surely holds its name in virtue of permission, not of insistence. Liberal theology is a haven for those who cannot believe in miracles. Mr. Chesterton treats it as a Torquemada for those who can.

Similarly, in another place, he totally ignores the distinction between preventive and retributive punishment, and treats a system which denies the use of the latter as though it denied the use of the former.[1] Again, in his attack on modern theories of evolution and progress, he poses as an exhaustive alternative an absolutely fixed ideal, or an ideal which completely changes. This gives him the occasion for excellent fooling, but does not meet the really rational exponents of the theory he attacks at all. Let me attempt to give my meaning in the author's own manner. If I say, " You must walk towards a fixed point on the horizon if you want to make progress. If, every time you look up, you change your direction and walk towards a different point in the opposite direction, you don't get on at all," I say what is very true. But such a remark is no reply to those who say that the nearer you get to your fixed point the more you see in its neighbourhood, and the further you see beyond it. So, too, to oppose change in ideals, as paralyzing, is an excellent reply to those for whom each fresh philosophy they read completely revolutionizes their estimate of the ideal aim to be achieved : but it is no reply to those who maintain a growth in its distinctness—a growing clearness in its explication. Again, when he tells us that to distrust a peasant's ghost story is necessarily either to distrust " the people " or

[1] Page 42.

to preach the intrinsic impossibility of ghosts, he is surely talking nonsense. I would pit the expert against the people in a problem of conic sections, and an educated man against a peasant in taking evidence for a fact in connexion with which popular superstitions are rampant among the peasantry. Yet this is not to deny the value of healthy public opinion. His alternative ignores the real question and reads like a mere joke.

The instances given above, though not the worst, have this special disadvantage, that the changes in the form of religious belief called for by changes in human knowledge have been ever since Galileo's time just the point on which the opponents of "orthodoxy" have something to say which has to be answered. It is a pity, therefore, that this something is here misrepresented instead of being met. It can only be met by admitting scrupulously the element of truth which is contained in their assertions, and showing that "orthodoxy" can admit the truth while it rejects its exaggerations. Mr. Chesterton, on the contrary, appears to exaggerate the intolerance of orthodoxy almost to the point of a literal *credo quia impossibile.*

Some of my readers will smile at these solemn criticisms on my part. They will say, "Of course; that is just Chesterton's way." But I point out these instances because I think it is not Mr. Chesterton's more usual way. His epigrams and sayings are far more often illuminating. In such instances they are on the whole misleading. I could quote other instances in which they are yet more misleading. And to class them all together is just one of the means whereby his critics give a false impression of his work. I do not ask for the omission of all such passages—this

would be too much. Mr. Chesterton moves onward
in his shirt sleeves, throwing out all the brilliant sayings that come into his head ; and to ask him now
entirely to change his manner and put on his coat,
would probably be to cramp his movements and lose
the best of him as well as the less good. I only say
that there is a gallery looking on which sees in his
best only what is to be found in his worst—only
paradox, more or less brilliant or surprising as the
case may be—and I should be very sorry if the
applause of that gallery ever became Mr. Chesterton's
test of the value of what he writes, or his inducement
to write.

I must not, however, exaggerate in my criticisms.
The pages I have just referred to have a serious
value in spite of their faults. They are not mere
brilliant paradox. If they are ineffective against
the more reasonable critics of *Orthodoxy*, they are
most effective against the popular excesses and
defects of the general movement they represent.
To read them brings home most forcibly the chaos
of thought and paralysis of effort resulting from
individualism—from thought ever beginning afresh,
and substituting for the old corporate faith an eager
alacrity to abandon the achievements of the past, and
beliefs tested by practical success. Such a method
makes construction impossible. It means ever hesitating or pulling down, never trusting or building.
The argument which in these pages is advanced on
behalf of a true creed and against a philosophy of
progress, exaggerating the immutability of the former
and the mutability of the latter, fails in that it does
not recognize the constructive and corporate elements
in modern thought, in the hands of its best exponents.

But it stands as a plea for the value of stability in conviction. Moreover, it shows the value of such stability even where the ideal and creed adhered to are largely wrong. And this is the application which Mr. Chesterton himself ultimately gives to his words. They are an apology for deep convictions, inspiring to action and hard to change—for strength of intellectual character. His view, perhaps, needs for its basis some of that very trust in the forces at work in progress which Mr. Chesterton lightly rejects. Or I should prefer to say that it needs for its basis a trust that we are fulfilling the designs of Providence in working hard for the best we can see.

The argument stands for conviction as against scepticism—as supposing not that all deep convictions are absolutely true, but that presumably they are partly true, and that to hold by them and to act on them in the first instance is a sounder principle than a ready scepticism. The former course will lead to their gradual correction as logic and experience test them in action. The latter foregoes the test of action and leads to an attitude of negation which is morbid and paralyzing. The sceptic is ever occupied in straining his eyes to examine what is deeper down than it is given us to see. Mr. Chesterton's argument is a plea against that blunder in reasoning which consists in carrying analysis too far—in the " exercise of thought in matters in which, from the constitution of the human mind, thought cannot be brought to a successful issue." As an argument for conviction against flabbiness, for action against inaction, for reform against stagnation, these pages are very powerful. As an argument against growth in the definiteness of the aim to be striven for, they miss the mark. But there is profound truth amid paradox in the criticism of a degree of intellectual plasticity which robs individual effort of intensity and makes perseverance impossible. The excessive openness of mind which is at the root of this tends not towards progress and reform, but towards its opposite—stagnation. For things can only be changed—change can only be planned—to suit a fixed ideal of something better. If such an ideal is not persistent or inspiring, the motive-power for change is gone. Over-great intellectual plasticity is thus the bulwark of stagnant conservatism. Here again we have a thought which is extremely interesting and among the most suggestive in the book : and the passage in which this conclusion is reached is an excellent illustration of the method in Mr. Chesterton's occasional madness, and the vivid light thrown by his most fantastic illustrations on important principles.

This is our first requirement about the ideal towards which progress is directed ; it must be fixed. Whistler used to make many rapid studies of a sitter ; it did not matter if he tore up twenty portraits. But it would matter if he looked up twenty times, and each time saw a new person sitting placidly for his portrait. So it does not matter (comparatively speaking) how often humanity fails to imitate its ideal ; for then all its old failures are fruitful. But it does frightfully matter how often humanity changes its ideal ; for then all its old failures are fruitless. . . .

. . . Let us suppose a man wanted a particular kind of world ; say a blue world. He would have no cause to complain of the slightness or swiftness of his task ; he might toil for a long time at the transformation ; he could work away (in every sense) until all was blue. He could have heroic adventures ; the putting of the last touches to a blue tiger. He could have fairy dreams ; the dawn of a blue moon. But

if he worked hard, that high-minded reformer would certainly
(from his own point of view) leave the world better and
bluer than he found it.  If he altered a blade of grass to his
favourite colour every day, he would get on slowly.  But if
he altered his favourite colour every day, he would not get on
at all.  If, after reading a fresh philosopher, he started to
paint everything red or yellow, his work would be thrown
away : there would be nothing to show except a few blue
tigers walking about, specimens of his early bad manner.
This is exactly the position of the average modern thinker.
It will be said that this is avowedly a preposterous example.
But it is literally the fact of recent history.  The great and
grave changes in our political civilization all belong to the
early nineteenth century, not to the later.  They belonged
to the black-and-white epoch, when men believed fixedly in
Toryism, in Protestantism, in Calvinism, in Reform, and not
infrequently in Revolution.  And whatever each man believed in, he hammered at steadily, without scepticism : and
there was a time when the Established Church might have
fallen, and the House of Lords nearly fell.  It was because
Radicals were wise enough to be constant and consistent ; it
was because Radicals were wise enough to be Conservative.
. . . Let beliefs fade fast and frequently if you wish institutions to remain the same.  The more the life of the mind is
unhinged, the more the machinery of matter will be left to
itself.  The net result of all our political suggestions, Collec-
tivism, Tolstoyanism, Neo-Feudalism, Communism, Anarchy,
Scientific Bureaucracy—the plain fruit of all of them is that
the Monarchy and the House of Lords will remain.  The
net result of all the new religions will be that the Church of
England will not (for heaven knows how long) be disestab-
lished.  It was Karl Marx, Nietsche, Tolstoy, Cunningham
Graham, Bernard Shaw and Auberon Herbert, who between
them, with bowed, gigantic backs, bore up the throne of the
Archbishop of Canterbury.

Taken as a whole, *Orthodoxy* is a timely warning
given to his contemporaries with a youthful force and

keenness by a convert to the aged creed of Christendom, which has passed its 1900th birthday. We learn how he has come to realize the inner force of its truth—"time honoured" for some of the philosophers, "effete" for others, ever young for Mr. Chesterton His pages are marked by the freshness and often by the insight of genius—no other word can be used. They have not the balance of an all-round philosophy. They do not show the fastidious taste and discrimination characteristic of the typical scholar. They have not the artistic finish of the poet ; and the true poetry of many a paragraph is marred by the transition from the sublime to the ridiculous. Yet in this there is meaning and method. It is a carrying into action of the view expressed in the epilogue to Mr. Chesterton's clever novel, the *Napoleon of Notting Hill*, that there are ever two aspects of the truth, the serious and the humorous. It is the utterance of a man for whom, to use Jowett's phrase, "things serious and profane lie near together, and yet are never confused." And the man who is more than his arguments must put himself into his writing. The book is the trumpet call of a reformer who, like all reformers puts his entire energy into his mission, and, therefore, cannot afford to be reflectively fastidious.

Nevertheless, it remains very singular that one so sensitive to the poetry which modern life has parted with, so greatly impressed by the loss of dignity which our commonplace surroundings have brought, should in his own writing apparently rejoice in just that destruction of dignity which commonplace images bring. Mr. Chesterton seems to have a dual personality ; and it is put together from the heroes of his own novel—Adam Wayne and Auberon. He

hates a red pillar-box ; he loves the robes of Becket.
Yet there is an enjoyment of incongruity which the
present writer at least, while enjoying its brilliant
displays, finds it difficult to reconcile with such tastes.
Something might be said as to Mr. Chesterton's
resemblance in this respect to Browning—of whom
Tennyson always said that he had a keen sense of
the music in poetry. Yet the unmusical rhymes he
loved seemed to show a very different side of him.
Both writers have asserted their individuality with
singular and unconventional boldness. Browning
carried the public with him in the end ; so, perhaps,
will Mr. Chesterton. Yet I am not convinced that
the manner of either is consistent with the truest
literary art.

However, a powerful individuality "maun e'en
gang his ain gait." And it is very many years since
so much individuality has been brought to bear on
controversies which are so largely long-standing ones.
*Orthodoxy* is a book to upset the pedant, to irritate
Mr. Chesterton's *bêtes noires*, the "dreary and well-
informed." Here it hits with wonderful precision the
one weak spot—the heel of Achilles—in some
ingenious but demoralizing system. There the reading of the relevant literature has been careless, and
the mark is missed—a lay figure is destroyed, a most
amusing play is enacted in the destruction, and so the
matter ends. The Casaubons of the age, and even
their betters, may find in the book much to criticize.
"A man," they will say, "ought not to have written
this page, who had not read this and was not familiar
with that." It is a book which makes a challenge
most unwelcome to the conventional philosophers—
"is this a brilliant charlatan or a man of genius?"

The former verdict must bring an uncomfortable sense of insufficiency. To the latter our age extremely dislikes to commit itself. The book can hardly fail to be a great force with the natural body-guard of reality and originality in literature —the abler spirits of the rising generation ; those who have not yet lost the instinct which detects and prizes vital thought, and sees through the shams which so often accompany highly conventional writing. In our own late day, a work on these well-worn themes rarely affords half a dozen passages which come upon one with the feeling that, in the sense above indicated, we have found something original. In this work one's pencil marks half a hundred. J. S. Mill told us, fifty years ago, that we must master the whole existing literature of these discussions before we are fitted to say anything new. But soon after he said it, signs were apparent of the advance of specialism at accelerated speed, of the consequent complete crushing of individual thought under the ever-growing weight of accumulated authorities. Our Davids did their best to put on Saul's armour, but it had become so heavy that before they had even got it all on their energies were spent. In philosophy and in theology it was the same. In Mill's time, the few experts could fulfil his test, and originality could, perhaps, emerge after the severe training. Now specialism has so greatly developed that it hardly can. Perhaps in Mr. Chesterton it would have done so, had his training been that of an expert. But it has not. And one of the very few men who could, I believe, have now fulfilled Mill's test, and remained original after the second half of a training—of which the first half is still good for all—has set the example of going forth with little of equipment over and above his own extraordinary force and skill—little beyond the stone and the sling. The result is, however, something which must be taken very seriously indeed; and if even half of what he says needs qualification and correction, that will not prevent the book giving us as a permanent legacy more of original and practically helpful suggestions than perhaps anything which has appeared in our own day on Chateaubriand's theme, " the genius of Christianity."

# V

# JOHN STUART MILL

THE publication of Mill's letters in 1910 made the picture of him attainable by the reading public as complete as in all probability it will ever be. The *Autobiography* and the *Criticism* by his intimate friend, Mr. Bain, told us much. The Letters and the brief diary appended to them go far towards filling in details of a portrait of which they do not change the general character. In reading these contemporary records we certainly get very near to the man who exercised in his generation an intellectual influence which was almost unique. That influence has been succeeded by the usual reaction. But it extended in its day to minds so various, and so far beyond the school of thought with which Mill was identified, that it is not likely that posterity will fail to do him justice—though his reputation may never again stand quite as high as it did in 1870. The letters have not been so widely read as they deserve to be, and I shall quote freely from them in the course of the ensuing observations.

Some forty years ago two comments on Mill used often to be cited, made by the two men who were then the most prominent figures in the English world of politics. Mr. Gladstone spoke of him (and, I think, also wrote of him) as the "saint

of Rationalism." Mr. Disraeli, whose attention was
called to Mill by his somewhat unexpected apparition
in later life in the House of Commons as member for
Westminster, when asked after a session's experience
of the new member what he thought of him, replied
with a shrug of the shoulders, " A political finishing
governess." Mr. Gladstone's verdict, that of one
who knew and valued Mill's work, was a profound
and true one; Disraeli's—passed by one who probably knew nothing of Mill beyond his speeches in
the House—was an obviously superficial one, indeed
not a verdict at all. But taken merely as what it was,
a statement of the impression made by Mill upon an
acute but superficial observer, who was all the more
alive to mannerisms because the real man was totally
beyond his purview, it suggests very truly the limitations of one who was in some respects a really great
man. These limitations appeared not in politics
alone. They were in fact the defects of those very
qualities which won Gladstone's admiration. Mill
had the educating mania, and it was largely inspired
by that religious zeal for the improvement of mankind
which formed part of his " saintship." From his
father he had early learnt to think that if only people
were thoroughly well educated and freed from the
dead hand of outworn institutions all would be well
with the world. And greatly though his views eventually changed, this early way of looking at things
left its stamp on him through life. His cult of
education issued in a certain priggishness and preciseness, and a detestation of anything vague and not
clearly communicable to those whom he would instruct
and help. It is to this side of his intellectual character that we may set down his admiration for the

French intellect and his extraordinary undervaluing of such German metaphysicians as Hegel and Fichte. To this again must be ascribed his intense joy in distinct classification—which made Dumont's redaction of Bentham (of which I shall speak later on) as inspiring and satisfying to him as Fichte and Hegel were almost physically distressing. It is the "finishing governess" element again which made his own unique and precocious early education for years the sole matter of interest to him, and led him afterwards to analyze its results with such painful care. Like a Jesuit confessor he regarded recreation only as a means to the accomplishment of his main purpose. In his autobiography he refers to frequent holidays as a boy of seven, eight, nine, and ten spent at the old baronial hall (Ford Abbey) rented by Mr. Bentham, as "an important circumstance in my education," and as contributing "to nourish elevation of sentiment." He saw the Pyrenees at the age of fourteen. This is interesting to him because it "gave a colour to my tastes through life." The interest of nearly every event in his life is determined by its effect on his mind and character.

The priggishness and preciseness which called forth Disraeli's saying were in part caused by those peculiarities of Mill's own early education. He had the ways of one who learnt in the first instance from books and in the schoolroom rather than, as Charles Dickens did, from the vivid impressions made by actual life on a boy's imagination. Mr. Bain tells us that to the end his hold on abstract principles was far closer than on the concrete—on the facts of life and the world. His extraordinary precocity was a hothouse growth, and he never quite recovered the

fulness of human nature. There was in Mill to the
end a certain thinness of sympathy and a deficiency
in geniality, though his sympathies were very intense
in their own narrow groove.[1] There was a lack of
full humanity. He had little sense of the ludicrous.
He did not enter into or understand the varieties of
human character, and he was wanting in virility.
These last two traits were evidenced in his believing
that all men were like himself and like one another in
the insignificant place which (as he maintained) the
sexual instinct normally occupied in the life of mankind. He traced obvious exceptions to this rule to
abnormal conditions. By a little management in
education the propensity in question could, he considered, be reduced to an almost negligible quantity,
and he once expressed to my father in conversation
the opinion that the human race would come to an
end by its ultimate complete disappearance.

It is also, I think, a mark of the " governess " side
of Mill's character that the published volumes of his
letters, absorbing though they are, exert something
of a strain on the logical faculty of the reader. There
is little or no imagination in them. Of humour there
is one gleam and only one—and it comes from no
words of Mill, but from a suggestion of Roebuck.
Mill's speeches in the House of Commons were (it
seems) weakened in their effect first by an impression
of hesitation as to the sequence of topics and arguments, and secondly by his manner of delivery. He
had a habit, in Roebuck's words, " of joining his
hands behind him and rolling from side to side like
a schoolboy saying his lessons." Possibly the general

---

[1] Here again he laboriously analyzed a deficiency which in him was
so marked. See *Diary*, ii. 360.

effect was somewhat similar to what many of us remember who have seen and heard another great writer, the late Mr. Lecky, addressing the House of Commons. Roebuck prescribed as a remedy that he should write out the heads of his speech on a card, and should stand every day, card in hand, for some minutes before a large looking-glass and rehearse the coming oration systematically.

The publication of Mill's letters on the whole confirmed the impression already created by the Autobiography. Sometimes the intimate personal address of letter-writing brings out a freshness of style which is wanting in writings designed for publication, and reveals qualities which are not apparent in conversation. It is not so with Mill. The letters do not give their readers any sense of exuberant life in the man, overflowing in self-expression. This stimulating quality is to be found in different forms in the correspondence of many of Mill's contemporaries— Carlyle, Macaulay (whom Mill despised), John Henry Newman, Ruskin—to name only a few writers of very different schools of thought. Mill, on the contrary, in his letters as in his published writings, is critical, analytic, practical, immensely painstaking, never spontaneous, rarely creative. The great modesty of the man, who ascribed all he ever did to his father's training, and placed his own gifts as " rather below than above par," must never be forgotten.[1] It almost disarms criticism, which is nevertheless necessary, in order to understand both his influence and its limitations.

In point of fact, his own account of all he owed to his father's method of educating him recognizes the

[1] See *Autobiography*, p. 17.

advantages of that method but not its drawbacks. The early hothouse forcing of a mind which was set to learn Greek at four and Latin at eight, and encouraged in destructive analysis of those natural sources of enthusiasm which most men find in national institutions and in religion, killed much while it developed much. It developed in an extraordinary degree the reasoning powers, but it tended to depress vitality and imagination, and to make the logical faculty unduly predominant. He associated little with other boys. He was never able to achieve any success in games or sport, and soon gave up the attempt to cultivate such pastimes. He spoke of himself as being in early life little more than a logical machine,[1] despising sentiment on principle.[2] Great though the change was which ultimately came over his attitude towards the cultivation of the affections and the imagination, these qualities of the boy did in some degree over-shadow him through life. He eventually desired to awaken the faculties he had despised, but it did not prove entirely possible ; they had become partially atrophied. Sentiment, when it came to him and was systematically developed, had always in it something thin, something hectic. He inhaled his oxygen not in the fields but artificially through an air pump. Passion and feeling were narrow though intense—intense in sympathy with the people and popular wrongs, with the ills of humanity, finding vent also in an idolatrous worship, without an atom of the normal passion of a man for a woman, towards her who became to him that ideal of worshipful womanhood with which Comte endeavoured to replace the Catholic *culte* of the Virgin Mother.

[1] See *Autobiography*, p. 62.          [2] *Ibid.* p. 64.

This is the general character of the limitations which are so conspicuous in his correspondence, and which were responsible for Disraeli's witty and unfair saying. And they were largely due to the way in which his father educated him.

A characteristic letter of Mill's boyhood given to the world thirty years ago by Mr. Bain in his *Criticism* of Mill, throws the vivid light of contemporary illustration on the unique story of the boy's education, which is so important as a clue to the man's characteristics. It is addressed to Jeremy Bentham's brother, Sir Samuel Bentham. The Benthams had known John Mill as a child. George Bentham had taken him at the age of five to see Lady Spencer—the wife of Lord Spencer, First Lord of the Admiralty—and Mill had kept up an animated conversation with her on the comparative merits of Wellington and Marlborough. When he stayed with the Benthams at the age of eight they found that he had already read in Greek Æsop's *Fables*, Xenophon's *Anabasis*, *Cyropædia* and *Memorabilia*, Herodotus, part of Lucian, and two speeches of Isocrates; also in English the histories of Robertson, Hume, Gibbon, Burnet's *History of his Own Time*, the *Arabian Nights*, *Don Quixote*, and quite as many more books whose names it would be tedious to enumerate. Curious to learn something of the further progress of this extraordinary experiment in education, Sir Samuel Bentham wrote asking for an account of his reading since they had last met. The solemn boy, just turned thirteen years old, consults his memory as to the events of his crowded life to ascertain how long ago that meeting was. He decides that it was six years earlier, and begins his reply as follows :

MY DEAR SIR,—It is so long since I last had the pleasure of seeing you that I have almost forgotten when it was,
but I believe it was in the year 1814, the first year we were
at Ford Abbey. I am very much obliged to you for your
inquiries with respect to my progress in my studies ; and as
nearly as I can remember I will endeavour to give an account
of them from that year.

In the year 1814 I read Thucydides and Anacreon, and,
I *believe*, the *Electra* of Sophocles, the *Phœnissæ* of Euripides,
and the *Plutus* and the *Clouds* of Aristophanes. I also read
the *Philippics* of Demosthenes.

The Latin which I read was only the oration of Cicero
for the poet Archias, and the (first or last) part of his pleading
against Verres. And in mathematics, I was then reading
Euclid ; I also began Euler's *Algebra*, and Bonnycastle's,
principally for the sake of the examples to perform. I read
likewise some of West's *Geometry*.

Aet. 9.—The Greek which I read in the year 1815 was,
I think, Homer's *Odyssey*, Theocritus, some of Pindar, and
the two orations of Æschines, and Demosthenes on the
Crown. In Latin I read the first six books, I believe, of
Ovid's *Metamorphoses*, the first five books of Livy, the
*Bucolics*, and the six first books of the *Æneid* of Virgil, and
part of Cicero's *Orations*. In mathematics, after finishing the
first six books, with the eleventh and twelfth, of Euclid, and
the *Geometry* of West, I studied Simpson's *Conic Sections*,
and also West's *Conic Sections, Mensuration and Spherics ;*
and in algebra, Kersey's *Algebra*, and Newton's *Universal
Arithmetic*, in which I performed all the problems without
the book, and most of them without any help from the book.

He proceeds to enumerate the books read in each
subsequent year—at the ages of ten, eleven, twelve,
and thirteen, which included the enormous list of
classical works set down in the Autobiography. Play-
fair's *Trigonometry* and Simpson's *Algebra*, Keill's
*Astronomy*, Robinson's *Mechanical Philosophy* are
read at ten and eleven. At twelve he read Hobbes'

*Logic* and several Latin works on the same science. Political economy followed next year, and he wrote an abstract of Ricardo. He also began to write various histories,—of the Roman government, as far as the Licinian laws ; of the United Provinces, from their revolt in Spain to the accession of William III. ; and some poems, including a tragedy. The general atmosphere of his home—the educational pressure under which his brothers more or less succumbed, and which, so far as we know, bore little fruit in his sisters (both younger than himself)—is brought before us in the concluding paragraphs of this letter :

I believe my sister Willie was reading Cornelius Nepos when you saw her. She has since that time read some of Caesar, almost all Phaedrus, all the *Catiline*, and part of the *Jugurtha* of Sallust, and two plays of Terence ; she has read the first and part of the second book of Lucretius, and is now reading the *Eclogues* of Virgil.

Clara has begun Latin also. After going through the grammar, she read some of Cornelius Nepos and Caesar, almost as much as Willie of Sallust, and is now reading Ovid. They are both now tolerably good arithmeticians ; they have gone as far as the extraction of the cube root. They are reading the *Roman Antiquities* and the *Greek Mythology*, and are translating English into Latin from Mair's *Introduction to Latin Syntax*.

This is to the best of my remembrance a true account of my own and my sisters' progress since the year 1814.

I hope Lady Bentham, and George, and the young ladies are in good health.

Your obedient, humble servant,
JOHN STUART MILL.

Sir Samuel Bentham invited Mill a few months later to accompany him on a visit to France. He was not yet fourteen when he left England. How completely, even amid all there was to see that was novel and interesting and to learn from what he saw, book-learning was still the one ideal and serious occupation we see from Mill's diary. The visit was an opportunity to learn the French language systematically—that was its chief advantage in his eyes. The following extract from Bain's summary of the diary (Mill's own words being in inverted commas) may be taken as a fair sample of the whole.

9th. "Breakfasted early and went with Sir S. and Lady Bentham in the carriage to Montauban ; took a volume of Racine in my pocket, and read two plays." On returning home he reads a comedy of Voltaire. 10th. "Before breakfast, learnt another [French] fable, and read some of Virgil. After breakfast, wrote some of my *Dialogue*, and some French exercises. Wrought some of the Differential Calculus. Read a tragedy of Corneille." 11th. "Learnt another fable ; finished my *Dialogue*. If good for nothing beside, it is good as an exercise to my reasoning powers, as well as to my invention, both which it has tried extremely." . . . "Wrote some French exercises ; began to learn an extremely long fable. Read a comedy of Molière, and after dinner a tragedy of Voltaire. Took a short walk by myself out of the pleasure grounds."

These extracts show the early form of the education mania impressed on him in word and in action by his father. It was a "finishing governess" very much in earnest with himself and with those committed to his care.

One trait in boyhood, however, which is more illustrative of Mr. Gladstone's saying is revealed in a letter from Lady Bentham to Mill the elder, written during the French tour. "Upon all occasions," she writes, "his gentleness under reproof and thankfulness for correction are remarkable." She adds that the correction is given by reasons illustrated by examples, and is designed to subserve his education for " commerce with the world at large."

In personal intercourse Mill appears to have been much what we should expect from his published works and his letters.

The letters of his mature days bring before the reader very little of Mill's personality. But we know from other sources what the man was like. Calm reasonableness and self-restraint were the dominant notes. Even an enthusiastic admirer like Mr. Bain leaves us under the impression that there was little or no personal magnetism at first meeting. At thirty-six Mill is described as tall and thin, with a somewhat bald head, fair hair and ruddy complexion. He was all through life a great reader, and he read either walking up and down his room in the East India Office (of which he was an official) or at the standing desk at which he wrote. His expression was sweet. His voice was thin, almost sharp. As he spoke there was a constant twitching of the eyebrows which arrested attention. His manner of conversation was cold and passionless as a rule. In his twenties he did not always impress people as a talker. " Though powerful with a pen in his hand," writes one witness, " he has not the art of managing his ideas, and is consequently hesitating and slow and has the appearance of being always working in his mind propositions or a syllogism." Even later some thought his conversation, " though remarkable enough in argument, wholly didactive and controversial. He had no humour, no talk, and, indeed, no interest in the minor concerns of life."

Mr. Bain's own account—that of an enthusiastic

disciple who from long experience of Mill's astounding kindness and high-mindedness saw the real man even amid mannerisms—does not give, I think, a very different impression, and his denial of the charge that Mill's manner—a somewhat hesitating manner—could be wearisome suggests the saying *qui s'excuse s'accuse.*

Mill's voice was agreeable  he writes , although not specially melodious ; it was thin and weak. His articulation was not very clear.  His elocution was good, without being particularly showy or impressive ; he had a mastery of emphasis ; his modulation was sufficiently removed from monotone, so that there was nothing wearying in his manner.  He had not much gesture, but it was all in keeping ; his features were expressive without his aiming at strong effects.  Everything about him had the cast of sobriety and reserve ; he did no more than the end required. . . . Although he did not study grand and imposing talk, he always aimed at saying the right thing clearly and shortly.

Mill was " wanting in momentum," adds Mr. Bain. He could tell a good story, as of the two Frenchmen conversing, both of them by nature addicted to monologue.  " One was in full possession, but so intent was the other upon striking in that a third person exclaimed, ' If he spits, he's done.' "  But such a story was told as an interlude.  There was no humour qualifying his general conversation.  He enjoyed the pleasures of botany and of scenery.  He had a taste for music and devised tunes for some of Walter Scott's ballads.  A few such pleasures, pale and restrained, did apparently make him smile.  But on the whole the impression we get from the records available is of laboured and almost painful earnestness.  Life was for him a most serious thing, and work and duty were all in all.  His favourite quotation was " The night

cometh when no man can work." Let it be added to
this picture of him that for many years his habitual
dress was the black swallow-tail coat worn in the 'fifties
by clergymen of the Church of England.

The collected letters nearly all belong to his mature
life. They are, therefore, imperfect illustrations of a
mental history which began to be interesting at sixteen.
But there are many passages in them and in the brief
diary of 1854 indicative of what I have said of his
character and temperament. And I will set down
some of these as a contribution to the picture of Mill in
his prime before speaking of the development of the
precocious boy into the man who so strongly influenced
his generation.

The pedantic or priggish side in Mill is especially
visible in his letters of advice to those who consulted
him. The following was written to a boy correspondent who asked his opinion on corporal punishment at schools. To most persons the subject
suggests some genial entering into the ways and
habits of the *genus* " boy." Not so to Mill, whose
reply has the dry solemnity, the touch of pedantry
which impressed Disraeli, though there is nothing to
be said against the advice it contains.

1. Severe punishments of some kind are often necessary
for boys, but only when they have been negligently or ill
brought up and allowed to acquire bad habits.

2. Assuming severe punishments to be necessary, any
other method of punishment that would be effectual is preferable to flogging. In the case, however, of certain grave
moral delinquencies, chiefly those which are of a cowardly
or brutal character, corporal punishment in that or some
equivalent form may be admissible.[1]

---

[1] *Letters*, ii. p. 48.

Of the physical distress wrought by German obscurity on one who was so anxious to make all things clear both to himself and to others the illustrations in his letters and diary are the more impressive because in the Autobiography he allows somewhat greater value to German thought.[1] The letters and entries were written when he was actually suffering from it. In his diary of 1854, when sighing to rescue men from misdirected labour and useless speculation, he suggests the advisability of "blotting entirely out the whole of German metaphysics."

When Bain recommends him to read Fichte, Mill communicates to his friend the results of his effort in the following words :

I cannot quite make out why you advised me to read the Fichte. I find nothing at all in it. It is a fanciful theory to account for imaginary facts. I do not see how his preconscious states can have had the merit even of suggesting to you or Spencer the first germ of what both of you have written, with a real science and philosophy, to connect our conscious with our purely organic states.

To the same correspondent he describes the quasi-physical repulsion produced by reading Stirling's *Secret of Hegel* and Hegel's own writings :

I have been toiling through Stirling's *Secret of Hegel*. It is right to learn what Hegel is, and one learns it only too well from Stirling's book. I say only too well, because I found by actual experience of Hegel that conversancy with him tends to deprave one's intellect. The attempt to unwind an apparently infinite series of self-contradictions not disguised but openly faced, really, if persisted in, impairs the acquired delicacy of perception of false reasoning and false thinking which

[1] *Autobiography*, p. 139 : "Along with much error they possessed much truth," etc.

has been gained by years of careful mental discipline with terms of real meaning. For some time after I had finished the book all such words as *reflection, development, evolution,* etc., gave me a sort of sickening feeling which I have not yet entirely got rid of.

We may remember in this connexion that Mill's able contemporary, James Martineau, after a prolonged study of German metaphysics, came to much the same conclusion as Mill, a fact which seems to suggest that there was something in the then state of the intellectual atmosphere in England which made obscurity especially unwelcome. Men were striving with the intense earnestness which characterized the middle of the last century to see clearly what could be proved as a legitimate part of human knowledge. They longed to help others and to be helped in turn by a clear statement whether of agreement or of divergence. The vague and indefinite were in such circumstances especially tantalizing.

But indeed it was in the intellectual candour and reality characteristic of that time, ministering in his own case to a passionate desire for helping mankind to act better and to think more accurately, that Mill was almost without a rival. The candour was largely an intellectual virtue. The passion for truth, and the intense feeling as to the duty of helping his fellow men to find it, meant a very high level of moral inspiration. This combination of the intellectual with the correlative moral virtues lay at the root of Mr. Gladstone's characterization of him as the "saint of Rationalism." The following words from the diary of this Agnostic kept in the year 1854 read like a passage from St. Ignatius Loyola or the *Imitation of Christ.*

> When death draws near, how contemptibly little appears the good one has done! how gigantic that which one had the power and therefore the duty of doing! I seem to have frittered away the working years of my life in mere preparatory trifles, and now "the night when no one can work" has surprised me with the real duty of my life undone.

Other entries in the diary remind us how completely he felt it to be his mission in life to provide mankind with a theory of life to replace the outworn beliefs of the "theological stage" which he, like Comte, regarded as a phase in human progress which was now superseded. The following may be quoted as a sample :

> There is no doctrine really worth labouring at, either to construct or to inculcate, except the Philosophy of Life. A Philosophy of Life, in harmony with the noblest feelings and cleared of superstition, is the great want of these times. There has always been talent enough in the world when there was earnestness enough, and always earnestness enough when there were strong convictions. There seems to be so little talent now, only because there is universal uncertainty about the great questions, and the field for talent is narrowed to things of subaltern interest. Ages of belief, as Goethe says, have been the only ages in which great things have been done. Ages of belief have hitherto always been religious ages ; but Goethe did not mean that they must necessarily be so in future. Religion of one sort or another has been at once the spring and the regulator of energetic action, chiefly because religion has hitherto supplied the only Philosophy of Life, or the only one which differed from a mere theory of self-indulgence. Let it be generally known what life is and might be, and how to make it what it might be, and there

will be as much enthusiasm and as much energy as there has ever been.

How little present reward he hoped for in the pursuit of his apostleship, how simple was his desire for the good of the race and not for his own fame or success in furthering it, is visible in many passages in the letters and diary. Sympathy from kindred spirits he did value, and while he courageously faced the loneliness which a thinker ahead of his time had (as he considered) inevitably to endure, he welcomed with intense thankfulness the appreciation of his work which he found in his own home. But to fame he was absolutely indifferent in the days of his maturity, having long outlived the never very great share of ambition which he had in boyhood.

Two interesting records of this attitude of mind are to be found in his correspondence—one in a letter of 1865 to F. D. Maurice, the other in his diary already referred to.

I sympathize [he writes to Maurice] with the feeling of (if I may so call it) mental loneliness, which shows itself in your letter and sometimes in your published writings. In our age and country every person with any mental power at all, who both thinks for himself and has a conscience, must feel himself to a very great degree alone. I should think you have decidedly more people who are in real communion of thoughts, feelings, and purposes with you than I have. I am in this supremely happy, that I have had, and even now have, that communion in the fullest degree where it is most valuable of all, in my own home. But I have it nowhere else ; and if people did but know how much more precious to me is the faintest approach to it, than all the noisy eulogiums in the world ! The sole value to me of these is that they dispose a greater number of people to listen to what I am able to say to them, and they are an admonition to me to

M

make as much of that kind of hay as I can before the sun gives over shining. What is happening just now is the coming to the surface of a good deal of influence which I had been insensibly acquiring without knowing it; and there are to me many signs that you are exercising a very considerable influence of the same kind, though you yourself seem to think the contrary.

In the diary we read :

The misfortune of having been born and being doomed to live in almost the infancy of human improvement, moral, intellectual, and even physical, can only be made less by the communion with those who are already what all well-organized human beings will one day be, and by the consciousness of oneself doing something, not altogether without value, towards helping on the slow but quickening progress towards that ultimate consummation.

The remedies for all our diseases will be discovered long after we are dead ; and the world will be made a fit place to live in after the death of most of those by whose exertions it will have been made so. It is to be hoped that those who live in those days will look back with sympathy to their known and unknown benefactors.

If ever there was a man whose temperament made a religion necessary to him as a support in his day's work it was one so profoundly pessimistic as to the present state and immediate future of the world, so little inspired by the desire for fame, and yet so scornful of the bare idea of living for personal pleasure, so exclusively devoted to public duty. Yet by an irony of fate John Stuart Mill's early education was in the hands of one, the main passion of whose energetic and able intellect was directed not only against Christianity but against belief in God. James Mill's religious history is related in his son's *Autobiography*. The turning-point in his rejection of

religious belief came when he read Bishop Butler's
*Analogy*. Butler's argument, that the difficulties
against Christianity were analogous to the difficulties
against believing at all in an all-wise and all-good ruler
of the universe, proved in the older Mill's case to be
a two-edged sword. James Mill accepted the premiss
that Christianity is as credible as Theism, but drew
the conclusion that Theism is as incredible as Christianity. His attitude is described by his son as
Lucretian—not one of indifference, but of hatred. He
regarded the established forms of religion as the great
enemies both of progress and of morality.

Brought up in this atmosphere it was long before
John Mill contemplated the possibility of turning
towards any form of Theism or of Christianity, though
his temperament and his view of the world cried
out for religion. He tells us in the *Autobiography*
that he regarded Christianity just as he regarded the
paganism of ancient Greece. Neither was of any
present concern to him. Descartes supported himself
while elaborating a philosophy of systematic doubt
by a *morale pur provision*—a creed which included
the acceptance of the current religion of his time and
country. This was for John Mill at first impossible.
That as time went on he did turn towards some of
the beliefs which he had been taught to despise, we
see from the letters, which confirm in this respect
what we already knew from the posthumous essays
on Religion. His ultimate conclusion was on the
whole in favour of a benevolent Deity limited in
power, to co-operate with whom in improving the
world was the most inspiring motive conceivable for
human action.

But, at an earlier time he cast about in vain for

any such inspiring motive as even this approximation
to Theism supplied. He looked for inspiration at first
in some ideal object for which he might live. Three
episodes of quasi-religious inspiration are visible in
the *Autobiography*. The first was his reading, in
1822, of Dumont's *Traité de Legislation*, containing
a redaction of Bentham's principal speculations which
made them come upon Mill with a new force and
practicalness.

> It gave unity to my conception of things [he writes]. I
> now had opinions, a creed, a doctrine, a philosophy ; in one
> among the best senses of the word, a religion ; the inculcation
> and diffusion of which could be made the principal outward
> purpose of a life. And I had a grand conception laid before
> me of changes to be effected in the condition of mankind
> through that doctrine. The *Traité de Legislation* wound up
> with what was to me a most impressive picture of human life
> as it would be made by such opinions and such laws as were
> recommended in the treatise. The anticipations of practicable
> improvement we studiously moderate, deprecating and dis-
> countenancing as reveries of vague enthusiasm many things
> which will one day seem so natural to human beings, that
> injustice will probably be done to those who once thought
> them chimerical. But, in my state of mind, this appearance
> of superiority to illusion added to the effect which Bentham's
> doctrines had on me, by heightening the impression of mental
> power, and the *vista* of improvement which he did open was
> sufficiently large and brilliant to light up my life, as well as to
> give a definite shape to my aspirations.

The second inspiring episode was his visit to
France during the Revolution of 1830, which renewed
his early dream of himself as a " Girondist in an
English Convention."

> It roused my utmost enthusiasm [he tells us], and gave
> me, as it were, a new existence. I went at once to Paris, was

introduced to Lafayette, and laid the groundwork of the intercourse I afterwards kept up with several of the active chiefs of
the extreme popular party. After my return I entered warmly,
as a writer, into the political discussions of the time, which
soon became still more exciting by the coming in of Lord
Grey's Ministry and the proposing of the Reform Bill. For
the next few years I wrote copiously in newspapers. . . . I
attempted, in the beginning of 1831, to embody in a series of
articles, headed *The Spirit of the Age*, some of my new
opinions . . . the only effect which I know to have been produced by them was that Carlyle, then living in a secluded
part of Scotland, read them in his solitude, and, saying to
himself (as he afterwards told me), "Here is a new mystic,"
inquired on coming to London that autumn respecting their
authorship, an inquiry which was the immediate cause of our
becoming personally acquainted.

But the third quasi-religious influence was by far
the most potent, namely, the friendship with the lady
who became Mrs. Mill, and the influence on him of
her memory after death. The story is well known.
He made Mrs. Taylor's acquaintance in 1831. She
was then but twenty-three, and he twenty-six. He
tells us in the *Autobiography* that he used to compare
her at that time to Shelley, "but," he adds, "in
thought and intellect Shelley, so far as his powers
were developed in his short life, was but a child
compared to what she ultimately became." Their
friendship ripened. It naturally led to difficulties.
His father accused him of being in love with another
man's wife. Mill replied that his sentiment towards
her was only what he would have had towards a man
equally able. External conventionalities, however,
were not attended to ; and Mill was criticized. Such
criticism he did not brook. His breach with Roebuck, with Mrs. Grote, with Mrs. Austin, with Miss

Martineau and with Lady Harriet Baring was in each case ascribed to their allusions to the subject.[1] Mr. Taylor, with curious chivalry, understood and accepted the exceptional situation. Mill asked none of his friends to visit her. But he passed much time in her society and she became the absorbing interest of his life. He regarded all he wrote as an inadequate attempt to express her thoughts. She was probably a remarkable woman. Carlyle speaks of her as "vivid" and "iridescent," and describes her as "pale and passionate and sad-looking, a living romance heroine of the royalest volition and questionable destiny." Mill's brother says, "a clever and remarkable woman but nothing like what John took her for." Mr. Bain suggests that in addition to the affinity which defies analysis, she attracted him intellectually by expressing ideas which she had really learnt from him. The thoughts he cherished came to him from the voice of the woman he loved, and he did not realize that it was from him she first learnt them. Whatever the explanation, she was to Mill the object of a passion remarkable for its purity and intensity. Twenty years after their first meeting her husband died (in 1851), and Mill married her. "What I owe even intellectually to her," he writes in the *Autobiography*, "is in its detail almost infinite."

When after the few years of their union Mrs. Mill died at Avignon, being taken ill in the course of a journey through France, the remembrance of the friend he had lost became the dominating influence and inspiration of the remainder of his life.

Since then [he writes] I have sought for such alleviation as

[1] In the case of Lady Harriet Baring Mr. Bain is not quite confident.

my state admitted of, by the mode of life which most enabled me to feel her still near me. I bought a cottage as close as possible to the place where she is buried, and there her daughter (my fellow-sufferer and now my chief comfort) and I live constantly during a great portion of the year. My objects in life are solely those which were hers; my pursuits and occupations those in which she shared, or sympathized, and which are indissolubly connected with her. Her memory is to me a religion, and her approbation the standard by which, summing up as it does all worthiness, I endeavour to regulate my life.

The inscription on her tomb at Avignon ends with the words : "were there even a few hearts and intellects like hers this earth would already become the hoped-for heaven." She had helped him much in the book on *Liberty*, which he brought out after her death with the following dedication :

To the beloved and deplored memory of her who was the inspirer, and in part the author, of all that is best in my writings—the friend and wife whose exalted sense of truth and right was my strongest incitement, and whose approbation was my chief reward—I dedicate this volume. Like all that I have written for many years, it belongs as much to her as to me; but the work as it stands has had, in a very insufficient degree, the inestimable advantage of her revision ; some of the most important portions having been reserved for a more careful re-examination, which they are now never destined to receive. Were I but capable of interpreting to the world one-half the great thoughts and noble feelings which are buried in her grave, I should be the medium of a greater benefit to it, than is ever likely to arise from anything that I can write, unprompted and unassisted by her all but unrivalled wisdom.

Grote's remark on this dedication was " no reputation but Mill's could survive it." But the general verdict of his friends ultimately was, that while on this one subject his judgment had been wholly carried away from its moorings, it remained sane and reliable in other matters. And if we compare the lover's vision with the reality in other cases this will appear the fairest verdict. The peculiarity of this particular instance is that whereas such judgments are generally hidden in the privacy of domestic life, Mill made his views public and associated them with his own writings, which were then so much before the eye of the world.

But while the memory of his wife was, as he says, a religion to him, while probably the thought of her was that which filled the purely emotional side of his religious nature, so inquiring a mind could not rest without a desire to answer the great questions with which religion in the ordinary sense is concerned,— the world behind the veil and the hope for the future which is reasonable for mankind.

And it is possible that the question of immortality took a new colour from the fact that one whom he so deeply yearned to meet again had passed from this earth. The feeling which he had expressed in reference to Sterling's death must have come yet more vividly when he lost one so far dearer than even Sterling.

There are many signs in his correspondence that Mill did, in the years following the death of his wife, earnestly desire to accept a form of Theism. One of the most interesting letters on this subject—written in 1860 to one who submitted to him some speculations on the subject—may here be cited :

It would be a great moral improvement to most persons

be they Christians, Deists, or Atheists, if they firmly believed
the world to be under the government of a Being, who, willing
only good, leaves evil in the world solely in order to stimulate
human faculties by an unremitting struggle against every
form of it.

In regard, however, to the effect on my own mind, will
you forgive me for saying that your mode of reconciling the
world as we see it with the government of a Perfect Being,
though less sophistical than the common modes, and not
having, as they have, the moral effect of consecrating any
forms of avoidable evil as the purposes of God, does not, to
my apprehension, at all help to remove the difficulty? I tried
what I could to do with that hypothesis many years ago,
that a perfect Being could do anything except make another
perfect Being, that the next thing to it was to make a per-
fectible one; and that perfection could only be achieved by
a struggle against evil. But then, a Perfect Being, limited
only by this condition, might be expected so to form the
world that the struggle against evil should be the greatest
possible in extent and intensity; and unhappily our world
conforms as little to this character as to that of a world without evil. If the Divine intention in making man was Effort
towards perfection, the Divine purpose is as much frustrated
as if its sole aim were human happiness. There is a little of
both, but the absence of both is the marked characteristic.

I confess that no religious theory seems to me consistent
with the facts of the universe except (in some form or other)
the old one of two principles. There are many signs in the
structure of the universe of an intelligent Power wishing well
to men and other sentient creatures. I could, however, show,
not so many perhaps, but quite as decided indications of an
intelligent Power or Powers with the contrary propensity.
But (not to insist on this) the will of the benevolent power
must find, either in its own incompleteness or in some external
circumstances, very decided obstacles to the fulfilment of the
benevolent purpose. It may be that the world is a battlefield
between a good and a bad power or powers, and that mankind
may be capable, by sufficiently strenuous co-operation with
the good power, of deciding, or at least accelerating, its final

victory. I know one man of great intelligence and high
moral principle, who finds satisfaction to his devotional
feelings and support under the evils of life, in the belief of
this creed.

What kept Mill from a nearer approach to
Christianity appears to have been partly the insufficiency of such Christian apologetics as he could
find.[1] Again, his moral sense revolted against the
attitude of the so-called orthodox in regard to honest
unbelievers. This enlisted the sentiment of moral
approbation, which is with so many a potent force in
favour of Christian belief, on the opposite side. He
considered that the best men he knew were among
the conscientious unbelievers. It was a time when
the anti-Christian fanaticism of the eighteenth century
had given place to something very different. The
sentiment expressed in *écrasez l'infâme* was diametri-
cally opposed to the feelings of one who had so strong
a wish to believe. The orgies of the mob which
placed a prostitute on the altar at Nôtre Dame was
the vulgar reflection and exaggeration of an attitude,
even among the intellectual, strangely at variance with
Mill's dream of perfect purity to be obtained by man
through philosophy. He himself had no passion
against Christianity. His passion was simply for
truth wherever it could be found. All his wishes were
on the side of definite religious belief. Doubt was
the sad necessity of the twilight of human life. He
preached in prose what Tennyson celebrated in poetry,

---

[1] So far as Theism is concerned, the *Essays* show this. On
Immortality we have a pregnant note in the *Letters* (ii. 381) on the
" bitter disappointment " which the alleged proof brings as being based
on the assumption that " the facts of the universe bear some necessary
relation to the fancies of our own mind."

the moral superiority of honestly avowed doubt to the shallow profession of creeds not profoundly or intelligently—in some cases not even sincerely—believed in. Moreover he regarded the ideal Theism which he and many of his friends held to—that is to say, belief in the duty of conforming one's actions to a rule approved of by an ideal God whose actual existence was at best uncertain—as superior morally to the actual Theism of many professors of Christianity whose conception of God was not moral, who conceived of Him as a Being revengeful and unjust, whom they nevertheless flattered, in the fear that otherwise He should punish them, by crediting Him in general terms with an infinite and absolute goodness which in particular actions they denied Him. It was in this connexion that he passed his well-known comment on Mansel's analysis of the character of the Deity, which Mill regarded as belief in a non-moral God.[1]

This passage made an immense stir, and the approach of Christian thinkers to understanding Mill's views was signalized by the fact that, although some

---

[1] "If," wrote Mill in answer to a criticism of Dean Mansel, "instead of the glad tidings that there exists a Being in whom all the excellences which the highest human mind can conceive exist in a degree inconceivable to us, I am informed that the world is ruled by a being whose attributes are infinite, but what they are we cannot learn, or what are the principles of his government, except that "the highest human morality which we are capable of conceiving" does not sanction them—convince me of it and I will bear my fate as I may. But when I am told that I must believe this, and at the same time call this being by the names which express and affirm the highest human morality, I say in plain terms that I will not. Whatever power such a being have over me, there is one thing which he shall not do—he shall not compel me to worship him. I will call no being good who is not what I mean when I apply that epithet to my fellow-creatures ; and if such a being can sentence me to Hell for not so calling him, to Hell I will go." (*On Hamilton*, pp. 123, 124.)

were shocked, several, including well-known Roman Catholics,[1] wrote to congratulate him on his protest against such depravations of Theism as extreme Calvinistic doctrines of election and reprobation were calculated to bring about.

J. S. Mill had none of that natural antagonism to the deepest principles of Christianity which his father and so many others have had. He had nothing of the pagan in him. To many some degree of emancipation from the strict Christian doctrines on purity and on humility appears necessary to make one's view of life really adequate to the length and breadth of human nature. Christian asceticism appears in both these matters one-sided. The ideal of such men is Greek, and they regard Christianity as savouring of Oriental asceticism. In short, they deny Tertullian's *testimonium animæ naturaliter Christianæ*. To Mill, on the other hand, the morality of Christianity did appeal —though its external evidences did not. He carried the principle of self-denial very far. As to purity his ideal was far more Christian than Greek. His efforts on this subject were directed towards the attainment of an ideal perfection which to ordinary mortals seems Utopian for the majority of men. His intellectual modesty had in it much in common with Christian humility. And it appears again and again in the *Letters* and in the *Autobiography*. Self is nothing; the great cause of working for mankind everything. He cared nothing (as I have said) for mere fame. He would not have his picture painted. He declined the honour of a visit at Avignon from the Princess Royal (the future German Empress). He shunned society

[1] Among these was my father, whom Mr. Herbert Paul curiously alludes to in his History as agreeing with Mansel.

which would have *fêted* him gladly. He had, indeed, very deep down a dislike of the luxuries and the flattery attending on a great social position. He had something of the saint in his unworldliness as in his asceticism. "We, like you," he wrote to Mazzini, "feel that those who would either make their lives useful to noble ends or maintain any elevation of character within themselves must, in these days, have little to do with what is called society."

An interesting picture of his life in his little country house outside Avignon is preserved in a letter from his friend Mr. Thornton to Henry Fawcett, and it brings before us his happiness in a secluded life, in which the chief physical pleasure was the lovely scenery which surrounded him :

In front of the house is an oblong garden with an avenue of sycamores and mulberry trees down the middle, and at the end a trellis-work supporting a vine which serves as a verandah to the dwelling. This is a small square building, whitewashed, with a tiled roof and green Venetian blinds without, and within, three small rooms on the ground floor and two on the floor above, all fitted up very simply, but with English comfort and neatness, and a mixture of French and English taste. Two of the lower rooms are the drawing-room and sitting-room, the third is my bedroom, at the window of which, looking into the garden, I am now writing. Above are the bedrooms of Mill and Miss Taylor, opening upon a terrace, from which is a view of green fields, backed by ranges of mountains of most graceful forms and constantly changing colours.

At eight o'clock we breakfast ; then, if there is no special plan for the day, Mill reads or writes till twelve or one, when we set out for a walk which lasts till dinner-time. In the evening Mill commonly reads some light book aloud for part of the time. This, I fancy, is his ordinary mode of life while here, but he is now laying himself out to entertain me, and almost every other day we make a long carriage excursion, starting directly after breakfast, and driving twenty or thirty miles on end and not returning till sunset or later. We have already visited in this way Petrarch's valley of Vaucluse, the Roman monuments at St. Remy, and the curious feudal remains of Les Baux, and to-morrow we are to go to the famous Pont du Gard. Mill tells me that they seldom let a week pass without making some such excursion, but that this year they have postponed all until my arrival. You may imagine how much I am enjoying myself, and no small part of my pleasure consists in seeing how cheerfully and contentedly, if I may not say how happily, Mill is living. I feel convinced that he will never be persuaded permanently to abandon this retreat, for here, besides the seclusion, in which he takes an almost morbid delight, and a neighbourhood both very interesting and, in its own peculiar way, very beautiful, he has also close at hand the resting-place of his wife, which he visits daily, while in his step-daughter he has a companion in all respects worthy of him.

I have dwelt somewhat fully on Mill's search for some source of inspiration to take the place of the old religions which he regarded as untenable—because the finding of a *Weltanschauung*, of a philosophy of life and adequate ideals of action, was clearly the chief object inspiring his own work and life. But, of course, his writings were not—except only the posthumous essays on religion—writings on the philosophy of life. They were contributions to the sciences or to the political problems of the day. The *Logic* and the *Political Economy* still hold their own as the best expositions of those sciences given us by any thinker belonging to his own school of thought. We may decline to admit that syllogistic reasoning is based on induction, or that "necessary truth" can be accounted for by experience ; but Mill's logic is far the best produced by any writer of the "experience" school, and much of it is invaluable to readers of every school. The canons of induction are never likely to be superseded. Much of the sociology of the sixth book has permanent value. If the *Political Economy* is vitiated by the assumption that men always act from self-interest, and some conclusions are therefore true only *ex hypothesi* and not in real life, this defect qualifies the value of only a small part of a great book. The *Liberty* is the most persuasive and moderate existing exposition of a theory in its totality fallacious. The *Examination of Hamilton's Philosophy* brings to an issue with unrivalled clearness the central points of debate between the schools of experience and of intuition. In virtue of the *Logic*, the *Examination of Hamilton*, and the *Liberty*, he was long the acknowledged leader of an important party in the world of thought. The *Dissertations and Discussions* are carefully made selections from his contributions to periodical literature, and there are among them essays of the highest value. Especially notable is the essay on Coleridge and Bentham. The little book on *Representative Government* is a really powerful piece of political philosophy which has been weighed and not found wanting by thinkers of many different political creeds.

The Letters show all the candour and independence in treating of the secular questions discussed by his contemporaries which are visible in his published writings. The resolute and honest individualism, the insistence on examining for himself and judging all traditional views, those of his own party as well as those of their opponents, which led Mill to make such considerable concessions to the religious party, placed

him also among the first to question and amend long-
standing verdicts in history, lazily acquiesced in by
the majority. The process of historical reconstruction
has, of course, been undertaken much more thoroughly
in our own day. But Mill's verdicts are often still
worth reading. The following brief estimate of
Voltaire's true position, as contrasted with the popular
view of him, may be taken as a sample of many fuller
ones :

I am now reading very sedulously Voltaire's correspondence : I never read it before. It throws much light upon the
spiritual character of that time, and especially of its literary
men. How strangely Voltaire's own character has been mistaken ; and how little does he seem to have been conscious
of what he was about, to have had even any settled purpose
in it. He certainly had no intention of being the patriarch
of any sect of destructionists, and if the priests would have
let him alone he would have let them alone. In the greater
part of his lifetime he seems to have been timid excessively,
and would have abstained from almost anything in order to
remain quiet at Paris. But after he had found the quiet he
sought, at a distance, it was the revival of persecution—as
evinced by the suppression of the Encyclopedia, the condemnation of Helvetius' book, the speech of Le Franc de
Pompignan at the Academy denouncing Voltaire himself
personally, the success of Palissot's comedy of *Les Philosophes*,
the abuse of the philosophers by various persons, etc., etc.—
it was these things which erected Voltaire after the age of
sixty-five into the leader of a crusade against Christianity ;
and it was then, too, that he seems to have found out that
wit and ridicule were capable of being powerful weapons in
his hands. He always seems to have despised the French,
and thought them incapable of philosophy or even of science ;
and he continually lamented that they insisted upon taking
to speculation, which they were unfit for, and neglected the
*beaux-arts.*

But when all is said as to the value of Mill's actual contributions to the thought of his own day we are brought back to Mr. Gladstone's verdict. The thinker was greater than the thought. It is the mental and moral quality of the "saint of Rationalism," shown even in works on purely philosophical or technical subjects, his infinite candour and teachableness, which gave his reputation its unique character in his own time and should make it lasting. The rare combination of assimilative power with independent criticism in his estimates and the justice of his verdicts were a powerful talisman. When he saw that the *Quarterly* did not venture boldly to recognize at its worth the rising genius of Tennyson, he wrote in the *London and Westminster* a courageous article which greatly helped to guide popular opinion on the subject. His recognition of Darwin's *Origin of Species*—given in one of the published letters—is a masterpiece of balanced criticism which could hardly be improved upon now after all the subsequent ebb and flow of scientific opinion on the subject. His criticisms of Voltaire, Machiavelli, and many another have also the freedom of an absolutely fair and independent mind revising popular verdicts, not from a dislike of acquiescing in established views, but because justice obviously demanded their revision. He claims with truth in the *Autobiography* to have been "much superior to most of his contemporaries in willingness and ability to learn from everybody." The strenuous conservative thinkers of that earnest day had the rare satisfaction of seeing their views appreciated by the "rising hope of the stern and unbending" Radicals of the school of James Mill and Bentham. Nay, more, they found him avowedly modifying the

N

extreme views he had learnt and was set up to defend. They witnessed the spectacle in all ages so rare of an almost professional partisan owning to half conversion, yielding to argument when it convinced him, and reforming his creed. This brought him into close touch with thinkers of many schools, and gave him great influence far outside the circle of his own direct followers.

Hence the record of the growth of his mind and character, given in the *Autobiography*, and copiously illustrated in its later stages by the *Letters*, is a more unique tribute to the greatness of the man than any of his published writings on technical subjects. In the religious bias (above referred to), which reacted against his father's atheism, we see, perhaps, the working of a peculiar temperament which sorely needed religion. But the story of Mill's mental progress, as a whole, testifies to an almost unique combination of moral earnestness and intellectual candour. And these qualities touched and drew to him the true *élite* of every creed and philosophical school—the salt of the earth. Let us recall the outlines of this story.

He admits (as I have already noted) to having been during two or three years of his later boyhood "a mere reasoning machine." [1] Benthamism undervalued imagination as simply misleading. But the Benthamite creed he outgrew before he was twenty, and spoke of it as "sectarian folly." Plutarch's *Lives*, Plato's pictures of Socrates, and still more Condorcet's *Life of Turgot* made him realize a wider range of ideas. Turgot disclaimed solidarity with the Encyclopedists as sectarian. And John Mill, at the age of eighteen, ceased to call himself a Benthamite. His

[1] *Autobiography*, p. 62.

new sense of the value of the cultivation of the
imagination and feelings came in the mental crisis (at
the age of twenty) in which he was rescued from the
slough of despond by a touching passage in Marmontel's *Mémoires*. He suddenly felt that the realization of all the objects for which he was working could
not bring him happiness. "The whole foundation on
which my life was conducted," he writes, "fell down
. . . I seemed to have nothing left to live for." After
six months of misery, during which all zest, and
all capacity for feeling, seemed to have left him, he
was deeply affected by reading the sad scene in which
Marmontel describes his father's death, the sadness of
the family, and his own sudden inspiration to be all in
all to them and to fill his father's place. The tears
which his reading drew from him wrought a cure
which reasoning had failed to effect. Life seemed
once more worth living. He found "enjoyment, not
intense, but sufficient for cheerfulness, in sunshine and
sky, in books, in conversation, in public affairs," and
"excitement, though of a moderate kind," in working
for the public good. He took the lesson to heart.
"The cultivation of the feelings," he tells us, "became
one of the cardinal points in my ethical and philosophical creed."

His emancipation from the sectarianism of his
early creed made it then essential to reform his
opinions, and in this task he displayed his extraordinary
openness to influence.

Wordsworth, Coleridge, Maurice, Sterling were
only a few of those whose views reacted on him. Of
Sterling he says, " He and I started from intellectual
points almost as wide apart as the poles, but the distance was ever diminishing." And new ideas were

not allowed by Mill to remain isolated. They meant further labour, for they had to be worked out in their effects on his own opinions as a whole.

> I found the fabric of my old and taught opinions giving way in many fresh places [he writes], and I never allowed it to fall to pieces, but was incessantly occupied in weaving it anew. I never, in the course of my transition, was content to remain, for ever so short a time, confused and unsettled. When I had taken in any new idea, I could not rest till I had adjusted its relation to my old opinions, and ascertained exactly how far its effect ought to extend in modifying or superseding them.[1]

Sterling's own appreciation of the change in his friend has been left on record :

> He has made the sacrifice of being the undoubted leader of a powerful party for the higher glory of being a private in the army of truth, ready to storm any of the strong places of falsehood even if defended by his late adherents.[2]

Mill thus exercised an immense influence on behalf of the intellectual candour which has distinguished the nineteenth century from the eighteenth. This characteristic was handed down to a later generation by the late Mr. Henry Sidgwick—but with the addition in the Cambridge thinker of a certain humorous pleasure in provisional demolition which Mill had not. To find wanting a theory which was seriously and ably advanced was ever, I think, to Mill a source of regret. The above named characteristic of the century is described by Mill himself in his diary, but naturally with no reference to his own large share in fostering and increasing it.

---

[1] *Autobiography*, p. 90.   [2] Courtney's *J. S. Mill*, p. 73.

In the last age (he says) the writers of reputation and influence were those who took a side, in a very decided manner, on the great questions, religious, moral, metaphysical and political ; who were downright infidels or downright Christians, thorough Tories or thorough democrats, and in that were considered, and were, extreme in their opinions. In the present age the writers of reputation and influence are those who take something from both sides of the great controversies, and make out that neither extreme is right, nor wholly wrong. By some persons, and on some questions, this is done in the way of mere compromise ; in some cases, again, by a deeper doctrine underlying both the contrary opinions ; but done it is, in one or the other way, by all who gain access to the mind of the present age ; and none but those who do it, or seem to do it, are now listened to. This change is explained, and partly justified, by the superficiality and real onesidedness of the bolder thinkers who preceded.

The tendency of Mill's age here described is to be seen in one of its aspects in Lord Morley's book on *Compromise*, in its deeper form and with a predominance of constructive conclusions in the works of Coleridge, and later on of F. D. Maurice. To Mill it was so congenial that the absence of it in such partisan writing as that of Macaulay made him almost blind to that writer's great talent. He can conceive nothing more damaging to the age in which he lived than that it should be "estimated by posterity as the age which thought Macaulay a great writer." It was an age when earnest candour was specially prized among the deep thinkers. And it was, moreover, an age, among the intellectual *élite*, of great changes of religious profession at the stern behest of newly won conviction. Carlyle left the Calvinism of his youth. Martineau ceased to be an orthodox Unitarian. R. H. Hutton travelled from Unitarianism on the opposite road—to

belief in the Trinity and orthodox Anglicanism. Newman joined the Catholic and Roman Church. Maurice
was the pioneer of a new theology for the Church of
England. Coleridge and Sterling both lived to hold
very different views on life and religion from those with
which they began. Mill was then the child of his time.
But his changes not only evinced his supremacy in
the intellectual virtue characteristic of the time, but
had in them something of the special quality which
attaches to the story of St. Paul, for his inherited
creed was not neutral, but intolerant. It was probably
the agreeable surprise he experienced when he found
real intellectual greatness in the defenders of views
which he had learnt from his father to regard as
morally depraved and intellectually beneath contempt,
which led him to do such ample justice to writers
like Coleridge and Wordsworth. A reader of the
article in the *London and Westminster Review*, on
"Coleridge and Bentham," finds it hard to realize in
fact that its writer was once a professed Benthamite,
and still declared Bentham to be on important points
nearer the truth than Coleridge. One of the most
interesting episodes referred to in these volumes is
his interview with Wordsworth, described in a letter
to Sterling of October 1831. It shows, for the time
at least, an attitude of more distinct dissociation from
radical principles than readers of the *Autobiography*
would expect to find :

> I went this summer to the lakes, where I saw such splen-
> did scenery, and also a great deal both of Wordsworth and
> Southey ; and I must tell you what I think of them both. In
> the case of Wordsworth, I was particularly struck by several
> things. One was the extensive range of his thoughts and the
> largeness and expansiveness of his feelings. This does not

appear in his writings, especially his poetry, where the contemplative part of his mind is the only part of it that appears; and one would be tempted to infer from the peculiar character of his poetry that real life and the active pursuits of men (except of farmers and other country people) did not interest him. The fact, however, is that these very subjects occupy the greater part of his thoughts, and he talks on no subject more instructively than on states of society and forms of government. Those who best know him seem to be most impressed with the catholic character of his ability. I have been told that Lockhart has said of him that he would have been an admirable country attorney. Now, a man who could have been either Wordsworth or a country attorney could certainly have been anything else which circumstances had led him to desire to be. The next thing that struck me was the extreme comprehensiveness and philosophic spirit which is in him. By these expressions I mean the direct antithesis of what the Germans most expressively call onesidedness. Wordsworth seems always to know the pros and the cons of every question, and when you think he strikes the balance wrong it is only because you think he estimates erroneously some matter of fact. Hence all my differences with him, or with any other philosophic Tory, would be differences of matter of fact or detail, while my differences with the Radicals and Utilitarians are differences of principle; for *these* see generally only one side of the subject, and in order to convince them you must put some entirely new idea into their heads, whereas Wordsworth has all the ideas there already, and you have only to discuss with him the "how much," the more or less of weight which is to be attached to a certain cause or effect as compared with others; thus the difference with him turns upon a question of varying or fluctuating quantities, where what is *plus* in one age or country is *minus* in another, and the whole question is one of observation and testimony, and of the value of particular articles of evidence. I need hardly say to you that if one's own conclusions and his were at variance on every question which a minister or a Parliament could to-morrow be called upon to solve, his is nevertheless the mind with which one would be really in communion ; our principles would be the same, and we should be like two travellers pursuing the same course on the opposite banks of a river. Then when you get Wordsworth on the subjects which are peculiarly his, such as the theory of his own art, if it be proper to call poetry an art (that is, if art is to be defined as the expression or embodying in words or forms of the highest and most reformed parts of nature), no one can converse with him without feeling that he has advanced that great subject beyond any other man, being probably the first person who ever combined, with such eminent success in the practice of the art, such high powers of generalization and habits of meditation on its principles. Besides all this, he seems to me the best talker I ever heard (and I have heard several first-rate ones) ; and there is a benignity and kindliness about his whole demeanour which confirms what his poetry would lead one to expect, along with a perfect simplicity of character which is delightful in any one, but most of all in a person of first-rate intellect. You see I am somewhat enthusiastic on the subject of Wordsworth, having found him still more admirable and delightful a person on a nearer view than I had figured to myself from his writings, which is so seldom the case that it is impossible to see it without having one's faith in man greatly increased and being made greatly happier in consequence.

Of Southey he writes also in the same letter, with appreciation but with somewhat less of sympathy, as a man of " gentle feeling and bitter opinions."

Mill's general conclusion is that in reforming the world he could ill dispense with the greater minds among the " speculative Tories."

If there were but a few dozens of persons safe (whom you and I could select) to be missionaries of the great truths in which alone there is any well-being for mankind individually or collectively, I should not care though a revolution were to exterminate every person in Great Britain and Ireland who has £500 a year. Many very amiable persons would perish, but what is the world the better for such amiable persons? But among the missionaries whom I would reserve, a large proportion would consist of speculative Tories : for it is an ideal Toryism, an ideal King, Lords, and Commons that they venerate ; it is old England as opposed to the new, but it is old England as she might be, not as she is. It seems to me that the Toryism of Wordsworth, of Coleridge (if he can be called a Tory), of Southey even, and of many others whom I could mention, is *tout bonnement* a reverence for government in the abstract : it means that they are duly sensible that it is good for man to be ruled ; to submit both his body and mind to the guidance of a high intelligence and virtue. It is, therefore, the direct antithesis of Liberalism, which is for making every man his own guide and sovereign-master, and letting him think for himself, and do exactly as he judges best for himself, giving other men leave to persuade him if they can by evidence, but forbidding him to give way to authority ; and still less allowing them to constrain him more than the existence and tolerable necessity of every man's person and property renders indispensably necessary. It is difficult to conceive a more thorough ignorance of man's nature, and of what is necessary for his happiness, or what degree of happiness and virtue he is capable of attaining, than this system implies. But I cannot help regretting that the men who are best capable of struggling against those narrow views and mischievous heresies, should chain themselves, full of life and vigour as they are, to the inanimate corpses of dead political and religious systems, never more to be revived. The same ends require altered means ; we have no new principles, but we want new machines constructed on the old principles ; those we had before are worn out. Instead of cutting a safe channel for the stream of events, these people would dam it up till it breaks down everything and spreads devastation over a whole region.

One word must be said concerning Mill's brief sojourn—between 1865 and 1868—in the House of Commons. In politics, as in the world of thought,

it was his frankness, candour, and moral elevation that
made a lasting impression. He was, as I have already
noted, a bad speaker. He was cold and not fluent—
often pausing for a painfully long interval to find his
appropriate word. Again the *bonhomie* and sympathetic manner that count for so much were wanting.
"The House listened to him with respect," writes
Mr. Courtney, "but he seemed like a man who
was performing a difficult and disagreeable duty in
addressing it." Nor was the matter of his speeches
always happy. He concentrated his main attention
on questions too subtle to arouse the interest of a
political party. In this he seemed to the average
politician something of a faddist. He did not play the
game of party popularity. In politics as in other
matters he was severely individualist. In religion he
had stood aloof both from all the religious sects and
from the sectarian agnostics. In his twenties he had
branded as "sectarian" his own early Benthamite
creed in philosophy. His brief party alliance with
Comte and the Positivists broke down when Comte
formulated his full creed and substituted an oligarchy
of men of science for a democracy. And in politics
too he declined party shibboleths. Even before
entering the House he had discarded under the
influence of patient thought some of his earlier
radical views. He opposed voting by ballot. And
while desiring an extension of the suffrage he
deprecated the undue predominance of the working
classes. He was optimistic as to the probable effects
of education in gradually fitting the British work-
man to use the suffrage wisely. But he was also
apprehensive as to the probable evil which the political
demagogues would work in corrupting him by flattery.

His independent attitude when first asked to stand for Westminster was very noteworthy. He declined to bear any of the expenses of election. Not Burke himself at Bristol was more emphatic in declining the very shadow of dictation from his constituents. He refused to concern himself with their local affairs. He did not consult them as to the measures they might desire him to support in Parliament.

He told them his views and said in effect, " Elect me or not as you please. I am totally indifferent. These are the views which if elected I shall advocate."

Two consequences are to be noted which had their counterpart during his career in other fields besides the political. First, the immense courage, honesty, and moral elevation of the man for a moment carried all before it. The working men voted for the candidate who publicly expressed his opinion that they were as a rule " liars " ; and Mr. Odger declared that they desired to be told their faults and not to be flattered. And the House of Commons itself immensely respected the new member. Mr. Gladstone's estimate of him is favourable to his tact as well as to his character. " He had the good sense and practical tact of politics," he writes, "together with the high independent thought of a recluse. . . . We well knew his intellectual eminence before he entered Parliament. What his conduct there principally disclosed, at least to me, was his singular moral elevation. Of all the motives, stings and stimulants that reach men through their egoism in Parliament no part could move or even touch him. His conduct and language were in this respect a sermon." Mill made some speeches that told, and used some phrases that stuck. It was he who coined the phrase " the stupid party " as applied

to the Conservatives and defended it in the House
as successfully as he defended his criticism on the
labouring classes outside of it: " I never meant to
say that Conservatives are generally stupid.  I meant
to say that stupid people are generally Conservatives."
In the debate on the Irish Church he used the
memorable sentence, " Large and bold measures alone
can save Ireland."

But, secondly, while his high character and
startling candour struck at the outset a strong vibrat-
ing note of sympathy in and out of the House, such a
line of action as his was not "to play the game " of
practical affairs.  A public assembly, like an individual
man of the world, is liable to be intensely touched for
the moment by nobility and quixotic heroism.  It will
accord to it a generous and impulsive recognition.
But this attitude does not last.  The novelty of the
spectacle of the " saint of Rationalism " in Parliament
wore off.  His speeches, long, technical, ill-delivered,
bored the House.  If his attitude was, as Mr. Gladstone says, a sermon, prolonged sermons weary human
nature.  Again, he did not quite work with his party,
while, as we have said, he largely ignored his constituents.  An independent and solitary personality is
out of place in the House of Commons.  When the
election of 1868 came Mill was defeated and returned
to the more congenial surroundings of Avignon.

I think that his parliamentary career suggests as
in a microcosm some important causes both of Mill's
great influence and of the subsequent re-action against
it.  In the world of intellect, as in that of politics,
" the Private in the Army of Truth," as Sterling
called him, who for conscience sake gave up the party
of which he had been leader, aroused a degree of

admiration, by his courage and honesty, which represented too high a standard of popular judgment to last. The Deists, Anglicans and Roman Catholics who congratulated him on his candid admission of some of their arguments and sang his praises as a just man in whom there was no guile, could not be his thorough-going supporters. And although he was still the unquestioned leader of the empirical school in philosophy, his followers long suspected that his attitude was not so iconoclastic as they desired.

Yet so long as he lived certain causes did prolong a popularity unusual in its nature. The high moral character and acknowledged eminence of the recluse who dwelt at Avignon got hold of the popular imagination. He was regarded as an oracle to be consulted by young thinkers much as Carlyle was consulted by them. And men of all schools would ask his advice and opinion because he was felt to be open to considerations from every side. He was the great living philosopher who taught all men to think candidly. Apart from the views he represented he was, as Lord Morley has said, eminently one who helped others to think deeply and truly. Again he still had, up to his death in 1873, a very powerful following as a philosopher, and still did represent an important school of thought, though not the Benthamite school as understood by his father. To many negative thinkers his arguments appeared all the more powerful and conclusive from his candour in recognizing the views of philosophical opponents. The *Logic* and the *Examination of Sir W. Hamilton's Philosophy* remained as thorough-going expositions of the empirical theory of knowledge. If he was no longer an out-and-out Benthamite he still represented

the philosophy of Hume and of his agnostic successors.
Thus he was at once a great living oracle, and the
leader of a powerful school of philosophy.

Both these sources of influence came to an end in
1874.   His death in 1873 destroyed the first.   The
publication of the posthumous *Essays on Religion* in
1874 destroyed the second.   Men like the present
Lord Morley and Mr. Leslie Stephen, who had
hitherto stuck to Mill though they recognized in
him greater sympathy than they themselves had with
the religious party, could no longer feel him to be
their leader after these essays appeared.   Perhaps
the essays recorded no fundamental change in Mill's
views as they had been rumoured in private conversation.   Indeed, Mill's letters show that this must have
been so.   But there had hitherto been vacillation ; and
while to some he had expressed his sense of the moral
value of belief in Theism and Immortality, he had to
others laid stress on the sufficiency for mankind of a
religion of duty and humanity—akin to Positivism
though divested of its extravagances.

But now a clear note was publicly sounded expressing the insufficiency of any religion which did not
contemplate the world beyond the veil.   The pride of
agnosticism was humbled.   The jubilant note expected
from a leader of the negative school was replaced by
its opposite.   It was in the third essay that the
matter for offence was found.   He went no further in
it than to admit a certain scientific value for reasons
on behalf of the probability of that qualified Theism I
have already described, and of a survival of the spirit
after death as its correlative.   But two things were
new ; and these were decisive in their effect on his
former followers.   First, he encouraged a religion of

hope and imagination in excess of the actual evidence. Secondly, his language concerning Christ was in the highest degree startling to such men as Mr. John Morley (as he then was) and Mr. Bain, still more to Mr. Huxley and Mr. Spencer, who were profoundly out of sympathy with Christianity and at war with its professed adherents.

On Theism and Immortality Mill wrote as follows :

To me it seems that human life, small and confined as it is, and as, considered merely in the present, it is likely to remain even when the progress of material and moral improvement may have freed it from the greater part of its present calamities, stands greatly in need of any wider range and greater height of aspiration for itself and its destination, which the exercise of imagination can yield to it without running counter to the evidence of fact ; and that it is a part of wisdom to make the most of any, even small, probabilities on this subject, which furnish imagination with any footing to support itself upon. And I am satisfied that the cultivation of such a tendency in the imagination, provided it goes on *pari passu* with the cultivation of severe reason, has no necessary tendency to pervert the judgment ; but that it is possible to form a perfectly sober estimate of the evidences on both sides of a question and yet to let the imagination dwell by preference on those possibilities, which are at once the most comforting and the most improving, without in the least degree overrating the solidity of the grounds for expecting that these rather than any others will be the possibilities actually realized. . . . It appears to me that the indulgence of hope with regard to the government of the universe and the destiny of man after death, while we recognize as a clear truth that we have no ground for more than a hope, is legitimate and philosophically defensible. The beneficial effect of such a hope is far from trifling. It makes life and human nature a far greater thing to the feelings, and gives greater strength as well as greater solemnity to all the sentiments which are awakened in us by our fellow-creatures and by mankind at large. It allays the sense of that irony of nature which is so painfully felt when we see the exertions and sacrifices of a life culminating in the formation of a wise and noble mind, only to disappear from the world when the time has just arrived at which the world seems about to begin reaping the benefit of it. The truth that life is short and art is long is from of old one of the most discouraging parts of our condition ; this hope admits the possibility that the art employed in improving and beautifying the soul itself may avail for good in some other life, even when seemingly useless for this. But the benefit consists less in the presence of any specific hope than in the enlargement of the general scale of the feelings ; the loftier aspirations being no longer in the same way checked and kept down by a sense of the insignificance of human life—by the disastrous feeling of "not worth while." The gain obtained in the increased inducement to cultivate the improvement of character up to the end of life, is obvious without being specified.

The passage on the personality of Christ is well known. The sting was to be found in its conclusion, which may therefore be here set down :

When this pre-eminent genius is combined with the qualities of probably the greatest moral reformer and martyr to that mission who ever existed upon earth, religion cannot be said to have made a bad choice in pitching on this man as the ideal representative and guide of humanity ; nor, even now, would it be easy, even for an unbeliever, to find a better translation of the rule of virtue from the abstract into the concrete than to endeavour so to live that Christ would approve our life. When to this we add that, to the conception of the rational sceptic, it remains a possibility that Christ actually was what he supposed himself to be—not indeed God, for he never made the smallest pretension to that character . . . but a man charged with a special, express and unique commission from God to lead mankind to truth and virtue ; we may well conclude that the influences of religion on the character which will remain after rational criticism has done its utmost against the evidences of religion are well worth preserving, and that what they lack in direct strength as compared with those of a firmer belief, is more than compensated by the greater truth and rectitude of the morality they sanction.

The change wrought by these passages in Mill's position with many of his old followers was parallel to the change in sentiment among enlightened Catholics towards a recently declared Modernist. As long as such a writer accepts Catholic dogma and respects ecclesiastical authority, while he strenuously endeavours to reconcile the acknowledged results of modern criticism with his religion, the abler Catholic readers are proud of his genius and open-mindedness. They regard him as the pioneer of an enlightened theology. But let him clearly overpass the lines of orthodoxy and there is a terrible reaction. His great position is gone in an instant. Thus Lamennais fell, from an eminence which was compared by Lacordaire to Bossuet's, to the insignificance of the beggary in which he died. The former followers of the Modernist are bitter—the more so because they had defended him as orthodox. They took him to depict the Christian Church as wise and comprehensive, ready to assimilate all truth. He is now seen to have been in reality depicting a Christianity which is discredited and can only be saved from positive destruction by the general adoption of his own personal views.

Something like this in kind, though far less extreme in degree and in its consequences, happened to Mill. So long the acknowledged defender of a negative philosophy of the sufficiency of enlightened

O

reason and imagination to supply the place of the old religions, he now appeared in a new light. The emancipated intellect of the nineteenth century was no longer in his pages proud and erect, jubilant as to its achievements and prospects ; it was prostrate and humbled at the recognition of an ignorance that could never be dispelled. Mill seemed to cast wistful and longing eyes at the ancient creed, towards which his followers were so supercilious. There was no note of confidence, of leadership. He was

> An infant crying in the night,
> An infant crying for the light,
> And with no language but a cry.

Many of us still remember the shock which this essay created. Mr. Leslie Stephen was reported to have paced the room in indignation which could not be contained, while his wife yet further angered him by the poor consolation of " I told you so. I always said John Mill was orthodox." Mr. John Morley, in the *Fortnightly*, did not disguise his profound disappointment. This was not the Mill whose henchman he had been, and whose praises he had sung so enthusiastically only a year earlier on the occasion of his death. Mr. W. L. Courtney testifies to the " consternation " caused " among those of Mill's disciples who had fed themselves on his earlier work " by an essay which seemed to recommend the renunciation of reason in favour of the twilight of faith. The religious press was, of course, jubilant. And the religious party scored heavily in a long-standing combat.

Almost contemporaneously with the shock of 1874 came another cause of the declension of Mill's

ascendency in the rapid growth in influence of the
evolution philosophy. Mill had fully recognized
historical evolution as formulated by Comte. But
even this was not one of his special subjects. And
the application of the theory to philosophy proper was
first made and with extraordinary thoroughness by
Herbert Spencer. This was a second reason which
led the negative thinkers to turn for guidance from
the man who had betrayed them in the theological
controversy to another. In the 'eighties Herbert
Spencer enjoyed much of the popularity which had
once been Mill's.

Then came the new influence of German philosophy in England, especially of Hegel. Mill had,
on the whole, despised Hegel and Fichte. And the
followers of the great Germans now had their revenge.
The thought of Oxford had been largely ruled by Mill
in the 'sixties. In the 'eighties T. H. Green's alliance
with his more orthodox Anglican pupils established
the predominance of a philosophy based largely on
Hegel. And the Hegelians were quick to retaliate
with the very note of contempt once sounded in their
own regard by Mill. Hegel stood far more widely
apart from Mill than from Spencer, with whom, indeed,
as with Comte, the German has real points of affinity.
With the change of dynasty came a great change in
fashionable modes of thought. Mr. Balfour decried
Mill's " thin lucidity." The passion for clearness in
expression, which still remained unabated in Huxley
and largely in Spencer himself, gave place in the
disciples of Green to a certain reverence for obscurity.
While in science proper and in historical criticism
lucidity was still recognized as a virtue and men
worked together to reach definite scientific results, in

higher thought a certain scepticism as to the value of human reason supervened, with faith as its correlative. Dim, half-expressed intuitions of deep truths commanded respect. Clearness was supposed to mean that the mind moved on a plane far below the highest problems. Philosophy itself became largely a faith though illustrated and developed by reason. The new attitude, which still largely survives, issued in its best exponents in some very suggestive and powerful thought. But in the rank and file it had grave disadvantages. The common measure of minds, to which Mill and his contemporaries had appealed in their dialectics, was disregarded, and no satisfactory test distinguishing seer from charlatan was substituted. A subtle contempt became the average critic's weapon of attack in place of the frank debates of an earlier day. The critic posed as a specialist, addressing outsiders, on subjects in which no consensus of specialists was in point of fact attainable. Criticism became very unperceiving, and was often shielded from being itself in turn fatally criticized by being wholly unintelligible, or at least by using as a loophole for escape an ambiguity which made not worth while any strenuous pursuit of views which if run to earth would be disavowed. Something startling, something new, or something indefinable, was needed to satisfy or at least to please the palate of a somewhat jaded generation. What was quite clear and generally persuasive was *ipso facto* discredited, as not only shallow but unworthy of being said at all. The antithesis to the ways and manners of Mill was complete. The old painstaking discussion in which you had first to prove your own capacity by restating an opponent's case and thus showing that you understood it, was no longer thought of. The

critics of whom I speak were too often incapable of
it. But they absolved themselves from all risk of
detection by disparaging such a procedure as a descent
from the heights on which alone true philosophic
contemplation was possible.

It is this modern repudiation of really adequate
analysis, this making professed analysis almost as
obscure as what is analyzed, which has been the *coup
de grâce* to Mill's influence. It is this which makes
his philosophy now so little read. Yet so exaggerated
a depreciation of candid and clear and often penetrating thought cannot last. Already there are whispers
that even the Germans are puzzled at the uncritical
worship in England of what they have themselves
found seriously wanting ; and Oxford is spoken of as
the place where good German philosophies go to
when they die. Moreover, where the world of
fact is concerned there is always a touchstone which
brings thought back to reality. Thus while the
*Examination of Hamilton* and most of the *Logic* have
long been quite neglected, students of political
economy have never wholly ceased to read Mill ; and
the wisdom of many of his political utterances has
recently been brought back to us with new power by
the circumstances of the time, just as Burke's speeches
of one hundred and fifty years ago are being read
with fresh interest. The *Liberty* and the treatise on
*Representative Government* are nearly as valuable now
as they ever were. When he comes to be widely
read again I believe Mill will be permanently recognized not indeed as a great constructive thinker, but
as a very great critical thinker, with the rare accompanying quality of remarkable sympathetic understanding. He himself did not believe that the

individual thinker was likely to reach finality in treating of the greatest problems. He certainly did not
reach it himself. It is the individual's office (he held)
to contribute the best he can to the general stream of
criticism and re-criticism. And in this task a critical
thinker almost without prejudices, of very acute and
penetrating mind, and of unexampled candour and
power of profiting by the thoughts of others, is not a
personage to be set aside as of little or no account.
" Who shall sum up Mill's collective influence as an
instructor in Politics, Ethics, Logic and Metaphysics ? "
writes Mr. Bain. " A multitude of small impressions
may have the accumulated effect of a mighty whole."

The *Autobiography* will ever remain as a most
pathetic human record, the story of an unnatural
experiment in mental vivisection, exercised on a little
child, issuing in a somewhat maimed and impoverished
nature, and of an heroic and partly successful attempt
at recovery. The figure it presents to us in mature
life is filled in by the letters. It is that of one
endowed by an almost unique sense of public duty
and indifference to personal motives, making the very
best of the powers that had been unduly developed
and of those which had been unduly stunted. Those
who knew him best set hardly any limit to his selfless
devotedness. And their testimony is on record.
" Like Howard in Bentham's felicitous eulogy," writes
an intimate friend, " Mill might have lived an apostle
and died a martyr." The saints are seldom universally popular, and the " Saint of Rationalism " will be
no exception. The constant exhibition of devotion
to duty is dull. And dulness is, to the present
generation especially, almost a crime. Indeed, it was
Mill's own living influence that helped to keep alive

the high moral standard of criticism which led to his full recognition. Unregenerate human nature will reassert itself when such guides disappear. Even candour will be assailed from time to time, as it was by Canning :

> Hail, most solemn sage,
> Thou drivelling virtue of this moral age.

But another generation as strenuous as Mill's own will place the moral virtues of his intellect very high and will reinstate his reputation. His philosophy indeed is not likely to revive. Parts of the *Logic* and parts of the work on Hamilton will consequently be read as little as the scholastic speculations on the *intellectus agens*, and *intellectus possibilis*. But even in the *Logic* his treatment of sociology and induction contain much of permanent value. I think that a certain want of virility and lack of imagination will always be felt by his readers. As we dwell on him we cannot conjure up the full picture of the hero or the great man who is born, not made. Much that was born was killed early by his one-sided training. Nearly all had to be made. But he was taught early how to make ; and we see him taking infinite and pathetic pains to recover artificially much that was irretrievably lost. One echoes his own sad words, " I never was a boy. I never learnt to play cricket. It is better to let nature have her own way."

Yet as one can deeply reverence a Christian saint and owe much to his influence though one sees that he is not a boon companion or even a gentleman, so it is with such a unique intellectual and moral character as Mill's. We admire, though the æsthetic pleasure afforded by buoyancy, richness, spontaneousness, creativeness of mind is absent. The ascetic sacrifices physical beauty and the realization of the many-sided possibilities of life and human nature in order to accomplish the all-important tasks prescribed by duty. A certain narrowness of direction makes for effectiveness. And something akin to the sentiment of admiration we give to the persistent religious devotee will, I am convinced, be accorded by posterity to Mill, in spite of all he lacked whether by nature or in consequence of his early training. When told that he was dying he spoke four words, " My work is done."

# VI

# CARDINAL VAUGHAN

IT is not too much to say that the publication of *The Life of Cardinal Vaughan* completely changed the estimate of his character that had been formed by the British public. To many, especially among members of the Anglican Church, Cardinal Vaughan had been simply the type of the masterful Roman prelate, proud, ostentatious, fond of flourishing the unwelcome claims of Rome in the faces of Englishmen, treading ruthlessly on the toes of his compatriots, constantly offending their national feelings. Phrases of the Cardinal's which were, perhaps, wanting in literary tact used to be repeated from mouth to mouth and their significance exaggerated. His commanding and handsome presence, his family relationship with aristocratic English Catholic houses, the state and circumstance of a Prince of the Church, doubled his offences. For a time there was revived in his person something of what had been the popular idea of Cardinal Wiseman in 1850. He was the embodiment of " papal aggression." He was the man who, with immense publicity and ostentation, dedicated England to St. Peter—as though England were his to dedicate ; who laughed at Anglican orders as " shivering in their insular isolation " ; who denounced to the Archbishop of

Toledo, in a letter which appeared in print, the "astute sect" of the Church of England which posed as Catholics ; who chose the moment when his co-religionists were longing to show their love for the great dead Queen of England to remind the public that she was a heretic for whom Catholics could not offer religious rites as for a member of the one true Church.

If the Cardinal's biography had presented something quite inconsistent with the popular idea of Herbert Vaughan, it would not have effected the complete change in public opinion of which I have spoken. It would probably have been regarded by the Cardinal's critics as a record bowdlerized out of all truthfulness. It is just because the book focuses, and puts in due place and proportion the offending features, because it explains the popular impression while correcting it, that it is so interesting and so effective a piece of apologetic.

I will not attempt at present to summarize in a few words the corrections of popular misconception which the book supplies—to set down categorically what is true and what false or vitiated by false elements in a conception of Cardinal Vaughan which has prevailed somewhat widely. It will be more convincing to endeavour first to place before my readers an outline of the picture given us by Mr. Snead-Cox—a picture made up almost entirely of actual facts and of the Cardinal's own words. Where analysis involves very subtle distinctions it may not be successful. But a true picture cannot fail to correct a false one.

The boyhood of Herbert Vaughan was passed at Courtfield—in the beautiful country traversed by the river Wye, near Ross. Here his ancestors had been settled for 350 years. His great-great-grandfather had a Spanish wife. One of the English Catholics who had fought for Prince Charlie in 1745, he left the country after Culloden, joined the Spanish Army and married a wife in the country of his adoption. The Cardinal's mother did not come of a Catholic stock. She was a daughter of Mr. Rolls of the Hendre, aunt to the present Lord Llangattock, and in childhood a strong evangelical. Becoming a Catholic she had all the intense piety of a devout convert. To their Spanish ancestry and their descent from one with antecedents so different from those of the old Roman Catholic families of England, may probably be traced the very marked and special characteristics of the Vaughans in the generation to which Herbert Vaughan belonged — their taste for romance and adventure, their immense energy and love of heroic and daring enterprise. The hereditary Catholics of England had for the most part the very different qualities and habits of a long-persecuted race. Some had, after two centuries of fidelity to the Holy See, conformed in the end to the Established Church. Some had grown lax in their allegiance to Rome, Cisalpine in sentiment as much as doctrine. The deep piety of others was of the long-suffering sort. The thought of daring enterprise and of great conquests for the cause of the Catholic Church was the last which came natural to a race well-nigh worn out with legal disabilities and persecution, and barely allowed to remain in the country. They were content to live in peace and say their prayers undisturbed — to live and let live.

The love of adventure and romance were from

the first strong in Herbert Vaughan—though the romance was so markedly limited in its direction that, as we shall see later, he seemed to many the most unromantic of men. His romance centred in the aims and ideals of religion, and was inspired by an extraordinarily vivid faith. His love of adventure, which later on was displayed in religious enterprise, found its first vent in his keen love of sport. So far as human affections were concerned, romance was visible mainly in his passionate love for his beautiful and saintly mother, who died while he was still a boy. In most other instances his very absorption in religious aims made him slight human affections as worthless and uninteresting. He was little given to descriptive writing. He lacked the gifts of a man of letters. But he has left on record the ineffaceable picture his " sweetest mother " left on him as he used to watch her praying before the altar as a little boy :

An hour in the morning was always spent in meditation in the chapel, which was her real home. She generally knelt, slightly leaning her wrists against the *prie-Dieu.* I do not recollect ever seeing her distracted on these occasions, or looking anywhere than towards the Blessed Sacrament or on her book. She often remained with her eyes fixed on the Tabernacle, and while her body was kneeling at the bottom of the chapel—her face beautiful and tranquil with the effects of Divine Love—her heart and soul were within the Tabernacle with her dearly beloved Saviour. . . . I used to watch her myself when in the chapel, and love her and gaze upon her. I used often to watch her from the gravel walk in the flower garden, and marvel to see her so absorbed in prayer.

Another deep and ineffaceable memory was his love of sport from boyhood upwards. His old home was for him to the end full of memories of his boyish

adventures with gun and horse. Walking at Courtfield with a friend in his later years he pointed out
place after place stamped by these keen early
memories.

In that pool in the river he had cast his first fly, but he
had never cared for fishing ; there he had been taught to ride ;
over that fence he had learned to jump ; under that hedgerow
many a time in the summer he had sat with his gun, waiting
for the rabbits to come out in the dusk, and saying his rosary
while he waited ; in that coppice how often he had gone
blackberrying ; and there—but that was later—he had killed
his first pheasant ; and in that field, on the brow of Coppet
Hill, he had almost shot his father—they were out partridge
shooting, and just drawing together under a tree for luncheon
when, putting his gun to half-cock, it somehow went off and
the whole charge whizzed past his father's head ; the Colonel
turned quickly, and, taking in the situation at a glance, said,
"Well, now let us unpack the basket." So the stream of
reminiscence went on until, stopping short, and moving his
arm as though to take in all the countryside, and letting his
voice fall almost to a whisper, he said, "And over it all is the
memory of what I went through before I made up my mind
to be a priest."

It was, indeed, the realization that sport was
becoming the sole interest of his life which largely
made him turn his thoughts to the priesthood. He
was an eldest son, and the priesthood meant for him
the abandonment of fortune and position ; but he
often said that it was the sacrifice of his life as a
sportsman that cost him most.

At sixteen his resolution to be a priest was taken.
And to him it meant from the first that he intended
to do, as he expressed it, " something intense " and
" something heroic " for God and the Church. Henceforth he applied himself to his books, and retained

grateful memories of being taught habits of systematic study at a French School at Brugelette, where he spent a year. His new and absorbing purpose made it no trial to him that he lived in this school a solitary figure among uncongenial French boys, who called him " Milord Roast Beef," while his cricket bat—the last relic of his taste for English games—was confiscated as a suspicious looking and probably murderous club. The school helped him to prepare for what had become the one object of his life, and he was grateful to it.

Passing to Rome, he gained there also deep and lifelong impressions—a quite special sentiment for all its relics of the past and for the Holy See, as those well knew who were ever in his company in the Eternal City. He lived at the *Accademia dei Ecclesiatici nobili* and attended lectures at the *Collegio Romano*, hearing, among others, the celebrated Father Passaglia, with whom he became intimate, and whom he describes as "kind and magnificent." He was present at the proclamation of the dogma of the Immaculate Conception. His dream—somewhat undefined as yet—was to do a great work as a missionary, perhaps in Wales, perhaps in foreign parts. He read eagerly at this time the lives of the saints, especially of the great missionaries. Such reading for him was not that of the day-dreamer who is content to dream and do no more. The healthy English boy who used to read Dick Turpin, when it first came out, was often too much inclined to try his fortune as a highwayman. And Vaughan had the same longing to translate into action his day dreams about the lives of the saints. Missionary work gave him extraordinary happiness. An expedition made in rough weather, in his youth at Courtfield, to help an old man who was taking to religion after a life of evil, stood out to the end as a bright spot in his life —as men of the world will remember to the last a moment of ideal love or of triumphant success. "The night was wet and cold and I was riding," he writes of it in his old age, "I had to cross the river and wind along the hill up home. The comfort and joy of that hour is inexpressible—it was sweeter than all the joys of the world—the joy within the heart making it feel confident in God who watches over it."

While in Rome he formed a close friendship with Henry Edward Manning. Manning had at that time a scheme for training the English Catholic clergy on the model of the oblates of the great Archbishop of Milan, Charles Borromeo. His strong influence with Cardinal Wiseman made the realization of this idea appear not improbable. For a moment, under Manning's influence, Herbert Vaughan turned aside from his visions of missionary work to join in promoting it. He was appointed by Cardinal Wiseman, when only twenty-two, Vice-President of St. Edmund's College, the successor in the South of England of the old Douay College, and the training ground for the secular clergy. He became at the same time a member of the congregation of the Oblates of St. Charles, which Manning had brought into existence, and induced some of the divinity students at St. Edmund's also to join this congregation and to further its special ends. The discipline of the college was to be reformed on "Oblate" lines.

The *imperium in imperio* thus created in the college, and the suspicion that Vaughan was there as Manning's secret agent, bent on gradually bringing

the whole college under the rule of the converted
Archdeacon of Chichester, who was far from popular
among the old clergy, made Vaughan's position an
impossible one.   At twenty-three he was undertaking
to instruct men of twice his own age, who were the
official superiors of the college.   Many of the divinity
students themselves were as old as he was ; some even
older.   Both "divines" (as they were called) and
Professors resented his presence.   He was, nevertheless, a hero with the boys.   They were proud of
his riding and his splendid presence ; and the story of
a highwayman who stopped him one day and found
that he had met his match, was long repeated in the
college.   His aim in accepting the Vice-Presidentship
was, however, defeated.   It may fairly be said that he
was inconsiderate and, in some degree, arrogant in his
bearing at St. Edmund's, and quite failed to understand the good elements in the system he meant to
reform.   But he unquestionably believed himself to be
aiming at a great work—at raising the ideals of the
clergy, at engrafting something of the strict discipline
and enthusiastic piety of the continental seminaries, of
which St. Sulpice was a notable example, on a somewhat apathetic English priesthood.   He seems, from
an entry in his journal, to have had some suspicion,
on thinking matters over, that he was (in his own
phrase) "proud and contentious" and inconsiderate of
the feelings of others.   Indeed, there was an innate
masterfulness in him through life which was again and
again rebuked in its manifestations by his touching
personal humility.   Whether in this instance he was to
blame, or whether Cardinal Wiseman commissioned
him to carry out an intrinsically impracticable scheme,
the position at St. Edmund's proved (as I have said)

impossible. The idea of bringing the clergy under Oblate domination, to be ruled by Dr. Manning, an Oxford convert of only four years' standing, was eventually disowned in express terms by Cardinal Wiseman himself.

To act merely as the Vice-President in an English ecclesiastical college which he regarded as unsatisfactory and deficient in high ideals, to carry on its humdrum routine, did not at all answer to Vaughan's dreams of a great " heroic " enterprise. Indeed, while he held the position he was a frequent absentee, more interested in visits to Wiseman at York Place and Manning at Bayswater, discussing with them the plan of campaign, than in the actual duties of a Vice-President. When, therefore, the original idea of a drastic reformation of the college under Oblate influences was definitely abandoned, he and the other Oblates left the college, and Vaughan turned his thoughts once again in the direction of missionary work—this time more definitely of converting the heathen. The dream grew in his mind for months. But, with his high views of a vocation, he needed both ecclesiastical sanction and some sign that he was following not his own whim and taste but the will of God. He gained the warm approval of Cardinal Wiseman in 1860, and after visiting the great shrines in Spain and Italy and praying for guidance, he went to his mother's grave at Courtfield. Here (he writes) " after several days of prayer an answer seemed to come to me in the chapel, saying distinctly, ' Begin very humbly and very quietly.' It came to me," he adds, " like a revelation, with all the force of a new idea."

The idea was deepened and quickened in the

following year by an incident which recalls the conversion of St. Ignatius Loyola, on his sick bed, and
his initiation of the great enterprise which led to the
foundation of the Jesuit Order. Herbert Vaughan
had a severe illness in the winter of 1861, and during
his convalescence he fed his imagination with the
lives of St. Francis Xavier, the apostle of Japan,
and St. Peter Claver, "the slave of slaves." With
him, as with St. Ignatius, the effect of vivid meditation
at a time of bodily weakness was decisive. Manning
—his Oblate chief—approved of his wishes, but
Vaughan soon saw that the Oblate community received
the idea with coldness and would not really take it up.
He had to act for himself. And this he did after a
period of depression, and what was to him the greatest
of trials—doubt and uncertainty as to his duty. The
immediate plan he formed was to make a voyage
across the Atlantic, in order to beg in America for the
funds which were needed to set on foot a training
college for missionary work among the heathen. And
this had to be done by his own unaided efforts,
with no help from human companionship or disciple-
ship. He spent six months in Rome in 1862, praying
for further guidance. His enterprise was to have all
the accompaniments of a great public work for the
Church. He pleaded his cause before Montalembert
and other Catholic leaders at the celebrated congress
of Malines in 1863, and the assembly passed a resolution wishing him godspeed. He went again to
Rome and gained the special blessing of the Holy
Father, and letters of approval for his American
campaign. The civil war was at its height, and
therefore the United States did not offer a promising
field. He set sail in December for California, receiving

on the eve of departure an affectionate letter from Wiseman—to whose large-hearted and enterprising nature the adventurous scheme especially appealed. Herbert Vaughan used to say that for thirty years he could never read, without tears, this letter, received by him at the moment of realizing his dreams of heroic enterprise for the one great cause—of a life really worth living.

Let one characteristic be here parenthetically noted which was well known to his intimate friends and was apparent in every work of his life, including the American expedition with its many adventures. Herbert Vaughan hardly knew what fear was, and had in his attitude towards death the spirit of his sister, the Poor Clare nun, who wrote, when the doctor pronounced her illness incurable, to inform her uncle of the "glorious news" which she was impatient to tell him, that she should soon be with her Lord in Heaven.

The sense of romance, which his American campaign aroused in Herbert Vaughan's friends, was inevitably intensified by his extraordinary personal beauty —far greater in his thirties than at a later period. There still remain photographs which bear out this statement. The portliness of later life and the slight heaviness of feature were not yet in sight. Slim of figure, his fearless blue eyes, aquiline nose, and firm-set mouth, the expression of sweetness and courage combined, made him in appearance an ideal Sir Galahad, setting forth in quest of the Holy Grail.

It would be tedious to relate the details of the American expedition. But the general story of his work there is most instructive and characteristic. It was a veritable realization of a chapter in some of

those lives of the Saints which had inspired him.
His absolute faith that the work he had undertaken
was God's work made his perseverance indomitable.
He counted on beginning to preach and to beg in
the wealthy town of San Francisco.  A crushing disappointment, however, greeted him at the outset.  The
Archbishop of San Francisco needed all the Catholic
money of the town for the requirements of his diocese.
He received Vaughan coldly, and would allow him
neither to preach nor to collect in the city.  This was
the first reminder he received of the hard world of
facts which had to be overcome before his dream
could be realized.  The Presentation nuns of San
Francisco were from the first his friends.  They
could give him all their sympathy and their prayers.
But they could give him no money.  Sympathy
Vaughan valued.  But prayer was, in his opinion, a
far more practically useful asset.  It was March—the
month consecrated to St. Joseph.  In simple Catholic
fashion he bade them lay siege to St. Joseph and give
him no peace until the Saint had changed the Archbishop's heart.  The nuns prayed.  But the last day
of March arrived, and there was no result.  " The
last day, but not the last hour of the day," was the
calm assurance prompted by Vaughan's confident
faith in prayer.  And sure enough, late in the evening,
he received a letter from the Archbishop, giving
permission for one sermon in each church in the city.

When once he was allowed to work and to speak
freely, the effect produced on his hearers by the
heroic character of his enterprise, by his own simple
faith, by the force of his personality, was irresistible.
Money came fast.  £200 was collected after the first
sermon ; £250 after the second, and these amounts

were long sustained. April brought a harvest: then things slackened. But May was the month of Mary. He prayed to the Virgin Mother for £1000 to found a "bourse" in her honour. The money came, but this time it came slowly.

The last day [he writes] I was minus 700 dollars and knew not where to turn for it—could not beg from the poor, and the Bishop only tolerated begging from the richer Catholics of the City. A man met me when I knew not which way to go and gave me 200 dollars, saying he wished to become a special benefactor. In the evening, I was minus 400 dollars. I went into Mr. Donohoe's bank to sit down. I told him my case: he had no sympathy for the work, and had given 250 dollars to please his wife. Said he would lend me 400 dollars. "But I can't lend them to the Blessed Virgin," said I, smiling. I told him I had not come with the intention of begging of him—he had given generously already. Finally, I said, "What interest do you require?" "Never mind that," he answered. "When do you want the principal back?" "Never mind that, either," said he. And so that night Our Lady had her bourse completed.

After five months in California, Vaughan went to Peru and Chili. Many curious experiences are recorded by him, and though his letters and diary show no great descriptive power, the keen sense of adventure is apparent through them all. The following extract from the *Life* contains a sample:

From Lima [we read] he journeyed into the interior, and on one occasion rode thirty-three miles before breakfast, starting at 2.30 a.m. Writing to Mrs. W. G. Ward, he says: "My last journey has been to Arequipa. It had the best Bishop in Peru, but alas! he was buried just before I reached there. It is south of Lima, and ninety or one hundred miles from the coast. The ride across the Pampa Grande, or great desert of Peru, was a great novelty. The road, or rather pathway, is strewn with the bones of horses and mules.  And after the great plain of sand is passed the track between and after the coast range of the Andes is covered with the remains of animals that have fallen by the way, exhausted by fatigue or thirst.   As soon as an animal can no longer go on, after he is relieved of his burden (everything that is carried into the interior has to be borne by mules—there are no roads for carts or carriages), he is necessarily left behind by his owner, and then, before the drove of mules is out of sight, great vultures, gathering from all parts, come down upon him. One alights upon his head—the poor animal seems to have lost all sense of self-preservation—and plucks out his eyes. The poor beast is soon despatched, and the next day the carcass is dried up and abandoned by both man and beast. Not always, however, by man, for whether it be to remind him of death, or as an ornament to the wilderness, these dried horses, mules and asses are made to stand up, some headless, some on one or two legs, in every shape and form that a dried, broken-up carcass can be turned into."

In Chili he collected 60,000 dollars, and the days of begging from rich and poor alike are thus described by him :

I went up and down the country, preaching in the churches, begging alms of the faithful from door to door. One day, as I was walking along the street, a man came up to me and said in Spanish, "Are you the person who is begging for the establishment of a Missionary College in London ?"  "Yes, I am," I replied.   "Then," said he, "take these hundred dollars."  "Who are you?" said I, "that I may put your name down in my book."  "I am nobody," he replied, and away he went and I saw him no more.   Another day I was begging from house to house, and I entered the house of a washerwoman.   She gave me the coppers that were standing by her soapsuds.   The next house I went into was that of a rich man.   I asked him for alms, and he put his name down for £1000.

On his way home he heard of the death of his dear friend, Cardinal Wiseman. He felt the loss deeply. He not only loved Wiseman, but he had ever looked up to the Cardinal as in many ways a model in his "large-mindedness and generosity," in his "ecclesiastical government, his forgetfulness of injuries, and his exhibition of Our Lord's doctrine of mercifulness." But more than all the loss to the cause of the Church weighed on him. "Who is to sit in his vacant place ? " he writes to a friend. "Who is to put on his armour? Who is to continue the work of which he laid the foundations ? " One man, and one alone, seemed to Vaughan capable of the work, Henry Edward Manning. Yet all probabilities were against the appointment. Vaughan prayed and prayed against hope. He went on collecting money, and got so much in Brazil that he felt his enterprise to be at last successfully accomplished. At Rio Janeiro he received from Mr. W. G. Ward the news that Manning was Archbishop, and he wrote at once a letter full of joy at the news.

A summons from the new Archbishop himself now cut short the American campaign. But Vaughan's work was really done. He returned to England and bought Holcombe House, at Mill Hill, to serve as a college for his first missionaries. Here again came one of those ventures of prayer in which he had learned to trust from his favourite lives of the saints, and one of the remarkable instances of seeming answers to prayer which accompanied him through life. The owner of Holcombe House at first declined to sell. The destination of the house as a Catholic College leaked out, and this increased his indisposition to meet the wishes of the would-be purchaser. An elaborate battery of prayers to St. Joseph was initiated. Vaughan surreptitiously left a statue of St. Joseph in the house itself, and told his friends that he was sure the Saint would do what was expected of him. March 19, the feast of St. Joseph, arrived, and that evening came the news that the man had signed the agreement to sell. These are not stories characteristic of England in the nineteenth century. But the facts are remembered by the Cardinal's friends, and he himself used to narrate them in all simplicity.

The college was thus founded; and the atmosphere of the lives of the saints was still apparent in its conduct, as it had been in the efforts which brought about its foundation. The ideal of the austerity befitting future missioners among the heathen had been kept alive during his campaign in America, where his own life had been one of hardship and privation of all kinds: and the same ideal was now to be stamped on the young men as it had been on their leader. Experience led him gradually to make concessions to what was practicable, human nature being what it is, in men capable of even heroic ventures. At the outset, however, he was quite uncompromising:

The first students at Mill Hill [his biographer tells us] besides being taught to regard cooked food as a luxury they could hardly expect, were from time to time subjected to such impromptu forms of discipline as the enthusiasm of their Rector might suggest. In the early days of the College, Father Vaughan's attention was drawn to the fact that there were some gold-fish in a pond near the house. It occurred to him that the capture of these little fishes might serve a double purpose—Father Cyril Ryder writes: "There was a pond in the garden full of gold-fish. These he wanted to sell; so he got his young men to wade into the water up to their middle, in their clothes, and to remain in this occupation for some hours. He told me it would harden them, and prepare them for crossing rivers when they became missioners. I am afraid I was profane enough to think that they would in all probability not survive their training, so that the only river they might be called upon to cross would be the Styx."

It was probably inevitable that a man of Herbert Vaughan's impetuosity of character and abandonment of devotion should be betrayed into some extravagances. They did little harm, for two reasons. With him it was always a case not of "Go on" but of "Come on." The youths who lived on tinned meat, or stood for hours numbed to the bone, using buckets to catch gold-fish in the garden pond, knew that the man who imposed these privations and penances had gone further than ever he was likely to ask them to go. And in him there was small fear of seeming inconsistent. If experience showed that a cook was necessary for a college, or that it was not wise to expose young men to damp and cold, he could be trusted at once to end the experiment. He would turn back as readily as if, trying to make a short cut across country, he was satisfied that the way by the road was quickest. We shall see many instances in his later life in which he disconcerted friends by the absolute simplicity with which, without casting about for excuses, he just reversed his policy. Once convince him that he was following the wrong track, and the order to reverse the engines came just as a matter of course. And so experience came as a corrective to many a theory in his work of founding a Missionary College, and his adaptability and readiness to subordinate his own preconceived ideas were never found wanting. The result is the St. Joseph's College, Mill Hill, of to-day.

The American War had brought to the front the question of the slave population of America: and Vaughan had himself witnessed scenes which had given him a horror of the attitude of the white man towards the negro in America. The first missionaries from Mill Hill were, with the sanction of the Holy See, to go to Baltimore with the special object of ministering to the needs of the black population, who were largely without any religion at all. Vaughan accompanied them, and took the opportunity of a voyage of discovery in the American States, with a view to the greater extension of the labours of his missionaries. There is much curious information in Herbert Vaughan's diaries in which he narrates his experiences. His first feeling was simply one of horror at the attitude of the white men, even the clergy and bishops, towards the negroes, whom they seemed to regard as hardly human. He once told the present writer of a visit he paid to a convent in which this feeling was only too evident. After receiving the most plentiful hospitality he gave his parting thanks to the Reverend Mother for her kindness in these words : " I shall pray that you may have as a reward a very high place in heaven." The Reverend Mother began to express her gratitude, but he cut her short, adding : " and that you may have a negro on each side of you for all eternity." Many years afterwards, when again in America, he visited the same convent, and the Reverend Mother—then an old woman—expressed great relief at seeing him once more, as she had something she had for years been longing to ask of him. " Do take that prayer off me," she explained.

His account in 1871 of the state of feeling towards the negroes is given in the following page of the biography :

From the local clergy he appears to have got a somewhat mixed reception, many of them, who worked unceasingly among the whites, regarded the blacks as hopeless, or at any rate outside their sphere of labour. From St. Louis, under date January 25, 1872, he writes : " The Archbishop thought all my plans would fail ; could suggest nothing for the negroes, and refused permission to collect and declined to give a letter of approval." A few lines further down he adds : " Father Callagan, S.J., who has for seven years worked for the negroes, disagrees with the Archbishop on this question. Speaks of the virtue and simplicity of the negro." In Memphis he notes : " Negroes regarded even by priests as so many dogs." What perplexed him more than anything else was the inequality before the Blessed Sacrament. There, before the altar, all men should be equal, and the colour-line should fade at the church door. In New Orleans he notes the case of a wealthy coloured man married to a white woman : " Pays for a pew in the cathedral—his wife sits in it, but he is obliged to go behind the altar." Perhaps the following entries, taken from the commonplace-book he kept at the time, may serve sufficiently to convey his impressions of the field of labour on which his missioners were to enter.

" A common complaint that white and black children are not allowed to make their First Communion on the same day. A coloured soldier refused Communion by a priest at the cathedral. Delassoize's inclination to shoot the priest. In a church just built here, benches let to coloured people which are quite low down. A lady—coloured—built nearly half the church, another gave the altar ; both refused places except at the end of the church. A Fancy Fair—coloured people allowed to work for it but not admitted to it. It is still unlawful in Alabama for coloured and whites to marry. Before the war it was unlawful not only to teach slaves, but even for coloured freemen to receive any education. During the slavery days the priest had no chance. A bigoted mistress would flog her slave if she went to any church but her own, and if she persisted in going to the Catholic Church, would sell her right away. I visited the hospital where there were a number of negroes. Talked to many in it and in the street. All said they had no religion. Never baptized. All

said either they would like to be Catholics, or something to
show they were not opposed to it.  Neither the priest with
me nor the Sisters in the hospital do anything to instruct
them.  They just smile at them as though they had no souls.
A horrible state of feeling!  How is it possible so to treat
God's image ?

   "In Georgia the State makes no provision for the education of coloured people, and refuses them admission into the
public schools."

A little experience made Vaughan somewhat
modify his views as to the desirability of treating
black and white men exactly alike.  He came across
cases where negroes had been treated with an
approach to equality, in consequence of the great
change wrought by the war, and saw for himself that
their education and habits, even their inborn character,
made them unfit for equal treatment.

   Visited the Legislature (Louisiana) [we read in his diary].
Half blacks, many unable to read—legs on desks, smoking,
eating apples, fourteen trying to speak at once.  In Senate, a
coloured man, Pinchback, President.

He found that so great an authority as the ex-
President, Jefferson Davis, took a very low view of
the capabilities of the negro :

   Called on Jefferson Davis [he writes].  He said the negro,
like a vine, could not stand alone.  No gratitude, but love of
persons—no patriotism, but love of place instead.  He says
that men are warring against God in freeing the negro, that
he is made to be dependent and servile ; that in Africa,
wherever a community does well an Arab is to be found at
the head of it.  I urged that this was a reason in favour of
our mission, that no one but the Catholic Church could
supply the guidance and support the negro's need.  Mr.
Davis quite agreed with this.  "The field is not promising,"

he said, "but you have the best chance. The Methodists and Baptists do much mischief among them."

Vaughan came eventually to hold that a certain separation between black and white men was necessary. However true it was that their souls were equal before God, there were both ineradicable prejudices and deep-set inequalities of mental and moral cultivation which made the idea of an amalgamation of the two races Utopian. He was in favour of their worshipping in separate churches. Thus, invidious distinctions in the presence of the Blessed Sacrament were avoided, while an impossible amalgamation was not attempted.

Extremely interesting is Father Vaughan's account —as summarized by his biographer—of the difference between the attitude of the inhabitants of the Northern and the Southern States, respectively, towards the negro.

Father Vaughan was struck with the fact that the feelings with which the North regarded the negro differed from those prevalent in the South, not in degree only, but in kind. He puts the case thus : "In the North the prejudice is against the colour ; while in the South it is against the blood." He instances a case in which children, apparently of white parents, have been excluded from school because, in spite of their appearance, they were known to have some taint of black blood in their veins. The distinction thus noted thirty years ago is true in its degree to-day, and is the outcome of different political conditions. Herbert Vaughan was quick to see that in the North, where the political or social supremacy of the negro is unthinkable, there is little hesitation to throw open all careers to him. That liberality, however, is accompanied and qualified by a very general feeling of repulsion for the person of the negro—a feeling almost unknown in the South. How could it be otherwise ? The sort of physical shrinking from contact with the person of a negro to which so many, whether in the Northern States of the American Union or here in England, would confess, can find no place among people who have had negroes around them all their lives—who from their earliest infancy have been accustomed to negro nurses and negro servants. The Southern prejudice is not, and never was, against the person of the negro. On the other hand, repugnance to the thought of the supremacy of the servile race, or even its existence on a footing of equality, amounts to a passion. In the North a white negro —there are white negroes as there are white blackbirds— meets with little prejudice. The fact that a man's lineage would show that in his blood he has a "touch of the tar-brush," would affect him as much and as little in Boston or New York as in London or in Birmingham. The visible marks of race disability are absent, and it is they that matter. In the South the mere question of colour counted for little. What mattered was the blood.

Before leaving America, Father Vaughan visited St. Louis, New Orleans, Charleston and other places and then returned to New York, in each place begging for money. In New York alone he raised £800. On his return from America, some of his friends observed not only his enthusiasm for much in the American character—as found in the Northern States especially —but even a slight occasional approach to the American accent in his speech, which always remained with him. "The American," he wrote, "is prodigal of money, health, home, lands and all. He will sacrifice all this for the sake of an undertaking." It was this American tenacity of purpose, this determination to succeed, no matter what the sacrifice to self, this combination of intense devotion with practicality, which so strongly appealed to him, and which he felt to be so invaluable when applied to the achievement of the great ideal objects of religion. It used to be said that there was something American in his way of looking at things for the rest of his life—something very practical, and for this very reason in small ways unromantic (for romance is apt to be unpractical), accompanying the intensely romantic love of adventure and devotion to the cause of the Church.

The college was founded and was an emphatic success. He loved it and visited it again and again after his direct connexion with it was severed.

He saw the seed-time and he saw the harvest [writes Mr. Snead Cox], and he knew that when he was gone others would continue to reap where he had sown. The college he built is there, and doing to-day the work he planned. His missioners, under their sentence for life, are at work to-day in the Philippines, in Uganda, in Madras, in New Zealand, in Borneo, in Labuan, in the basin of the Congo, in Kashmir and in Kafristan. In 1908 they gave baptism to nearly 10,000 pagans. In his busiest days, as Bishop in Salford, or Cardinal in Westminster, Herbert Vaughan was always glad when he could snatch a brief time for silence and retreat at Mill Hill. He went to the college when his time came to die, and he chose it for his place of burial.

I have dwelt thus long on the foundation of the College of Foreign Missions because I think no episode in his life was more characteristic of his greater qualities. The self-abandonment, the determination to persist through all discouragement, the life of adventure, through many phases and circumstances, the resolution to accomplish what seemed impossible and its realization, the life of absolute confidence in prayer, combined with an intensely practical energy—and, above all, the doing what he did quite single-handed, with none of the help which the sympathy of disciples affords—all these characteristics found their full play and manifestation in the establishment of Mill Hill College.

The story does not, however, call attention to the side of his nature in which he was less perfectly equipped. His campaign of preaching and begging gave ample opportunity for the display of his energy, his invincible tenacity of purpose, his power of sustained and arduous work for the great objects of religion without any help from human sympathy. It gave opportunity for the exercise of the personal influence he had in virtue of his high character and of a certain charm which made him as irresistible for those who felt it as he was unsympathetic to some who did not. He showed also in the actual working of the College a very considerable power of learning by experience, modifying extreme measures when he found them to be unworkable.

Where, indeed, he could choose the work to be done, and himself had the management of it, he had an extraordinary faculty for carrying a scheme through, for he knew his own limitations as well as his powers. But life presents comparatively few opportunities where this is possible. Men have to take their share in the movements of the time, originated by others, and representing the aims and ideals of others. They have to deal with circumstances created by very many diverse characters and natures. And their actions affect not only the few who are their instruments and whom they can guide, but many on whose lives they impinge incidentally. An immense and complicated machinery is already at work in human society. And where machinery is complex a slight action may have a very disturbing effect, while the greatest force and persistence may have no effect at all if directed

wrongly. A very slight movement of a child's finger
will make it necessary to send a watch to the watch-
maker before it will go. The utmost human force
that attempts to check the wheel of a steam engine
by pressing against it has no appreciable effect on it
at all. Accurate scientific knowledge is needed to
deal with a machine safely and successfully. The
driver can stop the engine or set it going with the
smallest exertion rightly applied. Here, then, is a
call for qualities other than those in which Vaughan
was pre-eminent. And the critic who attempts to
describe this remarkable man from the materials presented in his biography must give some indication of
the powers he had not as well as of those he had.

In honesty as in tenacity of purpose Cardinal
Vaughan was, as I have said, almost unrivalled. His
single-minded devotion to duty and desire to learn
and correct his own mistakes were as remarkable as
his zeal and energy, raising these qualities on to a far
higher plane than that of obstinate stubbornness.
Here was an immense initial driving force and a
potent principle of sustained action. But in dealing
with the movements of the day, in tracing their
sources and forecasting the probable issue of what
he did, our estimate of his powers must be more
moderate. When it was a case of carrying out a
policy already determined by his party—as in the
question of primary education for Catholics—he was
very successful. Catholic education was by the whole
Catholic community acknowledged to be a necessity.
The perplexing questions which may be raised in
connexion with partial concessions to the principle
of mixed education in order to suit modern exigencies
were beforehand ruled out of Court. The important

Q

thing was to estimate the practical consequences of proposed measures in their bearing on the fixed Catholic programme and the interests of Catholics, and to press insistently for what was essential. Here Vaughan's honest and straightforward mind, his absence of all *arrière pensée* to other interests and his good practical sense as well as his resolute persistence were invaluable. Again, when it was a necessity for the Bishops to protect themselves from encroachments on diocesan interests from the Jesuits and other religious orders, he was an admirable as well as an untiring advocate. Few chapters in his *Life* are more characteristic than the twelfth, which describes his long-drawn-out duel with Father Gallwey. When the line of action was fairly simple and was marked out for him he followed it with a success often almost equal to that which attended him in his own chosen schemes. It was where he had himself to review a difficult situation in which he might find himself, and determine on his own line of action, that his success could not always be relied on.

In his dealings, indeed, as a Bishop at Manchester, with business men, whose views and wishes were plainly avowed by themselves and understood by him, he was quite at home. Judgment had not in such cases to be very subtle. Straightforward and reliable action and a thorough knowledge of his own mind were great assets in his favour. But in a more complex society, or in fields to which he was more or less a stranger, he was less successful. The very clearness of his logic, the very habit of resting on a few simple ideal principles, which made him so successful when he could choose his conditions or thoroughly grasped the relevant circumstances, or when he held a brief for others, were sometimes obstacles in a more complex situation. When people's aims were mixed and their motives either unacknowledged or outside his own definite but restricted purview, he might totally misconceive the position of affairs, and consequences followed which he did not foresee or desire. The quick sympathy, the perception of the effect of word or action on others, must in such an atmosphere run faster than logic if mistake is to be avoided. Such perceptions exist in some men as a kind of instinct, and are perfected by experience of the world. Without them many danger signals are invisible. Logic advances the more fearlessly and impetuously from the clearness with which it sees its goal, while the obstacles are invisible to it. If only a few have the perceptions of which I speak sufficiently for conspicuous success, most men of wide experience acquire them so far as to protect them from obvious mistakes. Herbert Vaughan was not endowed by nature with these perceptions, and his experience of the world had been somewhat limited.

The almost intuitive appreciation of public opinion of which I speak tells a man where it must be yielded to if we are to guide it, how on Baconian principles it is to be conquered by obedience. Tenacity of purpose without it may be a positive evil, for mistakes are persisted in. In extreme instances (among which we certainly cannot place the late Cardinal) we are apt to recall Bossuet's words to Abbé de Rancé, "A good intention with little enlightenment is a serious evil in high places." In Vaughan's own case we need not go beyond his own judgment of himself. With a noble honesty which is rare indeed, and which

almost disarms criticism, he wrote himself to the
Pontiff before his appointment to the See of Westminster pointing out certain deficiencies in his equip-
ment for dealing with the great world.  " A person,"
he wrote, " may succeed in the subordinate position
of a Bishop in a provincial city such as Manchester,
and yet he may be unfit to be Metropolitan and fill
the See of Westminster.  The duties are of a very
different order and require very different qualifications.
I do not possess those high qualities. . . . It will be
very easy in such a position as the See of Westminster
to compromise the interests of religion by errors of
judgment—and the very quality of a certain tenacity
and determination would make those errors still more
serious."

I am far from denying that, even in the larger and
more complex world with which he was in contact as
Archbishop, his single directness did at times have a
great and salutary effect—the more salutary from its
contrast with the ways of the world on which he had
to act.  Straightforwardness rebuked crookedness,
singleness of aim and unselfishness rebuked worldliness and self-seeking, and made them ashamed.  But
if we are trying to paint the man as he was, to
depict light and shadow, it is to a certain want of
perception of the forces at work in a large and complex society that the less successful side of his career
is to be ascribed.  The absurd misconception of him
as an arrogant prelate, swaggering, loving display,
bent on enforcing Roman dominion, finds the explanation which is its best refutation in a certain want of
perception in him as to the effect of what he did on a
public which he did not wholly understand.  If a
certain external pomp realized in his mind what was

seemly for a Cardinal of the Holy Roman Church, he acted on his view. Such state was familiar to one who had spent so much of his early life in Rome. He did not realize the effect of a new departure in this respect on a community only just emerging from the ideas of Roman aggression, which had led even to bloodshed as recently as 1850. If his devotion to St. Peter prompted a public dedication of our country to the Prince of the Apostles, it never occurred to him to be anxious beforehand as to the effect of his act on the nation in whose presence his act of devotion was publicly advertised. If the case against Anglican orders seemed to him overwhelming, he spoke of them, with the contempt his downright logic warranted, as "shivering in their insular isolation." When Lord Halifax, as President of the English Church Union, wrote a letter to the Spanish Primate, in which his claim to be a Catholic might lead a foreigner to believe that he was in communion with Rome, Vaughan's comment was blunt in the extreme. The Cardinal did not hesitate to warn the Archbishop against the "subtle astuteness" of this "sect," which might "easily deceive him." Such phrases came from no wish to offend the Anglicans. He desired, on the contrary, to be sympathetic to them. But he did not realize their attitude of mind sufficiently to forecast how his words would wound them. It appeared to some even among his friends that he touched the raw when it was not necessary or useful. But he did not know it. He did not realize that he was causing keen irritation and damaging his own persuasiveness. Or he thought that irritation arose inevitably from the nature of the truth rather than from his peculiar way of putting it.

Guided by his own logic, based on the recognized teaching of the Catholic Church, he could realize in imagination hardly any other standpoint. He did, indeed, I think, realize the standpoint of the man of business to whom religion is nothing. But his genius being practical rather than intellectual, he fully grasped no standpoint but his own among genuinely religious men. The inquiring Agnostic, the Anglican, the liberal Catholic, the intellectual Catholic, were very partially understood by him, yet they were among the classes he had to deal with. He had, moreover, no sufficient protective realization of the probable effect of many arguments, convincing to himself, on the mixed multitude which reads the newspapers. Of this last gift he had, I think, enough for the blunt and practical Manchester public but not enough for a more sensitive audience or for a larger world with more various denizens. If others took real pains to understand *his* point of view, they would, in nine cases out of ten, find it clear and cogent, whether they agreed with it or not. But he could not himself move in a mixed crowd without jostling it sometimes too roughly to put it in the best temper for understanding him. And in religious controversy he had also at times too bad an opinion of his opponents' case even to try and persuade them. He tried, as it has been expressed, to "convict rather than to convince" them. In his funeral sermon on my father he spoke of him as "the champion of unpopular truth," and this, I think, was his ideal of his own duty. He was apt to ascribe his unpopularity in certain quarters to the inevitable unpopularity of high and unworldly maxims and truths with those who are without them and therefore resent them. And though there are not a few such cases, he included among them, perhaps, criticisms on his views which deserved attention. Finer shades of opinion were generally invisible to him. And, consequently, while his intentions were absolutely just, there were those who felt that in fact he treated them with injustice.

The lessons of experience made the defect of which I speak in reality far less noteworthy in later life than in earlier days ; but the great position he held as a Cardinal led latterly to its being in fact more noticed, while the years at Manchester presented comparatively few occasions when it was specially apparent or important. In such anxious controversies during his reign at Westminster as were raised by the Anglican movement and by the liberal Catholic utterances of Dr. Mivart and others, his grasp of principle was brought into play, but men felt at the same time a certain want of familiarity on his part with the forces at work. I shall not illustrate the above remarks primarily from such episodes, on which opinions are likely to differ widely as to the relative degree in which his strength and his weakness were respectively apparent. As my chief object is to obtain a psychological picture which will be generally recognized as accurate, I prefer to take as an illustration his conduct of the *Tablet* during the Vatican Council. His biographer gives a very frank account of this chapter of the Cardinal's life, and admits that a very large number of influential Catholics felt, at the time, that his action was unfortunate.

The critics of the proposed Definition of Papal Infallibility were intellectual and learned Catholics, like Bishop Hefele, Bishop Moriarty, Bishop Dupanloup and Dr. Newman, and liberal Catholics as Sir

John Acton and Professor Friedrich—two classes of his co-religionists into whose views Father Vaughan failed to enter with any understanding. He depicted these views in his own way, held up his hands in amazement at their perversity, and raised the standard of Catholic loyalty. Least of all could he understand Dupanloup and the moderate inopportunists.

He could not [writes his biographer] understand the attitude of men who, themselves accepting the Infallibility of the Pope, worked so hard to prevent the definition of the truth they believed in. All Catholics, to whatever theological school they belonged, whether styling themselves Liberals or Ultramontanes, held as an article of Faith that a General Council is under the direct guidance of the Holy Ghost, and that its decrees are necessarily and infallibly true. To be nervously apprehensive as to the consequences of decisions so arrived at, or to show a disposition beforehand to question the expediency of a decision so sanctioned and so certainly true, seemed to Herbert Vaughan illogical and almost uncatholic.

It was (Father Vaughan held) the duty of a Catholic editor simply to oppose these wrong-headed persons in the most effective manner possible. And he proceeded to do so.

It was a singular policy and a very simple one [we read in his Life]. Side by side with the vehement advocacy of Papal Infallibility as a doctrine recommended at once by reason and authority, and the almost universal belief of Catholic Christendom, was a resolute exclusion of any and every expression of the opposite view. As far as the *Tablet* was concerned, Herbert Vaughan deliberately set himself to strangle and suppress any and every utterance in favour of the Inopportunist Party. A search through the correspondence columns of the *Tablet* fails to show a single letter on the side of which, in this country, Cardinal Newman and the Bishop of Clifton (Dr. Clifford) were the conspicuous exponents.

Father Vaughan's policy was most unpopular. Many Catholics would no longer admit the *Tablet* into their houses. But Vaughan never flinched. It was a matter of pressing duty according to the simple view which he took of the case.

His conduct at this time [continues Mr. Snead-Cox] was governed by a great fear. . . . He not only believed in the Infallibility of the Pope, but was sure, and rightly sure, that it would shortly become an Article of Faith, binding on the conscience of every Catholic. There came in the fear— might not the Definition bring with it a new peril for souls ? And what an awful responsibility would be his who, through the columns of a newspaper, allowed the seeds of doubt to be scattered abroad—doubts which might ripen into such strength that not even the *fiat* of a General Council could still them ? What was the gagging of a newspaper by the side of the loss of a single soul ? The whole point of view is alien enough to the ordinary British reader, but, given the point of view, who shall quarrel with the conclusion ? It was humanly certain that the Definition would come—and Herbert Vaughan was in a position to judge rightly as to that ; it was supremely important that when it came it should be accepted *ex animo* and as of faith by every Catholic. The sands in the hour-glass were running low, but until the Council had actually proclaimed the Dogma there was still room and liberty for discussion. But how if some argument against the Dogma stuck, how if it carried conviction—might not the duty of submission then be made overwhelmingly difficult ?

This was a simple logical view of the case as it presented itself to one single class of mind among the scores existing in the Catholic Church. Vaughan seems to have contemplated solely the struggles of a simple mind—of one not already acquainted with any of the well-known controversies in historical and theological science, who would make his acts of faith happily if he read in the *Tablet* only reasons in favour of the Definition, but might be troubled and clouded and tempted if he read arguments on the other side. For such a mind he was, perhaps, right. A man of this kind, if he was able to read at all, had better not read discussions far beyond his comprehension in connexion with a doctrine which would probably be defined.

But such a simple struggle between faith and doubt did not represent the issues before the Catholic world at large—a world which included many educated men and many learned men. In that larger world a greater variety of human emotion and of thought was at work. Mrs. Augustus Craven used to ascribe her own opposition to the definition to the "odious and unchristian manner in which it was defended by" some amongst its chief advocates.[1] This was itself violent language, but it represented the impression of a good and able woman. The most prominent agitators for the Definition were the promoters of opinions which Dupanloup and Newman regarded as intolerant and at variance with Catholic theology. "Writers of a school which I thought excessive," exclaimed Père Gratry, when submitting to the actual definition, "were undesirous of limitation to infallibility *ex cathedrâ* as being too narrow." M. Louis Veuillot, in the *Univers*, was printing hymns to the Holy Ghost with "Pius" substituted for "Deus." He published a pamphlet called *L'illusion liberale*, in which he wrote as follows: "We all know certainly only one thing, that is, that no one knows anything except the man

[1] See *W. G. Ward and the Catholic Revival*, p. 259.

with whom God is for ever, the man who carries the
thought of God. We must unswervingly follow his
inspired directions." Another writer committed himself to the statement, "When the Pope thinks it is
God who meditates in him." In flagrant disregard of
the sacred and immemorial tradition of the Church
that discussion in Council was the normal means
whereby definitions of dogma had been in the past
accurately framed, the *Univers* laughed at the *Correspondant* for urging the importance of such discussion.
"The *Correspondant* wants them to discuss and wishes
the Holy Ghost to take time in giving an opinion."
Such was the sneer of the *Univers.* "It has a
hundred arguments to prove how much time for
reflection is indispensable to the Holy Ghost." [1] If
there seemed to be, humanly speaking, a danger lest
a definition of Papal Infallibility might represent such
views as these, or even be so framed as to give them
any countenance, a large body of the Bishops not
unnaturally judged the time inopportune for a definition, and considered their own opposition to it to be
the normal Providential means for averting it. They
declined to admit the assumption that the Holy Ghost
was on the side of untheological extremes. Again,
the spokesmen of this extreme "new Ultramontane"
school were not among the rulers of the Church.
They were, in many cases, laymen, whose extravagances had long been denounced by wise members
of the episcopate. Archbishop Sibour of Paris, an
Ultramontane of the school of Fénelon, had, some
years earlier, spoken as strongly against these
advocates of Papal absolutism as had Dupanloup, who

[1] The writings of this time are analyzed at some length in Chapter X.
of the present writer's work, *W. G. Ward and the Catholic Revival.*

was suspected of Gallican leanings. The zeal and piety of M. Veuillot were beyond question, and exaggerated language might, in the writer himself, be a symptom of its praiseworthy intensity. To take it literally as expressing Catholic doctrine and commit others to it was quite another matter, as though the lover, who may be readily forgiven his hyperbolical metaphor when he addresses his beloved as " My angel," should thereupon endeavour to make others act on the assumption that she has wings. In England itself this extreme language shocked the old clergy. It was contrary to the theology that had been taught—a theology which clearly separated the divine " assistance " which averted error in the final definition from positive inspiration—and recognized definitely the human element which might make the very arguments adduced in the preamble to a definition fallacious. Vaughan's straightforward and practical mind, on the other hand, saw in the inopportunist's position only the paradox, " Here is a doctrine I admit to be true. The Holy Ghost presides at a Council. Nevertheless I beg him not to define it, though He may judge it opportune, as it is in my (ignorant and arrogant) private judgment inopportune."

No single part of this rough-and-ready statement will bear the meaning he regarded as obvious. To admit Papal Infallibility to be true was not to desire such a definition of it as might seem to countenance the untheological errors of M. Veuillot. That the Holy Ghost presides at a Council does not mean according to the recognized theologians that he acts on it by way of direct inspiration. The Council takes the ordinary human steps for ascertaining theological truth, and the Holy Spirit does not

supersede the normal means supplied by Providence
because He protects the ultimate definition from
error.    To urge that the doctrine should not be
defined meant not to place the judgment of an individual against that of the Holy Spirit, but to contribute material to the human process of discussion
which the Holy Spirit blesses in its result.    The cry,
"It is inopportune," was raised by those who would
not have opposed a weighty and purely theological
movement for the definition of Ultramontane doctrine.
It was a war-cry, or a compendious statement expressing a protest against actually existing excesses
in the "new Ultramontane" movement.    In the
end the inopportunist arguments, so carefully suppressed in the *Tablet*, did issue in the addition into
the Vatican decree of words emphasizing the fact that
the Pontiffs used the human means supplied by
Providence for ascertaining what was in conformity
with Catholic tradition and received no direct revelation.    An historical introduction was prefixed to the
definition with the avowed object of making it clear
that the Pope "could not act in judging of matters
of faith without counsel, deliberation, and scientific
help."[1]    "I was confused," Newman once wrote,
"by the very clearness of the logic which was administered to me."    The logic of the *Tablet* had this
confusing effect.    For it shut out the world of actually
existing thought on the subject and confined itself to
the simple issues visible to such as scarcely thought
at all.    At the same time, it cannot be denied that
there was a disloyal spirit in the air among the
extreme Left which was fuel to the flame of Father
Vaughan's editorial ardour.    There were liberal

[1] See *W. G. Ward and the Catholic Revival*, p. 437.

Catholics who deserved both his blows and his boy-
cotting. But others were branded by him who did
not deserve it, and those were excluded from his pages
whose words would have been well worth reading.
Dr. Clifford, Bishop of Clifton, was excluded as well
as Professor Friedrich.

The late Count de Richemont has justly said that
the term "liberal Catholics," was most unhappily so
used as to include loyal Catholics like Montalembert
as well as free-lances like Professor Friedrich and
Professor Froschammer. It is noteworthy that
Montalembert, with whom Vaughan was personally
acquainted, was treated in the *Tablet* with the respect
he deserved. It was a remarkable instance of the
triumph of personal knowledge over that sometimes
most fallacious guide, the logic of a simple mind.
The abstract reasoning of the *Tablet* certainly
demanded Montalembert's execution. But personal
knowledge made the absurdity of such a sentence
in the case of so loyal and devout a Catholic too
apparent. It was just the absence of similar personal
knowledge in other cases—knowledge either of the
individual or of the type—which led at times to
censure as undeserved as would have been that of
Montalembert.

I will not speak of Cardinal Vaughan's anxious
controversy as Archbishop with the later developments
of liberal Catholicism. As to the Anglican movement
on behalf of corporate reunion, which figures so
largely in the biography, one observation may be here
in place. Words used by the Cardinal which stung
certain Anglicans as sarcastic and uncharitable were
in the speaker himself only the straight and simple
expression of the effect on himself of an attitude into

which he could not enter. All Vaughan's co-religionists, of course, feel the Anglican attitude to be illogical. But it is a real attitude, and admits of being stated persuasively. Cardinal Vaughan saw and stated it at its weakest and not at its strongest. He was, therefore, to many logically unconvincing as well as unpersuasive. Cardinal Newman never forgot the anomalous condition of the Church in the fourth century, when Arian Bishops presided over Catholic Sees and the laity had often to hold the Catholic faith against the views of the local Bishops. Here was a precedent which gave a superficial plausibleness to the position of High Church Anglicans. They professed to hold Catholic doctrine in spite of Protestant Bishops, in spite of State encroachments, waiting for better times. Vaughan had no such eye to history as could give him this clue to the Anglican mind. He showed up weak points in their logic very cogently. But probably his arguments would have been more convincing if, in place of adopting the sarcastic tone proper to something very perverse and extravagant, he had shown more of that sympathy which comes from and leads to understanding—if he had realized more fully what did actually persuade those he was criticizing that their position was tenable.

Yet any narrowness Cardinal Vaughan displayed was of vision rather than of temper or of heart. The friend and admirer of the large-hearted Cardinal Wiseman, he, too, was in his way a large-hearted man. He was eager to learn from experience, and experience did in many cases mellow and broaden his views. Again, a portion of the intolerance which angered some critics was the intolerance which the Church herself shows. To try and liberalize the

Catholic Church is to destroy its distinctive genius. There is sternness inherent in its doctrinal and moral code alike. So far as the spirit of Catholicism allows it, Vaughan was widest where he understood best. He was no stickler for red tape. On the contrary, he was by nature a reformer. His evening service at the Salford Cathedral, consisting of psalms chanted in English in place of the Latin vespers, was an instance in point. His championship, on the ground of exceptional qualifications, of a lay Professor of theology at St. Edmund's College was another. Both were innovations, justified, he held, by their utility in the special circumstances. That he was not an excessive ecclesiastical absolutist (as was sometimes said) is evident from the last letter of his life, in which he exhorted his successor to take counsel with the Catholic laity in important diocesan matters. " I do not know who may follow me," he wrote, " but I earnestly pray that he may gather all, lay and clergy, by union and consultation, in common action." In the intellectual controversies above referred to he was not by choice unduly conservative. Rather he enforced authority and tradition which he realized and understood against interests which were very vaguely visible to him. Few within the Church so combine insight into the singularly complex intellectual movements of the present day with full appreciation of the consequences of stern Catholic principles, as to take successfully an active part in those movements. In England Cardinal Newman long stood almost alone in this respect. And the caution and provisional toleration which are the alternative for one who is anxious to avoid excessive dogmatism were most uncongenial to such a nature as Vaughan's. His temperament prompted him to strenuous action. Strenuous action on liberalistic lines was clearly out of the question. Its danger was apparent in writings which were before his eyes. The tempting alternative for one who longed to be up and doing was to be active in counteracting these dangers. And this might easily drift into a policy of complete opposition to all that the popular cry associated with liberalism; the moderate and more discriminating view being dropped out of sight.

There is both largeness of heart and power of imagination visible in many of his letters—not least in one written in his last years to the President of a Conference of the Catholic Truth Society which ill-health forbade him to attend. The wistful note of farewell, the sympathy with the young democracy of the future, the dream of the fortunes of religion in the age to come, are all human, gentle, sympathetic.

We older members of the Society he wrote are beginning to move off the scene, some slowly and reluctantly, because the work is sweet and fruitful, and our interest in it is as keen as ever; some gladly, because they feel that their allotted day's task is nearly done, and they hear the loving Voice that is calling them home. But, whatever our feeling, we cannot help looking back to see who are following, who are going to take our place and fill up the ranks. For myself, I rejoice to see many zealous and intelligent members of the clergy pressing forward, especially among the younger clergy, and there is also a goodly and increasing number of men and women among the laity. . . . But, far off in the background, I see a great multitude of eager faces, I hear their voices like the sound of the waves of the sea. Who are these? They are the boys and girls in our public elementary schools; they are the strength, the hope, the population of the future. They form the young democracy that is going to

R

rule the country, to make or mar the future of Christianity.
These inspire me with the keenest interest. They are young
and innocent, they are eager and full of life, their minds and
hearts are plastic and ready to take any form, any direction,
you may impress upon them. If your influence is the first
with them, if you have captivated their ambition and filled
them with ardour to follow you, you will have secured the
success of your enterprise in the future.

We know not what may be before the Catholic Church to
accomplish during the present century. But we do know
that the future depends upon the child, and that it is impossible for us to render greater service to God and to religion
than by training the young to become Apostles of Catholic
Truth.

I think that the general view of the Cardinal's
qualities above suggested is confirmed, while it is
certainly supplemented, by the admirable analysis of
his character printed in his biography from the pen
of his spiritual director. Father Considine writes
from a special point of view, but he gives us
his own experience of the honesty, the unworldliness, the tenacity of purpose visible in the Cardinal,
and at the same time of a simplicity which made him
at times not fully realize the complex forces at work
in the world in which he dwelt. Father Considine
depicts him as no more completely at home in dealing
with the diplomatists than others found him in dealing
with the subtlest intellects. And in planning out his
manifold religious and social schemes his director
notes that habit of reckoning without full allowance
for the forces at work in the actual world,—a characteristic of which I have spoken in connexion with
certain ecclesiastical controversies of the day. This
analysis is so valuable that I give it almost entire :

I should put in the first place in any delineation of the

Cardinal's nature . . . his honesty—by which I understand his ingrained sincerity, his desire to see himself and to be seen by others exactly as he was—no better, no worse. He cherished no illusions about himself ; he was aware of his limitations and conversed quite simply about them. He laid no claim to any qualities or attainments he did not possess. Above all things, he loved plain dealing and plain speech, whether the outcome of it might be palatable to him or not. . . .

The Cardinal carried his frankness and directness into his intercourse with his Maker. He strove to be entirely above-board with Him, to hide nothing, even if he could, from Him whose eyes search the reins and the heart; it was a comfort as well as a duty to be open with Him, to let Him hear from one's own mouth the acknowledgment of one's guilt and promise of repentance. Common honesty seemed to require that much, and, besides, a loving son could not act otherwise towards the best of Fathers. And he expected that God would do by him in the same fashion. Indeed, it was this deep conviction of God's essential fairness and goodness that He would not be hard on any one who honestly meant to do right, . . . which made him so fearless in action and so unconcerned about temporary reverses and rebuffs. He had no doubt that all would come right at the last, let men meanwhile clamour and thwart as they pleased.

This leads me to speak of the little account he was disposed to make of public opinion, or generally of those things which men esteem most highly. He was at heart a thoroughly unworldly man. Not that he underrated the advantages of rank and wealth ; on the contrary, he was keenly alive to them, and knew how to use them for God's service ; but they did not dazzle him, they could not bribe him. He admired pomp and ceremonial if displayed on some fitting occasion, because he thought even a secular function should present itself to the eye and ear as worthily and impressively as possible, but he had no vulgar love of mere tinsel and glitter as such. And, of course, he rejoiced greatly in the seemliness and even magnificence of God's House and of all the vestments and ornaments allotted for its use. It was a delight and a comfort to him to have been allowed before his death to make provision for the solemn chanting of the Divine Office in his own stately Cathedral. However, worldliness does not consist merely in a love of finery and show, but much more in a habit of mind which puts the interests of this life above those of the next, which, in fact, has no outlook beyond the visible world, and therefore is necessarily, in its aspirations, feelings and aims, of the earth, earthy. It intrigues, overreaches, cajoles, plays a part, while professing to be sincere, but under all its disguises and through all its windings it is never noble and never ceases to be selfish. Now, diplomacy and chicane the Cardinal not only disliked, but could hardly understand; to him a thing was right or wrong, or true or false, and no juggling with words could make it otherwise. So a course of action approved itself to him or it did not—compromises, modifications, concessions might perhaps be necessary, but, nevertheless, they never quite satisfied him, as involving in some sense a betrayal of the right. Hence he moved in Society and dealt with great personages of the world as his position seemed to require, but he was too sincere and simple-minded to be really at home there. When he was translated to Westminster, particularly after he had received the Cardinal's Hat, he regarded it as his duty to appear and speak in public and to meet persons of all creeds in the intercourse of familiar life. Afterwards, however, he came to think that less good was done in that way than he had hoped. His motives were misunderstood and his conduct criticized, and in his later years he withdrew almost entirely from general society and was inclined to doubt whether he had not wasted much good time on it in the past.

His power lay in great ideas, in high thoughts which took possession of him, shaped his conduct, and found expression in his daily life, but which he was less successful in recommending by word of mouth or by the graces of personal intercourse. About the sincerity of his zeal for God's glory there can be no doubt—indeed, its very fervour seemed to become at times an obstacle to success. He yearned so ardently for the coming of Christ's kingdom upon earth that

he chafed at the barriers to it which men's passions and prejudices are setting up at every turn, and would have liked to
make short work of them, to clear them out of the way at
whatever cost to the susceptibilities of individuals.  Thus he
would outline some great plan for the spread of religious
truth or for social reform ; and when he had made up his
mind by what help and in what direction his scheme ought to
develop, he was too ready to assume that it must do so without fail, and he did not always foresee the inevitable checks it
must meet, nor was he over well pleased when they in fact
did occur.  In his conception of ecclesiastical problems he
sometimes resembled the abstract mathematician who reasons
of an ideal world, and prefers to deal with bodies and movements unaffected by the actual conditions in which we live.

Whatever view may be taken of Cardinal Vaughan's
success in solving some of the more difficult problems
with which he had to deal, I think that his letters
show that they cost him anxiety; that he was too
honest not to recognize their difficulty, and too earnest
to be quite happy in having to decide questions which
he felt to be in some degree, as he would express it,
"out of my line."  " I feel," he writes to the Duke of
Norfolk, "that I need the help of friends below as
well as of God above to keep such a one as I am at
all right and free from blundering on this critical and
dangerous pinnacle."  If we desire to see him exult-
ing in his strength and happy without a cloud of
misgiving, let us look at the last act of the drama of
his life.  It was the building of the Cathedral which
gave full scope for his zeal, energy, and imagination
in regions where he felt completely at home.  His
action was not delayed or hampered by any misgiv-
ings as to its direction.  He worked once more as he
had worked in early youth for the missionary college.
He placed the enterprise under the patronage of St.

Joseph, and in two years he had collected £75,000 for the great enterprise. He told the story in his speech at the laying of the foundation stone.

He said [writes his biographer] that at one time he had thought with anxiety of the large sum required. He put the whole matter in the hands of St. Joseph. From the moment he did so he found his task made quite easy; he wrote a few very simple letters, calling the attention of a certain number of his friends to the proposal. Without any persuasion on his part, only using the simplest words in his power, those friends at once, of their own accord, responded with all the generosity which had brought about the state of things concerning the Cathedral which had been witnessed that day, when the promoters had in their hands £75,000 towards the building.

It may be safely said [continues Mr. Snead-Cox] that that was a time of great happiness to Cardinal Vaughan. He knew that his dream was now certain to be realized. And surely it was no mean achievement to have secured for English Catholicism in so short a time a Cathedral of which generations unborn shall be proud. The Cardinal had the dimensions of all the great English Cathedrals and of many abroad at his fingers' ends, and knew that in scale and in stateliness his own might compare with the best. Something of the gladness and exultation he felt as he watched the walls slowly rising is reflected in an article written under his inspiration: "The style of the new Cathedral happily makes any invidious comparison with Westminster Abbey out of the question. Westminster Cathedral will join hands with an older time. The latest of the great ecclesiastical structures of the world, it will recall the earliest phase of directly Christian art. But though we cannot compare the new Cathedral with any building of the same type in this country, we may usefully contrast its general scale and dimensions with some of the historic fanes which are still the glories and the memorials of English Catholicism. In total area the Westminster Cathedral is upon much the same scale as

Durham and Salisbury ; and, of course, far larger than Hereford or Lichfield or Gloucester or Worcester or Peterborough. But in its impression of vastness it is likely to surpass even the few old Cathedrals which exceed it in actual superficial area. The length of the nave is exactly that of Durham. Those who recall the magnificent proportions of the great northern Cathedral will be able to form some adequate idea of the scale of the building which is now rising at Westminster. Only with this thought of Durham in his mind, let the reader also reflect that while at Durham the width of nave and aisles together is 82 feet, the width of nave and aisles at Westminster will be 150 feet. The length of the nave of the new Cathedral will be exceeded only in the cases of York, Winchester, Ely and ,Salisbury. In width it far exceeds them all, being 27 feet wider even than the great span of York. . . . As far as scale goes, at any rate, the last of the English Cathedrals may well challenge comparison with anything that has gone before."

Few instances are on record in which a man of genius so rapidly converted general hostility to enthusiastic admiration as did Mr. Bentley, the Cardinal's chosen architect for the Cathedral. In its early stages his work was the object of a depreciatory —even of a contemptuous—criticism, which was almost universal. When the building approached completion, admiration was as wide-spread. The element of tragedy, however, was not absent from the drama of the building of Westminster Cathedral. Bentley lived to see an unfavourable verdict reversed ; but he died in 1902 before his work was finished. The Cardinal wrote of his fellow-worker with feeling and appreciation :

The Cathedral will be his monument. For myself, I have a gratification in the thought that I gave him a free hand. Having laid down certain conditions as to size, space, chapels and style, I left the rest to him. . . . Mr. Bentley was a poet; he saw and felt the beauty, the fancy, the harmony and meaning of his artistic creations. He had no love of money, he cared little for economy; he had an immense love of art, a passion for truth and sincerity in his work. He was not ambitious to get on; he was not self-assertive; but he coveted to do well. He went in search of no work, but waited for work to come in search of him. He was exquisitely gentle and considerate in dealing with suggestions and objections; but he would have his own way whenever it was a question of fidelity to his own standard of artistic execution. I would not have singled him out to build cheap churches and schools, but he was the best of architects for a Cathedral, or for any work that was to excel in artistic beauty. He was no mere copyist, or slave to tradition; whatever he produced was stamped with his own individuality; it was alive and original, and he had a genius for taking infinite pains with detail. His reverence for God, for Our Lord, His Blessed Mother, and the Saints pervaded everything he did for the Church. In his judgments on art and style there was a critical but kindly humour; one always felt that there was an elevation, an inspiration, in his character that was due to his religious instincts and to his unworldly standard of life. It seems to me that it will be necessary for the perfection of the work Mr. Bentley left behind him, to retain his mind as a guide to its completion, as far as we can know it.

If, as the Cardinal said, the Cathedral is Bentley's monument, it is yet more truly his own monument, and a timely one, for he died in the following year, and his own *Requiem* was the first public service in the great Church he had built. He lived, like Moses, to see the promised land, but not to enter it. It was nearly completed, and he was living in the new Archbishop's House adjoining it when his own time came.

Mr. Snead-Cox, who writes not only with skill but with that genuine feeling for his subject which makes a biography live, gives a graphic picture of the Cardinal's final departure from Archbishop's House for Mill Hill, where he died.

On the morning of March 25 he left Archbishop's House for ever. He had sent me a message, knowing I should wish to be there. When I arrived I was shown upstairs, but outside the Cardinal's room I found the doctor chafing and impatient. "They are pestering him with papers," he said, "and he is not fit for it. He ought to be carried downstairs in an ambulance." At last the door opened, and the Cardinal, accompanied by Mgr. Johnson, appeared. The Cardinal was wrapped in a big Roman cloak and looking wan and pale, and as he stepped forward leaned heavily on his stick. A few whispered words, and then he slowly descended the stairs. At the bend of the stairs, as we faced the front door, there was a strange sight. When I had gone up, a quarter of an hour before, the hall was empty—now it was filled with people. News that the Cardinal was leaving had gone abroad, and all the priests and students of the Clergy House, servants of the household, and a number of friends were gathered there to take their last leave. As the Cardinal came forward, all that little crowd, as by a common impulse, went on its knees, and the stricken man, as he passed along through the lines of people, paused every few paces and raised his hands to bless. There were many eyes that saw dimly that morning, and I think we all knew he was going for ever.

The Cardinal died in June, 1903. *Ecce Sacerdos Magnus* is the Church's salute to her Prelates; and he was great in all the distinctive attributes of the priesthood. If in attempting some analysis of his gifts I have also endeavoured to ascertain what he had not as well as what he had, it has been partly in order to account for the fact that his great qualities were not universally recognized in his lifetime. One with a subtler power of influencing the public mind would have been more universally understood from the first. But in the long run character tells, and the whole man now stands before us visible to every reader of Mr. Snead-Cox's pages. His deficiencies are there seen to be largely the defects of great qualities. Indeed, from some readers this man of noble, single and complete nature will call forth greater sympathy than those who are strong where Vaughan was weak. The anxious thinker and philosopher who hesitates in his course because he sees much that is invisible to the world at large, is to many a far less stimulating figure than the man who sees only a few great principles, and acts on them with energy and heroic devotedness. Let such comparisons stand aside. Each has his own work— the thinker and the man of action. Each will be best appreciated on earth by those who see best that particular sphere which the action of each most successfully affects. In a world in which there is no twilight both will be seen to have done a work meritorious in proportion to the singleness of its aim, useful in proportion to its success in helping those whom their tasks most closely concern.

# VII

## TENNYSON AT FRESHWATER

THE Freshwater society of which Tennyson was the centre in the 'sixties and 'seventies approached, I think, nearer to realizing the purpose and ideal of a French *salon* than any social group I have myself known in England. It is, of course, startling to compare people who met in the most informal way in the green lanes of the Isle of Wight, and at the houses of friends who were for the most part in no sense people of fashion, with such a Parisian *coterie* as was grouped around Madame Récamier and Chateaubriand. Nevertheless, it appears to me that the ideal of the *salon*, which has proved so impossible to realize in London, was largely realized in Freshwater. We had our Chateaubriand in Tennyson, and, surprising as the comparison may be, we had our Madame Récamier in Mrs. Cameron. The essential work of gathering together the interesting people who were to form the Tennyson society, the enthusiasm for the hero and for genius in general, was Mrs. Cameron's part, as it was Madame Récamier's.

Mrs. Cameron, indeed, was no youthful beauty, but she was a woman of great originality and of most single-hearted devotion to genius. She was one of the gifted daughters of Mr. Pattle, a Bengal civil servant—a sister of the late Lady Somers and Lady Dalrymple. She had not the beauty of her sisters, but her appreciation of beauty was as keen as her appreciation of intellect. A beautiful woman who chanced to stay in Freshwater was soon discovered by her, and figured in her well-known and very artistic photographs. Thus beauty came to be well represented among those who formed the group of which I speak. It was a society for which personal qualities were the chief passport. The complications which the London world brings—in which rank, fashion, and official position are the chief titles to distinction—may prove fatal to the ideal of the *salon.* They make a wholly different ideal too prominent. Rank and fashion were indeed often represented among the visitors to Freshwater, who for the time joined the Tennyson circle ; but their representatives had to remember their true place in Tennyson-land—a subordinate one. It is, I take it, of the essence of the *salon* that the sense of distinction which is a part of its attraction, is given principally by the presence of acknowledged genius ; and the atmosphere prevailing must be that of recognition of genius as supremely interesting and important. These two qualities were given by the presence of Tennyson, and by the gift which Mrs. Cameron had for creating the atmosphere that was wanted. And the actual conversation was real, wide in its range, and often excessively interesting. It went beyond the mere snatches of serious conversation which one hears at a London dinner party.

The events in the literary world, and still more in the scientific world, interested the poet profoundly, and his judgments were always weighty. Details of

scholarship, and classical literature itself were also
welcome topics. And he would talk of them on equal
terms with Richard Jebb or Henry Butcher. Tennyson
had an excellent verbal memory, and the discussions
on English poetry which he would carry on with
Aubrey de Vere or Sir Henry Taylor were studded
with quotations. But he loved, too, to hear from
some traveller how men lived and what they believed
in parts of this wonderful world which he could never
himself visit. If Tyndall or Browning appeared on
the scene it was not merely that we saw great men as
one might see them at a large evening party. We
heard them talk, and not formally or for display, but
in undress. They "let themselves go" to a degree
rarely if ever possible in London society. We were
at leisure and the trammels of convention were
banished. In London the wings of the immortals
are clipped. The conversation at Freshwater was
stamped by the simplicity, directness, and wide range
of interests which marked Tennyson himself. He
gave the tone to his company. We all felt, moreover, in those days that we were in the making of
history. Tennyson was in the heyday of his fame
in the 'sixties. The *Idylls of the King* were being
written; the word would pass in Freshwater that a
fresh one was on its road, greater, it was usually
added, than any which had gone before. Thus
reported Mrs. Cameron or Miss Thackeray or Miss
Simeon who had actually heard the poet read it.
I myself used to hear the unpublished poems later
on; but the poems of the 'sixties, written in my boyhood, were greater events—even national events.

The group that gathered round Tennyson formed
a society from which unsuitable or unsympathetic

elements ought to have been rigidly excluded—more
rigidly even than they were. Outsiders with little
appreciation of literary greatness—who merely lionized
Tennyson as a famous man—were sometimes irritated
at the quality of our enthusiasm, and almost incredu-
lous of its sincerity. They could not enter into the
feelings of those who felt genius to be a far greater
thing than wealth or position. They knew a "lion,"
but not a prophet or seer. Tennyson was the first
to them, the last to us. Their account to others of
the poet and his friends would, therefore, strike a
wholly false note. Was there some French Sir
Gorgius Midas in the days of the first Empire,
and did he accidentally gain entrance to Madame
Récamier's *salon*? If so, we can fancy his annoy-
ance at finding Chateaubriand—"a conceited Frenchman, a writer he believed"—made so much more of
by the great ladies than any one else, including Sir
Gorgius himself with his millions, and (I had almost
said, for it marks the standard) his motors. Some
such note was occasionally struck when the wrong
people found themselves in Freshwater. And there
were some belonging to a better class than Sir
Gorgius Midas who proved to be "wrong people."
Such intruders had no instinct which could detect or
interpret the enthusiasm of Tennyson's true admirers.
They took stock of all they could see—namely, the
external signs—and traced them to the only source
their categories supplied, describing them as "adulation" of the poet. The distinction between lionizing
and hero worship was simply unintelligible to them.
It was such outsiders who were also mainly responsible
for the utterly false idea of Tennyson's attitude
towards his admirers, which is in some quarters

still current—as though he delighted in the conversation of flatterers.

On the other hand there were members of the great world, like the Duke of Argyll and Lord Selborne—and of Tennyson's intercourse with the latter I could speak from personal memory—who fell in completely with the tone and feeling of Freshwater when they came there. They realized as much as those to whom literature was everything, that there was a sphere in which Tennyson was a king. And they so treated him, intensely grateful for his poems, and eager to place a crown of laurels on his head.[1]

If one is to speak of the general atmosphere at Freshwater, not of exceptional incidents, I think no estimate could be more false than that of the rich Philistine. Our enthusiasm had the genuine ring which flattery never has. If it was sometimes indiscriminate, that was the intellectual fault of youth rather than a moral flaw. Tennyson's acceptance of the homage paid to him was the gratitude which sensitive genius could not have withheld without marked ungraciousness. Also Tennyson, it must be remembered, suffered keenly from bad criticism of his poems, as one may suffer from loud discordant sounds when one is playing a beautiful sonata. And he took, perhaps, some compensating pleasure when he saw that he was speaking no longer to deaf or dull ears, but to the perceiving and the grateful. This feeling no doubt had its place in his friendships but not a large place in his conversation. For the range of

---

[1] He was to Lord Selborne "the foremost man of all his generation and entitled to be ranked with the greatest of the generations before him." And the Duke of Argyll accounts his friendship as "one of the greatest honours of his life." (See *Tennyson's Life*, ii. pp. 458, 516.)

his talk was, as I have already said, very wide, and took in the most diverse topics wholly unconnected with himself.

I used to think his intimacy with Jowett a good index of the intercourse Tennyson most enjoyed. Jowett's unbounded admiration for Tennyson never even tended to obsequiousness, nor impaired the absolute freedom of his conversation. And I had many opportunities of observing their intercourse. I do not think any one worshipped the poet more sincerely than Jowett, and in using the word " worship " I do not exaggerate.

I recollect once at Farringford listening with Jowett after dinner to Tennyson's reading of his Ode on the *Death of the Duke of Wellington*. It was a poem which his peculiar chant made most moving, and he read the concluding lines with special pathos :

> Speak no more of his renown,
> Lay your earthly fancies down,
> And in the vast cathedral leave him,
> God accept him, Christ receive him.

Tennyson then turned to address some observation to Jowett, but no reply came, and we soon saw that the master was unable to speak. The tears were streaming down his cheeks. I ventured to allude to this some time later in talking to Jowett, and he said : " What would you have ? The two Englishmen for whom I have the deepest feeling of reverence are Tennyson and the great Duke of Wellington. And one of them was reading what he had himself written in admiration of the other ! " [1]

Yet Jowett would talk to Tennyson with the utmost freedom. He would make jokes to the poet's face on which few other people would venture. I

[1] *Tennyson and His Friends*, p. 227.

once heard them talk on the very subject of flattery. Tennyson was inveighing vigorously against flattery as representing a base side of human nature, and ended by saying : " No flatterer is a friend of mine." He looked at Jowett for assent, but Jowett did not reply. " Don't you agree with me ? " Tennyson insisted. Jowett smiled a little mischievously, and answered in his staccato tones. " Well, Tennyson, while you have been talking I have been reflecting that in this house and in this room I have seen a good deal of incense offered. And it was not unacceptable." The entire good humour with which Tennyson took this repartee carried to my mind complete conviction that it did not really hit him at all. He took the remark quite simply for the joke it was meant to be. His dislike of the *genus* " flatterer " was most genuine. I could quote instances of it ; and it was not appreciably qualified by such satisfaction as he, like other poets, might take in the signs that his genius was recognized. But, indeed, that satisfaction was below the average, not above it ; and Jowett hardly exaggerates, I think, in his written words on this subject which appear in *Tennyson's Life.* " Tennyson experienced," he writes, " a great deal of pain from the attacks of his enemies. I never remember his receiving the least pleasure from the commendation of his friends."

Mrs. Cameron had, as I have intimated, much to do with forming the society of Freshwater. She was a real social centre. And this was in itself remarkable. For her cottage of Dimbola seemed made for the simple life rather than for luxury or for entertainment. Everything about it was unpretentious and unconventional. But her keen, eager spirit, created

S

by its natural force a world of incident and interest. And by the true instinct which draws like to like, such men of genius as Tyndall, Darwin, Aubrey de Vere, Sir Henry Taylor, were among her visitors, and so many more that to attempt a list would be tedious. I have before me the inscription on one of her photographs of Tennyson which she gave to "Philip," as she called her dear friend Sir Henry Taylor—the author of *Philip van Artavelde*. It represents vividly the atmosphere of those days, and her place in forming it :

A gift transferred with much love to dear Philip. This photo done by my will against his will—a column of everlasting grandeur. June, 1863.

The " by my will against his will " is very significant. She not only insisted on photographing Tennyson, but used to make him show himself on occasion, and do whatever she thought suitable to his genius and position, while he often endeavoured, half annoyed, half pleased, to frustrate her designs. Sometimes her plans for symbolizing his greatness were extremely quaint. On one occasion (in 1873) she took it into her head that the great monarch of Freshwater ought, like the Doge of Venice, to wed the sea. She bade one of the Simeon family,[1] who was in Freshwater at the time, make a wreath of white and red may, to take the place of a ring, and proceeded with some friends in solemn procession to Farringford, to persuade the bard to do her will. In the end she succeeded in bringing him with her to Freshwater Bay, and making him throw the wreath into the sea and speak words worthy of the occasion.

[1] Mr. Stephen Simeon.

Tennyson loved Mrs. Cameron sincerely, and was amused at her intense hero worship. " All her geese are swans, and all her Taylors are gods," he once said.

She was almost an official mistress of ceremonies for those who desired an interview with Tennyson. The story has been told before now of her bringing some American visitors to Farringford at a moment when Tennyson was a good deal out of humour, and showed it to his guests too plainly. She rebuked him with the words : " Alfred, I brought them to see a lion ; they did not expect to find a bear ! '

Mrs. Cameron was profoundly interested in keeping the poet well, and fit for work. One evening a friend who was dining with her mentioned that there was small-pox in the neighbourhood. Mrs. Cameron started. " Alfred Tennyson has not been vaccinated for twenty years," she said. " We must not lose a moment." She went at once in search of the village doctor, took him to Farringford, and made her way to Tennyson's study. He was busy and did not want to see her, but she pursued him from room to room. In the end he said : " Madam, if you will leave me I will do anything you like." He was vaccinated. The sequel was told me by Tennyson himself. The vaccine proved to be bad, and he was not really well again for six months, so Mrs. Cameron's inter vention did not prove quite so fortunate as she had hoped.

Mrs. Cameron corresponded frequently with some of the great lights of science and literature—to Sir Henry Taylor she wrote almost daily. But, indeed, her general correspondence was enormous. There were certain days—I think just before the mail to

Ceylon—when the writing was at extraordinarily high
pressure. Then she stood at her high desk, completing letter after letter, and throwing each down on the
floor ; and even after the ordinary post had gone
there was a special messenger whom she called " Deer
Foot," who ran with her "overflow" letters to catch
the boat at the last moment. She photographed her
" lions " when they came to Freshwater. Those large
photographs, some of them real works of art, are still
to be seen in many houses in the Isle of Wight and
elsewhere—of Darwin, of Herschel, of Browning, of
Carlyle, and many another. She also photographed
her friends, and I was more than once the recipient
of her attentions in this respect. I remember being
photographed once as a Roman in a toga, and once
dressed as a Bravo. As a boy I wore my hair rather
long, and she was quite convinced that, as I was a
Catholic, my father and mother would make me part
with it all and be a monk when I grew up. So she
looked at the hair with a kind of sad fondness, as a
thing that must die young.

She chose her parlourmaids largely for their beauty,
and one of them in the end made a very good marriage.
There were two " Marys " whom she would sometimes
in the most unconventional way take with her into
society. On one occasion when the Simeons asked
her to come to the Cowes Regatta, somewhat to their
surprise the Marys appeared in her train. But the
result was most embarrassing to Mrs. Cameron, as
some of the more susceptible young men of the party
paid them attentions which made the duties of a
chaperon very onerous. She would show off to her
friends the Mary who was called, from the shape of
her face, " Madonna," using various devices to exhibit

her to the best advantage. " Mary, do stand on that chair and pull down that high curtain." Then, turning to her friend : " Isn't she perfect in that light, and in profile as you see her now ? " In the same way she would exhibit her wonderfully picturesque old white-haired husband. One went on tiptoe to the door of his study, a crack of which was opened noiselessly. " There he is, reading his Greek ; doesn't he look grand ? "

The high-water mark for interest in Freshwater society was perhaps reached in 1873 when G. F. Watts and Mr. and Mrs. Prinsep (the latter a sister of Mrs. Cameron) came to live at the Briery, close to Farringford. In 1874 Mrs. Cameron left the Isle of Wight for Ceylon.

Tennyson's brothers used occasionally to appear in Freshwater, and his sister—old Miss Matilda Tennyson. There was a very marked family likeness in all the Tennysons whom I recall to mind. The combination in them of strenuous hardiness, with a keen sense of the poetry in life, used to give me the feeling I had in reading La Motte Fouqué's stories of the old Noroemen. The brothers seemed to me to dress alike, and at a little distance off, Horatio Tennyson or Arthur Tennyson might easily have been mistaken for the poet. They all spoke, too, with a strong Lincolnshire accent. Something of their character is perhaps indicated in a chance remark of Arthur Tennyson's to a friend whom he met in the Freshwater lanes one fine April morning. In response to inquiries after his health (he was a man of 81), he replied : "I can't help being troubled by the terrible excitement of the spring." There was in the whole family something of the poet who is ever young.

As Isle of Wight reminiscences are to form the staple of my essay, I may say a word concerning Tennyson's old friend and my father's—Sir John Simeon. Tennyson's friendship with Sir John Simeon came to an end with his death in 1870, just before that with my father began.[1] Tennyson has spoken of his own friendship with each in his verse, and I may here record what I heard long ago, and have recently learnt in greater detail as to the writing of the beautiful verses *In the Garden at Swainston,* just before Simeon's funeral in 1870.

Tennyson reached Swainston some time before the cortège was to start, and he asked Sir John's eldest boy—a lad of 20—to give him an old hat and cloak of his father's, and his pipe. "Come for me yourself," he added, "when it is time to start, and do not send a servant." Young Simeon came when the hour had arrived, and found Tennyson smoking his father's pipe, and wearing his father's hat and cloak, stretched at full length under a tree in the garden, the tears streaming from his eyes, and the MS. of the poem written.

Concerning Tennyson's friendship with my father I may be allowed to quote some paragraphs from my contribution to Lord Tennyson's volume :

Tennyson's friendship with my father began at a date considerably subsequent to their first acquaintance. My father came rather unexpectedly into the family property in the Isle of Wight in 1849, when his uncle died without a son ; but he did not desire to leave the house Pugin had built for

---

[1] My father's own intercourse with Sir John Simeon, with whom he had been intimate in early life, almost ceased in the 'sixties, owing to Simeon's hostility to the Temporal Power of the Papacy, which was a great bone of contention among Catholics in those days.

him in Hertfordshire, where he had settled immediately after
he joined the Catholic Church in 1845. He and the late
Cardinal Vaughan were, in the 'fifties, doing a work for
ecclesiastical education at St. Edmund's College, Ware—a
work which came to my father naturally as the sequel to his
share in the Oxford Movement. Therefore, when Tennyson,
in 1853, came to live in the Isle of Wight, my father was an
absentee  He tried in 1858 for two years to live at his grand-
father's old home near Cowes, Northwood Park, but his health
broke down, and he returned to Hertfordshire. In the 'sixties,
however, he used to pay long visits to Freshwater, in the
scenery of which he delighted ; and on one of these occasions,
Tennyson was introduced to him by their common friend,
Dean Bradley. The meeting was not, I think, a great success
on either side. Later on, however, in 1870, when my father,
despairing of the Cowes climate, built a house at Freshwater,
he was Tennyson's near neighbour, and they soon became
friends.

Tennyson's friendship with my father grew up from close
neighbourhood, and from the fact that they had so much
more in common with each other than with most of their Isle
of Wight neighbours. It was cemented by my father's
devotion to Mrs. (afterwards Lady) Tennyson, who, in her
conversation, he always said, reminded him of the John Henry
Newman of Oxford days. Also they had many friends in
common—such as Dean Stanley, Lord Selborne, and Jowett
—who often visited Freshwater. They were both members
of the Metaphysical Society, and loved to discuss in private
problems of religious faith which formed the subject of the
Society's debates. They were also both great Shakespearians.
But most of all they were drawn together by a simplicity and
directness of mind, in which, I think, they had few rivals—if
I may say of my own father what every one else said.
Nevertheless, their intimacy was almost as remarkable for
diversity of interests as for similarity. It might seem at first
sight to be a point of similarity between them that each
revelled in his way in the scenery of the beautiful island which
was their home. Yet the love of external nature was very
different in the two men. It had that marked contrast which

Ruskin has described in his *Modern Painters*. Ruskin contrasts three typical ways of being affected by what is beautiful. There is first " the man who perceives rightly because he does not feel, and to whom the primrose is very accurately the primrose because he does not love it. Then, secondly, the man who perceives wrongly because he feels, and to whom the primrose is anything else than a primrose—a star, or a sun, or a fairy's shield, or a forsaken maiden. And then lastly, there is the man who perceives rightly in spite of his feelings, and to whom the primrose is for ever nothing else than itself—a little flower apprehended in the very plain and leafy fact of it, whatever and how many soever the associations and passions may be that crowd around it."

My father's imagination was of the second order, Tennyson's of the third. My father often perceived wrongly, or not at all, because he felt so strongly. Consequently, while the bold outlines of mountain scenery and the large vistas of sea and down in the Isle of Wight moved him greatly, he did not look at them with the accurate eye of an artist ; and the minute beauty of flowers and trees was non-existent for him. Tennyson, on the contrary, had the most delicate and true perception of the minute as well as the great. Each man chose for his home a site which suited his taste. Weston was on a high hill with a wide view. Farringford was lower down and buried in trees. The two men used sometimes to walk together on the great Down which stretches from the Needles rocks to Freshwater Bay, on which the boundary between Tennyson's property and my father's is marked by the dyke beyond the Tennyson memorial cross. At other times they walked in the Freshwater lanes. And there was a suggestion in these different surroundings of their sympathy and of their difference. The immense expanse of scenery visible from the Beacon Down was equally inspiring to both, but the lanes and fields which were full of inspiration to Tennyson had nothing in them which appealed to W. G. Ward. If he heard a bird singing, the only suggestion it conveyed to him was of a tiresome being who kept him awake at night. Trees were only the unpleasant screens which stood in the way of the view of the Solent from his house, and which he cut down as fast as they grew up. To Tennyson, on the contrary—as we see constantly in his poetry—there was a whole world of interest in Nature created by his knowledge of botany and natural history, as well as by his exceptionally accurate and observant eye. . . .

When Tennyson and W. G. Ward walked together there was then a most curious contrast in their attitude towards the Nature that surrounded them,—Tennyson noting every bird, every flower, every tree, as he passed it ; Ward buried in the conversation, and alive only to the great, broad effects in the surrounding country. . . .

W. G. Ward was himself not only no poet, but almost barbarously indifferent to poetry, with some few exceptions. He was exceedingly frank with Tennyson, and plainly intimated to him that there was very little in his poetry that he understood or cared for. But this fact never impaired their friendship. Indeed, I think Tennyson enjoyed his almost eccentric candour in this and in other matters, and he used, in later years, to tell me stories which illustrated it. . . . W. G. Ward's extreme frankness led Tennyson to remark to a friend : " The popular idea of Roman Catholics as Jesuitical and untruthful is contrary to my own experience. The most truthful man I ever met was an Ultramontane. He was grotesquely truthful." Tennyson would sometimes retort in kind to my father's frank criticisms, and once, after vainly trying to decipher one of his letters, observed that the handwriting was " like walking-sticks gone mad," a curiously true description of my father's very peculiar characters.[1] . . .

As with scenery, so with poetry ; my father only took in broad effects and simple pathos, and would single out for special admiration such a poem as the *Children's Hospital* over which he shed many tears.

Tennyson soon accustomed himself to my father's indifference to his poetry in general. But he hoped that, at all events, his metaphysical poems would interest his neighbour, and sent him the MS. of *De Profundis* when he wrote it ; but the reply was only an entreaty that he would put explanatory notes to it when it should be published. One exception,

[1] My own writing he compared to the " limbs of a flea."

however, must be made in favour of *Becket* which Tennyson read aloud to Ward, who, greatly to his own surprise,
admired it enthusiastically. "How do you like it?" Tennyson
asked, and the reply was, "Very much, though I did not
expect to like it at all. It was quite splendid. The development of character in Chancellor and Archbishop is wonderfully
drawn. Where did you learn it all?"

. . . When my father died Tennyson visited his grave in
company with Father Haythornthwaite, who spoke to me of
the visit directly afterwards. A cross of fresh flowers had
been placed on the grave until the monument should be
erected. Tennyson quoted Shirley's couplet:

> Only the actions of the just
> Smell sweet, and blossom in the dust.

And then, standing over the grave, he recited the whole of
the beautiful poem from which these lines are taken.

A few years later Tennyson published the memorial lines
in the volume called *Demeter and other Poems*, which show
how closely his observant mind had taken in the character of
his friend:

> Farewell, whose living like I shall not find,
>   Whose Faith and Work were bells of full accord,
> My friend, the most unworldly of mankind,
>   Most generous of all Ultramontanes, Ward.
> How subtle at tierce and quart of mind with mind,
>   How loyal in the following of thy Lord!

My father rarely mixed in general society in
Freshwater, or anywhere else, but both Mrs. Cameron
and Tennyson used often to bring their friends to see
us at Weston. A friend has lately reminded me of
one occasion on which we acted "dumb crambo," and
the word to be guessed was to rhyme with "tell."
After various exhibitions of her histrionic genius,
Mrs. Cameron reached her most triumphant height
when she entered the room, robed in a flaming red

cloak, and went through the most wonderful gestures and facial contortions, as of a tortured spirit, bringing rounds of applause, which betokened that she had discovered the word to be guessed—namely "hell." She was devoted to my father and used in her very original way to kiss his hand. She always addressed him as "Squire Ward."[1]

When Garibaldi visited Farringford, Mrs. Cameron was naturally among those most eager to make acquaintance with one who loomed so large in the English mind at that time. She arrived at Farringford after a morning spent in her usual occupation of taking photographs, with the result that her finger tips were deeply stained. She, of course, wanted to photograph Garibaldi himself. Her very original dress formed such a contrast to that of other ladies to whom Garibaldi was presented, that he thought this strangely clad and apparently dirty woman must be a beggar. She soon understood the situation, and not the least abashed, explained to him insistently, "This is not dirt, but art."

I have before now told the story of a very amusing meeting of hers and Tennyson's with one belonging to a very different world from Garibaldi. Cardinal Vaughan (then a Bishop) was staying with my father at Weston, and Mrs. Cameron and Tennyson came to tea to meet him. Mrs. Cameron was, at that time, photographing various people for the characters in the *Idylls of the King.* Directly she saw Vaughan's knightly face and figure, she called out to Tennyson : "Alfred, I have found Sir Lancelot." Tennyson,

[1] Mrs. Warre Cornish writes to me, "Mrs. Cameron used to say your father was such a great man that she *must* call him by a special title."

not seeing to whom she referred, replied in deep tones : " I want a face that is well worn with evil passion." The Bishop was greatly embarrassed, and the company a good deal amused. But the two men were afterwards introduced to each other and had much friendly conversation.

My own more frequent intercourse with Tennyson began after I returned from Rome, where I spent a year attending the philosophical lectures at the Gregorian University in 1878. While in Rome I read *The Holy Grail* very carefully, and had some correspondence about it with Tennyson's eldest son. When I returned to England I at once saw a good deal of the poet, and stayed with him, I think, every year at Aldworth until his death. I have elsewhere recorded various notes I made at diffcrent times of my conversations with him. I may say a word here as to the general character of his talk.

Tennyson's conversation was at its best out walking, and his morning walk was an event to which his friends always keenly looked forward. To one who had never met him it presented some surprises. When one first heard him speak one was startled by the strong Lincolnshire accent, which I fancy he deliberately cultivated. Huxley once said to me, " One thought it was his own Northern farmer." It took a little reflection on the actual words to observe the great beauty of his language. It was wonderfully simple, terse and clean cut, the words being, by preference, short and Saxon. His letters, so many of which are printed in his biography, give in this respect a very true idea of his conversation. He was a very good listener, and not in the least inclined to monopolize the conversation. He would find at once

the subject on which his companion had first-hand
information, and he would be eager to learn all he
could. He had a real passion for facts, and, in the
best sense, *la grande curiosité.* His memory for
details which he learnt, either in reading or in conversation, was most retentive, and I remember being
amazed at the array of exact figures he presented to
me one day after he had been reading Ball's *Astronomy,* as to the distances of planets, the rate of their
movement, and so forth. He also knew a great deal
about botany and natural history. But, indeed, his
passion for general knowledge (as I have already
intimated) struck one more than anything in talking
to him. There was no rash theorizing or generalization ; he had the true nineteenth-century instinct for
amassing details before he would proceed to an
induction. He liked, too, where he could, to see
things for himself, and within a year of his death I
remember his suddenly exclaiming, " I want to go
abroad and see the world."

Our national defences interested him very much.
About the year 1888 Mr. Stanhope, the Minister for
War, came to Freshwater to inspect the first trial of
Brennan's torpedo. A huge hulk, attached by a very
long rope to a small steamer, was dragged between
Colwell Bay and Hurst Castle, and the torpedo was
to blow it up. A good many of us assembled to
witness the experiment. I stood next to Tennyson, and on this occasion his silence of attention
was more eloquent than speech. We saw the hulk
dragged slowly along about 300 yards from the shore,
and when it got near the appointed spot, quite
suddenly, the torpedo started on its way from the
shore, making for a point just in front of the hulk. Its

course was shown by the flag attached to it, which was visible. As the flag darted rapidly onwards, jerking up and down, it had the appearance of something living. "It is like an evil spirit bent on destruction," Tennyson remarked. At last it suddenly disappeared, and a few moments later there was a huge cloud of smoke. When it was dissipated the hulk had vanished—blown to pieces. For some minutes Tennyson did not speak. He afterwards kept dwelling on what he had seen and several times recurred to the idea which had impressed itself on his imagination, that this engine of destruction, elaborated by nineteenth-century science, reminded him of the primitive conception of a malignant evil spirit.

Tennyson was, like many men of genius, moody. He was intensely highly strung, and when working at a poem was not the genial companion he was on other occasions. He could be abrupt and even rude. I have known him at such times unconsciously rude to strangers, and then make most gracious and kindly compensation when reproached for it, perhaps giving the person whose feelings he had hurt a copy of his poems with an autograph inscription. He had also the abruptness of great truthfulness. "He will say the thing that is in his mind," as Lady Tennyson once happily put it. There was in him (as I have said) a vein of childlike simplicity, and if the admiration of others sometimes made him appear self-conscious that was the cause. He was aware of it, and had not the sophistication of the man of the world, who would have pretended not to see it. He was extremely frank and simple in asking one's opinion on any poem he might be writing. Even when I was little more than a boy I remember his reading *Vastness* to

Mr. Frederick Locker[1] and myself at Aldworth before
it appeared in *Macmillan's Magazine*. In the course
of the noble couplets in which he presents the insoluble
mystery of the universe and of human life he read
one in which, as occasionally happened to him, his
sense of form had for a moment failed him. It ran as
follows :

> Love for the maiden crowned with marriage,
>   No regret for aught that has been ;
> Debtless competence, comely children,
>   Happy household, sober and clean.

Mr. Locker and I both smiled very visibly, and
Tennyson asked, " What are you laughing at ? " We
were somewhat confused, but I ventured to say,
" Perhaps, if it makes us laugh, it will make other
people laugh." Tennyson said, " That's true." He
folded up his MS. and read no more. Next morning
after breakfast he said to us, " I want to read you
something," and read the lines as they stand in the
published version :

> Love for the maiden crowned with marriage,
>   No regret for aught that has been ;
> Household happiness, gracious children,
>   Debtless competence, golden mean.

He used in the 'eighties very often to read me his
poetry, and I was among those who delighted in the
solemn chant with which he rolled out his lines. I
used to attempt to imitate it in reading his poems to
intimate friends, and I endeavoured to make the
imitation complete and to catch his somewhat provincial accent. " Some d—d good-natured friend "
tried to make mischief in consequence, as I discovered.

---

[1] The author of *London Lyrics*, afterwards Mr. Locker-Lampson.

I went to lunch at Farringford one day. More often than not Tennyson used to let me sit next him, and talked to me a good deal. On this occasion he came in late, and went at once to the other end of the table. I addressed one or two remarks to him, but he made no reply, and I saw him several times looking at me with a severe expression which I could not quite understand. Suddenly, during a pause in the conversation, he said, in his deep tones, "Wilfrid Ward, I'm told you mimic me!" It was rather a terrible moment, but I replied, "I think if any one has heard you read your poetry, the best thing they can do is to try and read it like you." "That's very true," he answered, with conviction, and the strain in our relations at once came to an end.

He was perfectly conscious of all that he added to the effect of a poem by reading it himself, and I remember on one occasion his reading to Sir Richard Jebb and myself *Come into the garden, Maud*, working up the passion of the concluding stanzas with extraordinary power, each line in a higher key than the one before it, and then his voice falling suddenly with the last words :

> Would start and tremble under her feet,
> And blossom in purple red.

He added, as the tears stood in his eyes and his voice trembled with emotion, "No one knows what *Maud* is till they have heard me read it." And it was perfectly true.

# VIII

## CARDINAL NEWMAN'S SENSITIVENESS

THERE is one feature in the temperament of Cardinal Newman which is very obvious to a reader of his correspondence, and somewhat exceptional. I refer to his extraordinarily sensitive nature, with certain defects of temper which were allied with it. His biographer was naturally somewhat anxious as to the result of publishing in his written life, as he has done quite frankly, documents in which this side of his nature is apparent. With hardly an exception, however, the critics of the Biography treated such symptoms with reverence, glancing only slightly at the defects of great qualities in a man of genius. And if its author desires now to offer a few words of explanation, it is quite as much in reply to the objections he himself felt at the outset to making public some documents which were specially intimate and personal, as in consequence of anything said by others.

It has been generally recognized that the somewhat exacting demands of modern biography may have called for revelations which would not formerly have been deemed necessary. That such demands are to be reckoned with I do not deny. The reserve of an earlier generation would not now be tolerated.

But there were in Cardinal Newman's case strong additional reasons which made a frank and full delineation of his personality an absolute necessity, if his biography was to be written at all. A selection of letters, full of wise counsel and conveying to the reader that sweet gravity and mellow wisdom which personal intercourse with the great Oratorian conveyed, might indeed have been published, leaving untouched the aspect above referred to ;—but not a biography. It is not merely that any biography must depict the personality of its subject, but in Newman's case the personality affects features of the life-story which are in many cases not directly connected with it. Even in describing Newman's views and mental outlook and the actual events of his career, the sensitive personality of the man must be studied intimately in order to give a true and intelligible account. Individual letters do not always convey his views truly. The mood and the circumstances, both of the writer and of the recipient of a letter, are necessary factors in its interpretation. Never was a man in whose nature the different elements were more closely knit together. The expression of his views in private letters often needs the personal equation for its translation into the real equivalents of the views themselves ; and these views, even when printed for all to read, are still impregnated with the writer's personality.

Let us consider this last point first—the personal element in relation to his speculative views even in their published expression. The intellectual side of a man's mentality may often—as in the case of some of the great schoolmen—be almost completely separated from his spiritual side and from his literary or poetic gifts. St. Thomas Aquinas was the author of the

*Lauda Sion*, and of the beautiful office in the breviary for the Feast of Corpus Christi. But the poetry and spiritual exultation which are so apparent in these writings are quite absent from the dry statements of the arguments against each thesis given in his *Summa Theologiæ* under the well-known formula *videtur quod*, or the luminous and dispassionate replies of the *respondeo dicendum*. With Newman it was otherwise. The personal touch on the mind of his readers, which makes them aware of the prophet, the poet and man of letters in the philosopher, is never absent. The subtlest essays he ever wrote on the difficulties which the rationalistic movement of the day presents against faith in the supernatural took the form of sermons "on the theory of religious belief" preached before the University of Oxford. They have none of the dry, objective, impersonal character of the arguments of Aquinas. They are masterpieces of literary style and they contain arresting images which speak as much of the poet as of the philosopher. Newman's own personality and spiritual perceptions hold a large place in these discourses. His own consciousness of this fact is suggested by the very title of one of the most striking of their number on " Personal influence as a means of propagating religious truth." In another of these sermons, " Love the safe-guard of Faith against Superstition," we have again the personal note introduced into an intellectual argument. The theory of "implicit reasoning," which is the keynote of these sermons, is avowedly the delineation of the action of a sensitive personality, with profoundly religious aims, directed and informed by the conscience, in reaching and holding to religious truth. And this theory was later on developed at a great length in the *Grammar of Assent* in its account of the "illative sense." The account is based on the writer's analysis of his own spontaneous reasoning. Here we have at once, in a sphere which seems at first sight concerned more than any other with dry intellect, the presence in action of the whole man who was at once prophet, poet and artist.

Once more, to speak still of this directly intellectual sphere of his work, Newman's peculiar personality breaks down the common contrast between the often adventurous representative of intellectual interests and the cautious protector of spiritual interests. We are accustomed, in reading of the controversies of the 'sixties, to think of Döllinger and the Munich School, of Lord Acton and his friends in England, as the great upholders of the interests of historical scholarship, of science, of philosophical thought within the Church. The Pastors of the Catholic people stand forth in contrast as full of tender consideration for the souls of men. Not by intellect alone they urge does the Christian people thrive. Why should men be scared and their faith shaken by the discussion of perplexing problems ; why should their pious meditations be disturbed and the simplicity of their traditionary ways of thought be invaded ? The point of view of the Pastor of the flock is thus popularly opposed to that of the scholar or thinker. But in Newman the two standpoints were united. It was precisely his tender consideration for the souls of men deeply desirous to hold the Christian faith and yet keenly alive to the difficulties which were familiar to thinking minds among his contemporaries, which prompted him in his most intellectual essays. His philosophy of faith never took the form of a dry-as-dust disquisition. It was a directly pastoral work. He could not admit that only the ignorant and the simple needed tender consideration for their spiritual interests. Such consideration was needed also by the men of thought and the men of learning to whom religious faith was as deep a need as it was to the simple. And in a sense their needs were the more important—for they were pioneers, and represented the necessities of the future. Thus it is impossible to deal with Newman's written words even on philosophy or on history, in their bearing on revealed religion, apart from the profoundly personal view of the situation which inspired them. That view likewise limited their scope. What hasty critics have sometimes set down as his intellectual limitations were often the limitations imposed by the law of charity. For he would not go beyond the practical need of those whom he strove to help, for the sake of satisfying an intellectual curiosity which was not really urgent.

We find in this predominance of the personal element the source of his strength and of his weakness in some of the actual theories he set forth. *Cor ad cor loquitur* was the motto he chose as a Cardinal, and his choice betrayed a true perception of his own genius. That a finely wrought and sensitive nature could convey to other like natures far more than could be put adequately into words was a fact on which he constantly insisted. Logical formulae are a very inadequate record of the reasoning of the human mind. The whole man reasons ;—his affections and his imagination, and his conscience, and his actual experience playing their part as well as logical powers. Other faculties supply the material for logic to work on. No one ever conveyed this great truth more cogently than Newman. The great General who rapidly takes in a strategical situation, foresees the movements of the enemy and anticipates them in his action, and chooses the psychological moment for a great counter move, is guided by faculties far more subtle and more multiform than formal logic can keep pace with or adequately compass. So too with the man of insight in other departments of action. In some measure the reasoning of such men is typical of the reasoning of all thoughtful minds in the urgent affairs of life. The "illative sense" is the phrase Newman used for that subtle power of the mind to take in and appraise the significance of relevant considerations. It sums up the complex of faculties utilized. Most men have this power in their measure, and he shows clearly that, much as men may differ in their capacity, every one has a power of reasoning far deeper and wider in its reach than is represented by the logic he has at his command. Informal reasoning includes many premises which elude the logical analyst. This fact is often a valuable refutation of the criticisms of the acute logician on convictions which really rest on grounds much more profound—though they may be unexpressed—than those of which the critic takes account. Yet, on the other hand, the theory has its weakness as well as its strength. If imagination and affection stretch out tentacles far beyond the reach of the logical *formula*, and seize instinctively on many profound truths, they may also, at times, lead the mind astray. In the hands of genius their action may be almost unerring. But not so with ordinary men. Yet that action passes to a region in which adequate verification is impossible. Newman's theory, though profound and largely new, was incomplete.

It was probably Newman's own extraordinarily acute perceptions which made him press the theory beyond the point at which it holds for ordinary men ; and we have in this abnormal acuteness of perception in most various departments a chief characteristic of the man, and the root of that "sensitiveness" which is named at the head of this Essay. His taste for wine was so delicate, though he drank sparingly, that he chose the wines for the Oriel cellars. His musical ear was keen, and music such an intense delight to him that when he played Beethoven's quartets on the violin, after an interval of some twelve years, he broke down and sobbed aloud, unable to go on. His sensitiveness to smell is apparent in a well-known passage in *Loss and Gain.*

This extraordinary physical sensitiveness was the counterpart to his sensitive intellectual perceptions (if the phrase may be allowed), and to his spiritual perceptions. In this latter sphere his sensitiveness gave an insight which, to the believer, was almost miraculously true ; yet to the unbeliever his "intuitions" appeared to be the suggestions of a morbid fancy. Here was a peculiarity which caused one of his deepest personal trials, and one which occupied a significant place in his history. He saw with almost a prophet's eye the issue of trains of thought which were leading men unconsciously to a denial of Christian faith and even of a belief in God. Yet the hold of his spiritual nature on the Unseen World was so close that while he keenly realized the reasonings which were affecting men so strongly in the direction of unbelief, they had no such effect on himself. He was thus in a sense isolated intellectually from both parties—from the believers and unbelievers alike.

He realized the mind of an Agnostic and the force
of the reasons which affected it to a degree which
alienated the sympathy of the orthodox who could not
tolerate the notion that unfaith was so plausible. Yet
his profound conviction of supernatural truth made
him completely out of sympathy with the unbelievers
with whose thoughts he was, nevertheless, in closest and
most understanding touch. These deepest problems
of his life had, therefore, to be dealt with in almost
total isolation. He seemed to one side to give away
too much, and to the other to be withheld by what
was in their eyes mere sentiment, from conceding
enough. The charge against him was the inevitable
one where incommunicable personality plays so large
a part. For there can be no adequate external test
of the validity of its conclusions. The question will
ever arise, Is this or that conviction due to the insight
of genius or to the aberration of a highly imaginative
mind? That charge was answered against him in
many instances by both camps. The unbelievers saw
in him a superstitious mind which they found it hard
to reconcile with unquestionable symptoms of intellectual insight and depth. The average Christian
theologian regarded his admissions as to the force of
agnostic reasoning and the melancholy anticipations
of the growth of the infidel movement in the world of
thought, as the suggestions of a morbid fancy, or as
signs of a dangerous tendency to religious liberalism.

It would be easy to show that what I have said
above, in regard to the part played by a sensitive
and unique personality in Newman's treatment of the
Philosophy of Faith, has its parallel in other fields of
thought.

But if his sensitive personality enters generally

into his intellectual views, its place is yet more
prominent and its quality more precise in the story
of the events of his career. It was the source at
once of his great achievement and of his failures, of
his greatest joys in life and his greatest suffering.
It was the personal magnetism due to his highly-
wrought nature and delicate perceptions which was
in great part the secret of his power at Oxford—a
magnetism felt in daily intercourse, which is often
quite absent in those whose power is publicly exercised, as Newman's was, from the pulpit. It needs
a close analysis of his personality to understand the
gift which enabled him to love each friend almost as
though he were the only one. This issued in the
almost unparalleled sentiment of loyalty which was
formulated by members of the Oxford School as
*Credo in Newmannum.* But Newman's faculty of
deep personal love, and of winning devoted loyalty
cannot be truly represented by giving only one side
of its manifestations. Gratitude for loyalty went with
resentment where loyalty was broken ; yearning love
for those who were "faithful and true" went with
a certain slowness to forgive what appeared to him
to be personal unfaithfulness. Again the years passed
as a spiritual leader among the men to whom he was
at the same time a most intimate and familiar personal
friend, years in which, as Mr. Froude has told us, his
every word was treasured as an "intellectual diamond,"
inevitably made the fact of his leadership almost like
a part of the course of nature. If he seemed and was
to some extent self-centred in the times that followed,
that was the direct consequence of a state of things of
long standing, of an acknowledged fact in the society in
which he so long lived, to ignore which would have been

profoundly unreal. No doubt from first to last those outside the group which felt the spell of the magician had something of a sneer both for the worship of his followers and for the leadership inevitably conscious of its own power. That sneer naturally reappears in some quarters now that the story has been fully told. But it represents the view of an outsider. Anyhow, the position of which I speak, with the personal qualities it involved, is an essential part of the life of the man.

But then again while his sensitiveness was thus bound up with his triumphs it was also an essential part of the discipline of trial under which he suffered for so many years after he joined the Catholic Church. His sensitiveness was the medium of purgative trial and the test of his resolute sanctity. He trod the path of duty at a cost not known to rougher natures; and persons who remember those days tell us that, profoundly though he suffered, he was in speech quite uncomplaining at the successive events which seemed to thwart all the aims he most cared for in life. Bishop Ullathorne once wrote that he appeared to be living under "a dispensation of mortification," but one who was a severe critic of Newman's, and long lived with him, said to the present writer that if Newman had a special claim to be accounted a saint it was the uncomplaining resignation with which he took successive and crushing disappointments which appeared to destroy the usefulness of his life. If the biographer has now let the world know, in the words written to intimate friends, something of what he suffered, it has been necessary in order that the full degree of chastening trial should be understood. But the reader must not forget that such complaints were comparatively few and private. Before the world at large he was silent and resigned. The extraordinary sensitiveness of his nature and his keen realization of his mission in life as a leader of men must be borne in mind that the story of these trials may be understood in its real significance. It was a nature which suffered tenfold from its own exceptional capacity of suffering.

Moreover, this temperament, so unlike that of a man of action, was partly responsible for some failures which reacted on it and further intensified its suffering. And if the story of the treatment he experienced at the hands of Dr. Cullen, Cardinal Wiseman and others, were told without even a minute description of the temperament of the hero of the tale, and of its share in causing the events which tried him so much, his opponents might seem to be almost monsters in human form. The difficulties with Dr. Cullen, the story of the offered bishopric and its withdrawal, the translation of the Bible and its abandonment, the scheme for an Oratory at Oxford, and the secret instruction from Propaganda against Newman's own residence in the university city, — all these events, if set down without a most careful analysis of the part played in them by Newman's sensitive nature, would involve the gravest charges against eminent and good men. In every case a certain want in Newman of the rough fibre and insistence of a successful man of action or a man of the world played a part in his failure. We may feel, indeed, that he was very hardly used, but we see also the point of view of those who ministered to his failure, and trace, in part at least, to circumstances and to Newman's own nature what was certainly something of

a tragedy.   The offer of the bishopric was clearly due
in the first instance to the impulsive action of Cardinal
Wiseman, who ought not to have made the suggestion without the full and deliberate concurrence of the
Irish Episcopate.   When, however, Newman's elevation had been publicly promised and announced, a
man of the world in Newman's position would unquestionably have declined to proceed in his work unless
the indignity done to him by its subsequent withdrawal
were cancelled.   In the whole Oxford scheme a more
practical man would have seen the hopelessness of
taking a line which militated in effect strongly against
the avowed policy of Rome and of the English hierarchy against "mixed education."   An understanding
with Dr. Manning was, as Cardinal di Luca pointed out
to Newman's friends, when they pleaded his cause in
Rome, an essential preliminary.   In both cases Newman was unquestionably very hardly treated, but probably in neither would events have turned out quite
as they did had he had the gifts of a man of action,
and had he not been handicapped by that peculiar
sensitiveness to which he owed so much of his joy as
of his suffering.   Again, in the projected translation
of the Bible, had he possessed something of Archbishop Kenrick's *sang froid* we should now have had
our new version of the Bible as the Americans have
theirs.   But resentment at the inconsiderate action of
Cardinal Wiseman (who was, however, as we know
from other sources, ill and preoccupied), and the
inaction which, in Newman's case, was not inconsistent
with resentment,—nay, was often caused by resentment—put an end to the whole project.   Here again,
as in the case of the bishopric, the sensitive nature
suffered profoundly but made no sign.   All these

years afterwards we know what he went through, but at the time he was silent. Had he then and there vehemently protested, in all probability the grievances would have been removed.

But it may be said—granted that the personal element must, for the reasons above indicated, be dwelt on to a considerable extent, there remains the question of degree. Could not Newman's sensitiveness have been indicated in general terms, and intimate documents written with no thought of publication have been omitted? The reply is that the man's nature was so complex and so subtle that the biographer dared not trust to such a summary. A subjective estimate must always be open to dispute. The documents must speak for themselves, for in some places they appear to present almost insoluble contradictions. An account could have been written of the Oxford scheme of 1865, illustrated by authentic documents, which would have given the impression that Newman never wished to go to Oxford, and was simply relieved when his mission thither was abandoned. Another account could have been written showing him almost broken-hearted when that mission was prevented. Letters could be given in which he seems to think that the authorities had on grounds of consistency and common-sense no choice but to put an end to the scheme; and other letters in which their action is severely criticized. He might be represented by selected letters as distressed and annoyed beyond measure at having to help in the conduct of the *Rambler* and as out of sympathy with its conductors. He might have been represented by other letters as considering it the most important work within his reach, undertaken in conjunction with men with whom on the whole he keenly sympathized.

His attitude towards the Vatican Council appears in
the letter he wrote about it to Dr. Bloxam, to be pre-
dominantly one of joy at the prospect. In other
letters we see his dismay at the tone and action of
some of its chief promoters. To analyze the excessively subtle distinctions which reconcile these apparently opposite accounts, as well as the changes of
mood and phases of thought which further explain
apparent contradictions, would be a difficult, perhaps
an impossible, task. At best it would be the biographer's personal interpretation open to vigorous
criticism from those who habitually choose one aspect
or another of Newman's attitude of mind as representing the real man. Personally I think that a profound
consistency of view is apparent under all the subtle
variations of mood and the interaction of his estimates
of different aspects of each case. But obviously a
field of endless controversy would be opened up by
any theory on the subject—or by any personal estimate of the outcome. Only the record of his own
self-revelations at different times and to different
persons could possibly meet the case and have the
necessary quality of objective fact. The publication
of documents telling only this way or only that way
would have been unfair. It is one of those cases in
which the situation is so complex and subtle, that
nothing but the truth minutely told will meet the case.
The result of substantial suppression would have
issued in a series of uncomfortable and partial explanations elicited in reply to successive criticisms—
explanations which would have borne to the eye of
the attentive reader incontestable marks of uncandour;
and it must have ended in everything coming out.
In such a case, emphatically principle and expedience

point in the same direction, and honesty is the best
policy.  To tell the truth at once is an intelligible
and dignified course, and though some may criticize,
most will respect it.  To have the truth wormed out
gradually, because evidences are detected that it is
being cloaked, is a gradual process in the course of
which both the biographer and his subject suffer many
things of which not the greatest is a loss of dignity.
This was, at all events, the conclusion to which the
writer of Cardinal Newman's *Life* was led after a pro-
tracted study of the material before him.  A less
closely knit nature or a simpler nature than Newman's
might have been otherwise dealt with.  Some biographies can be truthful without being intimate or
psychologically minute.  But in Newman apparent
contradictions form a part of the consistent whole to
be exhibited ; and it is only his most intimate revelations which give the clue to the real state of mind of
which partial aspects shown in letters to certain corre-
spondents so often appear to be simply inconsistent.

I will only add in conclusion that while the faithful
and accurate delineation of Newman's personality,
with its very peculiar forms of sensitiveness, was
necessary to the picture of his genius and of his life,
I was aware that even a few false strokes might, as
in the case of a painting, turn a reverently executed
likeness into a caricature.  And such strokes might
easily be added by a clumsy or hostile critic in reviewing the book.  The lines which determine the expression of a face are often few and slight—and pathetic
sadness may be changed to sneering bitterness by a
stroke of the pencil.

There are many obvious occasions for such a
travesty of my picture of Newman, but I will mention

one which is, perhaps, not among the most obvious. A subtle view held by Newman, or a view presenting different aspects, of which one is dwelt on in moods of joy, another in moods of depression, may by an illnatured or unperceiving critic be misrepresented as the changeableness of an egotistic mind which takes one view when vanity is hurt, another when it is gratified. Thus when Newman speaks on his elevation to the Cardinalate of his gratitude to the Irish people during his University campaign in Dublin, his language has been in fact by one journalist contrasted with his earlier complaints of the difficulties in Ireland which made his University scheme unsuccessful, and the contrast has been explained in the way just indicated. Yet the reader of the book itself will see in the contemporary letters, including those to the Irish Bishops at the time of his resignation, just that note of heartfelt gratitude to the Irish which is apparent in the address of 1879. Two Bishops are excepted— Dr. McHale and Dr. Cullen. And these two were certainly not acquitted in 1879. Personally he respected them both. But he held their action to be largely responsible for a failure which wasted years of his life. He was sad in 1857 and spoke of the causes of his sadness. He was happy in 1879 and ready to dwell on all happy thoughts. But not even a grain of inconsistency is to be found in the documents of these different dates in relation to this special point. Indeed, in this case, as in those above referred to—the Oxford Oratory scheme and the conduct of the *Rambler*—nothing is more remarkable than the consistency of view underlying variations of feeling and the recognition of opposite aspects of the same situation.

Considering the opportunity afforded to the perverse critic by such a picture as I have given, of making serious misrepresentations by means of touches of untruth in themselves slight, the biographer has been deeply impressed by the fact that in hardly a single instance has this opportunity been used by the English press. Reverence for the great Cardinal, and, perhaps also some chivalrous feeling as to the special unfairness of defacing a picture which has taken many years in the painting, have saved the work from such unworthy treatment.

# IX

# UNION AMONG CHRISTIANS

THE late Mr. Gladstone, who throughout his life was so profoundly interested in religious questions, said to the present writer in 1894 : " The most important need of our day is to obtain unity among Christians, that they may successfully withstand the inroads of modern infidelity. And I cannot feel very kindly towards your Church, for she appears to me to be the great obstacle to such union, from her exclusiveness and her unconciliatory policy."

Certainly if we look at one side of her action, the Catholic and Roman Church does appear to be little ready to fraternize with other Christian bodies or to make light of her differences from them. Catholics entirely decline to kneel in Protestant temples, or even to pray in company with fellow Christians outside their own communion to the Christ whom they worship in common. They decline to let their children learn the Bible except from members of their own Church, though they fully believe in the inspired word. They will not allow Catholic school children to be taught the Christian religion by any one except their own co-religionists, although the most important articles of the Christian faith are held by many others as firmly as they are held by Catholics themselves. Such peculiarities are often not unnaturally assumed to betoken narrowness unspeakable and to show that Catholics are unable to recognize any good outside their own Church. And such, apparently, was Mr. Gladstone's view of the matter.

Yet there are other obvious facts that may well make the hasty critic pause before passing such a verdict. For this exclusiveness, this apparent narrowness, is found not only among Catholics who belong to the more rigid school of Ultramontanism, but in those whose liberality is well known. It is perhaps natural for me to refer to a correspondence which I have for some years past been studying minutely—that of the late Cardinal Newman. Few readers of his published letters can, I think, have failed to be touched by those written in his old age to his Evangelical friend, Mr. Edwards—letters so full of the sense of brotherhood among Christians—in which he assures his correspondent that he has found in the Catholic Church the full realization of just that simple worship of Christ which he first learned in his childhood from Evangelical teachers. Again, when his old friend, Principal Shairp, of St. Andrews, died, Newman wrote to Professor Knight a letter he had not the strength to finish, in which he expressed his earnest hope that the future had in store that very union among Christians against infidelity on which Mr. Gladstone had set his heart. Yet we find in the record of Newman's intercourse with Mark Pattison in these very years a firm disclaimer of any such latitudinarian sympathies as should make light of distinctively Catholic dogma or treat it as a matter of comparative indifference. And to the same years belong his successful efforts to secure for the Catholic workers in a Birmingham factory facilities for the separate exercise of their religious worship and freedom from the obligation to attend the prayers of their Protestant fellow-workers. Such tokens would seem to show that the exclusiveness which some would ascribe to narrowness and to the absence of brotherly feeling towards other Christians may co-exist with an intense desire for union against the common foe and with keen sympathy with fellow Christians in the aims and ideals held by all.

But it may be said that Newman's mind was characterized by a liberality not shared by the average Catholic. It is the Catholicism of Manning rather than that of Newman—as we are often reminded—which represents the existing Church of Rome. Newman's fellow Catholics as a body have (it will be said) all his exclusiveness and little of his wide sympathy. In reply to this suggestion I would point out that it was Manning and not Newman who wrote in the early 'sixties the beautiful tract " On the workings of the Holy Spirit in the Church of England." While I do not deny that among Catholics, as among others, there are to be found many various degrees of breadth of sympathy in individuals, this is not determined by the difference between the more liberal and more Ultramontane schools of thought. The exclusiveness does not, in either school of religious thought, betoken narrowness of sympathy. It does not mean, as Mr. Gladstone so confidently supposed, any want of ability or disposition to co-operate with fellow Christians against the spread of infidelity. On the contrary, it exists in those to whom this is a specially cherished object. In the old Metaphysical Society, founded in 1869, the three Catholic members were all strict Ultramontanes—Manning, Father Dalgairns and W. G. Ward. Yet the avowed object of the society was that all its Christian members should act and argue in unison against the agnostic members, and the Catholics found themselves on the same platform as Dr. Martineau, Mr. R. H. Hutton and Dean Church. Indeed—and here I speak from personal memory of the enterprise—some of them used expressly to maintain that the Christian faith had in every age its special foe, and that the same militant spirit which made St. Dominic organize his " hounds of the Lord," his " *domini canes* " against the Albigenses should in later times inspire the united Christian phalanx against the agnosticism of the Huxleys and the Tyndalls.

What, then, is the true import and *rationale* of the exclusiveness of Catholics ? of their slowness to amalgamate with other Christians ? Why, if they wish to co-operate with others against the common enemy, are they not more ready than they actually are to put out of sight points of difference, to join in common worship, to send their children to schools in which the essence of Christianity is taught, though not the distinctively Catholic doctrines? Why do they seem so slow to recognize that in the great battle for Christian faith, forms of the creed are minor matters compared with its essence ? The reply may be put in various ways. The one which I think best appeals to the modern mind is the view which is illustrated in Cardinal Newman's *Essay on Development,* by his comparison of the Catholic Church to a living organism. An organism has many parts performing various functions which cannot be regarded as equally important elements in its life-work. Yet its power to do its life-work effectively depends on the whole being kept alive and vigorous. And for this object functions not directly connected with its most important work are indispensable. Cicero's digestive functions are certainly a very minor matter in our thought of Cicero as a world-power. Yet they may have played an all-important part in the general well-being without which he would not have left us the writings by which his greatness was established. The Catholic Church no doubt claims to be the one indefectible guardian of the Christian revelation. Her exclusiveness is largely based on this claim. But it has also much of its *raison d'être* in reasons which are the conditions of efficiency for any organism. Her creed and ritual and organization form a complete and living whole. Once you begin to tamper with it and to suggest that only those parts of her creed should be insisted on which she shares with other Christians, you threaten the vitality of the living organism and the individuality on which its power largely depends.

The same consideration holds in its measure with other Christian bodies. In point of fact, no denomination with any force in it is content with professing the common measure of Christian beliefs. Each holds them in its own way, with the associations and in the forms to which its history has given birth. Rightly or wrongly, on true lines, or on lines only partly true, or on false lines, each has developed into an organic system with a distinctive character. On this depends its *esprit de corps*. Tennyson once said, "You must choose in religion between bigotry and flabbiness." A sect maintaining only points of agreement with rival sects would be "flabby" and ineffective in its religion. *In point of fact, the very beliefs held in common have their edge and force in individual believers as parts of the different living systems in which they are found.* Thus the refusal to make co-operation depend on amalgamation in organization and in worship, or on the dismissal of what is distinctive of the several denominations and the retention only of what is common to all, may be grounded simply and solely on the interests of vitality in religion. To obliterate what is distinctive of the various communions means that even the doctrines which they *do* hold in common, and which are rightly considered the most important, lose three-quarters of their influence and effectiveness. There is not in existence sufficient agreement among Christians to enable us to create forthwith a new religious organism, a new corporate Church, which should inspire the necessary *esprit de corps.* We must utilize the existing *esprit de corps* in the sects. Therefore, if we would strengthen the force of common Christian beliefs it can only be by a co-operation between the denominations, which should not depend on destroying their distinctive and differing elements. It is a choice between an agreement amid difference in a religion which is inspired and alive, and an agreement pure and simple which is uninspired and comparatively dead and inoperative.

The above expresses, I think, one-half of the underlying principle on which Catholic exclusiveness is founded. It is one-half of the ground on which undenominationalism stands condemned of being ineffective as a religious force. Therefore, when I find the value of the denominational principle recognized as it is in the prospectus of the new *Constructive Quarterly Review,* which has been founded for the express purpose of promoting Christian union, I feel that Mr. Gladstone's forecast to which I referred at the beginning of my essay has met with a remarkable falsification. In place of finding in the Catholic exclusiveness the great enemy of effective union among Christians, experience and observation have taught the founders of this _Quarterly_ that to adopt the denominational or exclusive principle in its measure is necessary to any really practicable and successful common action among the Christian communions against modern unbelief.

Let us take, by way of illustration of what I have already said in general terms, a very prominent and distinctive Catholic ideal—that of the monastic life. If we take it in its fullest expression, as including the active as well as the contemplative orders, we have in this ideal the inspiring force of more than half the greatest achievements of the Catholic Church in the past. From the Benedictines in the fifth century to the Jesuits in the sixteenth you have in the history of religious orders the story of the greatest successes of the Catholic religion. These orders are all based on certain ways of carrying out the ideals of the New Testament. To Mr. Kingsley and to his successors in our time they seem poor and unmanly ways. Are we for this reason to waive the monastic ideal as unessential—as a point of difference which it would be well to sink, with the object of combining and agreeing with such as Mr. Kingsley against the infidel? Probably far more will be done to check infidelity by the zeal and _esprit de corps_ of even one among the hundreds of Catholic religious orders than by all that the religion in common between Mr. Kingsley and the Pope would be likely to effect—not because the points in common between them are not the most important ones, but because in the monastic vocation you have the inspiration and the faith that

can move mountains, while Mr. Kingsley and the
Pope are not likely to combine so as to create any
parallel *esprit de corps* or self-denying zeal in their
followers. Zeal is needed as well as truth, heat as
well as light. Nothing is more *important* than belief
in God. Yet a miscellaneous collection of theists
would probably be comparatively lukewarm and ineffective apostles. But if Mr. Kingsley or—to give
a more probable instance—Herr Eucken, of Jena,
publishes a fine essay against materialism and a great
vindication of man's spiritual nature, if Hegel writes
convincing words on "self realization by self denial,"
let us by all means stand by them and gladly use their
arguments and extend their influence. Do not, however, let us think that we shall do this more effectively
by abandoning the distinctive ideals which have created
our own heroes and done our work in the past.

It will certainly be objected to in the above remarks
that they ignore a principal difficulty in the path of
Christian union which the more liberal Christians with
whom Mr. Gladstone sympathized had tried to meet
by minimizing points of difference between the sects.
The difficulty in question is that in very many cases
these distinctive doctrines are doctrines which speak
of mutual hate and positive disunion. Luther protests
against the superstitions and corruptions of Rome.
This protest is what stirred up and still sustains the
*esprit de corps* of Lutheran Protestants. Rome anathe-
matizes the doctrines of Luther. The zeal of Alva is
fed by the bonfires with which he burns the heretic.
Sectarian tenets do not constitute merely that individuality of creed which gives edge to conviction and enables
agreement amid difference among believers to be the
more effective in the fight against unfaith. They are

a source or a direct consequence of mutual hostility between the believers themselves. If, then, you grant that the full force of religious zeal is largely dependent on the *esprit de corps* of the various religious communions, and that this *esprit de corps* would evaporate if their distinctive doctrines were dropped and only "our common Christianity" were retained, that is an argument not only, as it professes to be, against latitudinarianism, but against the possibility of any effective union among Christians. In emphasizing sectarian tenets you are encouraging those specific beliefs which tell directly for disunion—nay, for positive strife between Christians. You are breeding not effective "hounds of the Lord" to fight the infidels of the day, but rather Kilkenny cats who will fight until they have devoured each other.

It is to be hoped that the best detailed reply to this objection will be found in the future history of the *Constructive Quarterly*. Its promoters are confident that it will reveal a very real and effective sense of Christian brotherhood and a very sensible abatement of the hostile attitude which would a hundred years ago have made any scheme for union among the sects Utopian. But, speaking generally, the answer is, I think, implied in the second rule of the *Constructive Quarterly*, that each sect, while advocating its own views in full, should refrain from attacking its neighbours. Even the exclusive Church of Rome may recognize that there is an element of truth in the positive side of most heretical movements. Catholics are not concerned with maintaining that there were no abuses connected with the sale of indulgences in the sixteenth century. They condemn those who then worked for revolt, but they do not deny that element of justice in their protest which told of the need for reform. Indeed, the whole of the Catholic counter-reformation of the sixteenth century, associated with such names as St. Ignatius Loyola and St. Philip Neri, drew its inspiration from indignation in the Roman communion itself against those very abuses which led to the formation of the Protestant sects as a counterblast. The underlying principle of the *Constructive Quarterly*, as I understand it, is that many of these old controversies are not now actual or urgent, as they once were. For Catholics a new foe is more dangerous than Protestantism, for Protestants the same new foe is more dangerous than Catholicism. A new motive for combination exists which is likely to make the positive and true side of the tenets of each sect more prominent, while the negative and aggressive side is likely to grow less, and even to disappear in some cases, if all parties endeavour to bring this consummation about. The ideal aim is that every group of Christians should preserve its *esprit de corps*, but should at the same time refrain from mutual hostility. And though, like all ideals, this is not likely to be completely realized, some approximation may be made towards its realization. When a Catholic and a Calvinist have been fighting on the same side for a time in the battle against unfaith and have come to look at each other with friendly and understanding eyes, to be desirous each of finding in his fellow Christian's creed strong points telling for union and not weak points for attack, the Calvinist discovers that a good deal which he has been in the habit of regarding as his irreconcilable quarrel with Rome on Grace and Predestination is tolerated in the Catholic Church, and is found in the doctrine of St. Augustine and even in that of St. Thomas Aquinas. Protests against formalism and externalism in religion which inspired the zeal of Luther against Rome will be found to have inspired equally his arch-enemy, St. Ignatius Loyola, in fashioning the famous "Spiritual Exercises."

Nothing but experience can determine the exact issue of the endeavour before us. Therefore to discuss this matter further would be premature. Real but at present unconscious points of agreement will, it is to be hoped, come more clearly to light under the growing influence of a common zeal against the revival of pagan ethics and the destruction of faith in the unseen which now threatens the modern world. If the attention and energy of all Christians is concentrated on the crusade against those movements which threaten all religious belief and principle, the force and heat of religious zeal will gradually be transferred more and more to this common crusade. An immediate attempt to bring down the existing sects to a dead level of positive belief would, on the contrary, put out the flame instead of changing its direction. And, once extinguished, it might be hard to rekindle.

How far combination will be possible against a common enemy, how far allies who fight under the same banner will find that they have all along agreed more than they had supposed even in matters they had regarded as points of difference, how far good will and mutual trust can allay apparent differences which bad will and suspiciousness had a large share in creating, remains to be seen. I have said enough to show the nature of the experiment and the grounds on which it may commend itself to one like myself who is a member of the Ancient Church.

# X

# THE CONSERVATIVE GENIUS OF
# THE CHURCH

I wish to say a few words on a phenomenon apparent
on the surface of the history of the Church, which
has a very practical application to our own time.
And if for a few minutes I have to dwell on events
far removed from the present, I would ask you to
give them patient attention. Before concluding I
hope to show how closely they bear on problems
which are just now before the minds of many English
Catholics, and what light is thrown by the past on a
true solution of present difficulties.

The Church has from its beginning lived amid the
world, and had to face the characteristic social and
intellectual movements of each successive age. The
first thing that strikes one from the days of the very
first heretics—the Gnostics—to the days of the
Church's last assailants — the Agnostics — is her
attitude of uncompromising resistance to rival theories
of life, which strove to dictate to her and bend her to
their will. From the days of the Gnostics to those
of Abelard, from Abelard to Luther, from Luther to
Lamennais, the same thing has been apparent. The
Gnostics tried to force Christianity to identify itself

with a fanciful philosophical system, and banished the Old Testament and the historical groundwork of the faith ; Abelard—as St. Bernard bitterly complained in his letters—tried to base faith purely on the dialectics of Aristotle and on human reason, failing in his account to give their due place to the humility of faith, the sense of mystery apparent in the theology of the Fathers; Luther practically banished the office of the Church in mediating between God and the soul, and advocated individual private judgment in interpreting the Scriptures ; Lamennais wished to commit the Church to a theory of unfettered liberalism.   To accept any of these systems would have been for the Church to sacrifice her own authority, and her own individuality. In each case the Church was confronted with a form of *rationalismus*, or its twin sister *liberalismus*.   But there was only one *ismus* which she could accept— *Christianismus.*   She had to guard the revelation handed down.   Any system which professed to be complete and yet ignored the mysterious truth committed to her, or gave a rival account of life or of faith and presumed to dictate to her, was in the first instance met by her with the weapons of sheer resistance.

The second phenomenon is that all the systems she opposed contained elements which were good and true.   And from not one did she fail ultimately to assimilate something, in most cases a great deal, once their aggressive character had been broken by her resistance.   "She broke them in pieces," writes Cardinal Newman, and then he significantly adds, "she divided the spoils."   Readers of Cardinal Newman's *Essay on Development*, and of Professor Harnack's *History of Dogma*—which we value for

its facts, however often we may reject its theories—
know how much the Church adopted of the methods
and ideas which, in aggressive combination, formed
the Gnostic heresies. The very method of applying
the intellect systematically to the truths of faith,
according to both writers, originated with the
Gnostics. And dogmatic theology not only adopted
that method, but availed itself of much of the Greek
philosophy which the Gnostics had used against
orthodoxy. The dialectical method of Abelard
(again), and his devotion to the philosophy of
Aristotle, so strenuously opposed by St. Bernard and
the orthodox of the twelfth century, became in the
hands of St. Thomas Aquinas the instruments of
faith. Even Luther's undisciplined and exaggerated
pleas contained a protest against real corruption and
formalism within the Church ; and the counter-reformation of the Jesuits and their allies included a revival
of the inner life of the soul which showed that the
Church was ready to appropriate grains of truth and
salutary warnings even from her most implacable
enemies. *Fas est et ab hoste doceri.* Lastly, while in
the encyclical *Mirari vos* Gregory XVI. condemned
the liberalistic theory of Lamennais, we have seen
ever since its appearance among the most orthodox in
Lamennais' own country, from Lacordaire himself to
the Comte de Mun and M. Harmel, active sympathy
with the democracy. There has been a gradual
development of popular organization and freedom
of association (which Lamennais so strongly urged)
within the Church, although Lamennais' attempt to
identify the Church with the liberalistic and democratic
principle was crushed once and for all.

When I ascribe this double phenomenon in

Church history, of resistance and subsequent assimilation, to the conservative principle of the Church, I may at first appear to maintain a paradox. It may be urged that the first attitude—of opposition to aggressive novelty—is an exhibition of the conservative principle; but that the second—the subsequent assimilation of portions of what was rejected —is not. To this I would reply that to identify conservatism simply with the rejection of what is extraneous and new in form is to identify it with a principle of decay. To preserve a building we must indeed resist those who would pull it down. But we must also repair it, replace what is worn out by what is new, and fit it to last in the varying conditions of life. True conservatism involves constructive activity as well as resistance to destructive activity. Periodical reform and reconstruction belong to its very essence.

And now I think we have reached the heart of the matter. There are two classes of enemies to the true conservatism which would preserve for present use an ancient building—those who would pull it down, and those who would leave it untouched, without repairs, without the conditions which render it habitable in the present, superstitiously fearing that to alter it in *any respect* is to violate what is venerable and sacred. Had Napoleon bombarded Venice when he took it, a hundred years ago, and destroyed the Palace of the Doges, he would have ruined a noble and ancient building. But had the municipality in 1899 failed to note the undermining and sapping effect of the gradual action of the water in the canal, and omitted to take active steps for its repair and preservation, they too would have been destroyers. Their passivity and false conservatism would have

been as ruinous to the ancient fabric, as the activity
and aggressiveness of the most reckless bombardment.

And so the Church, with a true and not a false
conservatism, has in the past resisted both classes of
foes. The aggressive movements of the times she
has opposed. To yield to them would have been to
identify herself with partly false, partly one-sided and
exaggerated phases of thought, and lose her own
authority and her own individual character. But each
movement witnessed to a real advance of human
thought, new truth amid new error, and to fresh
developments of human activity. It supplied *material*
for repairs and reconstruction within the Church
although it was unacceptable as a whole. "The
sects," writes Cardinal Newman, "contained elements
of truth amid their errors." Had the Church been
content with a false conservatism—the conservatism
of mere resistance to innovation—and then remained
passive, having escaped the dangers of aggression,
she would have succumbed to the danger of decay.
She alternated instead, not between resistance and
passivity, but between resistance and the most active
process of adaptation and assimilation. The new
phases of thought which the various philosophical and
religious movements represented, the incidental truths
they brought to light, had all to be taken account of
and utilized. New conditions had to be met, new
secular truths assimilated. New methods which were
entering into the very life of the age had to be introduced into the Church.

The difference between the two processes is, as
Cardinal Newman has pointed out, that the first
process, of resistance, is the work of authority, of
Rome itself; the second, of assimilation, is the work

x

of individuals, authority only tolerating and not necessarily helping it, until it is so far tested that authority can more or less ratify what individuals have initiated.

The palmary instance of this assimilative activity —because the change was greatest—was the complete adaptation of theology to Aristotelian philosophy and to dialectical treatment by St. Thomas Aquinas. A reader of St. Bernard's letters would deem it almost impossible that, in the century following his time, a system should prevail in the Church containing so much which St. Bernard bitterly resented and condemned in Abelard. The feat was accomplished by a saintly theologian, who was devoted to and impregnated by both the Aristotelian philosophy and the Catholic tradition of the Fathers. The patristic tradition preserved the necessary conservative element in the new system. It was a gigantic scheme of conservative reform, a signal protest against the "fossilism," which calls itself conservative, the lines of the new system being mainly determined by the intellectual conditions of the time. Averröes and Avicenna, the Arabians, and Maimonides the Jew, had marked out the *terrain* of philosophical discussion. With the latter as an ally, and the former largely as opponents, St. Thomas went over the whole ground to be covered without flinching, and left the monuments of his work which we possess—the *Summa contra Gentiles* and the *Summa theologica*. What in Abelard had been negative and destructive became in St. Thomas's pages constructive. And the paradox was realized which Harnack describes in these words: "The negative theologian (Abelard) really laid the foundation for the classical structure of medieval conservative theology."

The fundamental difference between false conservatism and true conservatism is that the former is blind and passive, the latter open-eyed and active. Both recognize that the Church's business is to preserve the theological structure whereby the original revelation is protected, but the former tends blindly to cling to the *status quo*, the latter insists on surveying the building, renewing what is decayed, replacing what is worn out, examining intelligently whether a particular part of the construction now does the work for which it was originally intended.

And now to apply these remarks to our present conditions in England.

We are in some respects in a period of transition. The days when Catholics were excluded from public life—from Parliament, from the Universities, from the liberal professions—are, it is true, long past. But the habits which those days had created long survived. Catholics, until quite recently, passed all the critical years of education, apart from any non-Catholic influences, in their own schools and colleges. In after-life, to a very large extent, they held aloof from their fellow-countrymen. There was a Catholic club. There were in every class groups of friends, all Catholics, forming their own society. This state of things is giving place to another. In the Universities, in London clubs, in the general world, Catholics are more and more coming to associate freely with their neighbours.

One noteworthy consequence of this, with which I am here concerned, does not apply to all who attend this conference or to all members of the Catholic Truth Society. It applies especially to a comparatively small number, yet an important section. Those

who in the Universities or elsewhere are keenly
interested in the social, intellectual, or scientific movements of the time, find themselves face to face with a
number of problems which are freely discussed. And
they find it sometimes assumed as evident by their
non-Catholic friends that the Church is hopelessly
reactionary, and does not face or realize conclusions
which are, to those with whom they associate, the
assured conquests of modern science. To concentrate
our ideas by taking obvious instances, they see those
outside the Church busy adapting Christian teaching
to modern biblical criticism, and to the broad results
of the evolutionary hypothesis. They see that so far
as the Church herself has taken a public line in these
questions it has been almost entirely hostile. The
general drift of the Encyclical *Providentissimus* is
against the results and even the methods of the higher
criticism. The most notorious attempt of a Catholic
theologian to adapt the Evolution theory to Catholic
teaching—Father Zahm's work—has been condemned.

Now, if we realize the systematic action of the
Church in the past, to which I have called attention,
the difficulty presented by this attitude is far less
than appears at first sight. It is a patent fact that
both the Higher Criticism and the theory of Evolution
were first brought prominently before the European
mind in a form hostile to Christianity. The first
instinctive action of self-protection, of conservatism,
on the part of the Church has been necessarily to
oppose them. But while the broad, official, authoritative action of the Church is still maintaining an
attitude of opposition, many Catholics in England,
Germany, France, and elsewhere are, in the retire-
ment of their studies, working out a *modus vivendi*

between Faith on the one hand and the assured or probable results of Science and Criticism on the other. It is a very close parallel to what happened in the thirteenth century in reference to Aristotle's philosophy. Frederick Schlegel has described how in that century "the inclination of the age to absolute modes of thinking," and other causes, created an "irresistible rage for Aristotle, reputed as he was to contain the very essence of all liberal science and philosophy." And Aristotle was imported from the East with the comments of the Arabians Averröes and Avicenna, who gave a pantheistic character to his teaching. The danger to the faith of his Christian readers was great. The public, official action of the Church was largely hostile to the whole movement. The council of Paris in 1210 ordered Aristotle's metaphysical works to be burnt. Five years later, by order of Innocent III., Robert de Courçon, a papal legate, forbade the faithful to read them. A superficial observer, or an upholder of the principles of modern liberalism, might well have said that the Church was hopelessly reactionary, in opposing *the* characteristic intellectual movement of the time. But in those very years there was *also* proceeding a movement of assimilation. Albertus Magnus was already at work sifting Aristotle and adapting him to Christian theology. And before the century was finished all official opposition was withdrawn, and St. Thomas Aquinas had completed what his master began. The official opposition, which protected the Church from being overrun by a rationalistic and pantheistic movement, did *not* prove that in the event the Church could not come to terms with all that was good or even tolerable in the metaphysics which had been at first, from circumstances, dangerous

to the faith. And it is equally true now that while
the official attitude of the Church is suspicious or
hostile, the very best Catholic thought is effecting the
desired reconciliation. Both functions of the conservative principle in the Church are being carried on.

But now we come to a further difficulty. It may
be plausibly urged that the conditions of the nineteenth century are not those of the thirteenth; that
modern thought now inevitably penetrates to the
Christian people; that rapidity of discriminating
assimilation is now a far more pressing need; that
even temporary *intransigeance* may be unavailing and
disastrous. Authority (it may be said) is so intent on
opposition that it unduly retards the assimilative
action which takes place slowly in spite of it. It dis-
courages and opposes it. This is, I think, a fair
matter for investigation. If in this or that case the
particular form of opposition adopted is useless, if it
attempts to keep people from knowing theories which
every one must know, and with this impracticable
object forbids the freedom required for dealing with
them from a Catholic point of view, Catholics must
suffer. But assuming that there is some truth in this
supposition, those who desire that such a state of
things should be modified must not fail to bear in
mind, in their forecast of what is possible or practicable, the exigencies of the conservative genius of the
Church. Reform, adaptation to new circumstances,
may be needed now, as it has been so often in the
past, but it must be what I have called " conservative
reform." The principle of caution and resistance to
dangerous movements is not abrogated, because its
action, to be effectual, must be modified.

No doubt since the Reformation the forces of

resistance have been much more developed in the Church's theology than the forces of assimilation. The tremendous revolt of half of Christendom called for a strenuous movement, within the Church, of militarism and self-defence, and rendered very difficult the more liberal policy required for assimilation. The new state of things inaugurated in the present century, when many old controversies are practically spent, when we need the best and most open-eyed and fairest treatment of all contemporary thought, is at variance with the polemical and repressive habits which the Reformation of necessity inaugurated. The martial law which a state of siege necessitates would dwarf the normal development of the community in time of peace. This, I think, is very fairly maintainable. And thus we find Catholics in many countries urging the necessity of the cultivation of intellectual habits and training adapted to a new state of things. Authority is (presumably) glad to know the experience of those who are trying to serve the Church, and find themselves handicapped by conditions which are applicable mainly to a different state of society.

In general, if the Church is losing touch with or the power to control any deep movement in the hearts of men, something is probably out of repair in the machinery she employs. Such great orders as Dominicans, Franciscans, Jesuits, have owed their very foundation to temporary defect of this kind within the Church. They were new mechanisms to answer new needs. It is not (I need hardly say) a question of the Catholic faith, but of the effectiveness of some portion of the machinery used by the Church in dealing with the world around her.

The practical question in individual cases which

may concern us is how to deal with particular parts of
the machinery which may have become ineffective.
There are three programmes proposed which I will
state in homely popular language. The Radical says
in effect, "Cast it away as useless." The false Conservative says, "Leave it alone. It is impious to
touch it, or to examine whether it is in or out of
repair." The true Conservative reformer says,
"Thoroughly overhaul the machinery until you find
out exactly what is wrong; mend it and fit it for
existing conditions." For example, the question has
recently been asked—I mention it only to illustrate
my meaning—Do priests find the proportion of attention devoted in their training to scholastic philosophy
and the Aristotelian method a hindrance to their fully
understanding and influencing those whom they are
called upon to understand and influence? I am not
proposing to ask this question, which is outside the
sphere of our discussion here. I give it only as a
concrete example which illustrates the three programmes which have been proposed in such cases.
The Radical reformer will say—indeed, *has* said—
"Sweep the system away." That is to say, "Bom-
bard St. Mark's and the Doge's Palace, and build
a modern church and palace in their place." The
false Conservative will say, and has said, "Leave the
system precisely as it stands. The structure is sacred.
To consider its effectiveness under modern conditions
is a want of faith." That is to say, "Let the water
do its worst to the foundations. The Palace of the
Doges must last for ever." The advocate for conservative reform may claim the analogy of the Church's
action in the past in regarding both these programmes
as fatalistic and unintelligent. He has good precedents

when he urges, "Examine the structure. Repair it where it is necessary. Consider Scholasticism not as what it is not—a part of Revelation; but see intelligently what work it was intended by the Church to accomplish and how far it does that work now. Its *form* was originally intended not as the maintenance of something ancient and sacred, for it was entirely new—an adaptation to the times, to the *new* intellectual fashion. Nevertheless in that form the best theological thought and even parts of revelation have subsequently been expressed. *These* must be guarded as sacred. How far is it possible to preserve its permanent legacy of Catholic thought, and yet to make theology do in the most effective way what it was meant to do—influence and affect the religious thought of the day, now that medieval *form* does *not* appeal to the intellect of the age?" Here is an important and most practical problem which needs full consideration among those whom it concerns.

Take again the social movement. To press the theories of Socialism on the Church is to court rebuff from those in authority. It is exactly such an "ism" which the Church must oppose. Yet this is what Radical reformers would more or less attempt. But for the Church to hold its place and influence in a democratic age is a real and most practical problem, a problem which Leo XIII. has so boldly faced in the Encyclical *Rerum novarum*. Those who would simply resist the democracy are not real Conservatives. For simply to resist it is to fail to preserve the influence of Catholicism on the people. In this department as in others, the forces of contemporary thought and life would undermine the Church if the Church

did not deal with, understand, and partly assimilate
them.

Take, again, the modern cry for liberty of discussion and the liberty for all to read what they please.
The Radicals would simply open the door wide to
such a programme. The Church has always guarded
the faith of the weak, has always recognized the plain
fact that wild, random, unbelieving talk or reading
may upset their faith. "Novelty," says Cardinal
Newman, "is often error for those who are unprepared
for it, from the refraction with which it enters into
their conceptions." The Church cannot sweep aside
the principle on which she has always acted. The
real question is, Does the existing machinery for con-
trolling the dangers attendant on the free circulation
of heresy and dangerous reading do its work? The
days when the great aim was to prevent the reading
of any heretical statement were very different from
the present—in which practically many of us must
know most of what is said against the Church and the
faith, and our great desire is to find the most effective
antidote. An honest and able, though not faultless,
attempt to grapple with difficulties may save the faith
of many. If an over-scrupulous theologian finds one
statement of doubtful orthodoxy in far the ablest
Catholic work on the subject, and banishes the book,
it may well be that the loss is great, the gain infini-
tesimal. The faultlessly orthodox works on the
subject—so pleads one whose faith is tried—may be
colourless and inadequate ; excellent reading for those
who know nothing of the difficulties, worse than useless for those who know much. The forbidden book
may be the one useful one. This is but one aspect
of a large and important question.

So, too, with the higher criticism. Catholics cannot now ignore or simply oppose it. Its extremest conclusions already stand condemned by Christianity. It now remains to perform the second operation—to examine carefully and candidly what are the true conclusions to which it should lead us. And those who are attempting this work plead that for its effective performance a large measure of freedom for themselves, of provisional tolerance on the part of theological censors, is needed.

One word more. These and many similar necessities press upon many minds in England and America according as they come into contact with the special problems concerned. To one man biblical criticism seems all in all. To another receptiveness in philosophy appears most important ; to another the sympathy of the Church with the democracy. Our mixed populations belonging to many creeds, yet with many common aims and aspirations, help to bring about this condition of things. The people we meet raise the questions, and we desire to be able to treat them intelligently. We know that where Catholics live apart from their neighbours, such problems are less urgent. What is no irksome infringement of the liberty demanded for effectual action in a Spanish Catholic may be so for an educated Englishman or American. And general rules from headquarters which are obviously satisfactory in one case may be unsatisfactory in the other. In a vast empire like the Catholic Church this is at times inevitable. And it is beyond doubt that, when rules do not apply because they were made for other circumstances, the rulers desire full information as to the practical difficulties of the situation. Each man who finds such rules practically impossible to obey would be urged by them to make representations to that effect in the proper quarters.

And here we find a difference as to the appropriate method—a most important difference. We may either take the view of practical men : " Here is a matter of interest to us all, to the authorities as much as to ourselves. How can we best obtain full and fair consideration for it ? " Or we may simply grumble and abuse the authorities and the Church, and echo the slanders of her enemies, without taking practical steps to make difficulties understood, or reduce them to their true dimensions. This is the old programme of the born grumbler, to bury his talent and abuse his employer. " Lord, I knew that thou wert a hard master." There are constitutional methods of placing before the authorities local and special difficulties, and these are the normal means of obtaining consideration for them. And in what spirit should this be done ? Gregorovius, in his great work on *Medieval Rome*, has traced—in pages which, in spite of the writer's position as external to the Church, often make even the Catholic reader realize its genius in a new way—the grandeur and power of that medieval Christendom, with Rome at its head, which survives in the Catholic Church. The German historian describes the Christian Commonwealth as being the lineal heir to some of the greatest traditions of the Roman Empire, while it replaced the guiding spirit of old Rome by the Christian ideal. And the Empire would never have been what it was but for the loyalty of its citizens and their pride in the city of the Caesars. " *Civis Romanus sum*," " I am a Roman citizen," was the basis of their appeal where their liberty was infringed. But it was also a symbol of proud devotion and of loyalty to the city. And is it too much to hope that this double quality will always be preserved by the citizens of the greater Empire of the Catholic Church with Rome as its head, with Christian enthusiasm substituted for Pagan pride? If a Roman citizen saw that a provincial governor was about to violate such liberties or rights as the constitution allowed him, what was his redress? Did he at once malign the Caesar, sneer at Roman greatness, abuse the Roman people, unite with the enemies of Rome and conspire against existing authority? If so, the Roman lictors would have quickly ended his proceedings with their axes. On the contrary. His first protest was the expression of pride in Rome and trust in its protection: " *Civis Romanus sum,*" "I am a Roman citizen." His next was an appeal to the sympathy and protection, not of the enemies of Rome, but of the Roman people and their chief: " *Appello Caesarem ;*" "I appeal to Caesar." And is it too much to expect that the members of our own Imperial Church will have at all events as much trust and loyalty as their Pagan prototypes? Loyalty and faith in the representatives of the Church on earth, trustfulness that they will realize the ideal of their station, raises the Christian people and sustains its rulers. Petty cavilling and criticism creates distrust and dissension all round. To court the applause of the enemies of the Church by abusing its authorities is unworthy of the best Roman as of the best Christian traditions.

Emergencies may arise in times of transition. It may be lawful—it may be a duty on special occasions —to urge special or local necessities or to bring before those in authority the practical difficulties of the

situation. But a Catholic's final duty is to obey
authority in its rightful sphere. And at whatever
cost it should be his pride. If we desire the law to
respect our liberties, we must ourselves respect the
law. Justice may miscarry. Or he who has urged
the difficulties of the situation, and its requirements,
may have been unwise or wrong. In any case, the
ground of his appeal is the ground of his submission :
" *Civis Romanus sum*," " I am a Catholic."

# XI

## ST. THOMAS AQUINAS AND MEDIEVAL THOUGHT

A LEARNED Jesuit[1] once drew a very attractive picture of a Catholic University which should fulfil the functions of "a sort of boundary commission of physicists, historians, critics, philosophers and theologians, working with a common endeavour for the provisional adjustment of the contested frontier" between all these sciences at their present stage of development. There is no doubt that many learned men would welcome an institution with the functions and the authoritative *status* which these words imply. We suffer from the fact that this effort, so strenuously made in the thirteenth century, has never since been repeated with the same frankness or thoroughness. Consequently theological science, then developed with the aid of the best secular thought and learning of the time, and handed down with comparatively little change to our own day, is now in some danger of being cramped by the very elements that once gave it living relations with its intellectual environment; and we are apt to regard some of the peculiarities of form, which it then for the first time assumed, as part of its unchanging essence.

[1] Father Rickaby, in the Introduction to his translation of St. Thomas Aquinas's *Summa contra Gentiles*.

Yet if we read the great thirteenth-century school-men with an eye to the conditions in which they wrote, we cannot but see in their work—and notably in the works of St. Thomas Aquinas—a protest against this very tendency to petrifaction to which all intellectual systems are liable when their original meaning and purpose are forgotten. Aquinas was essentially a writer for an emergency. And the emergency for which he wrote was in some respects very similar to that which we have to face in our own day, in others, utterly dissimilar. Regarded from the point of view of his method of dealing with the problems of the hour, St. Thomas Aquinas is in some respects unrivalled and a veritable model for ourselves. " His marvellous grasp and subtlety of intellect seem to me to be almost without a parallel," writes a modern thinker, so far removed from the Saint's standpoint as Huxley.[1] But in the actual problems demanding attention two centuries could hardly be further apart than the thirteenth and the nineteenth. The *Summa contra Gentiles* is believed to be largely a *résumé* of lectures delivered in the University of Paris about the year 1260. The intellectual conditions of that time are familiar to students of its history. But they must be recalled and kept clearly in mind by the general reader who wishes to appreciate the qualities of the book and its lesson for us.

In spite of the difference between the actual problems debated, there were points of significant similarity between certain mental tendencies and social forces at work in the thirteenth and in the nineteenth centuries. The Oxford of the last century witnessed a very interesting struggle between the

[1] *Science and Morals*, p. 142. Macmillan.

upholders of what used to be called "liberalism" in religious thought, or a modified rationalism, and the conservative adherents of tradition. There were on either side men of veritable genius. Whately and Arnold, and later on more unmistakably Jowett, Mark Pattison, and Matthew Arnold, were the precursors of the liberal theology of to-day and the ancestors of those critical students of Christian "origins" and of the Bible itself, who are now exercising so great an influence.

Yet more marked was the genius of the leader of the conservative school in Oxford—John Henry Newman, who, following in the footsteps of Edmund Burke, defended the ancient ways against the acuter intellects of the hour. He upheld tradition and dogma as representing the wisdom inherited from our ancestors, the communication of rays of divine light to the prophets of old, and a message from One in whom the divine nature had become incarnate.

And Oxford, the microcosm, reflected in this battle England, the macrocosm. Every thinking man in the 'thirties and 'forties was in philosophy (according to the testimony of J. S. Mill) a Benthamite, belonging to the school of progress, or a Coleridgian, who upheld and analyzed the wisdom contained in the sacred traditions of the race.

Two tendencies, largely similar, were quite unmistakable in the thought of the twelfth and thirteenth centuries, and they are described with much picturesque detail and wealth of erudition, if not quite with critical accuracy or with the precision which needs a philosophical specialist, by the late Archbishop Vaughan, the author of the admirable *Life and Labours of St.*

*Thomas of Aquin.*[1] True, indeed, the theological liberalism of the Middle Ages was not allied, like that of our own day, with historical and biblical criticism and inductive science. But both forms of liberalism were attempts to carry into the domain of religious inquiry and faith those methods of reasoning which are applicable only to the regions of experience.

The monastic school, represented by St. Bernard and by Hugh of St. Victor, appealed, much as the school of Coleridge did, to the spiritual " taste" and instinct, as the true faculty whereby the inscrutable things of God are apprehended. Scholastic subtleties were abjured by them as irreverent and unprofitable. The things of God were too vast for the poor measuring tape of the human intellect. Faith was needed for their apprehension. Abelard, on the other hand, from his Chair in the University of Paris, applied his acute dialectic to all things. Reason must, he argued, precede faith, lest faith should be irrational. Reason again was invoked to investigate theological mystery itself, and the Trinity was made a subject for philosophical debate. He attempted to find a rational solution of all the minute questions which the imaginative brains of subtle and sceptical inquirers could formulate, in place of setting them aside—with the mystics—as belonging to a region above the reach of the human intellect. Describing to a Roman cardinal the Paris of Peter Abelard, St. Bernard writes : " Along the streets and in the squares people dispute about the Catholic faith, about the Child-bearing of the Virgin, about the sacrament of the altar and about the incomparable mystery of the

[1] The author, Dom Roger Bede Vaughan, a brother of the late Cardinal, was afterwards Archbishop of Sydney.

Trinity." [1]  The Oxford liberals of the 'fifties and
'sixties liberalized theology by rationalizing it.  And
so did Abelard after the manner of his time, although
he did not invoke in the process, as did the Essayists
and Reviewers, or Matthew Arnold and Arthur Clough,
the conclusions of an historical science which was
unknown to the Middle Ages.

The mottoes of either school in the twelfth century
might have been taken without change by their nineteenth-century successors.  The one freely quoted
from Isaias the words, " Unless ye shall believe, ye
shall not understand ; " the other from Ecclesiastes,
" He who believes quickly is light of heart and shall
be worsted."  In each period there were the compromises of those who saw elements of truth in both
tendencies.  Peter Lombard, the pupil of Abelard,
learnt also from the mystic pages of Hugh of St.
Victor.  So, too, Arnold was influenced by Keble.
And later on rationalism and idealism combined in
Thomas Hill Green, whose influence in return reacted
upon such successors of the Tractarians as Gore and
Scott Holland.  There were also, at both periods, the
extremes of the ultra-logical who passed on the one
side into obscurantism, on the other into Agnosticism
or Pantheism.

As time went on, indeed, in both cases the
prophecies of the conservatives as to the dangers of
liberalism were verified.  The mildly liberal theology
of Thomas Arnold developed into the rationalism of
his son ; and St. Bernard's warning, too, as to the
tendency of the dialectical method of Abelard seemed
to be realized.  The flood of new ideas, to which the
introduction of the Arabian and Jewish philosophies

[1] *Works of St. Bernard*, ii. 863.  Hodges.

and of the translations of Aristotle's physical and metaphysical works led in the thirteenth century, gave a strong anti-Christian direction to this method. The cultivation of the new learning, added to the unrestrained excesses of the fashionable dialectical tournaments, led, among thinkers, to an extensive abandonment of Christianity and of Monotheism itself. The general unsettlement it produced was somewhat analogous to the disturbing effect, during the first fifty years and more, of the flood of new discoveries in physical and historical science. Averröes, the Pantheist, had disciples in the university chairs in Paris during the space of half a century. The "liberal" tendency triumphed. The authority of Aristotle reigned supreme, and he was interpreted largely by the light of pantheistic Arabian commentaries, and of mistranslations which favoured such misinterpretation.

The medieval schools [writes Cardinal Newman] were the arena of as critical a struggle between truth and error as Christianity has ever endured ; and the philosophy which bears their name carried its supremacy by means of a succession of victories in the cause of the Church. Scarcely had universities risen into popularity, when they were found to be infected with the most subtle and fatal forms of unbelief ; and the heresies of the East germinated in the West of Europe and in Catholic lecture-rooms with a mysterious vigour upon which history throws little light. The questions agitated were as deep as any in theology ; the being and essence of the Almighty were the main subjects of the disputation, and Aristotle was introduced to the ecclesiastical youth as a teacher of Pantheism. Saracenic expositions of the great philosopher were in vogue ; and when a fresh treatise was imported from Constantinople the curious and impatient threw himself upon it, regardless of the Church's warnings, and reckless of the effect upon his own mind. The acutest intellects became sceptics and misbelievers; and the head of the Holy Roman Empire, the Caesar Frederick the Second, to say nothing of our miserable King John, had the reputation of meditating a profession of Mahometanism. It is said that, in the community at large, men had a vague suspicion and mistrust of each other's belief in Revelation.[1]

We are rightly anxious in our own day for a Christian and Catholic atmosphere in our own universities, and so we can sympathize with the distress of the rulers of the Church at what they witnessed in Paris in the ages of Faith. University professors taught that incarnations of the Divinity were many, or that the resurrection of the body and even immortality were incredible; or, by a blend of pantheism with positivism, that God was identical with creatures or with the creation,[2] or that Christian theology was based on fables. Certainly no positions more destructive of orthodox Christian faith have been upheld in our own day by rationalistic critics in England, or in Germany. The religious scepticism and eclecticism which Mark Pattison describes in his *Memoirs* as attending on the triumph of liberalism in the Oxford of the 'fifties—when men "questioned everything and were impatient to throw the whole cargo of tradition overboard"—was no whit greater than that which characterized the Paris of the early thirteenth century, and it was less openly avowed. There was, however, this difference—that the educated

---

[1] *Idea of a University*, by J. H. Newman, p. 383.

[2] See Gerson's testimony in *De Concordia Metaphysicae cum Logica*, iv. Compare also Ueberweg's *History of Philosophy* (English translation), i. p. 431; and Vaughan's *St. Thomas of Aquin* (Longmans), i., p. 406.

classes in the Middle Ages bore a far smaller proportion
to the whole population, and the danger was consequently less universal.

Authority, too, played its *rôle* in both cases. At
Oxford there were the condemnations of excesses on
both sides—in 1836 and 1845. In Paris, also, the
vagaries of mysticism were branded in David of
Dinanto, and those of rationalism in the followers of
Averröes. The mode of procedure was, however,
different. The "deprivation" of Dr. Hampden and
the "degradation" of Mr. Ward by convocation were
the attenuated survivals of a *modus operandi* which had
been extremely drastic in the Middle Ages, if not always
in the long run effectual. Amalric of Bena, as professor of logic and theology, had taught free doctrines
on the Incarnation. They took the form of excess,
and not defect. That God the Son became incarnate
in Christ, he willingly admitted. But so, too, he
taught, had the Eternal Father been already incarnate
in Abraham, while the Holy Ghost was still making
the whole human race incarnate gods.[1] Amalric went
to his account in 1207. But his doctrines spread, and
authority driven to bay acted decisively. Peter of
Corbeil, Bishop of Paris, convened a Council in 1209.
Amalric's teaching was examined and condemned.
His bones were dragged from their resting-place in
consecrated ground, and carted off to an unhallowed
grave. A fire was then lighted in the city, in which
ten of his most prominent disciples—some of them
priests—were burned alive.

The intellectual evils of the University were traced
by the authorities largely to the influence of Aristotle's

---

[1] See analysis of his doctrine in Ueberweg's *History of Philosophy*
(English translation), i., p. 431.

*Physics*, and the Council issued an edict that they were
not to be further read, publicly or privately.

It is a curious illustration of the obstinacy of human
thought at a time of intellectual agitation, that these
drastic measures failed. Not even the fear of being
burned alive could stop the speculations of the eager
philosophers, and the positions upheld by professors in
the succeeding years were quite as unorthodox as those
of Amalric. Though, in 1215, Robert de Courçon,
papal legate, supplemented the work of the Paris
Council by condemning Aristotle's metaphysical works
and prohibiting their use, yet the succeeding years
witnessed teaching as rationalistic as did the beginning
of the century. Archbishop Vaughan has collected the
propositions advanced by the heterodox, and protested
against by the orthodox, and his pages are very
instructive reading.

In the intellectual world it soon ceased to be a
struggle between the two methods ; for the dialectical
method had triumphed. Aristotle had acquired an
authority which could not be gainsaid. The Arabian
and Jewish philosophers—Avicenna, Averröes, Maimonides and the rest—were recognized powers, and
no one who did not appreciate and understand their
philosophy could exert intellectual influence on the
rising generation, any more than a man could gain
attention at Oxford or Cambridge as a competent
professor of philosophy, who did not know and treat
with respect the writings of Kant or Hegel. So long
as the existing intellectual fashion lasted, no philosophical teacher could revert to the attitude of
St. Bernard, for whom non-Christian philosophers
were simply ministers of evil. The practical alternative lay between quitting the world of thought, as

too far gone in perverse ways for remedy, or going fully into contemporary controversies, adopting the dialectical method which had prevailed, and treating respectfully the philosophers whose credit stood so high. The first alternative meant simply to leave alone questions which were crying aloud for an answer, for it was quite clear that, in spite of excesses, there were deep and true philosophical thoughts in the writings both of Aristotle and of the Arabians.

The conservatives did adopt the policy of simple abstention, and denounced not only the excesses to which the new methods led, but the methods themselves. They still held power and influence, but hardly in the world of thought. Even St. Bonaventure, whose whole temper of mind was mystical, was largely scholastic in method. The opposition to Aristotle's metaphysics and the dialectical method, where it was thorough-going, had now become simply the attitude of practical men, who saw faith being shaken by the intellectual ferment, but were not alive to the intellectual problems at issue. It was the conservative opposition, on the part of men of action, to the dangers incident to intellectual life. It lasted through the lifetime of St. Thomas, and gave an expiring kick after his death. Some years after that event—on March 7, 1277—another Bishop of Paris sat in judgment on the evil ways of the University which Bishop Corbeil had denounced in 1209, and condemned many propositions advocated by those who adopted the new learning and methods, including three which were taught by " Frater Thomas " himself. Albert the Great, now an old man of more than eighty years of age, came from Cologne to defend his friend's memory and avert the indignity of a condemnation, but to no purpose. The censure was passed, and not repealed until nearly fifty years later. It was endorsed in the following year (1278) in England, by Archbishop Kilwardby of Canterbury, himself a Dominican Friar.[1]

But, as I have just indicated, the plan of accepting the new methods and authorities was tried by St. Thomas, and with success. An Englishman, Alexander of Hales, the first friar to teach in the University of Paris, was the pioneer in this movement of reconciliation. He was acquainted with the whole of the works of Aristotle, and he adopted in his lectures the dialectical form, and the statement of arguments *pro* and *con* for each proposition. This was to abandon the old rhetorical exposition of earlier days. Alexander died in 1245. Albertus Magnus, the master of St. Thomas, took a similar line, and was the first scholastic to introduce Aristotle's philosophy into theology. In spite of strong opposition, this plan of action did eventually stem in Paris the tide of ultra-rationalism and licence of thought, which mere repression had been unable to arrest. The new generation found, especially in the works of Albertus and St. Thomas, a defence of Christian dogma which took account of all that was fascinating and persuasive in the intellectual life of the day. They were not called upon to renounce those methods which the world of thought universally accepted. Aristotle's Metaphysics were no longer proscribed, but on the contrary are to be found in 1254 on the official list of works required to be taught by the *Facultas Artium*.[2] And gradually the intellectual chaos was reduced to cosmos.

[1] See Lagrange's *Historical Criticism and the Old Testament* (English translation), Catholic Truth Society, p. 24. See also *Revue du Clergé Français*, 15 Juillet, 1905, p. 405.

[2] See Ueberweg, i., p. 432.

This policy of reconciliation between the new learning and the theology of the Fathers was, as I have said, adopted by St. Thomas' master at Cologne and Paris, Albertus Magnus, a fascinating figure in medieval history, a man of encyclopedic learning and a devotee of physical science as well as of metaphysics, an architect, a botanist, a mineralogist as well as a theologian. He was "a man so God-like in all science," writes his contemporary, Engelbert, "that he may suitably be called the wonder and miracle of our time." Albertus was born in 1193,[1] and was consequently just twenty at the critical time, to which we have referred, when the University of Paris seemed to be drifting away from Christian influences altogether. He outlived St. Thomas, dying in 1280 at the age of eighty-seven, when the long battle was practically won, and the new synthesis was gaining the assured position visible in the pages of Dante twenty years later. The learned Benedictine biographer of St. Thomas thus describes the views and work of Albertus Magnus :

There is no doubt [writes Archbishop Vaughan] that Albert took a wide and profound view of the conditions of the intellectual world of his day. A man does not labour as he laboured, nor strike out a novel course of teaching with the likelihood of being misunderstood, without having a grave reason for doing so. The very task which he set himself to accomplish points to the depth and the wisdom of his appreciation of the times. He saw clearly the immense influence which had been and still was being exerted by those vast intellectual powers represented by the Koran, the Talmud and the Stagyrite. Much truth thrown into philosophic form was on the side of the enemy. The power of the Greek thought, its precision, its clearness, its order, its logical force,

[1] Some authorities, however, place his birth thirteen years later.

together with the traditionary teachings of men of intelligence
as subtle as profound, could always make a respectable
appearance and often confuse those who were really seeking
after truth, and keep them from perceiving clearly the philosophy and beauty of the Christian religion. . . . It was not
without causing astonishment, and I may say not without
some scandal, that Albert set about his great work of bringing
Aristotle into the midst of Christianity. Had he contented
himself with hunting up old manuscripts, with laboriously
searching out the true text, and still more laboriously perhaps, eliciting the true meaning, by comparing one execrable
translation from the Arabic, with a still more execrable
translation from the Greek ; or, failing this, by comparing
one part of the author with another, or with Theophrastus or
Avicenna, men might simply have wondered at the extraordinary hobby of an industrious bookworm. But he did far
more than this : he actually had the boldness to modify and
mould Aristotle, by the light of Christian principles, into a
Christian form, to be set before Christian men as Christian
philosophy. And what is more, he made use of the position
he occupied of Public Professor of Theology and Philosophy
to instil his novel views into the minds of the rising generation. Never before this had Aristotle been made the special
subject-matter for lectures in the schools.[1]

Archbishop Vaughan does not fail to note the
fierce protests made in the name of orthodoxy against
Albertus' respectful treatment of the non-Christian
philosophers — Jews, Mahometans, Pantheists — and
especially of Aristotle. "Albert has," he writes,

[1] The fame of Albert was so far more universal than that of Alexander
of Hales that this passage probably represents truly the effect of Albert's
teaching. Moreover, Albert adopted Aristotle more completely than did
the Englishman. But, as I have said, the old uncompromising opposition
to Aristotle had already been dropped by Alexander, and the dialectical
method substituted for the more oratorical method of earlier times.
Alexander was the master of St. Bonaventure. See Vacant's *Dictionnaire
de la Théologie Catholique* (Paris, Letouzey), articles "Albert le Grand"
and "Alexander de Hales."

"been accused over and over again of 'introducing the philosophy of Aristotle into the very sanctuary of Christ,' of 'allotting to him the principal seat in the middle of Christ's temple'; of being drunk with the wine of secular science, human wisdom and profane philosophy; of uniting contentious, thorny and garrulous dialectics with most sacred and pure theology, and of teaching his followers a new and philosophic method of explaining and teaching the Holy Word. He has been called 'an ape' and 'an ass'; has been accused of sorcery and of witchcraft."

The great Dominican persevered in his efforts in spite of these charges against his orthodoxy, and in the early 'forties of the century he first came to know the man who was to continue and complete his work.

The Dominicans had been established at Cologne over twenty years when St. Thomas went there to attend the lectures of Albertus.[1] In 1245 master and pupil passed on to Paris, where Albertus was to occupy the professor's chair and don the doctor's cap. Already in 1228 Albertus had been (according to Archbishop Vaughan) invited to reform the intellectual condition of the University, and his second visit saw the continuation of this work. St. Thomas took his Bachelor's degree in 1248, and his duties at once included public addresses and disputations. His best early biographer, William de Tocco, describes his whole method as novel. There were "new propositions," a "new and clear method of deciding questions," "new reasons," "new opinions."[2] Eventually St. Thomas occupied the professor's chair in the

[1] I adopt Archbishop Vaughan's chronology.
[2] "A.SS. VII Martii (i, 661, F.) n. 15 apud Mandonnet, Siger de Brabant, et l'Averröisme Latin au XIII siècle, p. lxi (Freiburg, 1903)."

University more than once; and, as I have already said, the *Summa contra Gentiles* is believed to be based on lectures delivered before the University in 1260.

The reader who approaches the work with a mind fashioned by modern literature and philosophy cannot fail, I think, to be struck by two things—first, the extraordinary balance of mind, breadth of view, and absence of undue prepossession with which the Saint approaches the questions of which he treats; but, secondly, the marked peculiarities in the intellectual conditions of the time which determined the subjects chosen for discussion. The new method exactly fulfilled the definition of liberalism by its chief opponent at Oxford in the last century,—as the exercise of thought where "thought could not be brought to a successful issue." The old method of the Christian Fathers had been one of intellectual self-restraint in matters divine. The things of God were seen " through a glass darkly," and human reason could not scrutinize them. The Fathers had ever remembered the warning of St. Irenaeus against the Gnostics—that the inquisitiveness of the human reason in matters which are above it is waste of time and can lead to no good result; that God knows, but man can never know. Speaking of the monastic Platonism which long contested the ground with scholastic Aristotelianism, Archbishop Vaughan says that its devotee "would prefer, if he could help it, not to analyze, not to discuss, rather to push forward in knowledge that his love might be stronger." Even Anselm, the first of the scholastics, had held to this principle in his *Cur Deus Homo?* "The right order of things demands that we shall believe the deep things of the

Christian faith before presuming to discuss them by reason," he writes ; and he maintains that the intellect may often fail, even after its best endeavours, to reach the heights visible to the glance of faith. Very different was the temper of the later twelfth and earlier thirteenth centuries, which has so often been compared in acuteness and in universal inquisitiveness to that of a clever child. This temper, which completely prevailed after the dialectical method had become rampant in the early years of the thirteenth century, led to the formulation of some answer on every question propounded in the schools. The public disputations made this course a necessity. There was no limit set to the questions which a disputant might raise or the difficulties he might propose. And every question demanded an answer, every difficulty a solution. If he failed to reply explicitly, the defender of the thesis was defeated. The critical reader feels even in the *Summa contra Gentiles*—though far more in the later *Summa Theologica*—that if the questions were to be answered categorically, it is hardly conceivable that they should be better solved than they are by St. Thomas of Aquin. But some of them are questions to which, neither in the days of St. Irenaeus, nor in the days of St. Bernard, nor in our own time, a categorical answer would have been attempted. Even since Abelard's day the general confidence in the powers of the syllogism and in dialectic had very considerably grown, and it now amounted to a superstition.

If, as Schlegel tells us,[1] men were beginning to hope to discover the secrets of natural science by dint

[1] See *Philosophy of History* (Bohn's translation), p. 376: " A hope was secretly entertained that by the pretended magical power of these

of syllogistic reasoning, we can understand that to
decline the logical combat on any question, was
regarded as an obscurantist mistrust of the great
intellectual instrument of the time.

These considerations must be borne in mind if we
would account for the contrast between the persuasiveness of St. Thomas' treatment of some of the fundamental questions which belong to all times, and the
sense of inconclusiveness which will arise in the typical
modern reader as he peruses some of the fanciful and
subtle arguments on contemporary discussions. The
problems with which these attempt to deal were,
doubtless, often raised by ingenious devil's advocates
in the public debates then in fashion.

Even the Agnostic of the twentieth century cannot
read without a strong impression of candour, and
width and grasp of mind, such a chapter as that on
the necessity of teaching definite Theism among the
articles of Faith. St. Thomas holds, we need not
say, that the existence of God is the only truly
rational explanation of the world, and can be established by right reason apart from Faith. But living as
he did in a University where many professors upheld a
philosophy which taught that God was the world, and
that there is no God at all in the Christian sense, and
who invoked on their behalf the authority of thinkers
of world-wide reputation, St. Thomas treats the
philosophic aspect of the question with all the moderation of an educated man of our own day. Doubtless,
philosophical reason rightly used does eventually lead
to Theism ; but it is desirable, he argues, in practice
that the doctrine should be taught *per modum fidei*,

logical devices one might learn and obtain the mastery of many profound
secrets of nature."

because many are not capable of philosophical reasoning, because, also, such reasoning is a laborious and
long process ; because, again, the arguments and
authority of subtle philosophers of great name, who
are not Theists, may keep the ordinary mind from the
truth ; because, also, imagination and other weaknesses
of the individual reason may so affect us, as to mingle
what is false with what is true in our reasonings.

The passage shall be quoted in full as an excellent
specimen of the Saint's intellectual temper :

If a truth of this nature were left to the sole inquiry of
reason, three disadvantages would follow. One is that the
knowledge of God would be confined to few. The discovery
of truth is the fruit of studious inquiry. From this very
many are hindered. Some are hindered by a constitutional
unfitness, their natures being ill-disposed to the acquisition of
knowledge. They could never arrive by study to the highest
grade of human knowledge, which consists in the knowledge
of God. Others are hindered by the needs of business and
the ties of the management of property. There must be in
human society some men devoted to temporal affairs. These
could not possibly spend time enough in the learned lessons
of speculative inquiry to arrive at the highest point of human
inquiry, the knowledge of God. Some again are hindered
by sloth. The knowledge of the truths that reason can
investigate concerning God presupposes much previous knowledge. Indeed almost the entire study of philosophy, is
directed to the knowledge of God. Hence, of all parts of
philosophy, that part stands over to be learnt last, which
consists of metaphysics dealing with [divine things].[1] Thus,
only with great labour of study is it possible to arrive at the
searching out of the aforesaid truth ; and this labour few are
willing to undergo for sheer love of knowledge.

[1] Father Rickaby renders "divina" by "points of divinity." He
explains in a note, with which I concur, that "natural theology" is
meant ; but the phrase "points of divinity" seems to me to convey something quite different, namely, the superstructure of theology.

Another disadvantage is that such as did arrive at the knowledge or discovery of the aforesaid truth would take a long time over it on account of the profundity of such truth, and the many prerequisites to the study, and also because in youth and early manhood the soul, tossed to and fro on the waves of passion, is not fit for the study of such high truths ; only in settled age does the soul become prudent and scientific, as the philosopher says. Thus, if the only way open to the knowledge of God were the way of reason, the human race would remain in thick darkness of ignorance : as the knowledge of God, the best instrument for making men perfect and good, would accrue only to a few after a long time.[1]

A third disadvantage is that, owing to the infirmity of our judgment and the perturbing force of imagination, there is some admixture of error in most of the investigations of human reason. This would be a reason to many for continuing to doubt even of the most accurate demonstrations, not perceiving the force of the demonstration, and seeing the divers judgments of divers persons who have the name of being wise men. Besides, in the midst of much demonstrated truth there is sometimes an element of error, not demonstrated but asserted on the strength of some plausible and sophistic reasoning that is taken for a demonstration. And therefore it was necessary for the real truth concerning divine things to be presented to men with fixed certainty by way of faith. Wholesome, therefore, is the arrangement of divine clemency, whereby things even that reason can investigate are commanded to be held on faith, so that all might be easily partakers of the knowledge of God, and that without doubt and error (Book I. c. iv.).

[1] Father Rickaby weakens the passage, translating " remaneret " by " dwell long." I have restored the Latin phrase, not in any captious spirit, but because it is to me significant of the absolute candour of the Saint. I do not here enter on the question of man's natural knowledge of God, beyond reminding the reader that it is a distinct question from that of knowing God by philosophical reasoning. This subject was dealt with some thirty years ago in the pages of the *Dublin Review* by Dr. W. G. Ward.

This chapter does not stand alone in its critical
and moderate estimate of the effectiveness and
stability of the unaided human reason, and the
recognition on the part of the writer of the force of
disturbing influences which in practice vitiate its conclusions. In estimating and rejecting the famous ontological argument for Theism, the *Doctor Angelicus*
recognizes clearly the force of habit which leads men
to believe as proved by reason what is really only
rooted firmly by early associations. " Custom," St.
Thomas writes, " takes the place of nature; hence
notions wherewith the mind is imbued from childhood
are held as firmly as if they were naturally known and
self-evident." Again, Aquinas distinguishes between
arguments which may well be used " for the consolation of the faithful," and which presuppose faith
in those to whom they are addressed, and those which
are really cogent by themselves; and urges that the
former should never be used " for the convincing of
opponents, because the mere insufficiency of such
reasoning would rather confirm them in their error,
they thinking that we assent to the truth of faith for
reasons so weak."

Yet we find in the body of the work categorical
conclusions on the details of the world behind the
veil which startle our own habits of thought, and
appear to come strangely from so cautious a thinker.
The cause lies no doubt partly in what has already
been said—that the fashion of the day demanded *some*
categorical reply to every question which was raised :
the categorical form did not necessarily imply, as it
now would, that the position advocated was regarded
as demonstrably true. And questions which the
twentieth century would never even raise were asked

at that time because those were indeed the ages of faith, when God and the world behind the veil lived in the imagination of Christendom as undoubted realities, in spite of the scepticism of coteries. To inquire even minutely into a world which was so intensely real to the writer was an irresistible impulse, and was seconded by the conviction, already alluded to, that arguments in scientific form must lead to real knowledge.

To go further into this side of the work of which I am speaking, and to give the necessary qualifications to what has been said above generally, would need a separate essay. Many of the questions raised are the outcome of an inquiring imagination based on vivid faith in the unseen. Others are those which the Arabian philosophers had discussed, or which had been raised by Aristotle himself—specimens of the philosophical fashion of the hour, a fashion which has passed away, in many cases, as the intellectual fashions of our own day may pass too in their turn; and the most critical reader will, as we have said, rarely if ever be dissatisfied with the answers, assuming the canons of reasoning of the day to be valid, and the problems to be such as can be solved at all by argument.

But I should wish in conclusion to consider two questions. The first concerns the general character of St. Thomas' work viewed as a defence of Christian faith. I would ask, what is the relation of the task which now lies before the student of the Philosophy of Christianity to the scheme which St. Thomas elaborated; secondly, we may ask, what is the practical lesson we may learn from his as to the best method and temper for dealing with the problems raised by the intellectual fashion of the present hour?

As to the first point, we have seen that he found the University of Paris a chaos of rationalistic thought. The tendency manifest a century earlier in Abelard, who subjected such dogmas as the Trinity to rational examination, had assumed gigantic proportions in the course of succeeding years, and had resulted in a rationalistic treatment of the Incarnation, of the dogmas of Creation and of Immortality, and of the whole Christian theology, which ultimately threatened to destroy all faith in those who adopted it. St. Thomas' sharp distinction between truths known by faith and by reason stemmed the tide. Reason unaided might in the hands of an Amalric of Bena be made to prove that there were many incarnations, or, in the teaching of St. Thomas' contemporaries, that the resurrection of the body was incredible; but such beliefs are established in the pages of St. Thomas himself by Scripture, the Fathers and the tradition and definitions of the Church, and should, he maintains, be shut off from the sphere in which discussion on mere grounds of reason is admissible. Thus the rationalistic disputations on revealed dogmas were banished. And, as we have seen, by degrees the new rule prevailed in the lectures of the University professors. Dr. Ueberweg gives as the outcome of the labours of Albertus and Thomas "the complete accomplishment of the, until then imperfect, separation of natural from revealed theology," revealed doctrine " being now maintained on the ground of revelation alone, and withdrawn, as a theological mystery, from the sphere of philosophical speculation." [1]

[1] *History of Philosophy*, Ueberweg (English translation), i., p. 429.

But there was undoubtedly a rationalistic element
in the very method which had prevailed and which
St. Thomas in some measure had to adopt and correct.
The alternative system, which so long contested the
ground with it, is admirably described by Archbishop
Vaughan in his chapter on the school of St. Victor.
This school held to the monastic method which was
ultimately displaced by the scholastic. The reverent
attitude belonging to the old monastic method, its
distrust of all dialectic as applied to things divine, its
sense of human ignorance, its trust, on the other hand,
in the higher illuminated perceptions of the holy—this
was gone from the new mode of reasoning though,
as Archbishop Vaughan truly says, it existed in the
saintly mind of St. Thomas himself. His mind was
largely monastic and Platonic, though his explicit
method was of necessity scholastic and Aristotelian.
The *crede ut intelligas* of St. Anselm, the precursor of
Scholasticism, still preserved this earlier attitude—
this way of using the human reason in things divine.
It was something apart from the new distinction
between the premises applicable to truths of reason
and truths of revelation. It included that sense of
the inadequacy of our reason to penetrate into
mysteries beyond the world of sense, which is represented and exaggerated in modern Agnosticism.
And it included the recognition of a perception on the
part of the individual, whose spirit "tastes" the things
of God. This view is akin to that now represented
in modern theories of "religious experience," which
recognize that the grounds of religious belief must be
largely personal—though too often such theories
substitute mere instinct for illuminated reason. It was
indeed the rationalistic effect of the loss of this earlier

and higher philosophy of the Fathers which made so necessary the marked separation between the two kinds of truth. A reason, stretching out reverent hands towards things divine, might be allowed to touch the most sacred truths. But the meddling rationalistic reason of the thirteenth-century pantheists could not. It must be simply "hands off" for the rationalists so far as the hallowed ground of revelation was concerned.

The term "faith" is still used in our theological text-books only in St. Thomas' sense of belief on the authority of God revealing. But it stands in popular writings for something over and above reason, namely, that process or attitude of the spirit and mind of man, which leads him to believe in God Himself as well as in revelation. It recognizes at once the certainty of revelation and the inadequacy of the human mind fully to analyze its grounds or its contents. This attitude is recognized pre-eminently by St. Bernard, and even, as we have said, by the earliest of the scholastics, St. Anselm. The age of sharp distinctions, and of a dialectic which regarded only ground common to all minds alike, banished so personal an element from the *terrain* recognized by philosophy, though unable to banish it from life.

It has not perhaps even now returned to our theory of knowledge as fully as right reason demands. But Coleridge and Newman saw its importance, and it formed the staple of their philosophy of "faith." Just as Hegel analyzed "self-realization by self-denial," which had from the beginning been the secret of Christianity, so the task now lies before us of analyzing those attitudes of mind and instruments of knowledge, the different estimates of which issue, on the one hand in Theism and Christianity, and on the other in Agnosticism.

The method of Aristotle could not effectually penetrate beyond the world of sense, and the greatest brilliancy in the dialectical tournament could not enable the combatants to soar above the wrestling ground on which it was conducted. The wings needed to soar can only be given by that philosophy which underlies the Gospels themselves, a philosophy which finds partial expression in Plato, which lies at the root of St. Bernard's assaults on Abelard, which is lightly traced in St. Anselm's *Cur Deus Homo?* An appraisement of the personal apprehension of the Divine by the human conscience, and especially by the illuminated intelligence of the Saints, is essential to an adequate philosophy of religious belief. St. Thomas separated the sphere of faith from that of reason, and preserved the former from rationalistic treatment by a distinction which also shut off some of the earlier defences of revealed doctrine. But the process whereby the mind passes from the one sphere to the other needed for its full investigation the philosophy of the Fathers. Archbishop Vaughan rightly insists on the fact that that Philosophy was Platonic, while St. Thomas' method was Aristotelic. The spirit of the former the Angelic Doctor preserved in his own highest mental instincts. But its principles are not those of his explicit system. "His 'angelic' bias," writes Archbishop Vaughan, "was Platonic, his school gifts Aristotelic." [1]

But in the second and still more practical matter : How shall the Christian theologian deal with the secular learning of his time ? we have everything to

[1] *Life of St. Thomas of Aquin*, ii., pp. 671, 672.

learn from St. Thomas. Father Rickaby in a valuable essay has commended the *Summa contra Gentiles* as conveying, especially to contemporary theologians, a sense of the duty and necessity of keeping abreast of the thought and learning of their age. And this warning becomes the more impressive if what has been said above is true, namely, that the new learning and the movement of thought of the thirteenth century did involve elements which not all the genius of St. Thomas could make other than they were—elements of an essentially rationalistic method. Human reason, even aided by the authoritative premises which the later scholastics invoked, was unequal to the positive determination of many of the problems it attempted to solve. The distinction so strongly insisted on, between the two classes of truths, averted rationalistic conclusions, and preserved the sacred territory of revelation from rationalistic assault ; but it could not save a system at once sceptical and credulous, of universal inquisitiveness and of trust in the all-solving power of the syllogism, from being both unreasonable and rationalistic, if viewed apart from the strong antidotes supplied by the Saint. Nevertheless, this system had so completely got possession of the educated world that St. Thomas, with a singular and wise boldness, undertook the task of reconciling it with Christian theology.

And let us mark the result. He did not satisfy his contemporaries by any means universally. Certain propositions from his works were condemned by the bishop who presided over the very scene of his lectures, —by Bishop Tempier of Paris,—three years after his death. His lectures had not the magical effect of at once dispelling in the University an unruly movement of thought. Archbishop Vaughan recognizes the fact that the movement outlived the Saint. Yet the writings which he left behind him gave just what was needed for the rising generation, as his lectures had given it for his own immediate pupils. Those who were disposed to believe in the Christian theology, and yet were troubled by the antagonism between what they regarded as the genius and learning of the day, and the old theological writings which took no account of them, found rest in this reconciliation of the truths of philosophy and faith by one who united the reverent temper of a Saint with a mind of consummate ability. And when the generation incurably habituated to rationalistic discussion had passed away, the orderly structure of theological science provided by Aquinas prevailed so completely, that within fifty years of his death *il buon fra Tommaso* towers with almost the authority of an inspired writer over the epoch of Dante, as we plainly see in the *Divina Commedia* itself.

This is the lesson which appears to me to be at the present hour the more universally valuable, just because it speaks to those who are most alive to the perverse elements of the characteristic thought of our own time and to its excesses. Let it be granted that some of the extremely speculative conclusions put forth by exponents of the higher criticism are as extravagant as the medieval belief that the syllogism could discover the secrets of nature, that they are sometimes as unreliable from their extreme fancifulness as the replies to the most insoluble problems made by those medieval schoolmen whose excessive subtlety Leo XIII. gently reproved. Yet to proscribe the really scientific use of that critical method which has hold of all minds which think on such subjects, would be as ineffectual now as the bonfires fed by living rationalists were in the Paris of 1209. On the other hand, a strenuous effort to deal with modern criticism, to keep it within its reasonable limits, to restrain by its own principles a method which professes to be cautious and experimental, but which is constantly proving itself in the highest degree theoretical, speculative and adventurous, is just the medicine which will remedy the ills of the hour after the manner of Albertus and Thomas. If work in the field marked out by the "higher criticism" is occasionally touched by some of the defects of the method it has to use, that does not make it the less necessary. If those few who are competent to undertake it are afforded no scope for their energies, humanly speaking, the movement of criticism must lead widely to the destruction of faith, especially in those masses of half-educated people for whose especial benefit the avoidance of unsettling discussions is professedly designed. It is quite true that, in the earliest stages of such a movement, the simple are those whose faith is most easily overset on a first acquaintance with the new problems ; but questions which are now mooted in the *Daily Mail* and *Daily Telegraph* cannot be regarded as permanently the secrets of the learned few. And when such questions are widely raised, it is precisely the simpler souls, those least qualified to meet them rationally, who most need a recognized literature the work of men at once expert as critics and orthodox as theologians. Such a literature is the indispensable guide and authority for the average mind. Its very existence, and its recognition on the part of the official rulers, are a support to him. If it exists, his faith is saved. If it does not, humanly speaking, it goes.

# XII

## CARDINAL NEWMAN ON CONSTRUCTIVE RELIGIOUS THOUGHT

Cardinal Newman, in speaking of the scholastic theology which emerged from the new apologetic of St. Thomas, and from his attempt to reconcile the thought of his day with the essence of Christian tradition, points out that it "involved a creative act of the intellect." In the earlier period, popularly known as the Dark Ages, theology had been, he reminds us, mainly in the hands of devout Benedictine monks, whose "intellect attempted no comprehension of this multiform world." It had consisted in "a loving study and exposition of Holy Scripture according to the teaching of the Fathers, who had studied and expounded it before them. It was a loyal adherence to the teaching of the past, a faithful inculcation of it, an anxious transmission of it to the next generation." Theology was receptive, not creative. The period in question was not marked by that intellectual activity which makes on the one hand brilliant heresiarchs, on the other great constructive theologians.

But if we go back earlier again to the patristic period, we have once more a creative movement of thought. "Origen, Tertullian, Athanasius, Chrysostom, Augustine, Jerome, Leo," writes Cardinal

Newman in his *Historical Sketches*,[1] "are authors of powerful original minds, and engaged in the production of original works." Yet earlier we have another period of simple receptivity. The earlier sub-apostolic days had been in this respect like the later epoch of the monks. Theology had meant the anxious and reverent transmission of what had been received,—of the teaching of the Apostles. In the modern sense, indeed, theology did not exist. It did not profess to be a science. The Christian brotherhood belonged mainly to the uncultured classes and was one in mind. The first Pontiff had been a fisherman, and vivid faith rather than learning or intellectual subtlety characterized the community. Each man received in unquestioning simplicity what he was taught. Creative and constructive Christian thought was first demanded when this simple, unquestioning, unanalytical attitude of mind became impossible, because the character of the community changed. When thinkers and philosophers became Christians, and attempted, each in his own way, the intellectual explication of the faith, sects and heresies arose of necessity, and called in response for the work of the creative theologians. These men dealt with the philosophical theories broached by various thinkers, and rejected or assimilated them as the essential character of the Christian revelation demanded.

Origen, in writing against Celsus, notes this advance from the unity existing among the simple Christians of early days, to the divisions which speculation necessarily brought. "When," he says, "men, not slaves and mechanics only, but also many of the educated classes in Greece, saw something

[1] II. p. 475.

venerable in Christianity, sects necessarily arose, not simply from love of strife and contradiction, but because many learned men strove to penetrate more deeply into the truths of Christianity." [1]  It was this effort, then, which led to the development on the one hand of heresy, on the other of constructive Christian thought.

The original conservative spirit of Christianity was not, however, abrogated.  It remained as a check upon random speculation.  It traced deeply the lines of the original revelation which was a guide to the theologians in their work.  This conservative element was especially represented by the official rulers of the Church, the spiritual descendants of the Apostles. To guard the original revelation, the *depositum fidei* which had been committed to them, was their primary duty.  If Rome be regarded as the normal representative of tradition and stable rule, and of the conservatism which this implies, this function may be styled the "Roman" element in the polity of the Church.  On the other hand, new aspects of thought not expressly contemplated in the simple divine message, yet bearing upon its application and interpretation, could not but present themselves to active minds which were stimulated to inquiry by the philosophies of the day. And this force, pressing onwards towards change and necessitating further explication of the revelation in definite thought forms, may perhaps be spoken of as the "Greek" element in the Church.  While then the Roman element—that is to say, the force embodying tradition, rule, uniformity—was represented primarily by the authorities, the Greek element—that is, the force embodying vital thought—was asserted by the

[1] See Origen, *Contra Celsum*, III. 12.

adventurous thinkers who became heresiarchs, and by
the creative theologians. It is hardly an exaggeration to say that the whole history of theology is the
record of the interaction between these two forces.
The difference between the two representatives of the
Greek element was that the heretics recognized
insufficiently or not at all that higher knowledge
which should check or modify their own speculations,
while the orthodox theologians realized as thought
what the authorities guarded as law, namely, the
essential genius of the Christian tradition and revelation. This realization might almost be compared to
a chemical test, whereby they determined how far
contemporary speculations were or were not admissible
without endangering the faith that was committed to
the Church for ever.

Careful historians representing standpoints as
different as those of Cardinal Newman and Harnack
have pointed out that the very first thorough-going
exercise of the intellect on the Christian faith brought
into relief the phenomena of which I speak. The
Gnostics, as both writers agree,[1] were the first to
exercise the intellect systematically on Christianity.
In doing so they lost sight of the Apostolic tradition
and rejected the Old Testament. St. Irenæus opposed
to their bold speculations the original Christian rule
of faith, and rejected their theories as on the whole
unorthodox. Yet the influence of Gnosticism on
subsequent Christian thought is recognized on all
hands to have been very great, and Newman traces

[1] "The Gnostics," writes Newman, "seem first to have systematically
thrown the intellect upon matters of faith" (*Essay on Development*, p.
365). Harnack describes them as "the first to transform Christianity
into a system of doctrines" (*History of Dogma*, English translation,
Williams and Norgate, I. p. 227).

to the Gnostics ideas which were eventually accepted in a modified form by orthodox theologians, when once Christian thought had asserted its supremacy and vindicated the sacredness of tradition. "Gnosticism has left an enduring mark in the history of the Church," says a writer in the *Catholic Dictionary*. "The Arian heresy itself did not contribute more to the development of Catholic doctrine." "The scientific labours in the Church," writes Harnack, "were a continuation of the Gnostic schools under altered circumstances, *i.e.* under the sway of a tradition which was now more clearly defined and more firmly fenced round as a *noli me tangere*."[1] The Gnostic speculations were among those which supplied, as Newman points out, "the raw material" which the Church "had the power by means of the certainty and firmness of her principles to convert to her own uses."[2]

The contest between the Roman and Greek elements was more simple at the outset than it became later on. Conservatism, when that which was to be preserved was the divine revelation as the Apostles had handed it down, was hardly on the same plane with the speculative theories, which it nevertheless rightly checked and controlled. But when the first great creative period was over, when the theology of the Fathers with its large Greek element was accepted as authoritative, all the intensely conservative genius of Catholicism resumed its sway with a new consequence. It was not simply the divine revelation, the original *depositum fidei* committed to inspired Apostles, which was preserved by the faithful and by

---

[1] See Harnack's whole analysis of this interesting view of the case, *History of Dogma*, I. pp. 226 *seq.*

[2] See *Essay on the Development of Christian Doctrine*, p. 364.

the monastic theologians as sacred, but its exposition
by men—saintly and learned men, and of great genius
it is true—but still by men who were not individually in-
fallible, and whose thought was largely conditioned by
the intellectual characteristics of their own epoch and
determined by its controversies. The very definitions
of the Church were led up to and called for by those
controversies. And though vigilant theologians have
ever remembered this fact, and pointed out that not
the antecedent reasonings but only the definitions
themselves were divinely guaranteed, the mental effort
necessary for the thorough and accurate separation of
the divine from the human element in the theological
process of which they were the outcome, could not
always be successfully made. The existing theology
was preserved as sacred with its human and divine
elements together. This fact helped to make the
scholastic revolution of the thirteenth century widely
regarded at first as unorthodox in tendency, even
apart from the actual heresies to which it gave cur-
rency. For any great theological innovation appeared
to touch with rude hands the sacred structure which it
seemed profanation to examine with critical scrutiny.

But still more was the situation complicated when
the highly speculative movement of the thirteenth
century, having run its course as heresy and become
modified and regulated by Albertus Magnus and St.
Thomas into at first tolerated and then approved
orthodoxy, entered upon its last stage. The approved
writings of the Scholastics came to be regarded as
venerable oracles, and were received by the many
almost without question. A body of thought stamped
by the most marked peculiarities of the age in which
it was elaborated, was almost inevitably invested with

the sacredness belonging to the time-honoured theology which is the approved guardian of the deposit. Its jealous preservation was now the natural means of fulfilling the precept, *depositum custodi.*

For the restful life of devotion this was simply gain, for it meant the return to the normal and desirable Christian attitude of unquestioning and un critical belief. But rest for the faithful did not mean intellectual finality, and in the field of controversy this state of things brought obvious disadvantages. The separation of the divine and human elements became very difficult in a theological structure so complicated; indeed perhaps nothing short of an urgent intellectual necessity could make it even approximately possible. Thus a mass of minute reasoning came down to later times, accepted very largely on authority, and less capable in each succeeding generation of convincing the intellect of ages whose culture and axioms of reasoning became ever further removed from the medieval. Its developments became in some cases fantastic. Readers of the *Life of Sir Thomas More* know how even in the sixteenth century the disadvantages of this state of things were already felt. The scholastic writings then popular were in More's eyes like an acrobatic display, a system of guess-work, clever but unnatural, and by no means effectual in building up a strong and healthy Christian intelligence, which should (he maintained) rather seek its nourishment in Scripture and the Fathers. He thus addresses the typical representative of the system :

Let us suppose that Scripture is easy and your questions difficult, yet the knowledge of the former may be far more fruitful than the guessing at the latter. To dance, or bend double like an acrobat, is more difficult than to walk, and it

2 A

is easier to masticate bread than to grind potsherds between the teeth, but what man would not prefer the common processes of nature to such empty feats ? Which, then, of these disciplines is the easier I will not ask, but I cannot hear it said that these minute questionings are more useful than the knowledge of the sacred writings to the flock for which Christ died.[1]

More maintains that anything added by the schoolmen to the teaching of the Fathers and the Scriptures is not to be regarded as essential to a Catholic's belief. But, on the other hand, the systematic form adopted by the schoolmen had obvious controversial advantages, and the scholastic method flourished after the Reformation. More himself became less critical, and more alive to the dangerous consequences of dissatisfaction with the existing state of things within the Church. The ecclesiastical revolution gave new authority to all the forces of law and conservatism—and among them to the writings of the schoolmen.

I propose here to speak of a movement of Christian thought in the nineteenth century which suddenly gave to the Catholic intellect a new direction, —which developed what I have termed the "Greek" element in quite a new field. Scholasticism, which had represented the Greek element—that is, the living thought of the age—in the thirteenth century, had come, at the end of the seventeenth century, to be the most serviceable embodiment of the Roman element—the instrument for securing order and uniformity, the organ of reverent, unquestioning, uncritical, conservative tradition. The great schoolmen,

[1] See Father Bridgett's *Life of Sir Thomas More*, Burns & Oates, pp. 91, 92.

of course, as St. Thomas and St. Bonaventure, had
given to theology thoughts which were a legacy for all
time. Great truths were enshrined in the works of
Suarez, de Lugo and their contemporaries. But the
cast of their thought and expression did not belong to
and often did not appeal to the age. And the still
later scholastics, whom Lacordaire compared to Swiss
guides, who all follow the same fixed routes,[1] appeared
to their critics to repeat almost mechanically the
expressions of the earlier, not adequately realizing
either the thought of the thirteenth century or that of
their own day. Something else was needed to represent what I have called the Greek element—to be to
Catholic thought what the works of Clement and
Aquinas had each been in their own time. That something came, and had to fix its relations with the older
theology. The process of adjustment between the
two has not yet reached its term. Let us study its
beginnings, that we may be the better able to forecast
its future.

I have pointed out incidentally that what comes
ultimately to be spoken of as "theology" may be in
the making partly "Apologetic," and partly an attempt
at the reconciliation of contemporary thought with
Christianity. The earliest Christian writers, St.
Justin and his contemporaries, undertook Apologetic
against the heathen. St. Irenæus defended traditional
Christianity against the Gnostics. The defence of
orthodoxy against Pelagians, Donatists and other
heretics brought out some of St. Augustine's finest
work. Both the controversial and assimilative work
of the Fathers is familiar to readers of Newman's

[1] See *Inner Life of Lacordaire*, English translation, Burns & Oates,
p. 72.

*Essay on Development.* St. Thomas also first outlined his theology in his avowedly apologetic *Summa contra Gentiles.* And much of the greater and later *Summa Theologiæ*, which, in his own time, was undertaken as apologetic work, occupying a field considerably wider than theology as it was understood in still earlier days, became the model of the theology for the future. That is to say, it became the acknowledged scientific exposition of the Christian revelation in its consequences and in its relation to other fields of knowledge.

The "creative" religious thought called for by more modern inquiries has occupied a wider field than that contemplated in the theology of St. Thomas, just as his theology covered wider ground than the Patristic. The creative theology of the Fathers was the outcome of the work of thoughtful and learned Christians writing what they felt to be needed for existing circumstances. So, too, St. Thomas from his professor's chair at Paris had to expound the Christian faith to men imbued with the culture given by Greek, Arabian, and Jewish philosophy. The form of exposition was determined in each case by the emergency. Posterity saw in both a creative contribution to theology. For the writers themselves it was enough that they tried to meet the needs of thinking Christians.

I will here attempt an outline of a modern intellectual movement which has at least the qualities just quoted : (1) that it has utilized the characteristic thought of the day in expounding and defending Christianity ; (2) that it has been in one of its phases apologetic ; (3) that it is in another phase an attempt partially to reconcile Christian thought with modern

methods and modern science,—that it has striven
to unify from the Christian standpoint the general
knowledge represented in the Universities of the
nineteenth and twentieth centuries, as Alexander of
Hales and St. Thomas strove to unify that of medieval
Paris. This last work is that which is systematically attempted in the *Institut de St. Thomas* at
Louvain.[1]

Speaking broadly, the story of the nineteenth
century within the Catholic Church presents the
following sequences. Pius VII. came to the papal
throne at its dawn, when the Church was at a very
low ebb of power, and its dissolution was prophesied.
The papacy naturally welcomed support wherever it
could get it. Many eminent writers, some Catholic
in faith, some only in sympathy,—philosophers,
historians, writers of romance, as well as theologians,
arose at this supreme moment to place before the
imagination of the world the beauty and beneficence
of the Christian Church, of its saints, its thinkers, its
institutions. They carried triumphantly a movement of
reaction against the unjust and unphilosophical depreciation of tradition, in religion and in social life, which
had culminated in the philosophy of the Encyclopedists
and the French Revolution. While the allied powers
were combining to restore the venerable dynasties of
Europe, and the papacy itself, and to enlist against
revolutionary unrest all the dignity and stability of
historic claims, a somewhat similar work was being
done by a large section of European thinkers in
regard to religion. The value of the Church as a
social factor was recognized by many who did not

[1] The reader may be referred to the *Dublin Review* of July, 1913, for
an account of the Louvain philosophical system.

regard it as divine. The best intellect of the times combined to reinstate the ancient Church as it were with foreign bayonets, when its own soldiers had suffered defeat. Writers like A. W. Schlegel, Novalis and Tieck united with such Catholic champions as Chateaubriand, de Maistre, Frederick Schlegel and de Bonald. They restored the influence of historical Christianity and of Catholicism with the aid of considerations suggested by the intellectual genius of the hour, when the Catholic theological schools, cast in the medieval mould, had proved unequal to the task of influencing a world which had rejected their fundamental axioms and many of their canons of reasoning. A general movement ensued, of research and thought, inspired by that aspect of Christianity which appeared most significant to the time-spirit.

The story of the new apologetic at its headquarters, in the land of the great revolution, has been retold within the last few years by a writer who is in an especial sense an heir to its labours, the late M. Léon Ollé Laprune, in his book, *La Vitalité Chrétienne.* I shall here avail myself of the testimony of one who was so intimately acquainted with its details.

" The eighteenth century," says this distinguished French writer, "had banished Christianity from the cultivated world, from the thinking world. It was to be the work of the nineteenth century to bring it back." This was the aim of the new Apologetic. The eighteenth century had been for Catholic theology a period of inertia. The great struggle with Protestantism was practically over. The intellect of the age had passed on to free thought. The Church was despised by the thinkers.    She rested after her long battle almost unnoticed.[1]

And that battle had had one result, which lent itself to crystallization in her theology and her polity. It had been a vigorous defensive movement against the onslaught of the reformers on behalf of the existing system and existing authority and institutions. An immense effort of consolidation had been made. The tendency among Catholic thinkers of the early sixteenth century to assimilate much of the culture of the Renaissance epoch was abruptly checked by the stern necessity of defending the medieval theology. Men like Erasmus and More in different ways and degrees marked the transition.   Sympathetic in their earlier days to a wide culture, hostile to the dogmatism of a degenerate scholasticism, severe critics of abuses among the ecclesiastical authorities, and tolerant of new ideas, both of them recognized before they died that criticism must give place to union in the presence of the common foe.   For Catholics had before them a struggle *pro aris et focis*.   More declared that he would rather burn with his own hand his early criticisms on ecclesiastical abuses than that they should be used as a weapon against the Church.   The common danger demanded a united front for the defence of the very life of the Church.

The great theologians of Trent and their successors busied themselves in filling up *lacunæ*, in classifying and further defining dogmas, to make them bullet-proof against the enemy.   The accepted answer to current

[1] Ranke declares that no single work from the pen of an orthodox writer made any impression during the period which elapsed between the date of Louis XIV. and the Revolution (*History of the Popes*, vol. ii. p. 292).

heresy—the anti-Protestant limitation of dogma—
compactly stated, was the serviceable weapon for the
Catholic students.   Thus equipped they applied for
marching orders from their general.   Few, if any,
were able to carry on the deeper intellectual life,
receptive and assimilative, of peaceful civilization.
The creative genius within the Church seemed to
concentrate itself almost entirely on the movement—
at once spiritual and militant—represented by such
saints as St. Ignatius, St. Philip Neri, and St. Charles
Borromeo.   So far as intellectual effort was displayed,
its function was, as we have said, defensive and
practical, completing the statement of old positions
rather than surveying new ones.   The extreme of
intellectual completeness thus attained was in reality
in its very nature premature, and therefore its form
was temporary.   For Catholic thinkers needed time
to survey completely a new field in its relation to
ancient principles.

To some extent this "state of siege," as it has been
called, continued up to the eighteenth century, and
was then succeeded by a period in which the anti-
Protestant weapons were no longer an urgent necessity,
and yet remained the stock-in-trade of the orthodox
armoury.   The "Christian and Catholic idea," to use
M. Ollé Laprune's phrase, "the living principle of
further growth, found little expression in the France
of Louis Quinze."   It was, in the same writer's words,
"veiled by its own adherents."   A certain fatigue
after the long struggle perhaps contributed to this
result.   It needed freshness and energy to fight
effectively in the heavy armour which was no longer
needed.   But Christian thought arose again suddenly,
full of life and vigour, at the crisis which the closing

years of the century created, and seemed to shake off
its trammels and move freely as of old in a new intellectual medium.

The new apologetic, coming in upon the wave of
a great reaction against the French Revolution and
its intellectual harbingers, purported to blend the
" Christian idea " once again with the thought of the
times—to show that it was not a stranger or an enemy
to the lawful aspirations of the modern world, but was
even necessary for their satisfaction. This new movement of thought, says M. Ollé Laprune, had to " detach
itself from the immediate past," and derive its inspiration not from a period of torpor and numbness, following on another period of militant defence of positions
long since determined, but from epochs of life and
growth. It took up, for the most part, different
ground from the scholastic treatises, and appealed to
the original source of their life. The two great
creative epochs—the Middle Ages, and the Patristic
Era, when the Christian idea first worked out its true
relations with Greek thought—were the times to
which the glance of the new apologetic was turned,
not in a spirit of blind repetition of ancient phrases,
but, on the contrary, as a modern soldier gains from
the example of the " preux chevalier " who fought with
lance and shield, the spirit though not the weapons
with which he may approach his own campaign. To
realize the life which had created the medieval scholastic treatises must be to emancipate Catholics from an
unintelligent and rigid perpetuation of their inevitable
limitations ; from their " over-great subtlety " which
Leo XIII. once contrasted with the larger wisdom of
St. Thomas Aquinas himself. Only a dead body is
rigid. And its rigidity precedes decay. The living

Christian idea had in past times seized and penetrated the thought of the actual civilized world in which it moved. It had to do so again.

And with this object the Catholic thinkers of the early nineteenth century laboured at a time when the world was estranged from their faith. The conquests of physical science and the advances of critical research were slowly making definite that conception of the empirical method applied to the universe, regarded as a developing organism, which is characteristic of our age. The philosophy of history and its critical study received immense development. An ascertainment of the laws of progress, and of the relation of phenomena to their environment, based on an induction from the facts of science and from the story of mankind, was gradually being understood as the key to a scientific view of the world. Physical science, history, criticism, archæology, these were the fields in which modern thought and research were exercising themselves. In all those fields the Catholics laboured. Three men, as we know, were the pioneers of the movement— mainly in the field of history—Chateaubriand, de Maistre, and de Bonald. Chateaubriand brought the past of Christianity to life again and depicted its life-giving power and its beneficence. De Maistre and de Bonald in different ways seized upon the conception of evolution. De Maistre, in M. Ollé Laprune's words, "renewing the philosophy of history of Bossuet, applied it in living form to the present. 'Nothing,' he urged, 'is improvized in the social and political world.' He thus anticipates the philosophy [so-called] of evolution and Taine's manner of viewing history." Bonald's analysis of the individual reason as a factor in the universal reason, both exercised on the primitive

tradition which came from God, is another aspect of
the same philosophy.

The eighteenth century had seen the Church
identified with clerical officialism and a priesthood
which, though including admirable individuals, was on
the whole intellectually and even morally decadent.
It was depressed in general estimation. It could
never—Goethe had maintained at the time—hold its
own again among the great and cultivated. These
three champions of the Church, on the other hand,
were laymen, statesmen, men whose names stood high
in the world of intellect, noblemen of social influence,
great figures in the political world. De Bonald's
views were afterwards developed by Lamennais with
unique genius and eloquence. "The clergy adopted
Chateaubriand as their master. The author of *Du
Pape* was another leader to them." He was quoted
from the pulpit, and "a new view of politics drawn
from Christianity" was adopted under his guidance.
Lamennais, the successor of de Bonald, was hailed in
1817 as a second Bossuet.

During the years which succeeded, up to the very
middle of the century, the promise thus held out
seemed in a fair way towards realization. In spite
of the catastrophe of Lamennais' career the torrent
of Catholic genius was too strong to be stemmed.
Another layman, the Comte de Montalembert,
wore not unworthily the mantle of de Maistre,
and developed the work of Chateaubriand. Like
them he was a considerable social figure, a prominent
personage in the political world. He depicted, as
Chateaubriand had done, the glories of Christian history, his chosen field being the records of monasti-
cism. Ozanam, also a layman, continued the work of

drawing from history a view of the Christian Church which was comprehensive and free from unfair partisanship. Lacordaire was, in M. Ollé Laprune's opinion, the founder of a distinct class of apologists. And he might claim more truly than Lamennais to be a successor to Bossuet. Père Gratry brought into philosophy the comparative and historical method, and was "undeniably in France the great Catholic philosopher of the nineteenth century." Bautain, in his chair of philosophy in the *Collège Royal*, "created a philosophical and religious movement, sketched a system, brought about wonderful conversions, formed a school, and, what is better, a society of living thought and feeling [*d'esprits et d'âmes*]." Other eminent leaders and many distinguished followers were to be found working at the same time, with the same enthusiasm and the same object—the tracing of the Christian ideal in all fields of human activity. Ravignan, Père Félix, Dupanloup, Gerbet, Charles Lenormant, Dom Pitra, Comte de Falloux, Henri Perreyve, are only a few among those whom M. Ollé Laprune claims as all sharing in different ways in the same effort. De Tocqueville, too, though like Chateaubriand he had not the practical personal Christianity of the great leaders, took his share in the intellectual movement.

When Leo XII. succeeded Pius in 1823, this movement of ideas had begun to make itself felt; and it imparted a largeness and hopefulness of Catholic thought which was hailed with satisfaction in Rome. The writers had shown, together with the freshness of genius of a de Maistre and a de Bonald, that devotion to the Holy See which marked the *Du Pape*. And the Holy Father welcomed the volunteers who so

ably defended his cause. It was this spirit which
kindled the intellect and imagination of our own Cardinal Wiseman, whose mind was formed in Rome at
this very time.

M. Ollé Laprune regards the year 1835 as
marking the time when the movement first became
a veritable power in France. Lacordaire was
then thirty-three, Ravignan forty, Montalembert
and Ozanam in their twenties. It proceeded without serious let or hindrance up to 1852. It was
perhaps at its height in 1845. Lacordaire, then a
Dominican in the full maturity of his powers, was
giving his conferences in Nôtre Dame. Montalembert had just delivered his famous address on
behalf of the liberty of the religious orders and liberty
of teaching. Ozanam was at the height of his influence as professor of the Sorbonne. Ravignan, at the
instance of Dupanloup, had published his work on
the Jesuits. The genius of these men dominated
the French Church in the eyes of the world; and
French Catholics were apparently united in recognizing their leadership.

But the elements of division were all along present, though for the time they were latent. Men
will work together, however opposed in views or
temperament, to save from wreck the ship which
bears them all alike. But when the danger is over,
and they meet daily at meals, at work, at recreation,
without this strong uniting bond, personal antipathies,
or differences of tradition, of temperament, of view or
ideal, eventually become apparent. And so the bright
dawn of common constructive endeavour, at once
intellectual and spiritual, among Catholics, became
overclouded with the threatenings of dissension. The

allied powers of Christian genius reinstated the influence of the Church, which the weapons of officialism and a too conservative scholasticism had been powerless to defend against the "time-spirit." But in renewing the power of the Church they had renewed that also of the officials and the men of theological routine. The old Gallican clergy, especially representative of the eighteenth century defects were the official rulers in France. The old difficulty that a good deal of the traditional intellectual armoury was out of joint with the times was revived in an aggravated form. And if it was out of harmony with "the times," so, too, it was in a measure opposed to the genius of the new apologists. The elements both of numbing inertia and of blind repression were present. The conflict ensued, as old as the world, between those who were the real efficient intellectual support of Catholic doctrine in contemporary controversy, who had moreover restored the influence of Catholicism, and the representatives of an older intellectual and ecclesiastical aristocracy. The mayors of the palace had come to the front. But the representatives of the old order refused to become *rois fainéants*, or to give free scope to the newer school.

The machinery of ecclesiastical authority, for which the traditionalist and romantic thinkers had cleared the ground, resumed its accustomed groove. Incidental errors were sought out and condemned in the writings of Apologists who were defending the Church by novel lines of thought. By a curious irony of events Lamennais, who had done so much to increase the moral influence of the papacy, became, through his unbridled liberalism, the first victim of the weapons he had sharpened anew, and was censured by a papal encyclical. Hermes and Günther were condemned by the Holy See for excesses in the direction of rationalism. Bautain was condemned by his Bishop for the opposite extreme of " fideism." Rome condemned in Ubaghs, and in Bonetty, the exaggerations of that defence of the value of tradition which had been the very means of reinstating Catholic thought in the eyes of the world.

These condemnations were loyally accepted by all Catholics. But a marked difference of view became manifest in regard to the real bearing of such acts of authority on Catholic speculation. While to some they were signs that a loyal Catholic should desist from the endeavour to enter into the thought of the nineteenth century and meet it on its own ground, and should simply encase himself in the ready-made scholastic defences, to others they were but a reminder that in the first attempt, however useful and able, to adapt Catholic thought to new conditions, incidental error is almost inevitable. This latter class deprecated an attitude, visible in some of the excessively conservative thinkers, which confined its appreciation of the censured writers to the detection of their excesses or errors in thought and expression, and was not alive to the great importance of the intellectual movement among Catholics of which condemned propositions might be but incidental defects or exaggerations. St. Augustine's polemic against Pelagius was not the less invaluable because Jansenius could, by exaggerating portions of the saint's theory, form a heresy. Lines of thought which, in spite of occasional error or inaccuracy in their expression, were really calculated to influence the age, were thus regarded by one class as the intellectual hope for the Catholic schools in the future, to be pruned, amended, and freed from error, but pursued with loyal enthusiasm ;[1] by the other class they were viewed as suspect and tainted with heterodoxy and to be kept far at a distance. And these two views were the basis of subsequent developments.

The new intellectual life, which seemed welcome to Rome when Leo. XII. received Lamennais with honour, won less encouragement from ecclesiastical authority during the reign of Gregory XVI. Undoubtedly the political dangers of liberalism at this time had a share in the fear which supervened at Rome of all that appeared to savour of free thought. It was hard completely to dissociate the speculative movement from the practical. And the revolution of 1848 appeared to confirm the worst fears of the prophets of evil. After Pius IX.'s generous attempts to meet the liberal politicians of Italy halfway had failed, an intensely conservative reaction in philosophy and theology, as well as in politics, set in at Rome. Liberalism became a watchword which aroused such bitter memories and associations that the more discriminating judgments of an earlier time were for a while set aside by many influential Catholic writers of the school represented by M. Louis Veuillot, of the *Univers*. The new civilization had proved itself, it seemed, the enemy of the Church. The neo-scholastic revival followed. Some of its promoters

---

[1] This was of course the view of Cardinal Newman. So, too, M. Ollé Laprune, speaking on behalf of the French school of writers to which he belongs, says that "the errors which we are now able to discern and which the Church has condemned" are no reason for swerving from the attempt "to find out how the Church and this age can understand one another, love one another and reunite" (p. 76).

allied themselves to absolutist and untheological writers like the editor of the *Univers* in carrying out a policy of *non possumus* in the relations of the Church with the modern world. The profound injustice of the policy of Cavour and Victor Emmanuel, in their attack on the States of the Church a few years later, deepened the lines of this general policy, and made its pursuit among many Catholics a passion.

Still the most far-sighted thinkers—such as Dupanloup and Lacordaire—regarded the very worst episodes in contemporary history as quite insufficient to warrant any drawing back from the attempt to bring Catholic thought and learning abreast of the civilization of the hour. They held that an open-minded and candid treatment of all public questions was the one hope for Catholics, even if better days were far distant. It was, however, excessively difficult for Catholics who were suffering at the hands of an unscrupulous foe to adopt the serene impartiality of the critics whose standpoint was neutral, and who were for the most part thinkers rather than men of action. Catholics in France, Germany, England, and Italy came to be divided roughly into two schools of thought—those who attempted still to fit Catholic apologetics to influence the modern world, and those who, exasperated at the irreligious tendencies of the age, fell back on older intellectual forms and treated the modern world as an enemy. The works, which professed to represent scientific theology, and were still the text-books in the seminaries, made little or no systematic attempt to incorporate the thought of the former class of writers,—to assimilate the new apologetic. It was indeed still largely tolerated by authority ; but it was no longer, as it had been, in special favour in high places. It barely touched the theological schools,[1] which returned definitely to the old groove, to the form in which so much of the very best thought of the Church in the past was enshrined, but which, from its very logical completeness and absoluteness of method, did not readily assimilate a newer culture. The Munich Brief of 1863 tended to emphasize the wisdom of "standing in the old ways," and the subsequent Encyclical and Syllabus told in the same direction. The *intransigeants* of the *Univers* invoked these official utterances against the wisdom, and even against the orthodoxy, of the new apologists.

The attitude of which I have spoken as characteristic of the more conservative thinkers in the 'sixties, even if it was inevitable, was attended by serious dangers. The strenuous enforcement of the principle of authority from 1855 to 1870 became more and more closely bound up with the tendency to identify philosophical thought among Catholics with the obedient acceptance of a system. And that system, while its fundamental principles were profound and true, fell short in its very truths of many vital issues in the thought of the age. A loss of reality, and even of deep sincerity, in Catholic thought appeared to many to follow as a consequence. This danger was perceived by the abler thinkers of all schools. Among Englishmen, so devoted a scholastic theologian as Mr. Ward, of the *Dublin Review*, deprecated it in language quite as strong as was used by Mr. Simpson or Lord Acton in the pages of the *Rambler*.[2] It was not

---

[1] Perrone no doubt took some account of it. But it can hardly be said that he did so with special success.

[2] "Three-fourths of the arguments in ordinary text-books seem to me fictitious," writes Mr. Ward. "The writer never asks himself the question whether they are valid arguments, but merely whether they will

entirely overlooked even among the neo-scholastic philosophers themselves. Father Kleutgen urged, in his great work on Scholastic Philosophy, the necessity of supplementing that philosophy by a treatment of contemporary problems which should be living and real. "We have never asserted," he writes, "that all questions now raised were solved in times past, nor have we expressed a doubt that for their solution the ancient philosophy might derive advantage from the modern."[1]

On the other hand, the genuine thought and research of the new apologists had reached a stage at which a new difficulty was arising unknown to the early years of the century. The triumphant refutation of anti-Christian calumnies, by means of Christian genius and candid research, could not arrest itself at the moment at which the apologists' purposes were gained. Historical research once begun must be pursued. And history did not always tell a tale favourable to the Popes or to the views accepted among Catholic theologians or historians in the past. A movement more deeply in accord with the time spirit was succeeding to the first place of the new apologetic among Catholics—the candid and critical sifting of history, with trust that in the long run the cause of the Church must profit, but with the immediate prospect of revising not a few cherished traditions. From this many Catholics recoiled.

Its necessity was from the nature of the case not apparent to the multitude. Many of those in high

pass muster and impose upon ingenuous youth" (*W. G. Ward and the Catholic Revival*, p. 202).

[1] See *La Filosofia Antica*, esposta e difesa del P. Giuseppe Kleutgen Versione del Tedesco, Roma, vol. i. pp. 25, 114 ; vol. ii. p. 256.

places who had welcomed in the writings of de
Maistre and Lacordaire, direct apologetic, though it
was on new lines, as winning from the world at large
a new respect for Catholicism, shrank from the
vivisection of cherished traditions and long-received
historical positions which the new method was
inaugurating.   They could not believe that so painful
an operation was calculated to preserve and stimulate
life.   And the new conclusions affected in some cases,
not indeed theological dogma, but its explication.

Here we have the true beginning of the most
serious difficulties which still lie before us in our
own time.   At this point Lord Acton intervened.
He was a Catholic by birth, with a true loyalty
to his ancestral faith, but with no interest in theology proper.   In the days of his youth he showed
a passion for research which was in keeping with
his German descent, and laid the foundations of his
encyclopedic reading.   His enthusiasms were for
the modern ideal of liberty and for learning, and both
the optimism and the medievalism of the new apologists
irritated him.   The somewhat unfairly critical account
of their labours, which he published in 1861 in the
*Home and Foreign Review*, and his plea for work of a
different kind in the future, indicate the turning-point
in the Catholic intellect of the century from the work
of apologetic to that of an adaptation of Catholic
thought to the results of the new scientific and
historical methods.

A school of writers arose [so writes the *Home and Foreign
Review* concerning the nineteenth century] strongly imbued
with a horror of the calumnies of infidel philosophers and
hostile controversialists and animated by a sovereign desire
to revive and fortify the spirit of Catholics.   They became

literary advocates. Their only object was to accomplish the great work before them, and they were often careless in statement, rhetorical and illogical in argument, too positive to be critical, and too confident to be precise. In this school the present generation of Catholics was educated ; to it they owe the ardour of their zeal, the steadfastness of their faith, and their Catholic views of history, politics, and literature. The services of these writers have been very great. They restored the balance, which was leaning terribly against religion, both in politics and letters. They created a Catholic opinion and a great Catholic literature, and they conquered for the Church a very powerful influence in European thought. The word " ultramontane" was revived to designate this school, and that restricted term was made to embrace men as different as de Maistre and de Bonald, Lamennais and Montalembert, Balmez and Donoso Cortes, Stolberg and Schlegel, Phillips and Taparelli.

Learning has passed on beyond the range of these men's vision. Their greatest strength was in the weakness of their adversaries, and their own faults were eclipsed by the monstrous errors against which they fought. But scientific methods have now been so perfected and have come to be applied in so cautious and so fair a spirit that the apologists of the last generation have collapsed before them. Investigations have become so impersonal, so colourless, so free from the prepossessions which distort truth, from predetermined aims and foregone conclusions, that their results can only be met by investigations in which the same methods are yet more completely and conscientiously applied. The sounder scholar is invincible by the brilliant rhetorician ; and the eloquence and ingenuity of de Maistre and Schlegel would be of no avail against researches pursued with perfect mastery of science and singleness of purpose. The apologist's armour would be vulnerable at the point where his religion and his science were forced into artificial union. Again, as science widens and deepens, it escapes from the grasp of dilettantism. The training of a skilled labourer has become indispensable for the scholar, and science yields its results to none but those who have mastered its methods.

Herein consists the distinction between the apologists we have described and that school of writers and thinkers which is now growing up in foreign countries, and on the triumph of which the position of the Church in modern society depends. While she was surrounded by men whose learning was sold to the service of untruth, her defenders naturally adopted the artifices of the advocate, and wrote as if they were pleading for a human cause. It was their concern only to promote those precise kinds and portions of knowledge which would confound an adversary or support her claim. But learning ceased to be hostile to Christianity when it ceased to be an instrument of controversy—when facts came to be acknowledged no longer because they were useful, but simply because they were true. Religion had no occasion to rectify the results of learning when irreligion had ceased to pervert them, and the old weapons of controversy became repulsive as soon as they had ceased to be useful.[1]

The underlying weakness of this plausible programme is that it supposes a complete impartiality in the historical researches of the scientific world which has never had real existence, and least of all in 1861. That the bias which made irreligion pervert the results of learning was dead, is a supposition which subsequent events have not justified. The absolute dispassionateness of modern methods, while largely realized in physical science, has constituted an aim rather than an achievement in the fields of history and criticism.

Cardinal Newman never shared with Acton any such trust in the ideal justice of the conclusions of the intellect in any society of fallen men—even those most devoted to the sciences. Yet his intense sympathy with the impartiality and thoroughness of research advocated by Acton and his friends, made

[1] *Home and Foreign Review*, vol. i. p. 513.

him for years co-operate in some degree in their labours. His views on the subject are of material assistance in defining the true scope and method of a creative theology suited to our times, and I shall attempt to give some outline of them based on his writings of the 'fifties and 'sixties. They show, to put it briefly, a profound sympathy with the plea for thoroughness, impartiality and freedom of research, in the fields marked out by the individual sciences. But, on the other hand, the idea that freedom of intellect, in its survey of the whole range of knowledge and of life, is likely either to beget impartiality or to lead to the highest truth, is in Newman's eyes quite untenable. Pure unbiassed intellect is not an asset to be counted on in fallen man. Assumptions and prepossessions are not the monopoly of the narrow or the ultra-orthodox. As the heart of man must be renewed to make it love what is good and pure and congenial to our higher nature, so the intellect must be disciplined and purified—rather than left in a state of mere free-dom—to enable it to keep the simple eye for truth.

Let us first consider this last point which lies at the root of his teaching.

The modern spirit which inspired the liberal writers with such enthusiasm was in its *general* tendency, Newman held, irreligious. It tended to the simple negation of all religious truth. If it had led to the perception of new methods of ascertaining facts, and to the discovery of new truths, it had also lost both older and more sacred truths themselves and over-looked the clue to their discovery. It may be said that in religion as in art the highest perceptions may become less general owing to the circumstances of the time. In neither is there an absolute law of progress.

And if we use the word "liberalism" as denoting the spirit of the age, Newman maintained that it is nothing else than that "deep plausible scepticism" which characterized "the educated lay world." He regards this "scepticism" as being due to the absolutely free exercise of human reason. Reason left entirely to itself issues not in conclusions in the highest sense rational, but in rationalism. It attempts to decide questions beyond its competence. Rationalistic liberalism is the "exercise of thought on subjects in which from the constitution of the human mind thought cannot be brought to a successful issue." Newman speaks of this sceptical tendency as "the development of human reason as practically exercised by the natural man." He finds such an issue of the free play of human reason to be no new phenomenon, but only the repetition of what has already been visible in history. "Actually and historically," he writes, ". . . its tendency is towards simple unbelief in matters of religion. No truth however sacred can stand against it in the long run, and hence it is that in the pagan world when our Lord came, the last traces of the religious knowledge of former times were fast disappearing from those portions of the world in which the intellect had been active and had had a career." And this tendency of the intellect is still more marked in the educated world at large in our own times. "Outside the Catholic Church," he continues, "things are tending with far greater rapidity than of old time, from the circumstances of the age, to atheism in one shape or another."

His attack is of course not on the lawful use of reason, but on its constant abuse by fallen human nature if it is left entirely free. And if, still pursuing the method of close scrutiny of facts, of causes and effects, we seek for the source of this abuse, of this irreligious tendency of the human reason in existing human beings, we find it to be partly that reason left to itself in fact steps beyond its lawful province, and partly that it adopts the secular assumptions or maxims naturally resulting from the action on our imagination of this visible world, which is so urgent in its claim on our attention.[1]   Such a course, though foreign to the cautious and accurate use of the reason, is the constant result of the action of secular society, which perverts the best gifts of God.   "Assumptions and false reasonings are received without question as certain truths on the credit of alternate appeals, and mutual cheers and *imprimaturs*."   This was his reiterated expression of the same view in his eighty-eighth year.   Reason amid such influences easily ignores that inner voice of the "conscience" which testifies to the existence and holiness of God as "the shadow is a proof of the substance."[2]   Newman would seem to have shared the view urged with so much force by Professor Eucken,[3] that this age of science has obscured for our contemporaries the deeper significance of the moral consciousness and of the human personality.   The reason of the age moves on, gaining assurance from its own successes in the field of scientific inquiry, and forms its judgment of the world

[1] "This so-called reason is in Scripture designated 'the wisdom of the world,' that is, the reasoning of secular minds about religion based upon secular maxims which are intrinsically foreign to it."—*University Sermons*, third edition, p. 15.

[2] See private letter to W. G. Ward, quoted in *W. G. Ward and the Catholic Revival*.

[3] See *Revue de Metaphysique et de Morale*, 1897 ; article, "La Relation de la Philosophie au Mouvement Religieux du Temps Présent."

as a whole without taking due account of phenomena
which are all-important.   And then it transfers to its
defective view of the whole that self-confidence which
it has acquired from its powerful grasp of the part.
In its satisfaction it hardly looks for—at least it
fails to see—a large field of psychological phenomena
which are themselves intimations of great realities.
These phenomena are unmistakable, though bathed in
twilight.   They are visible to the truly philosophical
reason, but they escape the observation of those who
are most occupied with the lucid and successful processes of physical science, much as a man may from
the very intensity of the light covering one area be
apt to overlook the darker space adjoining it.   " The
religious man," wrote Newman, " sees much which is
*unseen* by the non-religious." [1]   " The main difficulty
for an inquirer is firmly to hold that there is a living
God, in spite of the darkness which surrounds Him,
the Creator, Witness and Judge of men." [2]

The tyranny of the world of science and of sense,
and its tendency to prevail in the counsels of reason
against belief in the impalpable realities of the supernatural world, were described by him in a famous
lecture delivered in Dublin in 1859.

The physical nature lies before us, patent to the sight,
ready to the touch, appealing to the senses in so unequivocal
a way that the science which is founded upon it is as real to
us as the fact of our personal existence.   But the phenomena,
which are the basis of morals and religion, have nothing of
this luminous evidence.   Instead of being obtruded upon our
notice, so that we cannot possibly overlook them, they are
dictates either of conscience or of faith.   They are faint
shadows and tracings, certain indeed, but delicate, fragile and

[1] In a letter to the present writer.
[2] *Grammar of Assent*, fifth edition, p. 497.

almost evanescent, which the mind recognizes at one time, not at another, discerns when it is calm, loses when it is in agitation. The reflection of sky and mountains in the lake is a proof that sky and mountains are around it ; but the twilight, or the mist, or the sudden storm hurries away the beautiful image, which leaves behind it no memorial of what it was. Something like this are the moral law and the informations of faith, as they present themselves to individual minds. Who can deny the existence of conscience ? Who does not feel the force of its injunctions ? But how dim is the illumination in which it is invested, and how feeble its influence, compared with that evidence of sight and touch which is the foundation of physical science ! How easily can we be talked out of our clearest views of duty, how does this or that moral precept crumble into nothing when we rudely handle it, how does the fear of sin pass off from us as quickly as the glow of modesty dies away from the countenance, and then we say, " It is all superstition ! " However, after a time we look round, and then to our surprise we see, as before, the same law of duty, the same moral precepts, the same protests against sin, appearing over against us, in their old places, as if they never had been brushed away, like the divine handwriting upon the wall at the banquet. Then perhaps we approach them rudely, and inspect them irreverently, and accost them sceptically, and away they go again, like so many spectres, shining in their cold beauty, but not presenting themselves bodily to us, for our inspection, so to say, of their hands and their feet. And thus these awful, supernatural, bright, majestic, delicate apparitions, much as we may in our hearts acknowledge their sovereignty, are no match as a foundation of science for the hard, palpable, material facts which make up the province of physics.[1]

The human intellect, then, if it is to be brought to

[1] This lecture is not one of the original series on " The Scope and Nature of University Education " delivered in 1851. It was delivered to the Dublin Medical School shortly before Dr. Newman ceased to be Rector of the University. It is reprinted in *The Idea of a University*, p. 514.

see deeply and in just proportion, must, like the rest of human nature, be rescued from the tyranny, from the blinding vividness of the world of sense and of science. It must be "reborn . . . bathed in a new element, reconsecrated to [its] Maker."

But where is the power which will enable us to effect this new birth ? We need, in the first instance, a force which shall effectually control and resist the rationalism to which our nature so fatally tends under the overpowering influence of the world of sense which is ever before our eyes. Where is the "concrete representative of things invisible, which would have the force and toughness necessary to be a breakwater against the deluge " ?

History shows that other forces have been trusted for this work besides the Catholic Church. And they have failed. Three hundred years ago established Churches were relied on. Now "the crevices of those establishments are admitting the enemy." Scripture was trusted. But experience has proved that a book, even a divine book, cannot do what needs an active living power ; "cannot make a stand against the wild living intellect of man."

Thus Newman turns to the one Church which takes the resolute stand involved in its claim to indefectibility, to rescue "freedom of thought . . . from its own suicidal excesses." If the representatives of the Church are on occasion harsh, peremptory, severe, absolute, even unwise in their uncompromising efforts to check intellectual excess, these are the defects of their qualities. For the Church is the "face to face antagonist" whose mission is to "withstand and baffle the fierce energy of passion, and the all-corroding, all-dissolving scepticism of the intellect in religious inquiries." In such a battle peremptoriness and a general policy which will be hard upon some individuals would be inevitable, even if ecclesiastical authorities were perfect. But, in fact, they themselves, though the instruments of a superhuman power, have the faults of human beings. It is the mission of the Church to keep insistently and peremptorily reminding the world, by her saints and by her visible polity and rule, of the truths which left to itself it forgets. The Church has two offices in this connexion. First it reminds men of realities which the atmosphere of secular thought leads them to forget or ignore. It "bathes" the human reason in a new atmosphere and new associations. But it has another also, which Newman insists on in some detail— namely, the healthy *restraint* of the speculative intellect, which is as prone to excess as any other faculty. There is the error arising from want of proportion or perspective, as well as the error of simply ignoring a true principle. We may pursue particular trains of thought or speculation so intemperately as to lose the sense of proportion between them and the whole, and to damage that "judgment" which Newman regards as the highest faculty of the intellect. Newman, like Fénélon, is alive to the dangers of what may be called intellectual gluttony. "The mind," writes Fénélon, "needs to fast as well as the body ; it is subject to an intemperance of its own . . . *sapere ad sobrietatem* is a deep truth." [1] The intellect is thus like other natural energies and passions, which are purified first by self-restraint and next by the positive influences of religion. Newman appears to hold that within certain limits the intellectual nature may benefit from a certain

[1] *Letters to Men*, p. 126 (Rivington, 1886).

restraining action of the Church, even if in the particular case ecclesiastical authority is unjust, or if the views whose expression is checked are largely true. Thus he speaks not only of the "false assumptions" of the reason adopted under the influence of secular thought, but of its "excesses" when left to itself, and of its health when it is restrained. "It thrives and is joyous," he writes, "under the terrible blows of the divinely fashioned weapon, and is never so much itself as when it has been lately overthrown."

So much may be said as to the intellect itself regarded simply as an instrument for ascertaining or preserving the truth on matters of religion. But Newman, in his analysis of the Church, regards her not only as the repository of *truth*, but as a polity to be ruled with a view to the religious welfare of her subjects. And that welfare includes primarily their devotional life.[1] Thus authority may rightly check the intellect not merely for falling into excesses which are untrue or misleading, but for pressing on the community speculations which upset the faith and devotional life of the masses. As a strong force, which if gradually applied would take us rapidly in the direction in which we want to go, may be so abruptly administered as to kill us by the shock, so truths may be so abruptly urged as to be dangerous to the Christian community.

These general principles, so often forgotten by the "liberal" Catholics, were, as it were, the preamble to Newman's views on the Church's attitude towards the scientific movement of our time, taken in its wider sense as including the scientific study of history and of biblical exegesis.

---

[1] This point is insisted on in the Preface of 1877 in the *Via Media*.

But when he passed to the definitely limited sphere of scientific inquiries themselves, he was prepared to go very far with the principles urged by Lord Acton in the *Rambler* and *Home and Foreign*, and was unable practically to agree with the ultra-conservative scholastics. Just as false and confident conclusions drawn in the name of science, but really beyond the warrant of science, were rightly checked by the Church as the guardian and embodiment of spiritual truth, so confident conclusions drawn in the name of theology, but really beyond the warrant of theology and outside its province, must be gradually rectified by the lessons of true science and experience. It was the colouring of scientific investigations by the spirit and tone of a secularist age that he regarded as unphilosophical. But absolute candour (and correlatively freedom) in scientific inquiry proper was not only not opposed to this view, it was even a part of it ; for the secularist assumptions were often themselves an uncandid addition to strictly scientific inquiries. Regarding then the intellect no longer as an active force, impregnated with the secular passions and associations of the hour, moving discursively amid the whole field of knowledge, and generalizing as to the meaning of life, but as our genuinely rational nature, disciplined and healthy, exercised in limited and isolated provinces of scientific and historical investigation, he advocated its freedom. " Free thought," commonly so-called, meant licence for all indulgence in intellectual passion, and prejudice in the sacred name of liberty, and its expression without regard for the effect of such utterances on the community. This was the high road to scepticism. But free discussions among the learned, dictated by

the sole desire for light, were on a different footing.
Without them no real adjustment between the religious
and secular sciences was possible.

"Free discussion," he wrote, "is simply necessary
for progress in science."[1]　Discipline and a degree of
thwarting might be valuable in imparting to inquirers
the caution which should keep the reason within its
lawful province.　But within that province freedom
for the trained and disciplined intellect was essential
in the search for truth.　And as to theological opposition, his quick eye noted that the maxims on which it
rested were in some cases framed before our new view
of the possibilities of the enlargement of empirical
knowledge was clearly contemplated.　This fact would
suggest the necessity of a revision, under the criticism
of science both physical and historical, of such maxims.
He illustrated the necessity for a change by a simple
and unanswerable instance.　The fundamental idea of
the Ptolemaic system, he pointed out, was regarded
by our ancestors as though it had been part of revelation.　"It was generally received," he wrote, "as if
the Apostles had expressly delivered it both orally
and in writing, as a truth of revelation, that the earth
was stationary."　This fact is of course the most
effective defence of the theologians who censured
Galileo in 1616.[2]　But the disproof of the supposition
on which they acted carried with it the far reaching
conclusion that theologians of the very highest
authority may regard as heretical what science subsequently shows to be true.　He thus entered a note of
warning against attaching such finality to the existing

---

[1] In his lecture on "Christianity and Scientific Investigation," 1855.
[2] In one of their propositions heliocentricism was condemned, not
merely as erroneous, but as formally heretical.

form in which the results of theological reasoning are authoritatively stated, as might first check the pursuit of true lines of research, and next give that shock to the faith of the many which arises from a statement being first identified with revealed truth itself, and then having to be explained away or dropped.

At the same time his deprecation of premature dogmatism in theology was allied not with any tendency to disparage theological science, but rather with a desire to make it living, deep and candid—to purge it of rigid bigotry, and to make its avowed principles approach as nearly as might be to the "wisdom of the perfect." He never limited the loyalty due from a Catholic in respect of theological literature to the acceptance of defined dogma. He never forgot that in matters of the highest import the great Fathers and schoolmen had left with us a legacy of thought which must always be preserved. Their writings embodied the wisdom of the Church, and gave the line of lawful development in revealed dogma, though in culture and in the treatment of secular knowledge those writings may smack of the soil on which they were born, of the times and places of their elaboration, of the prescientific period. "Catholic inquiry has taken certain definite shapes," he wrote, "and has thrown itself into the form of a science, with a method and phraseology of its own, under the intellectual handling of great minds, such as St. Athanasius, St. Augustine, and St. Thomas; and I feel no temptation at all to break to pieces the great legacy of thought thus committed to us for these latter days."

The outcome of all this was necessarily a resistance to premature dogmatism both in science and in

2 C

theology.   A similar discipline must cure both defects.
And that discipline, as he urged in an early sermon,
involves the patient trustfulness which marks alike the
true man of science and the typical Christian.

"It is," he wrote, "by a tedious discipline that the
mind is taught to overcome those baser principles
which impede it in philosophical investigation and to
moderate those nobler faculties and feelings which are
prejudicial when in excess.   To be dispassionate and
cautious, to be fair in discussion, to give to each
phenomenon which nature successively presents its
true weight, candidly to admit those which tell against
our own theory, to be willing to be quiet for a time,
to submit to difficulties, and patiently and meekly
proceed, waiting for further light, is a temper . . .
little known to the heathen world; yet it is the only
temper in which we can hope to become interpreters
of nature, and it is the very temper which Christianity
sets forth as the perfection of our moral character."[1]

The following pregnant passages from occasional
lectures at Dublin[2] illustrate the foregoing summary
of Newman's views.   Speaking of the attitude of a
thoughtful Catholic towards the bewildering multiplicity of speculations and hypotheses which arise in
the course of modern research, he writes :

He is sure, and nothing shall make him doubt, that, if
anything seems to be proved by astronomer, or geologist, or
chronologist, or antiquarian, or ethnologist, in contradiction
to the dogmas of faith, that point will eventually turn out,
first, *not* to be proved, or, secondly, not *contradictory*, or
thirdly, not contradictory to anything *really revealed*, but to
something which has been confused with revelation.

[1] *University Sermons*, p. 10.
[2] *Idea of a University*, pp. 428, 456.

The Catholic savant and thinker is the highest product of the Catholic university which " is deferential and loyal, according to their respective weight, to the claims of literature, of physical research, of history, of metaphysics, of theological science. . . ."

If he has one cardinal maxim in his philosophy, it is, that truth cannot be contrary to truth ; if he has a second, it is, that truth often *seems* contrary to truth ; and if a third, it is the practical conclusion, that we must be patient with such appearances, and not be hasty to pronounce them to be really of a more formidable character. . . . It is the highest wisdom to accept truth of whatever kind, wherever it is clearly ascertained to be such, though there be difficulty in adjusting it with other known truth.

In view of these general principles, while the scientific historian or physicist must beware of advancing conclusions in theology—a matter which he must leave to the theologians—or propounding " religious paradoxes " or " recklessly scandalizing the weak," he may claim freedom to pursue his investigations thoroughly and according to their own laws, without interference on the part of the theologians. Such freedom is the only path to further knowledge.

A scientific speculator or inquirer is not bound, in conducting his researches, to be every moment adjusting his course by the maxims of the schools or by popular traditions, or by those of any other science distinct from his own, or to be ever narrowly watching what those external sciences have to say to him, or to be determined to be edifying, or to be ever answering heretics and unbelievers ; being confident, from the impulse of a generous faith, that, however his line of investigation may swerve now and then, and vary to and fro in its course, or threaten momentary collision or embarrassment with any other department of knowledge, theological or not ; yet, if he lets it alone, it will be sure to come home, because truth never can be really contrary to truth. . . . This is a point of serious importance to him. Unless he is at liberty to investigate on the basis, and according to the peculiarities, of his science, he cannot investigate at all. It is the very law of the human mind in its inquiry after and acquisition of truth to make its advances by a process which consists of many stages, and is circuitous. . . .

In scientific researches error may be said, without a paradox, to be in some instances the way to truth. and the only way. . . . This being the case, we are obliged, under circumstances, to bear for a while with what we feel to be error, in consideration of the truth in which it is eventually to issue. . . . We can indeed, if we will, refuse to allow of investigation or research altogether, but, if we invite reason to take its place in our schools, we must let reason have fair and full play. If we reason, we must submit to the conditions of reason. We cannot use it by halves ; we must use it as proceeding from Him who has also given us Revelation ; and to be ever interrupting its processes, and diverting its attention by objections brought from a higher knowledge, is parallel to a landsman's dismay at the changes in the course of a vessel on which he has deliberately embarked, and argues surely some distrust either in the powers of Reason on the one hand, or the certainty of Revealed Truth on the other. . . . Let us eschew secular history and science and philosophy for good and all, if we are not allowed to be sure that Revelation is so true that the altercations and perplexities of human opinion cannot really or eventually injure its authority. That is no intellectual triumph of any truth of Religion, which has not been preceded by a full statement of what can be said against it ; it is but the *ego vapulando, ille verberando,* of the Comedy. . . .

Great minds need elbow-room, not indeed in the domain of faith, but of thought. And so indeed do lesser minds, and all minds. There are many persons in the world who are called, and with a great deal of truth, geniuses. They have been gifted by nature with some particular faculty or capacity ; and, while vehemently excited and imperiously ruled by it, they are blind to everything else. They are enthusiasts in their own line, and are simply dead to the beauty of any line *except* their own.  Accordingly, they think their own line the only line in the world worth pursuing, and they feel a sort of contempt for such studies as move upon any other line.  Now these men may be, and often are, very good Catholics, and have not a dream of anything but affection and deference towards Catholicity, nay, perhaps are zealous in its interests.  Yet, if you insist that in their speculations, researches or conclusions in their particular science, it is not enough that they should submit to the Church generally, and acknowledge its dogmas, but that they must get up all that divines have said or the multitude believed upon religious matters, you simply crush and stamp out the flame within them, and they can do nothing at all. . . . What I would urge upon every one, whatever may be his particular line of research, what I would urge upon men of science in their thoughts of theology, what I would venture to recommend to theologians, when their attention is drawn to the subject of scientific investigations, is a great and firm belief in the sovereignty of truth.  Error may flourish for a time, but truth will prevail in the end.  The only effect of error ultimately is to promote truth.  Theories, speculations, hypotheses are started ; perhaps they are to die, still not before they have suggested ideas better than themselves.  These better ideas are taken up in turn by other men, and if they do not yet lead to truth, nevertheless they lead to what is still nearer to truth than themselves ; and thus knowledge on the whole makes progress.  The errors of some minds in scientific investigation are more fruitful than the truths of others.  A science seems making no progress, but to abound in failures, yet imperceptibly all the time is advancing.

The intellectual and moral temper of the ideal Christian savant and thinker, absolutely candid, jealous of the interests both of scientific and of religious truth, patient of temporary perplexities and apparent contradictions, disciplined to discriminate hypotheses from established conclusions, conscious that each stage of intellectual inquiry is but a step on the road towards ultimate truth, seems by Newman to have been regarded as some participation in the *donum sapientiæ* granted to the Church as a whole and in the long run, and to be aimed at by all who would strive to reach such intellectual truth as is attainable in our present condition.

Here for the present I close my citations. I have quoted enough to show that Newman's ideal for thorough and constructive Christian thought in the future has a close coincidence with his generalizations from the story of the Church in the past. Thought at once active and creative is necessary now as in the days of the Fathers and the schoolmen. But it can only be guarded from the rationalism which marks the heretical spirit if thinking minds are disciplined by those influences which the Church is specially calculated to supply, as the representative of the unseen world, and the guardian at once of Christian tradition and of the original revelation. Creative thought in such conditions is the handmaid to theology; otherwise it makes for destruction and rationalism.

The above observations were written, for the most part, before the word "Modernism" was known. In these latter days, as in earlier ones, there have been "creative" thinkers who deserved our censure, and those who deserved our thanks. The *Institut de St. Thomas* at Louvain attempts "constructive thought" for the twentieth century as St. Thomas himself attempted it for the thirteenth—with loyalty alike to dogma, to tradition, and to the secular sciences. Its eminent founder once expressed the wish that theologians should also be men of science, for thus only can there be such effective knowledge of old and new alike as may combine to form a synthesis, modern, but not modernist. On the other hand, the extreme utterances which provoked the Encyclical *Pascendi* would seem to evince just that excessively speculative habit, and that disregard of tradition and authority which have in every age led heretics beyond bounds. Here we have, then, in our own time, both the use and the abuse of creative thought in religion.

# XIII

## REDUCED CHRISTIANITY : ITS ADVOCATES AND ITS CRITICS

In speaking of Mr. G. K. Chesterton's book on *Orthodoxy*, I hailed some of its arguments as an antidote to the "staleness" which infects even the greatest thoughts and beliefs after they have lasted many centuries. When Christianity came upon the world in all the freshness of novelty, its genius and wisdom at once stamped it in the eyes of many as divine and paved the way for its ultimate triumph. By Justin Martyr and other early apologists its ethics were depicted as the realization of the highest ideals of life imperfectly conceived by the philosophers. But the religion was something more also. It was the Gospel—the "good news" that God had visited his people—and gave a new sense of the value of life to a jaded generation. The Gospel is now no longer "news." And those who have ceased to realize how much which they value in contemporary civilization is really dependent on it have begun to question whether it is even "good." One supreme advantage possessed by Mr. Chesterton as an apologist was that he himself had at one time been an agnostic, and an agnostic with singularly little acquaintance with the teaching of Christianity. The Gospel came as good news to himself, as it did to the pagan world. He was thus able in recording his own personal experience to impart to thoughts and ideas which are familiar to most of us just that effect of novelty and freshness which made them so powerful in the early centuries.

Mr. Chesterton's great merit in carrying out this work is his keen imagination and his power of exhibiting principles in clear outline by vivid illustration. These gifts enable him to make others realize what he has felt. To many thinkers of the present generation a somewhat lethargic apprehension of Christianity is the starting-point. They are, therefore, open to the cheap platitudes of that class of critic which is by nature "agin the Government." And, in Newman's phrase, they "reject Christianity before they have understood it." Doctrines which, whatever difficulties they present, a little thought shows to be based on the nature of things, are discredited in their eyes by the most superficial criticisms. The obvious objections to such a dogma as that of vicarious sacrifice "how unfair and how impossible that another should bear the burden of my sins"; to the dogma of original sin "how unthinkable that I should suffer and be in some sense infected with guilt which is not due to my own personal fault";— such objections we see frequently set forth, with some pomposity, by the representative of modern enlightenment as considerations which must make a highly trained mind reject this religion of ruder ages. The modern critic is kind but firm, and he has half pitying smiles for the uneducated minds which fail to perceive that such flaws in the system are fatal. Mr. Chesterton's manner of approach is the opposite one. He begins not with so-called "flaws," but with the strong points of the system, which are in so many quarters not realized or simply overlooked. He shows how Christianity is concerned not with the philosopher's ideal world, but the actual world in which we live. The pompous critics have simply not faced the puzzling facts of life which make Christianity so helpful. What they prove to be unthinkable is not Christianity, but our own experience of life.

I cited in my former essay instances of Mr. Chesterton's method, and it may be used in answering the very arguments just mentioned. That our nature is prone to evil apart even from the results of our own personal wrong-doing is not a mere theory of Christianity but a fact of experience, and to many in its degree an almost crushing one. Christianity faces the fact : it does not invent it. If you preach the doctrines of original sin and of the Atonement you at least help people to encounter it. To find the cause of a disease and its remedy, even though neither cause nor remedy accord with our own preconceived view of things, is preferable to the fool's paradise which simply denies that we are ill because we cannot understand the illness. We do not profess in our small corner of the universe fully to understand the justice of man's lot as it is understood by Him who knows the whole. But the doctrines in question recognize obvious and trying facts. They help us to encounter such facts by a view which is coherent even though it be imperfect. This view is that mankind has something of the character of an organism, and the moral health of the individual is bound up with that of the whole. Christianity tells us that we are prone to evil because mankind has fallen from its pristine and normal state. Trouble for many arose

from the sin of one man, and One Man cancels its
effects and will save us if we trust in Him. A task
which seems hopeless to the individual is not really
hopeless : for what he cannot do of himself the God-
man will help him to do, supplying the defects which
even at best will remain in his attempt to get rid of
a burden which is too heavy for him. The crushing
effect of the undeniable facts of a mysterious world is
removed by doctrines which are no doubt themselves
mysterious. The objections to the doctrines are
equally objections to the facts of experience, while
the doctrines recognize the facts and make them more
and not less bearable and intelligible.

If there is no such thing as human sinfulness of
course the superior persons are right, and the Atonement and original sin are a very fanciful and improbable account of things.

I propose to consider further this line of thought
in relation to two other works representing both of
them schools of religious thought materially different
from Mr. Chesterton's. Dr. Neville Figgis's lectures
on *The Gospel and Human Needs* is apparently the
outcome, not of such a reaction as Mr. Chesterton's
against agnosticism, but of a new realization of the
depth of the Christian message on the part of one who
has never rejected it ; and the bowdlerized Christianity
of the superior person has been graphically painted in
Mrs. Humphry Ward's *Case of Richard Meynell*. To
consider one of these books helps us to consider the
other, for it is the growing prevalence of the " reduced
Christianity " of Mrs. Ward which gives occasion for
Mr. Figgis's argument. There is a considerable resemblance between Mr. Figgis's thought and Mr. Chesterton's, but Mr. Figgis faces much more explicitly than

Mr. Chesterton the questions raised by modern historical and biblical criticism which have had so large a share in arousing the intellectualist revolt against traditional Christianity. Mr. Figgis faces as frankly as Mrs. Ward the fact of modern criticism and the necessity of accepting its assured results. But his mental attitude on the subject is far more discriminating and far more philosophical than that of Mrs. Ward's hero, Richard Meynell.

To speak of these books means to speak of the philosophy of religious belief—a delicate and to many an irritating subject. What faith in Christianity is possible to a thoughtful mind? This question often irritates believers and unbelievers alike. The believer, Protestant or Catholic, whose mind moves in a fixed groove, hates all talk about reasons for doubt. "Christianity is there—let people take it or leave it," he is inclined to say. "Its proofs suffice for men of good will. If many reject them it is due to their own perversity." The aggressive unbeliever of the continental type, on the other hand, exceedingly dislikes the return into the field of debate of the superstitions that have so long misdirected the energies of humanity and diverted the attention of the ablest citizens from the great field for work open to them in this world. He and his friends have been doing their best to sweep away the traces of this medieval incubus. The *Via di San Marco* has become the *Via della Libertà* in his own city. The old monasteries are turned into barracks for soldiers. The former domination of the priests in the State is gone, and even in the schools it is fast going. Now suddenly a cloud is raised: the question is asked, "Is all of this really and for certain a movement of progress? Is not the assumption that

Christianity is antiquated and doomed premature ? "
The ordinary man of the world in England dislikes
the subject almost equally. " For Heaven's sake," he
is inclined to say, " do leave alone in your published
writings what is a purely personal question of no
public importance." He dislikes the note of urgency
and what he regards as morbidity on the subject even
more than the subject itself. He is quite content to
see all religions freely exercised in the national life,
but detests treating such controversies as matters of
public importance.

Yet just as with believers, in an age of faith, whose
religion has long ceased to be practical, circumstances
may suddenly arise which make it most actual to them,
so in an age of science the problem of religious belief,
habitually regarded as tiresome and merely speculative,
may suddenly become for any one a most urgent and
real matter.

No one can say what will bring the change of
attitude. Misfortunes may leave us unchanged in this
respect. Or they may suddenly and completely change
us. So with the consequences of sin. Such things
may leave us as we were, or they may give occasion for
such lines as Tennyson's :

> Through sin and sorrow into Thee we pass
> By that same path our true forefathers trod.

So with the advance of life and the nearer prospect of
that future which, if Christianity perchance be true, so
profoundly concerns our destiny. It may deepen us.
It may fail to do so. The loss of some one we love
will not necessarily make the change. But it often
does bring an overpowering realization of the question, Where is he—shall we meet again ? As with

conversion to God and the new sense it brings of the reality of what we had always professed to believe, so with the new urgency of the question, " What are we justified in believing ? " In some persons the two things are almost the same. With John Bunyan the process of conversion was for a time largely one with the struggle against speculative doubt. Lacordaire when he became serious and earnest found that reasons for belief which he had always known affected him in a new way. The turning to God and the returning to belief were one and the same act. Huysmans has said much the same thing in his account of Durtal's conversion. That wonderful change in Pascal, of which his own description can never be read too often, surely meant, in one of his sceptical temperament, at least quite a new firmness and vividness of belief as well as a deepening of the religious life.

I have purposely prefixed these observations to those that are to follow on the two books I have named because I am convinced that the sufficiency and value of the proposals discussed by each of the writers can only be truly weighed if the reader realizes, at all events in imagination, the conditions of life in which religion assumes real importance. Those will judge best in whom these conditions are actually present. We shall judge most justly when to our average neighbour we appear morbid, as a man who sees the danger signal will have a look of alarm which appears morbid to one whose face is turned the other way. We want to know not what aspects of Christian tradition will be interesting, suggestive, stimulating, worth setting down in an essay, but what will stand the test of the hard facts of life and actually help those who sorely need help. The discussion is not of vital importance while religion is regarded as a walking-stick to flourish in the hand. The important question is, How will it do as a crutch to lean on in the ugly circumstances of a maimed life in which you cannot walk? This is why brand-new theories are apt to make one impatient at a time of need, and the experience of ages as to what has actually helped suffering humanity to endure and to hope in evil days has an urgent claim to consideration in such discussion as is possible. An old religion carries the dignity and weight which an old hero of many campaigns carries in a discussion on tactics. I say " such discussion as is possible," because words can be no more than sign-posts pointing to states of mind which we can only recognize adequately each in his own consciousness. The prescriptions of our rival doctors can be quite decisively tested only by those who make trial of them.

If Mr. Figgis lacks something of Mr. Chesterton's extraordinary vividness in style he comes (as I have said) to much closer quarters with the modern literature of his subject and suggests a more practical programme in view of the most urgent and best established conclusions of the critics. There are many minds which incline to the dilemma—you must either be suspicious of the whole method of modern biblical criticism and the serious critical thought of the day on religious problems, or, if you allow it to have its due weight, you must be content with a Christianity so much reduced as to be revolutionized. Miracle must be eliminated, and the Christ of history will almost disappear. " Reduced Christianity " has become an accepted phrase. By its advocates Christian theology

is held to be defeated. If dogmatic formulae are kept
at all it is as venerable but empty symbols which, for
sentimental reasons, one would not rudely or abruptly
destroy. Some, perhaps, they would permanently
keep, for the same reason that M. Combes was
willing to keep the old French cathedrals—as monuments of the past—harmless so long as they no
longer harbour still living superstitions. Nay, more,
they may be valuable as symbols, apart from their
original significance. You still have (such thinkers
contend) the inspiring manifestation of the divine in
the *idea* of Christ as developed by His disciples quite
apart from its historical truth. You can still endeavour
to live a Christlike life, all the more happily because
you have cleared the ground of superstitions and
fables to which no thinking man can assent in his
heart, and which clouded the best minds with secret
suspicion of the whole system.

The above dilemma is throughout assumed by
Richard Meynell to exhaust the alternatives, and any
*primâ facie* force his views may have depends on its
being true that no more dogmatic belief than what
has just been outlined is possible to one who faces the
result of modern criticism. Meynell is persuasive when
he speaks as follows :

> The hypothesis of faith is weighted with a vast mass of
> stubborn matter that it was never meant to carry—bad his-
> tory—bad criticism—an outgrown philosophy. To make it
> carry [this matter]—in our belief—you have to fly in the face
> of that gradual education of the world, education of the mind,
> education of the conscience, which is the chief mark of God
> in the world. But the hypothesis of Faith in itself remains—
> take it at its lowest—as rational, as defensible as any other.

All this may have a perfectly true sense—a sense

in which it could be said with entire conviction by Mr. Figgis or by Cardinal Newman himself. *Dolus latet in generalibus.* It is not that bad history, bad criticism, or an outgrown philosophy is advocated by Mr. Figgis as necessary to Christianity and rejected by Richard Meynell. It is that when we come to ask what is meant by the "hypothesis of faith" and what by outgrown philosophy and bad criticism they differ *toto coelo.* Mr. Figgis, following here in the Cardinal's footsteps, suggests a third alternative which Meynell ignores.

Mr. Figgis opposes what I must call the credulity of Mrs. Ward—her wholesale and uncritical reaction from credulity in old legends to credulity in brand-new theories. A sifting process and time for sifting are necessary in respect of both alike. Richard Meynell, on the contrary, is ready to drop at once not merely legendary accretions which are clearly discredited, but the whole essence of the creed, in the panic raised by aggressive criticism. Mr. Figgis insists that this panic is irrational—that criticism and philosophy, apart from the naturalistic presuppositions which have led many able critics to their anti-Christian conclusions, have no such far reaching destructive effect. On the other side he holds that if the principles which "reduced Christianity" really admits are fully realized, they lead simply to Pantheism, or even naturalism. What is apparently added to this by the neo-Christian dissolves on close examination, part proving to be mere words and part to be untenable or unworkable. He points out, with Mr. Chesterton, that in their wholesale panic men are surrendering not by any means only what the advance of sober criticism and philosophy demands, but beliefs in which traditional Christianity goes far

2 D

deeper, and is far more in harmony with what we know of this strange and mysterious world than the "reduced Christianity" which promises us emancipation. The experienced facts of life and the wonders of Christianity are, in many cases as I have said, the problem to be solved and its solution. Reduced Christianity leaves the hardest part of the problem unsolved and then proceeds to deny its very existence. Many conclusions, which are advanced as the result of criticism and thought brought up to date, are really drawn from naturalistic philosophical principles assumed and inserted by the critics into the premises— a process of conjuring. Far from a deeper philosophy of life "reduced Christianity" offers us a shallower one, because it fails in the first essential of inductive reasoning, a frank survey of the facts to be explained. In a word, while its advocates hope timidly that. a niche may be found for a remnant of Christianity in the great temple of modern thought and learning, Mr. Figgis holds that Christianity may well keep its own temple and go on boldly in its own course, and can perfectly assimilate all genuine results of criticism without essential change in its doctrines. This method reverses that of the modernist. It recognizes at the outset the value of the Christian revelation tested by long experience, and treats it as being in possession until it is disproved. The corrections made by the advance of science in the human traditions which form its setting, are to be made cautiously, and with care, with the eye of a philosopher who knows how fashions tend to run to excess and then to change. The neo-Christian, on the contrary, starts by making the existing fashion in the world of thought and science his oracle—regardless of the fact that experience witnesses to nothing more certainly than the constant changes in what the critics advance at first as certain results. He starts by displacing Christianity from her position of vantage, as hereditary possessor of the land, with a great record of practical success as a religion, and then places her on her knees as an outsider and a suppliant, asking only to reinstate a few unimportant, unintrusive survivals of her former self in a system of thought and belief to which she is on the whole quite alien. It is surely clear that whatever opinion may be held as to the nature of the final result, it should be reached by Mr. Figgis's *method* and not by Mrs. Ward's—by conservative development and not by panic-stricken revolution.

Mr. Figgis's strength lies in his readiness to concede to historical criticism all that is necessary, and his firm resistance to superfluous concessions and panic. His attitude towards doubt is particularly interesting. He is clearly not one of those who have little sympathy with the doubter or his difficulties. But, nevertheless, he points out that life is for action, and he prescribes for the doubter a moral tonic. Let the doubter be up and doing. Let him act one way or the other. Let him have the courage of his doubts and realize the logical consequences of unbelief. This may clear his path. If he abandons cloudy phrases and mere reverie and assumes that practical attitude which befits us in an urgent crisis, he is likely to see and feel how little his doubts leave him to rest on in the conduct of life. He must either acquiesce in this result or give himself another chance of realizing fully the wisdom of the Christianity of the Gospels which he has rejected, only perhaps half mastering its philosophical depth. The shock thus administered may prove just what is wanted to knit his intellectual and moral frame together, and give him the insight necessary for belief.

Mr. Figgis's plea for an undiluted Christianity is advanced under four heads : First, he pleads for a miraculous revelation. He holds that it has been dismissed, not on grounds of evidence, but in consequence of a sub-conscious naturalistic philosophy which is widely influential and yet does not really accord with the facts of experience. The enormous strides made in our day by natural science which is based on uniformity of cause and effect are responsible for this naturalistic tendency. The freedom of the human will is an obvious exception to such uniformity. Therefore naturalism does not square with the facts of life. A miraculous revelation is at least in harmony with this feature of our experience. But so much are we swayed by imagination that if we allow subconscious naturalism to discredit miracles, we are in danger of losing belief in freedom itself and regarding ourselves as " cogs in the great machine " of Nature. A miraculous revelation interposed in the history of the human race by the freewill of God proclaims aloud that the spirit is free amid the uniformity of material nature, and thus gives to the individual heart and imagination to realize and use his own freedom.

Secondly, Mr. Figgis pleads in general for the recognition of mystery in religion ; and here he gives us the plain man's common-sense argument which goes far nearer to the heart of things than the reasoning of the dilettante philosopher :

The plain man's readiness to accept the mysteries of God's grace rests at once on his ignorance and his knowledge. He feels that in all things there is mystery, and that what is the constant factor of his inner being is somehow part of the stuff of the universe. He places no reliance at all upon the optimistic faith of men who, like Du Bois Raymond, look forward to the day when the world can be reduced to a mathematical formula ; or in the more common assertion that the whole of being is penetrable to thought, for even the delight in a poem or a piece of music can prove the contrary. He knows that, though men may explain the world, he remains inexplicable to himself. On the other hand, he feels that there must be reality in that love and joy and willing resolve which are the deepest and most real things in his life. The Christian faith asserts this truth at once of the mystery of things, of the eternity of love, of the infinite worth of choice, as does no other creed. And this is its warrant.

Thirdly, Mr. Figgis urges—making another appeal to the needs of the plain man—that the actual historical Christ who died and rose again from the dead and is believed by Christians still to live and to hear and to help those who ask for help, is clearly a power and succour in the life of an ordinary man which an imagined ideal figure can never be. Moreover, the rejection of the old belief on this head is far from being really *due* to exact thought. It is rather due to a panic and to prejudice. Because some religious traditions have been disproved by the critics, therefore even the unproved theories of the critics are to be allowed to sweep all before them. Christianity is to be regarded as falling like a house of cards. Again, the modern mind, with its bias against the miraculous, does not view the evidence for such an alleged fact as the Resurrection even impartially. It approaches such evidence with an enormous presumption against its sufficiency.

But we have the contrast between reduced Christianity and genuine Christianity most vividly in Mr.

Figgis's last contention—the reality of sin and of forgiveness. J. A. Froude long ago saw that this was the turning-point in the discussion. And Mr. Figgis goes over much of the ground covered sixty years since by Markham Sutherland's reflections in Froude's *Nemesis of Faith*. Of all the doctrines of traditionary Christianity sin is the most uncongenial to the modern temper. The reality of sin is not a thing which modern biblical criticism can disprove. The objection to it comes from a philosophy of life and of human nature to which it is uncongenial. Yet surely—as I have already said—this is a philosophy which says if facts don't square with it *tant pis pour les faits*. It has been in the past the experience and urgency of sin which more than anything else has made men welcome the good news of the gospel. Sin does undoubtedly jar most unpleasantly with an optimist philosopher's theory of life. Newman once described the ideal human nature present to the Greek mind—as though that nature were perfectly balanced, perfectly healthy and could " dance through life." Nevertheless history records moral excesses which were fearfully prevalent in Greek society. Mr. Figgis quotes Sir Oliver Lodge as bidding sensible men "not to worry about their sins, but to be up and doing." All very well if men are so happily constituted that they can lead an ideal life of action untroubled by their lower nature. Such things as sin and the evil tendencies of nature are unseemly and depressing and undignified, and the philosopher looks away from them. They are too ugly a blot in any scheme of life for his complacency. The advocate of " reduced Christianity " also passes them by with scarcely a glance. Traditional Christianity, on the other hand, is too practical to ignore them, and brings from another world the mysterious explanations which enable us frankly to face such mysteries in this.

The question is [writes Mr. Figgis], Is it *there*, this sense of sin ? not, How did it get there ? Do we as a fact experience this sense of guilt, of weakness, of a diseased will ; and are we most conscious of it when we are most conscious of the call to the higher life ? And to answer this, each of us can only appeal to his own consciousness ; he can go no further. St. Paul had to go to himself for his evidence : "We know that the law is spiritual, but I am carnal, sold under sin. For that which I do, I would not ; what I would, that do I not ; but what I hate that do I. . . . To will is present with me, but how to perform that which is good I find not ; for the good that I would I do not, but the evil which I would not, that I do. . . . Oh, wretched man that I am, who shall deliver me from the body of this death ! "

Either these words awaken an echo in our hearts, or they do not. They may seem to represent our own deep and constant experience ; or we may feel ourselves members of that fortunate band who can say with a different teacher, "the higher man of to-day is not worrying about his sins ; he wants to be up and doing."

It is only if St. Paul's words represent the facts that the Gospel has any foothold in my soul.

For myself I find them true, and the other not true to my inner life. It is that very "worrying" about sin which I cannot escape that obstructs all my desires to be up and doing and blights even my highest and purest thoughts. Doubtless I might be happier, could I feel myself a man of the new dogmatic, not "essentially a sinner"! But I cannot. I cannot help it ; I have this burden, like Christian in the story, and I cannot roll it off except at the foot of the Cross. Miserable and well-nigh hopeless in face of the future, I have to live. Taught by oft-recurring failures to distrust my best resolves, and finding sincerest love and all the hardest sacrifices vain, stained with the past, frightened in face of the tempter, aware how easy it is to yield and what little rest he

gives, tortured with lustful passions, a prey to pride and
malice, contemptible even more than odious in my weakness,
divided in my inmost being, torn every hour between God
and the devil, to whom shall I go? What must I do to be
saved? Alas! I know that I can do nothing. I have no
*quid pro quo* to offer God, and cannot win my pardon by any
virtue or gift ; I am naked, beaten, prostrate.

> Nothing in my hand I bring,
> Simply to Thy Cross I cling :
> Naked, come to Thee for dress ;
> Helpless, look to Thee for grace ;
> Foul, I to the fountain fly ;
> Wash me, Saviour, or I die.

Mr. Figgis, in words written before the appearance
of Mrs. Ward's book, depicts the position of Richard
Meynell and his friends very aptly.

Finding in orthodox Christianity great difficulties, they
purpose, by what seem to them changes of detail, to make it
once more acceptable to the cultivated intelligence. Thus
they are in their own view apologists. They look for a great
revival. Once more will the Church go forth conquering and
to conquer, purged of its grosser elements, the relics of pagan
and oriental error ; refined to the modern taste, relieved of its
ignorant love of marvels, its feminine submission to priests,
and its really rather vulgar preoccupation with sin and matters
which decent people do not think about.

Mr. Figgis remarks most pertinently that Christianity does not exist only for the benefit of decent
people and of the cultivated classes. It is addressed
primarily to the poor and to sinners. Its marvels
were recorded by its Divine Author, " The blind see,
the lame walk," and the climax of these records is
reached in the fact that " the poor have the Gospel
preached to them." Again, our Lord tells us " I came

to call not the just but sinners." And it is, with any
of us, at the moment when we are hard hit and have
some of the trials of the poor and of sinners that we
most need it and can best understand it.

If we go to Mrs. Humphry Ward's pages we find
that Meynell retains as his positive religion nothing at
all in the shape of belief which can inspire moral action
in the many. Most of what Mr. Figgis would retain
as the "hypothesis of faith" is carted away by Meynell
as discredited by bad criticism and bad philosophy.
Mr. Figgis's presumption is (as I have said) that the
Christian tradition remains in possession as the "hypothesis of faith," though you must subtract from its
setting what is clearly shown to be the outcome of
bad criticism. Mrs. Ward's presumption is that all
the "higher criticism" of German theologians and
most of the speculations of anti-Christian philosophers
and critics are true, and that only what remains to
traditional belief after what they dismiss is subtracted
may be retained as "the hypothesis of faith"; and
this is mainly, so far as I can see, an enthusiasm for
moral action -for the higher life of the spirit in its
war against the animal life. And though a helpful
impulse is to be derived from the traditional story
of Christianity considered apart from its historical
truth, there is uncertainty as to how much of the
life of the spirit, as enforced in the evangelical
counsels, is to be allowed to stand in the new Christianity. Certainly the ideal of self-denying charity
towards our fellow-men is retained. But the complete
other-worldliness of the Gospel ethics does not accord
readily with Meynell's language. It would be rash to
say that Richard Meynell accepts the unearthly
teaching of the eight beatitudes, though he certainly

accepts the ideal of cultivating the rational nature in man and fighting against sheer animalism. But when we ask for the *beliefs* which are to inspire the neo-Christians in this battle with some of the force which made the early Christians die rather than deny Christ our search is vain. Sanctions we do not find in the system. It knows little of what Christ was in this world, nothing of His present existence in another. We find in it no tangible convictions to inspire our philanthropy and help us in the fight against the lower nature—not even a clear belief in a God accessible to prayer and ready to help us, still less in a future life in which we shall be rewarded or punished. It provides only an agreeable imaginative *stimulus* for refined minds and well-ordered characters—for those, that is, who stand least in need of religion. For all her claim to speak in the name of exact thought and criticism, Mrs. Ward accepts quite uncritically the intellectual fashion of the moment, while she is at the same time the victim of the Christian associations of her youth. These throw a halo round the Christian story and give it still, in spite of destructive criticism, theoretically accepted, an inspiring force for her imagination which it cannot have for those who have no such associations to disguise the consequences of Meynell's conclusion that it is simply a "tale and a symbol."

The most definite information Meynell gives us as to what is meant by the "hypothesis of faith"—that is, the positive side of religion—is the following :

What the saint means by it I suppose in the first instance is that there is in man something mysterious, superhuman, a Life in life, which can be indefinitely strengthened, enlightened, purified till it reveal to him the secret of the world, till it toss him to the breast of God, or again, can be weakened, lost, destroyed till he relapses into the animal. Live by it [adds Meynell], make the venture. *Verificatur vivendo.*

But this is the very difficulty. How, if the ideal of the life is not defined, can it be lived? If a path is not traced it cannot be followed. And, moreover, even if the ideal were clearly depicted how can the struggle its attainment involves be undertaken or sustained if you give up belief in what makes the struggle worth while? That action, inspired by certain beliefs, may make both those beliefs stronger and the future path of action clearer, may be readily granted. In this sense we may believe in order to know—*crede ut intelligas.* But when many paths professing to lead to a higher life exist, you cannot choose from among them without some initial belief to guide you in your choice. Moreover, the sanctions added by Christian belief which make the harder struggles of life possible to the ordinary man as well as to the philosopher, are simply swept away.

However much may be desirable in the way of getting rid of really bad history and criticism (a very different thing it must be remembered from adopting confidently all the most recent theories in both departments), the definite outstanding beliefs of the Christian creed are necessary both to define what *is* the " Life in life " which we are to " strengthen and purify," and to understand in general what is the world scheme which makes such an aim worth our while—which makes it the truly rational course and not merely the gratification of a mood which comes at times to most of those who have found pleasure unsatisfying and degrading. This large gap in Mrs. Ward's scheme of religion—so large that it means the absence of all the most essential ingredients of religion—is filled up both in her own case and in that of her hero by sentiments begotten of an early Christian training. But these sentiments can hardly find a place in a scientific statement of religion which dispenses with their original exciting cause. Her positive creed—as distinct from the enthusiasm for destroying what is rightly or wrongly judged to be superstitious and antiquated—is simply emotional. One appreciates the sacred feelings associated in her case with the historic Church and its historic cathedrals—feelings naturally created in the course of a Christian childhood. One sympathizes with her distress at being asked to part with what is made precious by these treasures of memory. So, too, one sympathizes with the hero of Miss Edgeworth's story who has been brought up as the scion of an ancient family and discovers in mature life that he was a changeling. But in both cases sympathy and duty point opposite ways. You cannot claim a share in associations and possessions the right to which is proved not to be yours.

I have above spoken of Mrs. Ward as credulous and uncritical in her acceptance of modern theories, and as the victim of sentiment in her desire to retain a place in the Christian Church for those who do accept those theories. I venture to plead for a clearer realization of the issue in both cases. Meynell might well keep his place in the Christian Church if his attitude towards modern criticism were more scientific; but if he accepts wholesale and quite uncritically a new theory of life essentially different from the Christian he should at least like Comte form a new Church. Nothing is more obvious to the careful critic of the "higher criticism" than its constant departure from the caution of the true scientific method. And students of the monuments of antiquity have often protested against its unphilosophical preference for theory to observed fact.

The arrogancy of tone adopted at times by the "higher criticism" [writes Mr. Sayce] has been productive of nothing but mischief; it has aroused distrust even of its most certain results, and has betrayed the critic into a dogmatism as unwarranted as it is unscientific. Baseless assumptions have been placed on a level with ascertained facts, hasty conclusions have been put forward as principles of science, and we have been called upon to accept the prepossessions and fancies of the individual critic as the revelation of a new gospel. If the archæologist ventured to suggest that the facts he had discovered did not support the views of the critic, he was told that he was no philologist. The opinion of a modern German theologian was worth more, at all events in the eyes of his "school," than the most positive testimony of the monuments of antiquity.[1]

On the other hand, if Mrs. Ward and her hero are right in their wholesale acceptance of destructive criticism and of a naturalistic philosophy, it would surely be more satisfactory to frame a religion which accords better with her intellectual position. Sentimental affection for the old and intellectual acceptance of the new are not uncommon. But in so serious a matter conviction and not feeling should determine the religious creed and the nature of the Church.

Auguste Comte was in essentials far more reasonable than the "reduced Christians." He had evidently, like Mrs. Ward, a sentimental attachment to the ceremonial, the worship, the organization of the Church in which he was born and bred. The French writer, like the English, realized the value of a devotional

[1] Sayce, *The Higher Criticism and the Monuments*, pp. 5, 6.

system and high examples in history in the struggle of man against his lower nature. But he made the effort which reason demanded to reconcile intellect and feeling. Having found in science the great guide to life, and having dismissed as unattainable all definite knowledge of the supernatural, he made his Church correspond with these convictions and did not call his system Christianity or keep the old forms of worship which belonged to an ideal he had rejected. His priests were the men of science. His Calendar of Saints presented the embodiments of ideals far more varied than those of Christianity—ideals which Mrs. Ward also accepts. His new Church frankly admitted these modern conceptions of human excellence, and did not preserve forms associated with more exclusive ideals and beliefs which he had definitely rejected. In ritual, devotion and organization, his " Church of Humanity," while it derived some inspiration from the Christian Church, was based on those facts only which Comte recognized as intellectually knowable. If we eliminate certain points of detail, in which the Frenchman's lack of sense of humour makes us smile, the general conception was rational and consistent. Mrs. Ward attempts to disguise the extent of what is lost by using old forms which imply that Christianity is in some sense retained. This may be English compromise, but it can hardly be lasting, and at best is a policy which the far-sighted must see to be but the stepping-stone to acknowledged Positivism.

It may be said that Mrs. Ward speaks of " God," but it is doubtful to the present writer whether the God of Pantheism which she recognizes amounts to more in her religion than the Positivist " Humanity controlled by Nature " in the religion of Comte.

It is hard, then, to think of Meynell's system as genuine Christianity. Even, however, if it should gain in frankness and cease to claim Christ as its founder, it would still remain, like Positivism itself, ineffective as a religion for the many.

But further, if we take Mrs. Ward on her own ground and consider mainly the sufficiency of her religion for the cultivated classes themselves, her book is surely permeated by one profound fallacy. Its picture of the enthusiasm of the Meynellites is undoubtedly true to life. The present writer has seen similar enthusiasm in many well-known zealots for the new theology in different communions. It consists in a passionate zeal for reform—for purging the Christian Church of what they regard as harmful superstition. The movement has in it something of the zeal of an apostolate. All this I concede. Am I not then, it will be asked, conceding all that Mrs. Ward maintains? By no means. The enthusiasm I recognize is that which belongs to the work of reformation, not to religion. When this work of reformation is accomplished and has lost its novelty, enthusiasm can only be maintained by the positive religion that remains. And it is in respect of this that, as I have pointed out, the creed is bare to nakedness. When the Puritans had destroyed " Popish superstition " they kept an evangelical faith both inspiring and helpful. On this they lived and not on the zeal for destruction which was sated. But when Meynell's reform is accomplished, there remains to him no such religion to hold the enthusiasm of his followers. The few remnants of Christian tradition which Meynell preserves include no beliefs which can substantially help men in the wear and tear of life. The Puritans broke the statues, but kept the Bible. Richard Meynell's fanaticism is that of an iconoclast. This will inspire men until the images are actually broken, but it will not persuade them afterwards to worship the fragments.

Surely, then, if the Higher Criticism has reached some of its most destructive results by an unscientific disregard for facts which are inconsistent with them, and if Mr. Figgis is right in holding that the Church of England can still remain the home at once of learning and of traditional Christianity, it cannot be justifiable to open its doors, as Richard Meynell demands, to men who preach so meagre a gospel as that of "reduced Christianity," driven thereto not by hard facts but by ingenious theories. Pantheism and optimism are congenial enough to human society in the heyday of life : the Christian Church has been forcibly depicted by Newman as the providential antidote against them—as set up to remind us of "the hateful cypresses"—of death, sin, judgment, and of the beliefs which are needed to face these ugly facts. If the Church of England can share in this work and still be a bulwark or breakwater against infidelity, can it be wise to cripple her power in this respect by admitting to her ministry those who go so very near to holding the very attitude towards life which Christianity is set up to oppose—and this (I repeat it) not under pressure from the consensus of experts in science but in deference to the dogmatism of extremist leaders and the credulity of their followers ? If, as Meynell maintains, "reduced Christians" are already admitted to the ministry but dare not as things stand openly avow their beliefs, surely reform should be in the direction of the exclusion of what is alien to Christianity and not of capitulating openly to the enemy ?

In appending a few words to compare Mr. Figgis's apologetic with methods more familiar to Catholics, I wish to build a bridge between the two in order to prevent misconception. Mr. Figgis says in many places that it is not on "reason" but on "life" that religion is built up, and he has much to say of "religious experience" as justifying belief. To a hasty reader such language may appear to savour of pragmatism or of subjectivism. But this would be a great misconception of the writer's meaning. I do not care to defend all Mr. Figgis's phrases, but his general drift is quite clearly other than this criticism supposes. Mr. Figgis strongly repudiates pragmatism, and in his preface he clearly locates his argument as belonging to the region in which the subjective element has no tendency to issue in subjectivism, namely, the personal frame of mind of the individual in approaching the proofs of religion. "I have tried," he writes, "to remove difficulties which prevent the evidence producing its proper weight." A man, as our theologians express it, is "led prudently to believe" in consequence of certain evidence. The conclusion is "credible" and "certain" but not "evidently true." It is not such as to preclude the possibility of doubt, though the doubt which remains possible is not the doubt of a "prudent man." There is some danger lest Mr. Figgis's expressions just referred to should be considered as referring directly to what is regarded in technical theology as "evidence of credibility," but in point of fact they concern rather the "prudent" attitude of mind, and the disposition of the will, which are the final determining cause of belief. Lacordaire, as I have noted above, said that the reasons for his conversion to Christianity were reasons he had always known; but a personal change came to him, which led to their affecting him differently. His own personal reaction on the reasons changed; and, to use the expressions of theology, the imprudent doubt or disbelief was exchanged for the belief of a prudent man. When Mr. Figgis talks of "life" and "experience" as contributing to bring about belief and to justify religion to the individual, he is dealing primarily with this matter of psychology, with the variations of the dispositions of the will brought about by the experience of life and not substituting religious feeling for the "notes of the Church." All theologians admit that we need the *pia affectio voluntatis*. But an experimental examination into the variations of the disposition of mind and will in individual cases is obviously most important.

This is a matter perhaps too little considered by apologists, and presents more varieties in a society where believer and unbeliever are constantly exchanging views than it does either in an age of faith or for those who live in a society where such questions are not discussed. Moreover, it must never be forgotten that while to base belief on "religious experience" is dangerous, the opposite extreme of denying the reality of such experience would be to discredit half our hagiology and to set down St. Teresa and St. John of the Cross as dreamers. The reality of communion with God in prayer may not be appealed to technically as evidential. Yet it is not a fact which either Popes or congregations have been disposed to deny. And the effect of such experiences on the moral dispositions is a fact for which there is room in every variety of the analysis of faith.

The reason why theologians are cautious and

authority rigid in respect of loose language about "religious experience" is because it runs so easily into mere subjectivism in religion. No one could protest more emphatically against this danger than Mr. Figgis. On the other hand, if we avoid all reference to "religious experience" in the lives of individuals and in the determination of their beliefs, we must bowdlerize our saints' lives and condemn as heterodox all mystical theology.

In one respect, however, a Catholic must approach the whole subject dealt with in these books from an opposite standpoint from Mr. Figgis. Mr. Figgis is attempting to restore to the Anglican Church much which the Catholic Church has never lost. It is hard for him to gain from the Church of England the support of an objective witness to religious truth as a remedy for subjectivism because he and his friends are but a party in that Church, urging their particular way of viewing things. The chief compensating advantage to him, from a controversial point of view, is that one who constructs a new system is free to select the arguments which appeal most forcibly to the present age. On the other hand, the Catholic and Roman Church has jealously excluded those currents of thought which have caused the disruption of the Church of England. Our strength lies in our conservative principles. We only relinquish traditional beliefs or apologetic methods and arguments when it is plainly necessary. Therefore it is harder for us to make changes even when the advances of criticism do call for them. The decrees against Galileo were repealed only in the nineteenth century. Our first principles have, in their appeal to the world, all the dignity and force of what has been consistently acted on. But our history also makes harder those modifications in detail which are necessary in order that our apologists should have due influence with the more thoughtful contemporary religious inquirers. We certainly gain more than we lose. "Things seen are mightier than things heard," and "example is better than precept." To act on true principles continually and from time immemorial is a more forcible proof that those principles can stand the test of life than to recommend them by persuasive arguments. But the isolation from the modern world of thought which has been the condition of their preservation has also, perhaps, made us insufficiently alive to the new points of view familiar to that world. It is a question whether we are not in consequence becoming unable to make those without see the force of views which were they within the Church they would feel in fact to have the marks of what is deep and true. For the world reads what we say in its own context and the context of the Church is very different.

This is why I venture to think that we might all study with profit—though not with complete agreement—such works as those of Mr. Chesterton and Mr. Figgis, who often express in a manner which appeals forcibly to the modern world ideas which find their fullest expression in action within the Catholic Church itself.

# XIV

## PAPERS READ BEFORE THE SYNTHETIC SOCIETY

### I. THE AIM OF THE SYNTHETIC SOCIETY.[1]

THE thought of forming the Synthetic Society first occurred to a few persons differing from each other in theological opinion, and yet equally desirous of union in the effort to find a philosophical basis for religious belief. It is generally felt that more than a century of destructive criticism has at least impaired the effectiveness of the traditionary systems of natural theology. The religious inquirer is no longer able to view them as exhaustive and practically irrefragable demonstrations of Theism and Immortality. The absolute ascendency they long enjoyed would seem in part to have been due to those very Christian influences for which they professed to be a philosophical foundation. They are the lineal descendants of the systems in vogue in medieval Christendom. The first principles whence they start, whether or no they may prove, on thorough consideration, to be exact, have at least been so far questioned as to disprove their claim to be unquestionable. They are such as to have been readily accepted in a society in which

[1] This paper was read at the inaugural meeting of the Society, on February 28, 1896.

dogmatic belief was the intellectual characteristic.
Further, the logical progress from these first principles
to conclusions already imbedded in the daily life of
such a society was not likely to be viewed critically.
*De facillimis non est hic disputatio* were the words
in which one scholastic doctor excused himself from
even entering into the proof of Theism. Unsparing
hostile criticism has since shown, at all events, that
the systems in question needed much fuller philosophical consideration and elaboration than they had yet
received alike as to premises and as to proofs. The
problems they treated as simple and solved so sym-
metrically were found to be complex and encompassed
with difficulty. It was not to be expected that this
should be generally seen at a time when the universal
ascendency of Christian beliefs made a philosophy of
Theism seem to the multitude almost a superfluous
concession to the lovers of methodical argument. But
as a soldier whose reputation has been won by neatness of uniform and perfection of drill in time of peace
may fail when war tests his endurance and nerve, so
these symmetrical proofs may be found inadequate to
bear the brunt of the battle when religious belief is
seriously assailed.

The Natural Theologies, then, shared the fate of
those *à priori* philosophies with which they were so
closely connected. A rigid scrutiny of the facts of
human experience, physical and psychical, and of the
limitations of the human faculties of knowledge, discredited them with many. No attempt can here be
made to trace the history of their decline. What had
been threatening since the rise of the inductive philosophy took substantial form in the last century. Hume
and Kant may serve as landmarks. The shock given

to believers by the destructive method of Hume received an additional impetus from its practical endorsement in the speculative philosophy of Kant, and from his rejection as theoretically invalid alike of the Ontological, the Cosmological, and the Teleological proofs of Theism. This result was not at once counteracted by the hopes held out in that philosopher's ethical works and *Critique of Practical Reason*. It became widely maintained that the religious philosophy of medieval times was in reality largely due to a temper of mind which accepted dogmatic first principles uncritically, and to an ethical atmosphere which supplemented any defects in the argumentative processes commonly employed. A society which was largely a Christian Theocracy was not likely to question readily the very basis of its constitution.

This admission appeared perhaps for a time tantamount to a triumph for the destructive critics. Religious belief seemed to have been due, not to its professed philosophical basis—which was unsatisfactory—but to certain peculiarities in the mental and moral atmosphere which prevailed in the Middle Ages. Those elements, at all events, which separate Christian Theism from an unpractical Deism appeared to fall outside the sphere of truths whose philosophical character was generally admitted. An intellectual fashion of individualism and negation succeeded. The empirical principles on which it rested were handed down in our own land from Hume to the two Mills. They were popularized far and wide by Huxley in the memory of us all.

Our own time, however, has become increasingly sensitive to the inadequacy of the various systems of destructive philosophy, as failing to account even for universally acknowledged truths, and as incommensurate with the facts of human nature. Above all things its inability either to explain, or to explain away, the religious aspirations or the religious consciousness has been increasingly felt. This defect had indeed been noted from the early days of its influence. It suggested at the outset to Kant his practical philosophy which restored those beliefs which his *Critique of Pure Reason* had failed to justify. It was likewise the basis of the traditionalism of a Catholic thinker like De Bonald, who to some extent accepted the criticisms passed by Locke and Hume on the old *à priori* thinkers and appealed to the traditions of society as evidence of the interference and guidance of a power more than human. It formed a basis of agreement between such opposite thinkers as Comte and Lamennais, both of whom abandoned the *à priori* methods and sought for a philosophy of religion elsewhere than in individual introspection. One found it in the purely emotional and ceremonial system of the Positivist worship; the other in Catholicism as representing the corporate decisions of humanity. The history of the Church was to Lamennais the summing up of the spiritual traditions and experiences of the race. The human race in its corporate aspect could grasp what eluded the intellectual apprehension of the individual.

These are early instances of the refusal to acquiesce in the negations of empiricism and of attempts to frame, on those convictions which remained alike unaccounted for and undestroyed by the negative systems, a constructive philosophy to replace the old natural theologies. In more recent years such attempts have been many and various. Thinkers of various schools have vindicated for some of those ethical elements in the individual and in society, to which the destructive critics had traced religious belief, a really philosophical character. Kantian doctrine and an appeal to the principles of social philosophy have in some cases combined, and both have tended to admit the sceptical results of purely speculative thought in the individual, and to regard a true philosophy as wider and more practical in its scope.

The evolution theory, though ushered in under the banner of Agnosticism, seems to many to give new meaning and perhaps new promise to the attempt to construct, by the consideration of mankind corporately, a basis for beliefs which it is difficult to justify, at all events with irresistible cogency, by a purely individualistic philosophy. The greatest of the medieval schoolmen urged the necessity of teaching Theism and not leaving it to individuals to ascertain it by philosophical reasoning—an attempt, he added, in which very few would practically succeed, however cogent in the abstract the proofs of God's existence might be. Were the individual mind left without external teaching of this great truth (he declared), "the human race would remain in the greatest darkness of ignorance." What was here stated as a practical fact of human experience in days when philosophy was limited in its scope by technical restrictions, should, we suppose, be taken into account by any philosophy which professes to be commensurate with human nature. If the actual causes of important convictions are to be found historically in the social influences surrounding the individual, and if our knowledge and our very faculties of knowing have been developed by the social environment of successive generations, the study of sociology and of evolution is clearly necessary to an adequate philosophy of the existing human mind. And if, after all, the philosopher must finally come back to a form of individualism ; if the thinker is reminded that after doing his best to appraise all corporate influences and all causes of belief, his final decision must remain his own ; if he is even led back to some of the first principles which he had previously dismissed as unduly dogmatic, the road he has traversed may well have been instructive. He has made an advance parallel to the Kantian transition from dogmatism to criticism, though with a different result. First principles, which were unjustifiable when they professed to be obvious axioms, vouched for solely by the direct insight of the individual mind, may acquire a securer basis by the consideration of their origin, of their results in history and in society, and again of the results of their denial. What seemed at first arbitrary may be found to be indissolubly linked with what even hostile critics perforce admit. Its denial may be found to involve the questioning of principles without which the human mind is unable to work at all. In such a case the character of a primary axiom may be restored from the reflected light thrown back by the fuller examination of results.

Again, the full consideration of the social or historical standpoint leaves its effect on the intellectual attitude of the inquirer. The philosopher feels, at the end of the process, far more a learner, far less a judge. He should have acquired some of the humility which generally follows the prolonged application of the experimental method. This may show itself in various ways. To remember the speculative efforts of his ancestors, with their repeated failures, is a cure for philosophical egotism or eccentricity in the individual. He learns from the experience of others the direction of least resistance, and his own contribution becomes better regulated if more modest. Again, the study of the sources of conviction in others makes a man aware of the impalpable forces influencing his own mind. Familiarity with the recurring cycle of the history of thought, and with the numerous and subtle influences in society actually causing belief, must give both a caution and a discriminating receptivity which were wanting to the dogmatist. If, for example, the same alternate tendencies to scepticism and dogmatism have recurred in the same order repeatedly, as though by a kind of natural law, the thinker who remembers the law has an advantage which is wanting to him who follows the tendency of his own mind regardless of surrounding influences. Such a thinker allows for a current which may carry the other all unconsciously away. And the presence around us of a large variety of systems of religious thought, each embodying some instructive human experience, none without some characteristic truth, each yet presenting, in the eyes of its opponents, likewise characteristic error, must, we suppose, call for a similar combination of criticism and receptivity.

But to pursue such a suggestion further, or to define it with greater precision, would be beyond the purpose of this sketch. Lotze's *Microcosmus* is an example alike of a philosophy having regard to both standpoints—the social and the individual—and of the mental attitude to which such a philosophy naturally leads.

We have spoken so far mainly of the doubt thrown

on the old natural theology by a new realization that much of its influence depended on convictions proper to a special time and a special society. A change in some respects similar is taking place in regard to the Scriptures. The recent advances in biblical criticism have, we suppose, brought home to an increasing number the circumstances of time and place which had their influence in the production of the Scriptures as we receive them. It has been the defect of an uncritical age not to take these circumstances sufficiently into account in estimating the nature of the knowledge we may expect to derive from the Inspired Word.

Again, the study of comparative religions has become more general, and has necessarily had its bearing on our view of Christianity. These two sciences will fall within the scope of the Society, it is to be supposed, exactly so far as they are required to illustrate the truly philosophical attitude in their regard at which the religious inquirer should aim—the change in theological analysis which the advance of such sciences must involve, and the compatibility of such change with permanent religious convictions.

It may be added that the phrase "working philosophy of religious belief," used in the rules of the Society, is designed to indicate that our ultimate object is a practical one; and that while technical metaphysics will obviously have its place in the discussions, it will be open to those who think that the best working philosophy is to be found in a direction other than the purely metaphysical to say so. Indeed, in the case of metaphysical speculation, as in that of the consideration of comparative religion, it is to be hoped that its treatment will be guided by the degree to which it can be helpful in attaining our main purpose.

It is not expected that the point of view we have attempted to indicate will prove to be precisely that of other members of the Society. But what has been said may serve to show the light in which a problem as to whose urgency many are agreed has presented itself to a few.

The promoters of the Society are well aware of the wide divergence to be looked for among different thinkers who are equally desirous of a constructive philosophy adapted to existing circumstances. But it is hoped that the unity of aim will give to the discussions a useful and critical, rather than a polemical, character. Whether any approximation to general agreement will be attained remains to be seen. At any rate, it is hoped that discussion with a common object will promote good feeling amid such theological differences as exist, and may be a step towards that real union among those desirous of maintaining the religious basis of human society, which at the present time is so far from existing, and is yet so greatly to be desired.

## II. THE SOCIAL OR HISTORICAL STANDPOINT

The object of this Memorandum is to elucidate the distinction, drawn in the paper on the *Synthetic Society*,[1] between the social or historical standpoint and the individual standpoint in philosophy, and to indicate its possible utility in reference to problems which may come before the Society. The writer will endeavour to illustrate his meaning by simple instances taken from the controversy with empiricism.

[1] The paper referred to was the preceding one, read at the preliminary meeting of the Society.

One prominent matter of debate in the papers of the old Metaphysical Society was the attempt of the empiricists—from Hume to J. S. Mill—to deny to the mind the power of intuition, and to trace all our knowledge to sensible experience. The method used by the intuitionist in this controversy was that of individual self-analysis. He appealed to beliefs accepted as valid by intuitionist and empiricist alike ; analyzed their logical basis ; showed that this *must* include certain primary intuitions irreducible to experience. The empiricist was challenged to examine his own mind, to apply the intuitionist analysis, and to show if he could that the conclusion was not inevitable—that the beliefs in question rested on intuitions. The crucial part of the process, on either side, was individual introspection. The case was decided by the verdict of accurate self-analysis. The standpoint on either side was that of the individual examining his own mind.

Among the issues fought out by this method were the intuitive character of memory, the intuitive basis of necessary truth, the nature of the primary ethical perceptions. Huxley had traced our confidence in memory to our *experience* of its truthfulness. The intuitionist challenged him to analyze his own mind more accurately. He could not know that memory *had* been truthful in the past without *first* trusting its own avouchment. Nor could any argument justify our trust in the most positive assertions of memory as to recent events. To *understand* an argument you must trust that memory which connects the first part of a sentence with the last. It is a condition of all coherent reasoning that the memory should be trusted. Our trust in it is therefore ultimate.

So, too, it was argued in the case of the empirical theory that belief in necessary truth is based on induction. You must necessarily admit that the belief that the truths of geometry obtain universally is more than an induction from experience, because to observe carefully one instance in which a trilateral figure is triangular proves to you that all trilaterals *must* be triangular.

Again, you must admit (it was argued) the simplicity of the idea of "moral worth"—that it is something distinct from the idea of "beneficial to the race" to which some of the older utilitarians reduced it—because you yourself must recognize that to say "whatever is beneficial to the race is good" is far from being the tautologous proposition "whatever is good is good."

So far (I repeat) each party appealed to the analysis of the individual mind—to instances in which mental experience is the same, and the only question is of true and false analysis; and the intuitionist claimed that by the inevitable confession of his antagonists his own analysis was shown on these points to be the true one. He claimed a victory, and set down as admitted first principles that our trust in memory is ultimate and intuitive; that the acceptance of necessary truths is not of the nature of an induction, but is intuitive, or derived from intuition; that the idea of moral worth is a simple idea, and not identical with "beneficial to the race," or with other suggested analyses of its import.

If the controversy ended here, if to show that Hume and the Mills had denied what the analysis of the human mind clearly establishes, were tantamount to a philosophy of religion, it might be unnecessary to consider another standpoint. But this is not so.

The admission of certain axioms as primary, and even as known by intuition, does not necessarily involve the admission of all the axioms postulated in a Theistic philosophy. You may bring the empiricist, as Mill was brought, to admit memory as an ultimate means of knowledge, but he may stop short, as Mill did, of the intuition of causation. You may prove the inadequacy of the idea " beneficial " as an explanation of " good "; but you still have before you subtler explanations of the ethical judgments, referring conscience to the early fear of father and ruler, or to the associations created early in life by punishment for a certain class of actions, or to the still more complicated genesis suggested by the evolutionists. Again, the endeavour to connect the moral perceptions with knowledge of God may raise further questions in which no agreement can be obtained between the analyses of different thinkers. You may have won the admission that geometrical truth is necessary ; but you have yet to win assent to the proposition that space is objective—that necessary truth is more than subjective consistency in the à priori elements which the mind brings with it as a condition of experience. And both the objective character of space and the objective validity of synthetic à priori judgments are important elements in more than one version of the philosophical basis of Theism.

And here arises the problem which first suggests what I have called the social or historical standpoint at its narrowest angle of departure from the individual standpoint. Hitherto beliefs have been considered in which the decision of all minds is really similar, and in the case of which apparent differences are resolvable into a true and a false analysis of similar convictions. Thus a direct issue was possible from the individualistic standpoint. All men really trust their memories in certain cases, as an ultimate trust, assumed in the very attempt to offer proof that there are prior motives for the trust. All men really hold particular geometrical truths to obtain universally, on the examination of one instance, and not as an induction from many. Here the empiricists had simply failed in their analysis of experiences common to all.

But when we get to the further questions just referred to it is otherwise. Is the use of the causation argument for Theism valid ? Does causation really involve more than succession ? Does the human mind affirm with right the objective character of space ? These questions are found to involve ultimate differences, not of analysis, but of first principles. Individualism comes to a deadlock. Its weapons no longer apply. Either we abandon all hope of agreement, and end with the statement on either side that "orthodoxy is my doxy," or we make some attempt to trace the history of differences between mind and mind, hoping to discover their source, and thus to effect a reconciliation, or to join issue on a prior stage in the argument. We leave the study of the individual mind and take up the social standpoint.

The philosopher no longer merely analyzes his own mental experiences, treating this process as a final appeal, stating it that others may apply it to their own minds, and test how far it reveals defects in *their* analysis. He employs a different method. He questions his own most positive and ultimate convictions by comparing them with those of others. He

2 F

looks on himself from outside, as a unit acted on by
social influences ; and questions the source of the first
principles he has accepted.   He looks along the line
of history to see if he can ascertain a reason for ultimate differences between one mind and another, and
if that reason can throw any light on the question—
which of the opposing first principles is right ?   He
becomes provisionally a doubter, where he had been
positive.   The thinker who is thus hesitating between
the two views (above referred to) concerning causation
and space may undoubtedly learn something from
tracing the history of the controversy between the
empirical and the *à priori* schools.   He may come to
the conclusion that the early success of the empiricists
was due to the fact that a dogmatic age had been too
ready to multiply dogmatic first principles, which it
was really beyond the power of the human mind law-
fully to affirm ; that the protest of Bacon, echoed by
Locke, against the theorizing of the *intellectus sibi per-
missus* had in it a measure of obvious justice ; that the
subsequent reaction against empiricism was due to a
similar exaggeration on the part of such empiricists as
Hume, who, in their zeal to expose the false preten-
sions of the advocates of " innate ideas," eventually
denied to the mind powers which must really be
assumed as valid in the simplest and most obvious
reasoning processes—powers which can be justified by
no external test, as the human mind has no test at its
command which it can apply without using the very
powers and processes whose validity is to be tested.

Here, in an instance I have chosen for its great
simplicity, a glance at history does reveal the *root* of
divergence in first principles.   Neither party was
wholly right ; yet both held a characteristic truth.

The dogmatism of scholastic days and the caution bred by the rise of induction each formed a temper of mind which tended, one to exaggerate, the other to minimize, the power of the human faculties to rise above sensible knowledge. The individual who had been influenced by the maxims of either age had to correct his mind's spontaneous decision by allowing for the current.

Here it is at least possible that this slight, historical survey may come to the aid of the inquirer, in such a deadlock as I have indicated between the views of Mill and of the intuitionists as to causation; or between the views of Kant and of his opponents as to the objective character of space. The thinker may come to the conclusion that the extensive dogmatism of medieval philosophy, which tended to the exaggeration of the mind's powers of active perception, had led to a violent reaction, in which the analysis of passive impressions as the exclusive road to truth had become an intellectual fashion; that the sober common-sense of Locke had kept this tendency from extremes; but that Berkeley and Hume, each in his own way, had carried it so far as to question all active elements in mental perception. This extreme had in it (our thinker may conclude) the perverse untruthfulness of an exaggerated reaction. When Hume "waked Kant from his dogmatic slumbers," Kant was, no doubt, considerably affected by the new vividness with which Hume and Berkeley had brought out the extent of the merely phenomenal in our knowledge; and though Kant was too clear-sighted to deny to the perception of geometrical truths the character of synthetic *à priori* judgments, he was, nevertheless, so far a child of his time as to refuse to ascribe an objective character to our perceptions of space—a refusal due to the pressure of an intellectual fashion which tended to paralyze confidence in the *active* perceptions of the mind, and in its power of knowing any *objective* truth.

In a similar way, the student contrasting his own sense of power in causing the movements of his own body with Hume's view that causation is *mere* succession, may find in the story of the origin of empiricism good ground for ascribing Hume's position to a one-sided temper of mind—a fashion of distrust of the mind's active powers—and for returning to the intuitive view. That the empirical temper is one-sided he concludes both from the history of its origin, and from the fact that it has led its votaries, in their distrust of all professed intuitions, to positions in regard to memory and to necessary truth which were suicidal. Such untenable results throw grave doubts on the initial method to which they were due, and discredit as morbid the degree of questioning and caution as to the mind's spontaneous decisions to which empiricism leads.

Here, then, are two instances in which it is conceivable that a thinker who had failed to make the controversy yield a satisfactory issue so long as the method of self-introspection had been exclusively applied, may come to a definite result if he supplement the individualist method by the social and historical.

And surely a like method may be usefully applied on a more extended scale.

Passing the eye along the history of philosophy, and comparing his own self-analysis with that of others, often tracing the differences to ascertainable social causes, the thinker modifies and corrects the conclusions which commended themselves to him while he adopted the purely individualist standpoint. The ascertaining of the causes of the varying convictions of philosophers at least gives him an additional means of testing his own accuracy. So far as they have been due to misunderstanding, he learns to avoid such ambiguity as has been found misleading. So far as they have been due to opposite first principles, he learns what has led different minds to take up varying positions in their ultimate decisions, and what tests of truth or falsehood may be found in the causes thus discovered. Even in the present—and apart from the marked differences of intellectual habit which history presents in different ages—a man with a scholastic education differs widely from one with a scientific education. The one from his deductive habit readily assumes first principles ; the other is cautious, ever mindful of the disillusions of experience. The process of mutual correction by contact between such minds is valuable. Far more valuable, surely, is the correction of individual idiosyncrasy to be attained by the study of the history of thought all along the line—that is, by the social and historical method.

And, it may be added, if there is to be any progress in philosophy, such a method seems to be indispensable. It will leave, indeed, a sufficient number of deadlocks—of inevitable differences—to keep up the distinction of schools of thought. But to register the lessons of experience—the primary differences, the solved problems, the explanations which have passed, the topics which still appear to offer hope of further elucidation—is surely essential to real progress. Otherwise history blindly repeats itself

We each knock our head against the wall, whose hardness in proportion to the human skull has been experienced again and again by our ancestors.

No doubt a man must ultimately apply his researches to his own mind ; and the final result is that he gives his own contribution to philosophy based on them or corrected by them. Thus he returns to the individual standpoint. But his provisional position, while studying the variations between different minds, is different from the standpoint from which he analyzed his own mind, and showed, by his own analysis of it, that conclusions common to him and to others necessarily presuppose certain first principles which must therefore be admitted by all. In the latter case he regards the decision of his own mind as without appeal ; in the former he is, by a reflex act, questioning the origin and working of his own mental machinery—and this by comparing it with other minds. No doubt it is still his own mind which institutes the investigation and decides as to its result ; but the materials it uses are different, and are such as may make him modify his former decisions, and enable him to judge of their value from a wider survey.

Of course it may be said that in the very act of writing down your own analysis, and inviting another to give his, you are comparing notes and taking up so far a social and not a purely individual standpoint, though it be limited to a comparison between two minds. And again, by the fact that the most complicated studies from the social standpoint issue in a conclusion which is individual to yourself, it may be shown that they are in the last resort only the materials for an individualistic philosophy. No doubt the distinction may thus be made to vanish ; as I have fully implied in my former paper. But considering that the processes are so widely distinct in kind, the one regarding comparatively and from outside the variations of thought in history and in the world, the other regarding from within the immediate analysis of one's own mental operations, and considering that these two ways of looking at the problems in hand are opposite for the time being, and mutually corrective, it seems useful to contrast the standpoints, while allowing that both standpoints are taken up by one individual.

And now we have to consider the fact that the social standpoint, first suggested by the differences between philosophers in first principles, is also called into request by the actual considerations as to the scope of human knowledge, which have been urged by the later empiricists, who appeal to evolution. The attempt to explain the intellectual and moral faculties by the association of ideas is transferred by them from the history of the individual to that of the race. The development of the faculties in the course of evolution is considered. Conscience is maintained to be an instinct, commanding in its tone, telling what makes for the life of the race. The intellectual faculties are dealt with as the gradual development, in the course of evolution, of the sensible faculties— not different from them in kind.

Then, concurrently, there is the attitude towards religious conviction, which says, in effect, "We will not attack you ; we will explain you." We have the ghost theory, and other similar theories, to account for the origin of belief in the supernatural ; and the old demarcation, so convenient for the purposes of abstract philosophical discussion, between natural and revealed religion, is blurred by tracing the actual convictions of Christians on natural religion to the influence of Christianity itself, while the Christian evidences are discredited by the myth-theory of modern criticism.

And here we are unable to escape the consideration of the social and historical standpoint. The allegation is that in fact the belief in Theism and Immortality in a large number of men is due to the subtle ethical influences of a Christian society. No doubt we may reply that, allowing this to be so, these beliefs can also be justified by a true philosophy of the human mind, which leaves these special influences out of account. But, as St. Thomas Aquinas says in a famous passage, such a philosophy is not likely to be directly influential with the mass of men. Granted even that it is the justification of the few philosophical minds, and that it has indirect influence on the less philosophical through their instrumentality, you must perforce consider the question, How far has the average man ground for believing that in surrendering himself to this influence he is acting wisely and reasonably, and in a way which gives a presumption that he will not be misled? And here we are again driven to the social standpoint.

But, in point of fact, besides this influence of the philosophical few on the many, there *is* the influence of the atmosphere—spread by Christianity around each unit in the Christian society—of the contagiousness of the belief of his fellows, of the response which the truths of Natural Religion professed by the community find in his own moral nature.

It would surely be unsatisfactory and untrue to

fact to dismiss these influences as simply misleading, to confine the philosopher's efforts to an abstract philosophy of the individual mind, which can only really satisfy the majority in consequence of their trust in those who expound it ; and at the same time to exclude entirely from the sphere of rational causes both that trust itself and the other influences which actually sustain the belief of the community.

I am not denying that there is a process, reasonable in its degree, whereby less philosophical minds do rise to the conception of God apart from external teaching ; but, in point of fact, man lives in society and cannot be independent of its traditions, which he learns, and which must have their effect on his beliefs. Therefore, in order to assure the average man that his belief is well founded, it is useless to appeal exclusively to a process which cannot practically take place in him—namely, the movement of his mind in response to the visible world apart from any social influences. If social influences for or against belief have been acting on him from earliest childhood, and if inherited predispositions are likewise due to external influences exerted on his ancestors, he cannot appraise the reasonableness of his belief without in some degree estimating the value of these influences, which effectively sway his mind in one way or another.

And in view of the incompetence of the average individual to do this in a trustworthy fashion—to stand outside himself, and appraise dispositions which have become part of himself—we are led to the conception of a Society or Church in which the more spiritual and profound spirits support the weaker and guide the Society. In some degree the inequality of minds is compensated by the influence of one upon

another.   A schoolboy can learn the law of gravita-
tion from a Newton, and be taught to prove it by his
own intellect.   But he could not have discovered it.
Thus the greater minds bring out the rational faculties
of the smaller ; and an influence in one sense social
gives knowledge which is truly rational in the
individual.

And this may surely be so likewise in the
philosophy of religion.

If a true philosophy of the individual mind leads
the philosopher to attach importance to the moral
intuitions, to the sentiment of moral approval and
disapproval, to the more complex judgments and
sentiments summed up in the word "conscience" ; if
these acts or phenomena of the mind form an important link in the chain of arguments for Theism ;
then those in whom the moral nature is more highly
developed—the saints and moral heroes—give point
and additional force to the argument.   Society gives
in a more unmistakable form, by the most developed
instances, this ethical aspect of human nature which
philosophy considers to be significant.   We remember
Browning's account of the momentary flashes of the
spiritual nature from which the most sceptical are
not free :

> Just when we are safest, there's a sunset touch,
> A fancy from a flower-bell, some one's death,
> A chorus-ending from Euripides—
> And that's enough for fifty hopes and fears
> As old and new at once as Nature's self,
> To rap and knock and enter in our soul. . . .

It is tolerably clear that such glimpses do not
necessarily differentiate themselves unmistakably from
mere excursions of the imagination.   Place him who

experiences them in isolation, and they may carry him no further. They are glimpses of what might be—"the Great Perhaps"—but no more. They may seem, perhaps, chiefly suggestions from the æsthetic nature rather than from the deeper moral conscience. Place him, on the other hand, in contact with those whose ethical perceptions are steady and constant, and two results follow. Firstly, his own moral perceptions, such as they are, assert themselves more distinctly ; and, secondly, he comes to attach more importance to them by seeing the quality of more developed instances. Tennyson expresses this in the *Ancient Sage*. The dissolute sceptic says of the glimpses of moral light which come to him :

> Idle gleams may come and go,
> But still the clouds remain.

The Saintly Seer replies :

> Idle gleams to thee are light to me.

And he suggests that their significance would grow in the other by a sustained course of moral action.

Without attempting to decide on the rational value of this element in the basis of Theism, it seems, at least, clear that a " working philosophy " of religious belief cannot leave out of account what has so much influence as a cause of belief, and what has certainly in it at least some of the rational value attaching to the argument from man's moral nature to the existence of a moral author of the universe and of humanity. To reject the study of other minds in such a case, and to confine one's self to the individual mind—whose moral faculties may be abnormally

undeveloped—would be to lose sight of the full force
of the argument.

But I may add—to avoid misunderstanding—that
this function of what I have called the social standpoint is necessarily guided by the moral intuitions of
the individual which it strengthens and confirms. It
is not to a *merely* external comparison of different
manifestations of religion—to an exclusively social
method—that I have appealed. It is the recognition
that perceptions in ourselves have their counterpart
more highly developed in others, which is the guide
in this appeal to evidences of Theism derived from
minds other than our own. That the moral consciousness is significant we learn from our personal
experience—even though that experience be due in
part to the action on ourselves of greater characters
than our own. The *degree* of its significance may be
seen, as far as the individual is capable of seeing it,
only by doing his best to use his mind as a reflector
of the higher perception of others, and adding to his
own direct perceptions the testimony of those who see
more, whom he can reasonably trust, but whose direct
knowledge he can never fully share.

In the considerations I am here suggesting I am
raising questions which it would carry me far to discuss
fully. But I trust I have said enough to show that
the conception of gaining aid for a working philosophy
of religious belief from the religious experiences of
others and of the race is not unreal or purely mystical.
If we have any faculties which lead us to the conception of God as the ultimate satisfaction of our rational
and moral nature, we are more likely to see the full
significance of these faculties by having regard to men
of moral genius, than by looking solely at ourselves

The greatest truths—scientific and mathematical—are known to the individual through his appreciation of the lead which genius offers to give him. His own faculties are educated and directed by studying the mind of a Newton or a Laplace. And so it may be with religious truth. And if revelation professes to have culminated in One in whom an absolutely Divine nature has been manifested, and whose teaching is calculated to draw forth moral aspirations and perceptions of a higher order than any which mankind had previously known, such a profession would be in harmony with the hierarchy of knowledge and the means of attaining to it which we find in human society. The union of our own perception with trust in the guidance of One who sees fully and clearly what we could only discern imperfectly and by glimpses, the increased confidence in our own glimpses due to His fuller explanation of their sources and import, would be a fresh instance of an order of Grace which follows more perfectly the order of Nature.

## III. MR. HALDANE ON AUTHORITY IN RELIGION [1]

How far would the lines of Mr. Haldane's paper on "Authority in Religion" coalesce with a line of thought suggested by the evolution theory as explained by Spencer, Huxley, or Wallace? It is an Hegelian saying that "Nature attains to self-consciousness in mind"; and the same idea may be said to underlie the conception of evolution.

[1] This is a criticism on a paper read to the Society by the present Lord Haldane in February, 1897.

From the development of the lowest forms of sentient life onwards, organic evolution is the gradual unfolding of the universe to the animal consciousness. This process has already reached the comparatively rich experience of man ; and it is possible enough to conceive of it as indefinitely continuing—and issuing, in fuller and fuller manifestations of conscious knowledge, until full self-consciousness should be attained by nature, and the subject, having got rid of all the limitations attaching to knowledge in the individual, should find itself to be, as Hegel maintains, identical with the object. On this hypothesis, experience would be the "ultimate and the real," and individual self-consciousness might be regarded as "a phase that comes in only as a stage in the logical arrangement of knowledge."

But leaving this imagined conclusion of the process out of the question, we may consider the process itself. At each stage of this growth of experience from the very earliest, the question stated by Mr. Haldane arises, "To what extent is a real feature in experience being recognized ?" There is at each stage, as the information given by the senses becomes wider, the alternative—Is this new phase of consciousness fresh experience, or is it partly (or wholly) an illusion ? And the question which concerns us here is, How far are the ideas of God, Freedom, and Immortality, which have arisen so generally in the human consciousness, truly correlative to real features in experience? Empirical Agnosticism would regard them as (so far as we can know) *mere* illusions. Mr. Haldane claims, at *least*, that they are "symbolical of a beyond to which experience points us."

Perhaps some light as to the true interpretation of

this phase in human consciousness may be gained by considering an earlier stage in animal experience. The most remarkable transition in the evolution of sensible experience came with the development of sight, which has given to sentient beings in this small planet a direct relation with the solar system and fixed stars. The problem of the origin of the eye gave Darwin to the last, he used to say, "a cold shiver," from the difficulty of accounting for the origin of a sense which gave ultimately such far-reaching relations with the environment. If we trace the eye from its earliest rudiment in the lower forms of sentient life— pigment cells covered with transparent skin—to the first appearance of the optic nerve, then onward to the appearance of the lens, and then onward to the complete vertebrate eye, it is clear that there has been a gradual advance in sensible experience, from *mere* sensitiveness to light to a confused recognition of external objects, which steadily became more and more exact until it reached the comparatively perfect vision of our own eye. It is tolerably plain that at each stage there was a growth of real experience and concurrently a growth of illusion. Even at the final stage our own accurate vision gives by itself, until corrected by reason and observation, many fresh illusions, one of the most obvious of which is the idea of the position and movement of the stars conveyed by sight alone. Sight so rudimentary that it could not descry the stars at all would have been free from these particular illusions. To other optical illusions also individuals are liable, as in judging of distances ; to others, again, from special defect, as with the colour-blind. Of course at an earlier stage there would probably be illusions as to the distance and position of neighbouring objects, still more marked and more various.

If we conceive rational endowment to have come at a low stage in the development of the visual organs —for instance, if we imagine the first appearance of the optic lens to have come to beings with minds—we should have in some respects a parallel case to the present one of our religious consciousness. In the early stages of sensitiveness to light there might have been the agnostics as to vision. They might have maintained the whole of this new kind of experience to be illusion. Others, noting the universality of the new ideas and their coincidence with undeniable experiences in touch, might have maintained that this new phase (to use Mr. Haldane's expression) " pointed us to a beyond," but that all further definition must be regarded only as giving " symbolical images."

Here, be it observed, already a great point would be won beyond the admission of the Agnostic. If my sight of the stars is admitted to be a real growth of experience, as contrasted with the lower developments of sight, I can go on by further observation and reasoning to *correct* its attendant illusions, to reach the Copernican hypothesis—that is, to ascertain more exactly what knowledge experience does give by its fresh advance.

And so too in religious as in visual experience : once we admit, as Mr. Haldane does, that the existence of a reality beyond previous stages of experience is being disclosed, though the forms in which we conceive of it may be illusive and merely pictorial, we have some reason for hoping that illusion may be dispelled and the nature of the further reality more clearly discerned.

And it is here that I should endeavour to begin where Mr. Haldane ends. He notes the discrepancies of the symbolical images in which the religious consciousness expresses itself—the varying theologies and mythologies of different times and places. He appears to say—the idea of a Beyond is common to all, therefore it is valid ; in all else different times and places present different conceptions, therefore all else is made up of illusive pictorial forms.

I should reply that once we admit the reality of the " beyond," it is not too much to hope by comparison and observation to do something towards the purification of the pictorial forms from the elements of illusion which they contain. While the discursive reason and the processes of observation and comparison are powerless to attain a knowledge new *in kind,* they may be, here as elsewhere, invaluable in correcting and dispelling illusions in experience itself. Reason and observation could never *give* sight, but they can correct it. Moreover, the development of visual experience has not been exactly equal in all individuals at the various stages of advance. Comparing our own experience with that of others whose visual experience is more developed may be of great value in interpreting our own.

Thus, instead of saying, with Mr. Haldane, that " the foundation of the authority " of the religious ideas is " no more than this—that they are symbolical of a beyond to which experience points us," and regarding the variety of religious ideals as a sign that no further truth is attainable, I should ask if we can learn no further lessons as to the new reality—the beyond—parallel to those which rational beings with imperfect sight could have learnt concerning the

2 G

results of higher visual experience, by observation, reasoning, and intercourse with those whose visual faculties were more developed than their own. I should appeal once more to the testimony of religious and ethical genius, and to the results of closer observation under their guidance. And here an argument urged by the Bishop of Rochester[1] and Dr. Bigg comes to the rescue. The convictions thus gained would receive further proof from the fact that they give coherency and definiteness to unmistakable but only rudimentary perceptions which we all share in common. Some of these Mr. Haldane himself recognizes as, at all events, universal and fitting in with experience; for instance, the reality of moral obligation.

The analytical reason, then, has for its task the purification from illusive elements of the ideals which arise from religious experience. And this (I suggest) is not done by eliminating as illusive what all minds do not yet possess in common. Such a process would reject new knowledge as well as new error. The testimony of religious genius would be rejected as well as the eccentricity of the fanatic. A more discriminating scrutiny is required to discern those new perceptions which are involved in the genesis of very various religious ideas—perceptions which further define the reality to which the rudimentary faculty common to all obscurely points.

And, if this is so, we may come to recognize advancing accuracy of religious knowledge—an indication of the true nature of the beyond of which Mr. Haldane speaks—in the gradual development of the idea of a Deity or deities into that of one

[1] Dr. Talbot, now Bishop of Winchester.

Personality, the realization of our ideal of moral good. Religious evolution on this hypothesis becomes, like evolution in other departments, a gradual increasing adaptation of the mind to reality. Mr. Haldane's pictorial forms remain, indeed, to the end partly symbolical and untrue, but yet the necessary vehicle of new truths, containing the illusion attendant, in this as in other cases, on advance towards a higher stage of experience. Every such advance, while it helps to correct the illusions proper to an earlier stage, brings also its own indistinct perceptions—the rudiments of a still higher phase, which for a time the imagination fills up with illusive pictures or the reason completes with inaccurate deductions.

THE END